Psychological Perspectives on Early Childhood Education: Reframing Dilemmas in Research and Practice

The RUTGERS INVITATIONAL SYMPOSIUM
ON EDUCATION SERIES

O'Donnell/King, Eds. *Cognitive Perspectives on Peer Learning*

Vitello/Mithaug,Eds. *Inclusive Schooling: National and International Perspectives*

Golbeck, Ed. *Psychological Perspectives on Early Childhood Education: Reframing Dilemmas in Research and Practice*

Shimahara/Holowinsky/Tomlinson-Clarke,Eds. *Ethnicity, Race, and Nationality in Education: A Global Perspective (In press)*

Psychological Perspectives on Early Childhood Education: Reframing Dilemmas in Research and Practice

Edited by

Susan L. Golbeck
Rutgers University

LAWRENCE ERLBAUM ASSOCIATES, PUBLISHERS

2001   Mahwah, New Jersey   London

Lawrence Erlbaum Associates, Inc., Publishers
10 Industrial Avenue
Mahwah, New Jersey 07430

The camera ready copy for this book was provided by the editor.

Library of Congress Cataloging-in-Publication Data

Psychological perspectives on early childhood education : reframing dilemmas in
research and practice / Susan L. Golbeck, editor.
    p. cm. – (The Rutgers invitational symposium on education series)
  Based on original papers presented by the authors at the symposium on creating
environments for learning in the early years, Nov. 6, 1998, in New Brunswick, NJ,
at the Rutgers Graduate School of Education.
  Includes bibliographical references and indexes.
  ISBN 0-8058-3228-9 (cloth: alk. paper)
  1. Early childhood education–United States–Psychological aspects–Congresses.
I. Golbeck, Susan L. II. Series.

LB1139.22P79 2001
372.21'01'9–dc21

                                        00-057280

Books published by Lawrence Erlbaum Associates are printed
on acid-free paper, and their bindings are chosen
for strength and durability.

Printed in the United States of America

10 9 8 7 6 5 4 3 2 1

This book is dedicated to the memory of Robbie Case.

Contents

Contents

Series Foreword

Louise Cherry Wilkinson
Dean and Professor of Educational Psychology
Rutgers Graduate School of Education
November 1, 1999

The profession of education was shaken to its roots nearly two decades ago when national attention focused critically on education and educators. Beginning with the highly publicized *A Nation at Risk* (1983), often contradictory criticisms, analyses, and recommendations on American education appeared from virtually every segment of contemporary U.S. society. Critics and friends have raised basic questions about our profession, including whether educators have successfully met the challenges that the students and the schools present and, even more fundamentally, whether we are *able* to meet those challenges.

In this explosion of concern and ideas for educational reform, there has been a need for a national forum in which the problems of education can be examined in light of research from a range of relevant disciplines. Too often analyses of complex issues and problems occur within a single discipline. Aspects of a problem that are unfamiliar to members of the discipline are ignored, and the resulting analysis is limited in scope and thus unsatisfactory. Furthermore, when educational issues are investigated by members of only a single discipline, there is seldom an attempt to examine related issues from other fields or apply methods developed in other fields. Such applications may prove to be illuminating.

The national debate on educational reform has often suffered from a myopia as problems and issues are identified and analyses and solutions often are proposed within the limited confines of a single disciplinary boundary. In the past, national discussions have been ill informed or uninformed by current research partly because there are far too few mechanisms for interdisciplinary analyses of significant issues.

In response to the call for educational reform in our country, the faculty of the Rutgers Graduate School of Education developed the *Rutgers Invitational Symposia on Education*, RISE, which is both a live forum at Rutgers and a published scholarly series. Taking a multidisciplinary and interdisciplinary perspective, the *Symposia* focus on timely issues and problems in education.

x

Because there is an accumulating corpus of high-quality educational research on topics of interest to practitioners and policymakers, each symposium focuses on a particular issue, such as potential teacher shortage, how to assess literacy skills, the optimal structure of schools, or the effects of cognitive psychology on teaching mathematics. Each volume in the *Symposia* series provides an interdisciplinary forum through which scholars interpret and disseminate their original research and extend their work to potential applications for practice, including guides for teaching, learning, assessment, intervention, and policy formulation. These contributions increase the potential for significant analysis and positive impact on the problems of educational improvement for American children.

The present volume, the 12th symposium, is dedicated to early childhood education. This volume is based on original papers presented by the authors at the symposium on *Creating Environments for Learning in the Early Years: From Research to Practice*, November 6, 1998, at the Rutgers Graduate School of Education in New Brunswick, New Jersey. This topic, which focuses on a unique and increasingly significant educational program dedicated to improving children's preparation for schooling, could not be more timely. As we celebrate the millenium, there is increased awareness of and interest in universal preschool education in America. In this context, the 12th *RISE* is an important contribution to our understanding and improvement of children's learning. It is with great pleasure that we contribute this volume to the series, *The Rutgers Invitational Symposia on Education*.

EDITOR'S PREFACE

As we enter the new millennium, the public is clamoring for bold reforms in our public education system. One component of reform is the implementation of prekindergarten programs on a widespread basis. With the call for universal prekindergarten, researchers and scholar practitioners have been asked to identify which programs will most effectively facilitate children's learning. This is not a new question. Early childhood education has a relatively short, but rich history of instructional innovation grounded in the field of applied developmental psychology. Teachers and researchers have looked to the field of child development and developmental psychology for guidance in answering their query: How can we best help children learn? The purpose of this edited volume is to present some examples of current thinking on this topic in a manner that will be useful to teacher scholars, policymakers, and researchers struggling with questions of how to optimize preschool education.

Several dilemmas are explored across the chapters in this volume. The prevailing concern focuses on identifying strategies that support the child's self-regulation of learning while providing the teacher with a clearly defined role in teaching or guiding learning. All of the authors address this issue as they explore the limitations in earlier conceptions of instruction in the early childhood classroom. Everyone agrees that the child-centered versus teacher-centered dichotomy is overly simplistic and that more sophisticated conceptions of early childhood instruction are needed. The authors included in this volume assume a constructivistic stance as they apply current research in children's cognition to classroom practice.

A second concern focuses on content. How can we be sure that all young children are indeed *ready to learn* socially, emotionally, and cognitively? What kinds of experiences should be included in programs to ensure children's learning across such content domains as literacy, reading, science, social studies, and the arts? The volume is organized to deal with this issue head on. One section of the book focuses on foundations for pedagogy addressing issues in children's social, emotional, and cognitive development (e.g., Case, Griffin, & Kelly, chap. 2; Stipek & Greene, chap. 3; McCune & Zanes, chap. 4; Hyson & Molinaro, chap. 5; Klein, chap. 6). Another section focuses on the practice of pedagogy in specific content domains (e.g., DeVries, chap. 7; Ginsburg, Pappas, & Seo, chap. 8; Morrow, chap. 10).

A third issue is implicit in the organization of the volume. Recent years have seen a critique of the field of child development as a basis for early childhood practice. However, much of this criticism has ignored recent research in the field of developmental psychology. Recent theory and research is far more context sensitive and presents a more fine-tuned analysis of the role of experience in children's learning. The research programs described here clarify the role of experience in the early childhood classroom from the perspective's of both child and teacher. This clarification points the way toward more effective programs for young children.

This volume should be of interest to readers with a practical orientation who are interested in a sophisticated analysis of problems in the early childhood classroom. The contributors are leaders in the field of child development, all actively studying young children's learning in classrooms. The volume should also be of interest to scholars in the fields of early education and developmental psychology. For the former, the book provides a coherent overview of psychologically based work on children's learning. For the latter, the book provides a good illustration of a current problem in applied developmental psychology.

In the Introduction, Golbeck provides a context for contemporary problems in early childhood education. Past research on competing models of instruction are overviewed, and the rationale for a child-regulated/teacher-guided pedagogy in early education is spelled out. The remainder of the volume is organized into two sections. Part I addresses the psychological foundations for instruction and pedagogy in early childhood. Case and his colleges (chap. 2) present a neo-Piagetian model of cognitive development. Stipek and Greene (chap. 3) explore the problem of achievement motivation in the early childhood classroom. McCune and Zanes (chap. 4) discuss the role of children's play and focused attention in classroom learning. Hyson and Molinaro (chap. 5) address the significance of emotions in the early childhood classroom. Finally, Klein (chap. 6) discusses children's conceptions of their early school experiences. Part II addresses issues of pedagogy. DeVries (chap. 7) discusses the role that adults play in promoting sociomoral development; she describes classroom environments that promote it. Ginsburg and his colleagues (chap. 8) consider pedagogy in mathematics by describing a ground-breaking study of preschool children's mathematical thinking in classrooms. Liben and Downs (chap. 9) explore the meaning of geography education for young children in an insightful discussion of symbols, spatial representation, and mapping. Morrow (chap. 10) discusses critical issues in early literacy. Rosenberg (chap. 11) considers the arts in her discussion of children's creative expression. Finally, Frede, Barnett, and Lupo (chap. 12) discuss a system for observing teaching practices with special needs children.

Special appreciation is extended to Louise Cherry Wilkinson, Dean of the Graduate School of Education, Rutgers University for making the 1998 Rutgers Invitational Symposium in Education and this book possible. Thanks are also owed to Naomi Silverman, Senior Editor at LEA and to Lori Hawver and Art Lizza at LEA for their assistance with many aspects of production. Finally, thanks are extended to Sandy Chubrick of the Graduate School of Education, Rutgers.

INTRODUCTION

1

INSTRUCTIONAL MODELS FOR EARLY CHILDHOOD: IN SEARCH OF A CHILD-REGULATED/TEACHER-GUIDED PEDAGOGY

Susan L. Golbeck
Rutgers - The State University of New Jersey

Which instructional approach is best for the preschool years? What is the role of play, child initiative, and creative activity in the curriculum? How can young children's literacy and numeracy skills best be promoted? How are new instructional approaches to be reconciled with traditional perspectives such as those provided by Montessori and Dewey? These are enduring questions asked by researchers, teachers, and parents. However, they will take on renewed importance in the next decade. The concept of universal prekindergarten programs, funded through the public school system, is moving from discussion to reality (Clifford, Early, & Hills, 1998; Hicks, Lekies, & Cochran, 1999). As policymakers and administrators from the public schools make decisions about educating preschool-age children, it is more important than ever that early childhood educators effectively articulate the theoretical and empirical basis of their pedagogical practices. Furthermore, the call for standards, as exemplified by Goals 2000 (Short & Talley, 1997), has created a renewed focus on academic achievement.

As states move toward the implementation of standards-based assessment and curriculum reform, discussion has focused on academic goals in the subject area disciplines. Early childhood educators have often thought in a child-centered holistic manner rather than in a discipline-oriented way. Although it is widely recognized that these two points of view are complementary (Neuman, Copple, & Bredekamp, 2000; American Association for the Advancement of Science, 1999), their integration requires a solid understanding of the pedagogical and instructional practices proved to be effective with young children. As we stand at the brink of the new millennium

3

and we anticipate dramatic changes in our system of early care and education, it is appropriate to review what is known about contrasting models of instruction in early childhood education.

In this chapter, I attempt to create a context for current questions about instruction in early childhood education by reviewing research on preschool children's learning and development in school settings. The work I discuss was conducted over a 30-year period beginning the late 1960s. Many things changed during this time period. The value of preschool education for disadvantaged children was accepted by the public. The infrastructure of the early childhood profession developed. The knowledge base in educational psychology ballooned. The strengths and limitations of quantitative research were closely scrutinized. However, important questions about instruction in the early childhood classroom remain unresolved.

I begin with a discussion of early childhood programs emerging from the Head Start era. These programs were shaped by theory and research in developmental psychology. Developmental psychology in the mid-1960s was characterized by an interest in *grand systems* or overall theoretical models of development (Damon, 1998; Dixon & Lerner, 1999). *Carmichael's Manual of Child Psychology* (Mussen, 1970), a compilation of state-of-the-art essays, includes a detailed presentation of Piaget's cognitive developmentalism, psychoanalysis, and learning theory. Like psychological theory at the time, the new early childhood programs were ambitious. Many included comprehensive curriculum models designed to foster children's cognitive, linguistic, perceptual, and socioemotional development. Little mention was made of children's learning in particular content areas such as reading or mathematics, although close scrutiny of the programs shows that these topics were not ignored. Although much has changed since these programs were conceived, many have an enduring value because programs and participants were the targets of longitudinal evaluations (Barnett & Boocock, 1998), some of which are still underway (e.g., Schweinhart & Weikart, 1997). Findings emerging from this research continue to shape debate and direct policy decisions (Frede, 1998).

By the 1980s, research in early childhood education had taken a new turn. Of particular interest were specific instructional practices-especially those termed *developmentally appropriate*. Discussion of this forms the subsequent section of the chapter. This later generation research differs from the earlier work. First, community-based programs, rather than experimental sites, were usually the targets of study. Second, rather than focusing on a single comprehensive model curriculum, specific practices, such as opportunity for child-initiated activity, positive social climate, or academic emphasis, were studied.

The orientation of developmental psychology today, is decidedly different from the late 1960s. The grand systems have all been shown to be deficient. Developmental psychologists have taken to smaller scale theories useful for understanding particular aspects of psychological functioning. New models of learning and development address microgenetic as well as broader level changes within the individual (Lerner, 1998; Scholnick, Nelson, Gelman, & Miller, 1999). At the same time, psychologists have recognized the significance of the social context or the ecology of the development at multiple levels. The field of early childhood education has also changed dramatically. The field is far more multidisciplinary, and research methodologies are correspondingly more diverse (Genishi, Ryan, & Ochsner, in press). However, this diversity is unified by a common interest in young children's learning and development as well as a concern for how adults can best optimize learning. I conclude by arguing for a new model of instruction--a child-regulated/teacher-guided approach. This approach blends the best of child- and teacher-centered approaches in the design of young children's educational programs.

INSTRUCTIONAL MODELS FROM THE HEAD START ERA

Research on instructional models in early childhood education finds its origins in the Head Start era. This was a time of highly productive collaboration between developmental psychologists and early childhood educators. By the early 1960s, developmental psychologists in the United States were making important strides in understanding the development of young children's intelligence, recognizing that intelligence was profoundly influenced by experience (Bloom, 1964; Hunt, 1961). The relatively recent resurgence of interest in Piaget's theory within the United States had prompted intense debate between traditional experimental psychologists committed to mechanistic approaches to learning and development and developmental psychologists committed to the more organismic approaches of Jean Piaget and Heinz Werner (Langer, 1969; Overton, 1984; Reese & Overton, 1970). (The reader today may wonder about Vygotsky's place in these discussions. It is worth noting that only Vygotsky's first book, *Thought and Language*, was translated into English at this time, and some of his most powerful ideas were unknown to most American developmentalists.) These theoretical debates provided an important context for emerging programs in early childhood education. In some cases, new early childhood programs were devised from theory (e.g., Bereiter & Engleman, 1966; Lavatelli, 1973; Weikart, Rogert, Adcock, & McClelland, 1971) and seen as an opportunity to further test contrasting points of view regarding children's learning and development (Peters, 1977).

The 1960s was also the era of the War on Poverty. In 1965, the federal government launched Project Head Start, a major initiative to improve children's lives through early education, health care, services to families, and community involvement. This novel program was grounded in a rather small body of empirical data from developmental psychology including a few experimental intervention programs designed to increase cognitive functioning through preschool (see Zigler & Valentine, 1979). The linkage to psychology was demonstrated through reliance on psychological theory to justify and further develop early childhood programs, supportive services to families, and community development through community participation.

Given the size of the Head Start Program, the speed with which it was implemented, and the lack of an infrastructure for early childhood education, it is not surprising that the first evaluation of Head Start was disappointing (Spodek & Brown, 1993). The first Head Start programs in the summer of 1965 looked to traditional nursery school practice as a guide (Sales, 1979). Broad guidelines for programs were issued, but specific models for delivering the program were not specified. One initiative for improving Head Start focused on *curriculum* or the preschool education component of the program. A wide variety of program models were developed, and interest in identifying the most effective program for young disadvantaged children grew. These program models are frequently referred to as *curriculum models* in the early childhood literature (Day & Parker, 1977; Epstein, Schweinhart, & McAdoo, 1996; Goffin, 1994; Miller, 1979; Peters, Neisworth, & Yawkey, 1985; Spodek & Brown, 1993), although the term *instructional models* actually seems more appropriate today. Some models were traditional (e.g., Bank Street, Montessori), but many were newly devised. One source notes that as many as 40 models were available. Eleven were selected for funding and evaluation under Head Start "Planned Variation" (Miller, 1979).

Program models in Head Start differed dramatically in assumptions about learning and development, recommended instructional strategies, and the believed sources of educational disadvantage among poor children (Miller, 1979). One analysis by Miller (1979) applies to programs developed more than 25 years ago. However, there is a striking similarity to contemporary concerns (e.g., Goffin, 1994; Stipek,1991).

Three points are noteworthy. First, drawing on Bruner (1972), Miller (1979) identified a distinction between context-free and context-sensitive orientations. Context-free orientations emphasized the similarities in development among all children and tended to ignore differences produced by such variables as social class, ethnic membership, and family lifestyles. Program models in this group would have included the Bank Street Traditional Approach, The High/Scope Cognitively Oriented Curriculum, and the Open Classroom Model. In contrast, context-sensitive theories emphasized the crucial role that culture and subculture play in determining cognitive abilities. The context-sensitive models at the time would have included Bereiter Engelmann's DISTAR Approach and Karnes's Ameliorative Program. (Recall that much of Vygotsky's work was not yet available.) Second, preschool approaches differed in explanations of cognitive change. In DISTAR, Karnes's approach, and Susan Gray's DARCEE program (Gray, Ramsey, & Klaus, 1982), change was viewed as a cumulative process in which learning occurred incrementally. Such orientations emphasized the value of careful task analysis and a specific sequence of instructional activities. Other approaches such as Bank Street, High/Scope, and Montessori emphasized the notion of change occurring more slowly and following a broad stagelike progression. Further, it was believed that both lateral and vertical progress occurred in learning. A third difference identified by Miller was the assumed relationships among cognitive, social, and emotional development. Some [e.g., Bank Street (Biber, 1977)] argued that the concept of the self as a competent, successful, independent worker affects interactions with all problem-solving situations. Others (e.g., Bereiter & Engelmann, 1966) argued that a sense of competent self followed from academic success.

The systematic comparison of curriculum models in early childhood programs occupied the attention of researchers during the 1970s. Several excellent reviews of this work exist (Clarke-Stewart & Fein, 1983; Goffin, 1994; Miller, 1979; Peters, 1977; Powell, 1987; Stallings & Stipek, 1986). In short, researchers sought to demonstrate which theory-based curriculum model would best optimize young children's learning. Identifying the most effective approach was an explicit goal of the Head Start Planned Variation Studies as well as numerous other experimentally based programs around the country. As is often the case in experiments, the findings from the early studies lacked the clarity the researchers had desired. Furthermore, a decade after Head Start began, the political landscape had changed. The value of *any* early childhood intervention was seriously questioned, and funding for programs diminished. Whereas the early studies of the Head Start era programs followed children through the initial years of elementary school, the Consortium for Longitudinal Studies was created in 1975 specifically to extend the study of children included in early cognitive intervention projects of the 1960s. Through a meta-analyses of long-term outcomes and indicators of life success, researchers sought to establish the value of preschool for poor children (Condry, 1983). Hence, an early focus on comparing models shifted to a focus on simply showing that preschool mattered.

I describe three studies comparing instructional approaches in early childhood education. In each study, researchers compared programs in an effort to identify the most effective preschool model for young economically disadvantaged children. The three studies described here were originally designed to follow students from preschool through early elementary school. All three were extended in 1975 as part of the Consortium for Longitudinal Studies. Taken together, these three studies lay the groundwork for the contemporary discussion of instructional practices.

Louisville: Four Approaches

The first study included Head Start children in Louisville, Kentucky from 1968 to 1969 (Miller & Dyer, 1975; Miller & Bizzell, 1983a, 1983b). Four well-known approaches to preschool instruction were examined. These included: (a) the traditional nursery school approach emphasizing enrichment and socioemotional growth, (b) the Montessori approach taught by trained Montessori teachers using Montessori didactic materials in the prepared environment, (c) Bereiter-Engleman's innovative direct instruction through patterned drill in arithmetic and reading (known as DISTAR), and (d) another newly developed program called DARCEE, which combined an emphasis on preacademic skills with support in developing appropriate attitudes toward learning (Gray & Klaus, 1965; Gray, Ramsey, & Klaus, 1982). Both the Traditional and Montessori approaches emphasized slower paced, individualized, child-centered learning, whereas the DISTAR and DARCEE programs were more preacademic and teacher centered, and emphasized small-group, teacher-led sessions. The preschool classrooms were observed, and differences in practice both within and across programs were documented. Also the effects of the four programs on children's cognitive, motivational, and perceptual development were measured (Miller & Dyer, 1975). Children were assessed several times during preschool and early elementary school. An additional assessment occurred in adolescence as part of the Consortium Study (Miller & Bizzell, 1983a, 1983b).

Based on program model descriptions, Miller and Dyer focused on eight program dimensions. Programs were hypothesized to differ in practice along these lines. These included: (a) feedback and the use of reinforcement, (b) modeling and imitation, (c) the role of play and criteria for toys in the classroom, (d) the significance of sensory stimulation in the classroom, (e) language and informal conversation in the classroom, (f) manipulation of materials in the classroom, (g) sequencing of content, and (h) ecological dimensions of the classroom, including grouping and the number of ongoing projects in the classroom. Observational systems for measuring these program dimensions were devised including categories of teacher and child behavior. Coded observations were analyzed in discriminant analyses.

In general, programs ordered as expected on the dimensions observed. In some cases, there were obviously four distinct models. In terms of *activities of children*, the four programs were clearly different. Much verbal recitation and little role playing ordered models from highest to lowest: DISTAR,

Montessori, DARCEE, and Traditional. On other dimensions, the four programs fell into two groups. For example, in *classroom structure*, DISTAR and DARCEE appeared highly similar as did the Traditional and Montessori programs. DISTAR and DARCEE were both teacher-directed, fast-paced didactic treatments in a group format involving high amounts of positive reinforcement. DISTAR was characterized by requests for group performance, teacher modeling, more setting of academic standards, and more correction. DARCEE was characterized by verbal instruction, requests for individual performance both verbal and role playing, and lower amounts of error correction. Only DISTAR was characterized by more teacher contact with groups than individuals. In contrast, Montessori and Traditional were child-centered, individualized, and slower paced treatments. Montessori was characterized by more didactic teaching through giving information to individuals, low amounts of either positive or negative reinforcement, and much child conversation and materials manipulation. Traditional Nursery School was characterized by low amounts of didactic teaching and teachers communicating primarily through verbal requests for individual performance as children conversed and played. In general, programs differed from each other in practice, and they were also largely consistent with the program developers' expectations.

Cognitive, motivational, and perceptual measures were administered in prekindergarten, kindergarten, first grade, and second grade. At all four testing occasions, children received a general IQ test (Stanford-Binet), The Basic Concept Inventory, The Peabody Picture Vocabulary Test, and several motivational measures (Dog and Bone Test, The Curiosity Box, The Replacement Puzzle, The Behavior Inventory). In addition, children were given the Embedded Figures Test in preschool and kindergarten and the California Achievement Test in first and second grades.

The prekindergarten assessment measured the immediate effects of the early childhood programs on children. In general, the immediate impact of each program was consistent with program emphasis. The effects of the DISTAR program were largely confined to cognitive and academic areas. Effects of DARCEE were more diffuse and most evident in areas of motivation and attitudes. The two didactic programs (DISTAR and DARCEE) produced higher scores on the Stanford-Binet, arithmetic, the Basic Concept Inventory, and sentence construction. DARCEE also influenced motivational measures such as achievement ratings, ambition, and verbal social participation. Montesorri children improved more than others in inventiveness and curiosity. Children in the Traditional program showed the highest level of verbal social participation.

By the end of kindergarten, the Montessori children were high on two subtests of the Metropolitan Readiness test: alphabet and numbers. Montessori and DARCEE children were higher on inventiveness than the other two programs. At the end of second grade, Montessori and DISTAR children were superior to the other groups on reading. The highest group was the Montessori males. Montessori males were highest on IQ. DARCEE and Montessori children continued to score high on divergent thinking, whereas DISTAR and Traditional children were still low. DARCEE and Traditional children were higher in verbal social participation. All groups declined in IQ, but the decline was steeper for DISTAR children and for females.

The results from the long-term follow-up are reported by Miller and Bizzell (1983 a, 1983b). By seventh and eighth grades, only a small number of children were performing at or above the 50th percentile for their grade level. Of those that were, about half were from the Montessori preschool. Although there was no significant *main* effects for program in seventh or eighth grades, there were several interactions. Males from the Montessori program received significantly higher scores than other groups. A similar pattern was shown on achievement measures. The boys from DARCEE received the lowest scores. The pattern for females was quite different. On achievement, girls fared best in DARCEE, although they did not do as well as the Montessori boys. All groups, with the exception of the Montessori boys, declined in IQ from second to eighth grade.

Miller and Bizzell (1983a) concluded that differences among programs seem to have been more pronounced for boys than girls. Within programs, sex differences were most pronounced in Montessori and DARCEE. On achievement tests, the middle school advantage for the Montessori children, for example, existed primarily for boys. The DARCEE program produced consistently higher achievement test scores for girls rather than for boys. Miller and Bizzell further noted that their findings regarding gender differences are consistent with other work by Gray, the developer of DARCEE, as well as work by Karnes and colleagues.

Thus, it would seem that the boys *may* have especially benefited from the child-centered, individualized format, which also permitted a high degree of physical manipulation and conversation. It is noteworthy that the boys did not particularly benefit from the Traditional program, at least as implemented in this research. This program was also child centered and individualized. The results from the classroom and videotaped observations are particularly useful here for identifying what actually transpired in these two different preschool models as implemented in Louisville. One difference appears to be in the activities of children. Children in both DARCEE and Montessori were more actively engaged with materials through physical manipulation and informal conversations with teachers and other children. It is intriguing that the gender-by-program interaction does not emerge until second grade and that, in the short run, the high-structure program appeared to benefit boys as well as girls.

In summary, boys fared the best in the Montessori program, whereas girls fared best in DARCEE. This conclusion relies on the long-term data. There was a striking difference between the short-term findings and the long-term findings from middle school. Early results favored the highly structured, teacher-centered programs, especially DISTAR. However, these effects faded. By middle school, the beneficial effects of the child-centered approach became evident.

Illinois: Five Approaches

Concurrent with the initiation of Project Head Start, Merle Karnes launched a research program comparing five instructional programs for preschoolers. According to Karnes, models were chosen on theoretical as well as practical grounds to represent different levels of structure. "The teacher child interaction was considered to be the paramount ingredient of structure, and the degree of structure was contingent upon the specificity and intensity of that interaction" (Karnes, Schwedel, & Williams, 1983, p. 135). According to Karnes, as the specificity and intensity of the interaction increased, so did the structure. Two programs represented the less structured end of the continuum--the Traditional and the Community-Integrated programs. These programs had a similar theoretical orientation, but the Traditional program included only disadvantaged children, whereas the Community-Integrated program enrolled primarily middle-class children along with two to four disadvantaged children in each class. Third was the Montessori program. This shared some features of the Traditional program but followed the Montessori methodology. Finally, there were two highly structured classrooms. The Ameliorative Program developed by Karnes and her associates emphasized psycholinguistic skills and made use of the Illinois Test of Psycholinguistic Abilities (ITPA) as a reference point for organizing instruction (see also Karnes, Zehrbach, & Teska, 1977). The Direct-Verbal or DISTAR Program was developed by Bereiter and Engelmann.

Karnes measured intellectual functioning, language functioning, and school achievement. The Stanford-Binet Intelligence Scale, the Illinois Test of Psycholinguistic Abilities (ITPA), the Metropolitan School Readiness Test, and the California Achievement Test were all administered at the end of kindergarten, the end of first grade, and the end of second grade. Unfortunately, little data about program implementation are reported by Karnes, Schwedel, and Williams (1983), although program developers were involved in program implementation. Later on, when Karnes and her group joined the Consortium for Longitudinal Studies, additional measures regarding family background were added.

Of primary interest to Karnes and her colleagues were outcomes of the five preschool programs. At the end of the preschool year, significant differences in intellectual functioning favoring the Ameliorative and the Direct-

Verbal Programs (DISTAR) were found. These groups gained about 14 IQ points, whereas the other three groups gained from 5 to 8 points. Similar results favoring these two groups were also found on the ITPA. Karnes argued that program structure would predict change, and her results are partially consistent with this. Although the high-structure groups showed the greatest change, children in the Traditional program showed more change than those in the Montessori program. Karnes noted that this is inconsistent with her expectation because the Montessori program was more structured than the Traditional. She attributed the poor performance of the children in Montessori to the absence of verbal interaction in that program. It is not clear whether this statement is based on observation of classroom interactions or is an inference based on written program materials.

From kindergarten through Grade 4, only children in Ameliorative, DISTAR, and Traditional programs were followed. Tests of reading achievement at the end of first grade showed that the children in the Ameliorative program and the DISTAR program outperformed those in the Traditional program. By the end of third grade, only the Ameliorative group was at grade level, whereas the children from DISTAR and the Traditional programs were slightly below grade level. A similar pattern was evident in mathematical achievement. Hence, at the end of first grade, it appeared that the highly structured programs were more effective in supporting school achievement. However, as students progressed in school, differences among groups became less apparent (Karnes, Schwedel, & Williams, 1983).

An additional perspective on these programs is added by the longitudinal follow-up conducted by Karnes and her colleagues in conjunction with the Consortium for Longitudinal Studies. Because the purpose of the Consortium study and the longitudinal follow-up conducted in 1979 and 1980 was to examine the effects of preschool intervention on disadvantaged children's overall life success, several indicators of school performance were studied. Indicators of school success included placement in special education classes, graduation status, and grade retentions. It is interesting to note that the Montessori group contained the highest percentage of high school graduates (75%), with children in the Traditional program close behind (70%). Relatively low rates were shown for the other groups. The Montessori group also contained the highest percentage of students never retained in grade. On a composite indicator of overall school success, the Montessori group scored the highest. The Traditional program was ranked second, and the Ameliorative was slightly below at third. The children in the DISTAR program scored relatively poorly on this overall indicator.

In reflecting on the performance of the Montessori children, Karnes suggested that perhaps working independently and persisting, components of the Montessori experience, provided a special payoff. She noted that these children actually had quite low IQ scores at age 16, but suggests that independence and persistence may be qualities that are viewed positively by teachers and may have particularly benefited these children. In retrospect, it is unfortunate that more data about these students were not gathered at earlier phases of the study.

High/Scope: Three Approaches

A third curriculum comparison study was initiated by the High Scope Foundation in the 1960s (Schweinhart & Weikart, 1980; Schweinhart, Weikart, & Larner, 1986a; Weikart, Epstein, Schweinhart, & Bond, 1978). This study was initially conceptualized to evaluate the Cognitively Oriented Curriculum developed by Weikart and his colleagues as part of the Perry Preschool Project in Ypsilanti, Michigan. In this study, three curricula were compared: the High/Scope Cognitively Oriented Program, the Bereiter-Engelmann DISTAR program, and a Traditional Child-Centered Thematic-Based Approach. Weikart and his colleagues characterized the DISTAR approach as *programmed learning*, in which the teacher plays an active role and the child plays a passive role. DISTAR stands in contrast to the traditional child-centered approach, in which the child actively initiates and the teacher plays a more passive role. Weikart characterized the High/Scope Cognitively Oriented Program, or Open Framework Approach, as the only one in which both the child and teacher play an active, initiating role (Hohman, Banet, & Weikart, 1979). This focus on joint initiating activity is important and is discussed again later in this chapter.

The 68 child participants were randomly assigned to the three preschool curriculum groups. Children were followed across their two years of preschool (an unusual feature of this study was that children began preschool at age 3) through elementary school to the fourth grade. Children were assessed for intellectual performance and school achievement during the preschool and elementary years. At age 15, children were assessed on these measures as well as measures of social competence, social behavior, and attitudes. Schweinhart, Weikart, and Larner (1986a, 1986b) reported IQ scores for all groups each year from ages 3 to 10. They also reported California Achievement Test Scores for first and second grades. Across all three preschool programs, IQ scores rose dramatically for one year of preschool. Scores then dropped somewhat. The smallest dropoff occurred for the DISTAR group, and the difference between this group and the High/Scope and Traditional programs was significant. Although the DISTAR group continued to outscore the other two groups in three of the four subsequent years, the differences failed to reach significance. A comparison of the California Achievement Test scores across the three groups at ages 7 and 8 also failed to show a significance difference. In summary, with the exception of IQ after one year of preschool, which favored the DISTAR program, type of curriculum was unrelated to children's cognitive performance and school achievement in elementary school.

However, a different pattern emerged from the data gathered from the preschool program participants when they reached adolescence. At age 15, Schweinhart and colleagues assessed the former preschool participants for *adult functional competence*. A self-report measure was developed to assess juvenile delinquency and other areas of social behavior. The DISTAR group differed significantly from the other two groups on the High/Scope Delinquency subscale. They also differed in other social activities such as, less frequently participating in sports, less frequently holding a school job or office, and less often reporting having read a book in the last week (Schweinhart, Weikart, & Larner, 1986a, 1986b).

In reflecting on these findings, Schweinhart and his colleagues noted that there is no evidence that the youngsters in the DISTAR program engaged in more delinquency than they would have if they had not attended preschool. They noted the incidence of self-reported delinquency was no higher than it was for children in the control sample. They emphasized that the social goals inherent in the High/Scope program as well as the Traditional program served to produce favorable long-term social development goals (see Gersten, 1986, for an alternative interpretation of these findings). These findings have been largely maintained in a subsequent follow-up at age 23 (Schweinhart & Weikart, 1997).

Conclusion: Groundwork for Child-Regulated/Teacher-Guided Instruction

Taken together, these three comparisons of instructional models lay the groundwork for a child-regulated/teacher-guided approach to preschool instruction. Looking only at the relatively short-term results, one might conclude that, for disadvantaged children, a high-structure, teacher-directed program is the best choice. Indeed, all three of these studies, to the extent that they showed any differences across prekindergarten programs at the beginning of elementary school, tended to favor the more teacher-directed approaches. However, looking at the long-term picture, one sees that the children who fared the best were those whose preschool experience emphasized child choice and initiative through hands-on manipulative activities. In all three studies, children, especially boys, in the DISTAR program received slightly higher scores on either IQ assessments or achievement tests immediately following preschool. However, in all three studies, these early advantages eroded. By middle school, these children were floundering more than their counterparts in at least some of the child-centered preschool programs.

Although these studies present a variety of methodological limitations, taken together there is a compelling pattern. The late emerging benefits of the child-centered programs were not hypothesized by any of the researchers. Although these findings were happily embraced by the early childhood research community, most child-centered programs advocates had expected to see their approaches outshining the preacademic, high-structure programs early on. The success of the Montessori models included in the study by Miller and her colleagues as well as in the study by Karnes merits closer scrutiny. Results from both studies show a slight early advantage for children in the fast-paced, teacher-centered programs in academic areas. However, this advantage appears to fade as children continue in elementary school. In contrast, the benefit of the Montessori program emerged later. Miller found that boys in Montessori actually outperformed children in other programs at seventh and eighth grades. Karnes reported that children from the Montessori program showed the highest levels of school success, although they did not necessarily show the highest IQ scores (Karnes, Schwedel, & Williams, 1983). This model remains controversial within the mainstream early childhood community despite it's demonstrated success. The findings described here suggest that the Montessori approach should play a larger role in current discussions about instruction in early childhood classrooms.

A closer look at the old DARCEE approach is also needed. This approach is little known today and its original conceptual foundation is outdated. Recall that this approach, although characterized as teacher centered and preacademic, was the most effective with girls in the Louisville study. Miller and Dyer noted some similarities between DARCEE and Montessori. Both emphasized sensory stimulation, manipulation of materials, and teaching through modeling of skills concepts. For example, in both programs, the teacher introduces a concept by building a tower or a design with blocks, which the child is asked to copy (Miller & Dyer, 1975). Both also place a heavy emphasis on supporting the child's motivation to learn, although they use different means to achieve that goal. DARCEE also emphasized informal conversation. Although conversation is not emphasized in Montessori, it is not discouraged, and the implementation data from Miller and Dyer (1975) show that it occurred more often there than in other programs. Both approaches include a tightly planned didactic curriculum and instructional plan.

There may be similarities among some of these instructional strategies and the currently popular Vygotskian notion of *scaffolding* (Berk & Winsler, 1995; Bodrova & Leong, 1996). Although the role of the teacher is often downplayed in Montessori and the role of the child's interactions with the materials is emphasized, the Montessori teacher keeps extensive observational notes on individual children. She makes a decision to introduce new materials through a demonstration lesson when she feels the child is ready. She carefully directs the child forward to materials that are structured to require minimal guidance after the initial demonstration. She seems to scaffold from a distance. In contrast, the DARCEE teacher appears to play a more immediate scaffolding role, spending more time directly interacting with the children around the materials.

In summary, findings from these three studies are consistent with an approach that emphasizes opportunities for the preschool-age child to regulate ongoing activity in the classroom through informal discussion, child choice and initiative, and interaction with hands-on manipulative materials. There is also a clearly defined role for the teacher as an active planner and implementor of carefully planned and sequenced instructional experiences.

REEXAMINING APPROACHES: BACK TO BASICS VERSUS DEVELOPMENTALLY APPROPRIATE PRACTICE

Concurrent with the release of the Consortium Study described earlier (Lazar & Darlington, 1982), the general public was expressing a renewed interest in early academics and *back to basics*. Interest came from two groups--middle-class families seeking academic acceleration and advocates for disadvantaged children. Some argued that early formal academic instruction was a valuable enrichment experience for young children (Gersten & Carnine, 1975; Veras, 1975). Others condemned the *pressure* and *hot housing* of young children. For example, Elkind (1987) was highly critical of early formal instruction in reading and math, arguing that excessive early academic pressure runs counter to the child's natural predisposition to learn by exploration and activity. The imposition of excessive adult learning priorities on young children interferes with the child's self-directed learning, creating anxiety, guilt, and the stifling of intrinsic motivation. These views were echoed by many others (Kagan & Zigler, 1987; Sigel, 1987).

Reductions in federal funding led to the scaling back of social programs. Increasingly, state and local governments included early childhood programs in the public schools (Spodek & Brown, 1993). This was accompanied by concern from the early childhood community about inappropriately pushing down practices employed with primary level children. The NAEYC Position Statement on Developmentally Appropriate Practices (Bredekamp, 1987) was especially targeted at programs created in this new era of preschool expansion into the public schools (Kagan & Zigler, 1987).

Although *developmentally appropriate* and *developmentally inappropriate* are not curricula, they are descriptors of instructional approaches and learning environments. Highly academic programs such as DISTAR, even when well implemented, would have been considered *inappropriate*, whereas a well-implemented version of a traditional Bank Street Approach, High/Scope, or other Piagetian model would be considered *appropriate*. The value judgments associated with the labels *developmentally appropriate* and *developmentally inappropriate* precipitated a flood of controversy within the field of early childhood education (Goffin, 1994; Kessler & Swadner, 1992; Lucek, 1996; Wardle, 1999). It is interesting to note that both the Montessori and DARCEE programs present challenges to the developmentally appropriate/inappropriate classification scheme. In the revised edition of the NAEYC Guidelines for Developmentally Appropriate Practice, Bredekamp and Copple (1997) modified the recommendations to better account for the role of instruction in the curriculum content areas. However, the debate about these guidelines continues.

In the next section of this chapter, research on the effects of varying instructional practices on young children's learning and development is explored. A number of psychological outcomes have been considered including stress, interpersonal reasoning, motivation for learning, and, of course, academic outcomes. This work differs from the research described in the last section in three ways. First, most of the work was carried out in community-based programs rather than sites funded for research and development. Second, specific philosophies and instructional practices are explored rather than comprehensive curriculum models. Third, child participants represent a wide range of socioeconomic backgrounds.

Instructional Practices and Stress

Asking whether an academic orientation in preschool serves as a challenge or pressure to young children, Rescorla, Hyson, and Hirsch-Pasek (1991) considered the role of parents' and teachers' attitudes on program choices and child outcomes. They also measured features of early childhood learning environments and their effects on children. Using the original NAEYC Guidelines as a reference, Hyson and colleagues (Hyson, Hirsch-Pasek, & Rescorla, 1990) devised a measure of the developmental appropriateness of the preschool classroom environment. Ninety 4-to-5-year-old prekindergarten children and their mothers were included. Fifty-six children were followed and investigated at the end of kindergarten. Children attended preschools varying widely in teaching philosophy. Rescorla and colleagues concluded that highly academic preschool environments had no effect on academic skills within this relatively affluent sample. They were, however, modestly related to less creativity, higher levels of test anxiety, and less positive attitudes toward school.

Concurrently, a series of studies emerged from a research group at Louisiana State University exploring relationships between teacher beliefs and practices and stress behaviors in young children. Charlesworth, Hart, Burts, and Hernandez (1991) developed a questionnaire based on the NAEYC Guidelines for Developmentally Appropriate Practice in Early Childhood Education to assess teachers' beliefs and perceived classroom practices. Stress behaviors exhibited by kindergarten children in classrooms labeled *developmentally appropriate* and those labeled *developmentally inappropriate* through the teacher questionnaire were subsequently examined by Burts, Hart, Charlesworth, and Kirk (1990). Children in the developmentally inappropriate classroom showed significantly more stress behaviors (e.g., daydreaming, teethgrinding, ignoring friendly overtures, ear pulling, rocking, stuttering, inappropriate laughter) than children in the developmentally appropriate classroom. Burts and colleagues also noted marginal gender differences, with males exhibiting more overall stress behaviors than females.

In a follow-up study, Burts and her colleagues extended this initial study to a larger sample and also considered socioeconomic status (SES) and ethnicity of the child (Burts et al., 1992). Teacher questionnaires (including teacher beliefs and instructional activities) were distributed to 219 (94% of the total) kindergarten teachers in a medium-size southern city.

Teachers with standardized factor scores at least 1 standard deviation above or below the mean (of all kindergarten teachers) were contacted for further participation. These 20 teachers were then observed on the Checklist for Rating Developmentally Appropriate Practice in Kindergarten Classrooms as a cross-validation on their self-reports. Twelve classrooms were finally selected for participation. Two hundred and four children (89% of those in the 12 classes) participated. Children were observed for evidence of stress while in their classrooms on at least six nonconsecutive days during a variety of daily activities. Overall results show that males in inappropriate classrooms exhibited more stress than males in appropriate classrooms. There were no differences in stress for girls across the two types of classrooms.

In summary, these and other findings support the contention that children participating in programs characterized as *developmentally inappropriate* and placing a heavy emphasis on drill, worksheets, and preacademics, while minimizing choice and decision making, show higher levels of stress in school. These effects appear to be most pronounced among boys and to some degree among poor and African-American children. The work by the Louisiana State group suggests some of the costs that might have been associated with the slightly increased test scores observed in the DISTAR classrooms described earlier. More observational work on children's classroom behavior in relation to specific instructional practices is needed. More longitudinal follow-up is also sorely needed.

Instructional Practices and Interpersonal Reasoning

A somewhat different approach to studying the impact of an early childhood program was followed by DeVries (DeVries & Kohlberg, 1987/1990; DeVries & Zan, 1994). The work of DeVries and her colleagues underscores the notion that all developmentally appropriate programs are not the same. In a series of small-scale studies, DeVries and her colleagues examined the effects of a Piaget-based, constructivist early education program on children's interpersonal reasoning. DeVries's constructivist early education program builds on the epistemological assumption that knowledge is actively constructed by a knower who interprets experience, making sense of it in terms of what she already knows and how she already reasons. Constructivist education fosters development through activities that appeal to children's interests, involve experimentation with phenomena of the physical world, and create the need for social interaction leading to cooperation (DeVries & Kohlberg, 1978/1990; DeVries & Zan, 1994; Kamii & DeVries, 1977). A key component to the constructivist program is the promotion of autonomous moral judgment (see DeVries, chapter 7, this volume). One vehicle for promoting this goal is through social interaction, both between the child and her peers and between the adult authority figure and the child. The teacher in a constructivist classroom strives to establish a democratic atmosphere in which children vote, make their own classroom rules, and discuss what to do when rules are not respected. The teacher attempts to mediate children's conflicts, helping them to consider other's perspectives and develop new strategies for dealing with conflict.

In an early study, DeVries and Goncu (1987) reasoned that experience in a constructivist classroom, which encouraged social interaction and conflict resolution, should promote children's interpersonal understanding. They compared a group of children in a DeVries' constructivist classroom with a group of comparable children enrolled in a Montessori school. This is an interesting comparison because the Montessori program shares certain similarities with the Piaget-based program. Both encourage child initiation and choice of activity, and both downplay whole-group, direct instruction. DeVries and Goncu found that children in the constructivist classroom evidenced more sophisticated patterns of interpersonal reasoning in a social problem-solving situation.

In a subsequent set of studies, DeVries and her colleagues compared teachers' enacted interpersonal behavior (DeVries, Haney, & Zan, 1991) and children's sociomoral development as evidenced by enacted interpersonal behavior (DeVries, Reese-Learned, & Morgan, 1991) in constructivist, eclectic (an approach based on a mixture of practices lacking in conceptual coherence), and direct instruction (DISTAR) classrooms. DeVries and her colleagues expected that the sociomoral atmosphere of the three classrooms would differ and would be manifested in part through teachers' enacted interpersonal understanding. The study of teachers' enacted understanding included a discourse analysis of all the talk over the course of two days. Teacher-child interactions were coded microanalytically for the use of negotiation strategies and shared experiences. Interpersonal understandings were categorized at four levels. Consistent with expectations, the constructivist teacher evidenced the highest number of shared experiences. She also showed a greater percentage of high-level (Level 2 and 3) negotiations. The direct instruction teacher showed a higher percentage of low-level (Level 0) and a lower level of shared experiences than the other teachers. According to DeVries and her colleagues, the direct instruction teacher evidenced a strong authoritarian orientation and a strong academic emphasis. The constructivist teacher showed a cooperative orientation and an emphasis on stimulating reasoning. The Eclectic teacher fell in between.

In a parallel study, DeVries, Reese-Learned, and Morgan (1991) studied the enacted interpersonal understanding of the children in the three different types of kindergarten programs. Pairs of children were observed as they played a game. Interactions were coded for social understanding in the use of negotiation strategies, at three levels, and in shared experiences. Children were also interviewed about life in classrooms. Specifically, they were asked about rules, misconduct, interpersonal problems, classroom activities, and reasons for school. Results show that all children predominantly used Level 1 negotiation strategies, the constructivist group consistently had the highest percentage of Level 2 negotiations, and the direct instruction group had the lowest. The constructivist group was more interpersonally active, having a greater number and variety of negotiations and shared experiences than the other groups. One interesting difference between the three groups was the degree to which children continued to function effectively and independently when the teacher briefly left the room. Only the constructivist class evidenced no disruption in activity. Although academic achievement was not a focus of this study, DeVries and colleagues noted that the direct instruction group had shown higher scores on a preschool screening test and on an achievement test at the end of first grade. However, by third grade, these differences had disappeared.

Instructional Practices and Motivation for Learning

Yet another line of research on early childhood programs and their effects on young children was conducted by Deborah Stipek and her colleagues at UCLA (Stipek, 1991; Stipek, Daniels, Galluzzo, & Millburn, 1992; Stipek & Greene, chap. 3, this volume). Stipek created an empirically based approach to differentiating early childhood programs with regard to a broad array of instructional practices along the same lines as Miller and Dyer (1975) and Stallings (1975). She devised a complex observation protocol focusing on variables relevant to social and motivational development. Sixty-two prekindergarten and kindergarten classrooms from diverse settings were observed. Observers spent 1 day in each program and made 27 judgments about each organized (teacher-planned) activity. Judgments focused on the nature of the activity (e.g., intellectual, motor, discussion) and how it was implemented (e.g., were children allowed to work with peers, how much discretion children had about carrying out teachers' instructions). In addition, 36 summary judgments of each teacher were made (e.g., teachers' warmth and responsiveness, the diversity of activities, whether playtime and worktime were clearly differentiated, and how frequently social comparisons were made). Variables were then grouped conceptually and empirically into six subscales that differentiated classrooms. These included *child initiative* (children choose activities in a playlike atmosphere, social interaction), *teacher warmth* (teachers were nurturing, accepting, respectful, and responsive to children), *positive control* (positive approaches to maintaining student engagement in sanctioned activities), and minimizing behavior (clear instructions, novel, interesting activities, without ridicule, threats, or punishment). The *academic emphasis* subscale included items about differentiation of subject matter, large amounts of time on focused academic topics, frequent use of commercially prepared materials such as worksheets, frequent use of closed-ended tasks and absence of embedding content in practical or personally meaningful context. The *performance pressure* subscale included items about negative evaluations and criticism and an emphasis on outcomes rather than the enjoyment of learning. Finally, the *evaluation stress* scale measured the use of external evaluation and rewards.

Although each of the six subscales showed internal consistency, they were not independent. A nonorthogonal factor analysis showed a single factor with the first three scales loading positively (i.e., child initiative, warmth, and positive control). These were labeled the *social context* subscales. The second three subscales loaded negatively on the same factor and were referred to as *teacher-directed instruction*. Hence, the empirical analyses suggested a unidimensional characterization of early childhood programs. The poles of this continuum are consistent with the characterizations by early childhood experts, child centered (low in direct instruction, high in positive social context), and didactic (high in instruction, less positive social context). Stipek noted that the unidimensional picture was supported by the results of separate cluster analyses for preschool and kindergarten. For each, three clusters emerged: child-centered programs, didactic programs, and an in between group. Stipek's results suggest that the dimensions identified in the Louisville experimental programs described earlier also characterized the community-based programs in Los Angeles nearly two decades later.

In subsequent work, Stipek and her colleagues examined the effects of these two different instructional approaches on children's socioemotional, cognitive, and motivational outcomes. In one study, Stipek, Feiler, Daniels, and Millburn (1995) assessed 227 four-to-six-year-olds from diverse backgrounds. Children attended 1 of 39 preschool or kindergarten classrooms that varied on the previously described dimensions. Classrooms were clearly classifiable as child centered or didactic. Child-centered and didactic kindergartens and child-centered preschools were roughly half public and half private. All didactic preschools were private. Children were assessed for basic skills achievement (using the Woodcock-Johnson Achievement Test or the Peabody Individual Achievement Test), self-perceptions of academic ability, expectations for success, enjoyment of school and school like activities, dependency and need for approval, preference for basic skills and challenge, anxiety, and pride in accomplishment.

Results show that children in didactic programs stressing basic skills had significantly higher scores on the letters/reading achievement test, but not on a numbers achievement test. Being enrolled in a didactic early childhood education program was associated with relatively negative outcomes on most of the motivation measures. Compared with children in child-centered programs, children in didactic programs rated their abilities significantly lower, had lower expectations for success on academic tasks, showed more dependency on adults for permission and approval, evidenced less pride in their accomplishments, and claimed to worry more about school. The overall effects of type of instructional program were similar for economically disadvantaged and middle-class children. Also effects of instructional program were similar for preschoolers and kindergartners.

A follow-up study reported by Stipek et al. (1998) replicated the earlier study of the relationship between instructional experiences and child outcomes. They tested preschoolers and kindergarten children, but added several new features. Specifically, they added a pretest assessment; included a broader mix of early childhood programs by incorporating classrooms with instructional practices falling midway between the poles of child centered and direct instruction; extended measures of cognitive skills to include conceptual grouping, problem solving, and flexibility of thinking along with achievement measures; assessed motivation in the classroom context through observation; and included a subsample of children posttested 1 year later. The results show primarily negative effects on both cognitive and motivation outcomes of preschool programs emphasizing basic skills using structured, teacher-directed approaches in a relatively negative social climate. For kindergartners, both positive and negative achievement outcomes were associated with both types of programs. The findings from the second study differed somewhat from the earlier study. In the second study, preschool and kindergarten children evidenced different reactions to the two instructional approaches. Results on both the cognitive and the sociomotivational measures suggest that the preschool-age children fared better with the child-centered approach. However, at the kindergarten level, the structured, teacher-directed program appeared to increase basic skills, whereas the child-centered program promoted motivation and problem solving.

Stipek and colleagues stressed the mixed picture offered by the findings from these studies. Although results generally favor child-centered approaches, some useful skills may be effectively taught using didactic methods. They interpret their findings as a call to seek out a broader array of instructional approaches and specifically a better meld of didactic and child-centered approaches, such as a didactic environment, which also includes a positive nurturing social climate. Such an environment would emphasize both an active role for the teacher and the creation of a positive social climate through instructional conversations, thought-provoking questions, and encouragement to test hypotheses and draw inferences. Such an approach, she and her colleagues argue, would be consistent with the revised NAEYC Guidelines (Bredekamp & Copple, 1997), which emphasize a Vygotskian, social-constructivist approach to learning and instruction.

Teacher-Identified Instructional Approaches

A recent study by Marcon (1999) illustrates an alternative approach to examining the differential impact of preschool program on children's development and learning. Marcon studied inner-city children in a large urban school district. She examined the relationships between teachers' support for an academic orientation in preschool, a child-initiated approach, or a mixed approach and child outcomes. Marcon identified program models by surveying teachers about their beliefs and practices. The brief survey of all teachers in the district focused on: (a) scope of developmental goals, (b) conception of how children learn, (c) amount of autonomy given to the child, (d) conception of teacher's role, and (e) provision of possibilities for learning from peers. Teachers were asked about beliefs and practices. Based on survey responses, teachers clearly belonging to one of each of the three model orientations were identified. Unlike earlier studies, program identification emerged exclusively from teachers' self-reports about their beliefs and practices. Child outcomes were assessed through the existing school district achievement measures as well as the Vineland Adaptive Behavior Scales.

Marcon's results support the hypothesized differential effects of the three preschool models on children's development at the end of the preschool (Head Start or prekindergarten) experience. Comparisons between three preschool approaches (teacher-centered direct instruction, child development, and eclectic) indicate that children in classrooms where teachers held beliefs that corresponded with a single, internally coherent theory of how young children learn and develop (based either on a didactic learning approach or a more traditional developmental orientation) fared better on a standardized measure of development than children whose teachers attempted to blend aspects of theoretically diverse approaches in a less coherent way. The combination approach was ineffective. In addition, at this early age, children's development was not notably hindered by the strong academic focus represented by the direct instruction model, although receptive and expressive language skills, personal and interpersonal relationship skills, and gross motor skills of those children were lower than expected. Children who enrolled in the more child development-oriented model actually mastered more basic skills. Marcon noted that the benefits of child-initiated learning were especially notable in African-American children's performance.

Marcon's findings complement Stipek's work in an interesting way. If early childhood professionals seek to develop an integration of direct instruction and child-centered approaches, they must do so in a way that preserves logical coherence. Marcon showed that haphazard eclectic approaches are unlikely to be effective. Rather, what is needed is an approach to instruction that is logically consistent and comprehensive. One such approach may well be grounded in a dialectical-cultural approach to learning and development, such as Vygotsky's or some other contemporary approach to cognitive development emphasizing domain-specific and domain-general changes (e.g., Case,1998; Case, Griffin, & Kelly, chap. 2, this volume). Marcon's conclusions echo the rationales for theory-based programs of the Head Start era (Day & Parker, 1977; Evans, 1975).

FINDING NEW MODELS OF INSTRUCTION

Enduring Conflicts

The history of science has shown that conflicting findings provide the context for the generation of new theoretical explanations (Kuhn, 1970). The research on instruction in early childhood education has no shortage of conflicting findings, and the need for new theoretical models could not be more strongly felt (see Barnett & Boocock, 1998; Clarke-Stewart & Fein, 1983; Genishi, Ryan, & Ochsner, in press; Goffin, 1994; Powell, 1987; Spodek & Brown, 1993). The purpose of this chapter has been to overview some of these findings in an effort to set the stage for new approaches to young children's classroom learning. Several key sets of conflicting findings have been explored. Although some of these issues have been raised before, the time is right to reexamine them and identify new approaches for solving the puzzle they present.

Short-Term Versus Long-Term Outcomes. The first set of conflicting findings concerns the longitudinal research on curriculum models in the 1960s. This work is illustrated by Miller and her colleagues in the Louisville study, the Karnes curriculum comparison study, and the High/Scope study. All three of these studies show relatively short-term cognitive gains as measured by achievement or IQ for teacher-directed instructional programs. Yet long-term results show no support for DISTAR style teacher-centered instruction. Rather long-term results favor child-initiated approaches. Two of these studies, Miller and Bizzell (1983a, 1983b) and Karnes, Schwedel, and Williams (1983), suggested that the Montessori program is particularly effective. The dilemma of long-term versus short-term findings is a recurring concern for early childhood educators, developmental and educational psychologists, and policymakers (see Barnett, 1998; Barnett & Boocock, 1998).

Child-Centered Versus Teacher Centered. A second set of conflicting findings is evident in Stipek's research as well as some of the research on developmentally appropriate practice. Stipek (1993) presented an excellent analysis of this issue, and it is discussed further by Stipek and Greene (chap. 3, this volume). Community-based early childhood programs can generally be described as either slow paced and child centered or fast paced and teacher centered, and the bulk of the evidence in programs for 4-year-olds favors the former. However, there is evidence favoring the more teacher-centered approaches when some specific academic skills are the concern. There seems to be a conflict between a positive social climate and strong instructional goals. This conflict is also illustrated by the work of Charlesworth and colleagues (1991). Children in developmentally inappropriate environments are more stressed. How can early childhood educators simultaneously support children's academic goals and their socioemotional well-being? The recent work by Marcon may begin to clarify this conflict. She has shown that the least effective environment is one in which the teachers operate from an eclectic, inconsistent conceptual framework. Perhaps all teacher-centered programs are not the same. However, it remains to be seen whether the children in Marcon's teacher-centered classes will hold their own in the long term. Will their gains disappear as did those of the children in the early DISTAR programs? Or will they endure as did those of the girls in DARCEE?

Cognitive Development Versus Character Development. A third conflict is described by DeVries (chapter 7, this volume). Paralleling some of the earlier discussion on DISTAR, DeVries makes clear that instructional practices that promote interpersonal understanding are not consistent with the authoritarian orientation of a teacher-centered classroom. This conflict is not really an empirical conflict. It may reflect conflicting educational goals and conflicting values. Is it possible to promote autonomy and standards-based achievement simultaneously? Is it possible to enforce standards without being authoritarian? Some, including Kohn (1997), argue that these two concerns cannot be reconciled. [But see Glanzer (1998) for another view]

Signposts Toward a Resolution: Child-Regulated/Teacher-Guided Instruction

A search for resolutions to these dilemmas is the goal of this book. Research discussed here makes clear that a new model of instruction capable of synthesizing these findings must meet several criteria.

Child-Regulated Learning. First, the evidence points to the importance of a learning environment calling for an active child. There appear to be long-term positive effects of the so-called *child-centered approaches*, especially High/Scope and Montessori. (The Traditional or Bank Street Approach is also child centered, but it seems to take more varying forms and showed less evidence of long-term effectiveness.) Common to all of these orientations is an emphasis on an *active* child. Typically this includes slower paced activity that is child initiated. However, it may be that what is critical is not child-initiated activity per se, but rather the child's ability to regulate activity. Learning environments that fail to allow the child to regulate the pace of interaction may undermine learning and development. Child-regulated interaction with the environment is critical for brain development, language development, and many aspects of cognitive growth. Environments that are poorly matched to the child's ability to self-regulate will not foster learning and development. Related issues are explored in the chapters by McCune and Zanes (chap. 4, this volume) and Hyson and Molinaro (chap. 5, this volume).

A focus on child-regulated activity suggests that environments with too little structure as well as environments with too much structure can undermine children's intellectual development. Hence, the Traditional program described by Miller and Dyer (1975) contained too few opportunities for stimulation and active engagement with materials, whereas the DISTAR environment described in Miller and Dyer (1975), DeVries, Reese-Learned, and Morgan (1991), Schweinhart, Weikart, and Larner (1986a, 1986b), and elsewhere probably contained too much direction and control by the teacher. Although the latter setting did lead to learning in the short run and facilitated children's performance on standardized tests, cognitive changes were not enduring. New models of instruction for early childhood education must permit the child to regulate the pace of instructional interactions in a flexible environment, rich in opportunity for intellectual engagement and responsive to the child's individual interests and temperament.

Teacher-Guided. Second, there is abundant evidence pointing to the influence of early childhood teachers on young children's academic performance. Weikart and colleagues described the active teacher, although the *active teacher* in High/Scope is quite different from the *active teacher* in the DARCEE program. In both programs, teachers interacted with children in planned small-group experiences, but the DARCEE teacher was more directive. The teacher in DARCEE was less dominating, however, than the teacher in DISTAR. Although DISTAR had short-term positive effects, the long-term effects were negative. The less domineering DARCEE teacher, who made use of manipulative materials, taught concepts through modeling, and made much use of informal conversation, was more successful in the long run. The Montessori teacher also had a very active role in implementing the curriculum, although it was quite different from High/Scope, DARCEE, or DISTAR. The Montesorri teacher demonstrated the appropriate use of materials through modeling, ensured that the environment was properly prepared, and engaged in intensive observation of children. This is not a teacher-centered instructional model, but is clearly a teacher active model. Another approach to this active teacher is to view the teacher as a guide. The teacher plays an active, guiding role in instructional interactions.

An Understanding of the Disciplines. Third, the active teacher must have a rich understanding of the disciplines (Gardner, 1999). She must understand how to link young children's experiences to the structure of disciplinary content. It is insufficient to simply identify engaging activities for young children. The teacher must know what the child can learn from those experiences. Often this is the downfall of the Traditional child-centered preschool curriculum. The linkage between children's learning and the structure of the disciplines is discussed in the recent volume on learning in math, science, and technology (American Association for the Advancement of Science, 1999), the recent volume on learning to read and write from NAEYC (Neuman, Copple, & Bredekamp, 2000), and in the recent volume *Classroom Lessons* (McGilly, 1997). This issue is further explored by Ginsberg, Pappas, and Seo (chap. 8, this volume); Liben and Downs (chap. 9, this volume); Morrow (chap. 10, this volume), and Rosenberg (chap. 11, this volume).

A Scientific Model of Learning and Development. Fourth, a scientific model of learning that links the broad integrative stagelike principles of cognitive development with domain specific learning is needed. Vygotskian and neo-Piagetian models of learning and development will meet this criteria. Theory in children's cognitive development and learning has changed dramatically since the development of the instructional models in early childhood described at the beginning of this chapter. There has been an explosion of interest in neo-Vygotskian orientations to learning and development (Berk & Winsler, 1995; Bodrova & Leong, 1996; Rogoff, 1990, 1998) as well as Piaget's later work and neo-Piagetian theories of learning and development (Case, 1998; Case, Griffin, & Kelly, chap. 2, this volume; Fischer, 1980; Scholnick, Nelson, Gelman, & Miller, 1999). This work provides a basis for integrating learning and development in a dynamic fashion. Others have emphasized the importance of microgenetic change (Fischer & Bidell, 1998). These new models of development can meet the need for both a child-regulated and a teacher-guided approach.

New models of instruction for early childhood must synthesize components of a traditional child-centered approach with this contemporary research into learning and development. Case, Griffin, and Kelly (chap. 2, this volume) refer to these essential components as play and meaning-making activities that are natural to early childhood. However, they must also include opportunities for didactic interaction with more knowledgeable others in which children jointly acquire the knowledge of the culture. Such interactions may take a variety of forms and are illustrated by Case, Griffin, and Kelly (chap. 2, this volume), and Ginsburg, Pappas, and Seo (chap. 8, this volume).

Ecology of the Child's Learning and Development. Fifth, there is a need to consider the context or ecology of the child's development in the design of instructional models for early childhood education (Eccles & Roeser, 1999). Context can be viewed as existing at three levels. The first level of context is *within* the child. This means that cognitive development and mastery of academic content must be considered within the context of the child's overall development. Social, emotional, and neurophysical development must be considered with intellectual development. In a recent discussion of Head Start, Raver and Zigler (1997) called for supporting children's social and emotional competence within Head Start. They also emphasized the continuing need to support these aspects of development. These notions are also underscored by the research on instructional models described earlier. Within this volume; DeVries (chap. 7), Hyson and Molinaro (chap. 5), McCune and Zanes (chap. 4), Stipek and Greene (chap. 3) and Frede, Barnett, and Lupo (chap. 12) explore closely related issues.

The second level of context is within the classroom. Work from a variety of sources suggests that it is important to consider social relationships within the classroom when designing instructional environments (see O'Donnell & King, 1999; Pianta, 1999). Stipek's work shows clearly that preschoolers in early childhood classrooms scoring high on positive social climate (child initiative, warmth, and positive control) showed higher expectations for success, evidenced more pride in their accomplishments, and worried less about school. Furthermore, DeVries has shown that the nature of the instructional environment is related to children's interpersonal negotiation skills. These points are discussed in later chapters by Stipek and Green (chap. 3), Hyson and Molinaro (chap. 5), Klein (chap. 6), and DeVries (chap. 7).

The third level of context refers to the child in the family and community. It is increasingly clear that models of instruction must account for the varying cultural contexts in which children and their families live. It is no longer appropriate to assume that learning and development follow an unvarying course for all individuals (see Cole, 1999; McLoyd, 1998). As Case, Griffin, and Kelly (chap. 2, this volume) point out, our schools must account for the dramatic differences between children's experiences prior to school entry. Models of instruction must accommodate these differences and seek to maximize all children's likelihood of success in adult life.

CONCLUSION

Standards-based reform in American education has emerged from a different climate and context than did the War on Poverty and Project Head Start. However, both time periods are characterized by a great hope for our educational system as a source of social change and an equally great fear that the system is not equipped to meet the challenge. The first goal, identified in Clinton's Goals 2000 (Short & Talley, 1997) is, "All children will enter school ready to learn." One response to this challenge has been the call for universal prekindergarten in the public schools (Schulman, Blank, & Ewen, 1999). As we move toward full implementation of universal prekindergarten in the public schools, it is imperative that educators and policymakers employ the extensive knowledge base that exists regarding instructional models for early childhood.

It is critical that programs be implemented and evaluated thoughtfully and rigorously, and that the knowledge gained from such evaluations be cycled back into programs for design improvement. Past research suggests that teacher-centered instructional models for preschool education must be scrutinized carefully and implemented with great caution. Research shows that most teacher-centered instructional models emphasizing direct instruction for young children have a short-term payoff and long-term costs. This is particularly dangerous because politicians are always tempted by short-term payoff. Unfortunately, important benefits of child-centered approaches may not appear until after program evaluations are completed. This speaks to the need for longitudinal evaluations of preschool programs grounded in psychological theory. Research and theory from psychology has much to offer educational practitioners. The remaining chapters in this volume make this clear.

ACKNOWLEDGMENT

The author is indebted to Jody Eberly, Ellen Frede and Elisa Klein for their thoughtful comments on an earlier draft of this chapter.

REFERENCES

American Association for the Advancement of Science. (1999). *Dialogue on early childhood science, mathematics and technology education.* Washington, DC: Author.

Barnett, W. S. (1998). Long-term effects on cognitive development and school success. In W. S. Barnett & S. Boocock (Eds.), *Early care and education for children in poverty: Promises, programs and long-term results.* Albany: SUNY Press.

Barnett, W. S., & Boocock, S. (Eds.). (1998). *Early care and education for children in poverty: Promises, programs and long-term results.* Albany: SUNY Press.

Bereiter, C., & Englemann, S. (1966). *Teaching disadvantaged children in the preschool*. Englewood Cliffs, NJ: Prentice-Hall.

Berk, L., & Winsler, A. (1995). *Scaffolding children's learning: Vygotsky and early childhood education: Vol. 7. NAEYC Research into Practice*. Washington, D. C.: National Association for the Education of Young Children.

Biber, B. (1977). A developmental interaction approach: Bank Street College of Education. In M. C. Day & R. Parker (Eds.), *The preschool in action: Exploring early childhood programs*, 2nd ed., pp. 421-460. Boston: Allyn & Bacon.

Bloom, B. S. (1964). *Stability and change in human characteristics*. New York: Wiley.

Bodrova, E., & Leong, D. J. (1996). *Tools of the mind: The Vygotskian approach to early childhood education*. Englewood Cliffs, NJ: Merrill.

Bredekamp, S. (Ed.). (1987). *Developmentally appropriate practice in early childhood programs serving children from birth through age 8*. Washington, DC: National Association for the Education of Young Children.

Bredekamp, S., & Copple, C. (Eds.). (1997). *Developmentally appropriate practice in early childhood programs* (rev. ed.). Washington, DC: National Association for the Education of Young Children.

Bruner, J. (1972). Poverty and childhood. In R. K. Parker (Ed.), *The preschool in action: Exploring early childhood programs* (pp. 7-35). Boston: Allyn & Bacon.

Burts, D., Hart, C., Charlesworth, R., Fleege, P., Mosley, J., & Thomasson, R. (1992). Observed activities and stress behaviors in developmentally appropriate and inappropriate kindergarten classrooms. *Early Childhood Research Quarterly*, 7, 297-318.

Burts, D., Hart, C., Charlesworth, R., & Kirk, L. (1990). A comparison of stress behaviors observed in kindergarten children in classrooms with developmentally appropriate versus developmentally inappropriate instructional practices. *Early Childhood Research Quarterly*, 5, 407-423.

Case, R. (1998). The development of conceptual structures. In W. Damon (Ed.), *Handbook of child psychology* (5th ed., pp. 745-800). New York: Wiley.

Charlesworth, R., Hart, C., Burts, D., & Hernandez, S. (1991). Kindergarten teachers' beliefs and practices. *Early Child Development and Care*, 70, 17-35.

Clarke-Stewart, K. A., & Fein, G. (1983). Early childhood programs. In P. Mussen (Ed.), *Manual of child psychology* (pp. 917-999). New York: Wiley.

Clifford, R. M., Early, D. M., & Hills, T. W. (1998). Almost a million children in school before kindergarten: Who is responsible for the services? *Young Children*, 54(5), 48-51.

Cole, M. (1999). Culture in development. In M. Bornstein & M.Lamb (Eds.), *Developmental psychology: An advanced textbook* (pp. 73-124). Mahwah, NJ: Lawrence Erlbaum Associates.

Condry, S. (1983). History and background of preschool intervention programs and the Consortium for Longitudinal Studies. In *As the twig is bent: Lasting effects of preschool intervention studies* (pp. 1-31). Hillsdale, NJ: Lawrence Erlbaum Associates.

Damon, W. (1998). Preface to the handbook of child psychology. In W. Damon (Ed.), *Handbook of child psychology* (5th ed., pp. xi-xvii). New York: Wiley.

Day, M. C., & Parker, R. (Eds.). (1977). *The preschool in action: Exploring early childhood programs*, Boston: Allyn & Bacon.

DeVries, R., & Goncu, A. (1987). Interpersonal relations in four-year old dyads from Constructivist and Montessori programs. *Journal of Applied Developmental Psychology*, 8, 481-501.

DeVries, R., Haney, T., & Zan, B. (1991). Sociomoral atmosphere in direct-instruction, eclectic, and constructive kindergartens: A study of teachers enacted understanding. *Early Childhood Research Quarterly*, 6, 449-471.

DeVries, R., & Kohlberg, L. (1987/1990). *Constructivist early education: Overview and comparison with other programs*. Washington, DC: National Association for the Education of Young Children.

DeVries, R., & Reese-Learned, H., & Morgan, P. (1991). Sociomoral development in direct instruction, constructivist and eclectic kindergarten programs: A study of children's enacted understanding. *Early Childhood Research Quarterly, 6*, 449-471.

DeVries, R., & Zan, B. (1994). *Moral classrooms, moral children: Creating a constructivist atmosphere in early education*. New York: Teachers College Press.

Dixon, R., & Lerner, R. (1999). History and systems in developmental psychology. In M. Bornstein & M. Lamb (Eds.), *Developmental psychology: An advanced textbook* (4th ed., pp. 3-46). Mahwah, NJ: Lawrence Erlbaum Associates.

Eccles, J., & Roeser, R. W. (1999). School and community influences on human development. In M. Boornstein & M. Lamb (Eds.), *Developmental psychology: An advanced textbook* (pp. 503-554). Mahwah, NJ: Lawrence Erlbaum Associates.

Elkind, D. (1987). *Miseducation*. New York: Alfred Knopf.

Epstein, A., Schweinhart, L. J., & McAdoo, L. (1996). *Models of early childhood education*. Ypsilanti, MI: High/Scope Press.

Evans, E. (1975). *Contemporary influences in early childhood education* (2nd. ed.). New York: Holt, Rinehart & Winston.

Fischer, K. (1980). A theory of cognitive development: The control and construction of hierarchies of skills. *Psychological Review, 87*, 477-531.

Fischer, K., & Bidell, T. (1998). Dynamic development of psychological structures in action and thought. In W. Damon (Ed.), *Handbook of child psychology* (Vol. 1, 5th ed., pp. 467-561). New York: Wiley.

Frede, E. C. (1998). Preschool program quality in programs for children in poverty. In W. S. Barnett & S. Boocock (Eds.), *Early care and education for children in poverty: Promises, programs and long-term results* (pp. 77-98). Albany: SUNY Press.

Gardner, H. (1999). *The disciplined mind: What all students should understand*. New York: Simon & Schuster.

Genishi, C., Ryan, S., & Ochsner, M. (in press). Teaching in early childhood education: Understanding practices through research and theory. In V. Richardson (Ed.), *Handbook of research on teaching* (4th ed.). Washington, DC: American Educational Research Association.

Gersten, R. (1986). Response to "Consequences of three preschool curriculum models through age 15." *Early Childhood Research Quarterly, 1*, 293-302.

Gersten, R., & Carnine, D. (1984). Direct instruction mathematics: A longitudinal evaluation of low income elementary school students. *The Elementary School Journal, 44*(6), 28-31.

Glanzer, P. (1998, February). The character to seek justice: Showing fairness to diverse visions of character education. *Phi Delta Kappan*.

Goffin, S. G. (1994). *Curriculum models and early childhood education: Appraising the relationship*. New York: Merrill.

Gray, S., & Klaus, R. (1965). An experimental preschool program for culturally deprived children. *Child Development, 36*, 887-898.

Gray, S., Ramsey, B. K., & Klaus, R. A. (1982). *From 3 to 20: The Early Training Project*. Baltimore: University Park Press.

Hicks, S. A., Lekies, K., & Cochran, M. (1999). *Promising practices: New York State Universal Prekindergarten* (January 1999). The Cornell Early Childhood Program, Department of Human Development, Cornell University, Ithaca, New York.

Hohnam, M., Banet, B., & Weikart, D. (1979). *Young children in action: A manual for preschool educators*. Ypsilanti, MI: High/Scope Press.

Hunt, J. McV. (1961). *Intelligence and experience*. New York: Ronald.

Hyson, M. C., Hirsch-Pasek, K., & Rescorla, L. (1990). The Classroom Practices Inventory: An observation instrument based on NAEYC's Guidelines for Developmentally Appropriate Practices for 4- and 5-year old children. *Early Childhood Research Quarterly, 5*, 475-494.

Kagan, S., & Zigler, E. (1987). *Early schooling: The national debate*. New Haven, CT: Yale University Press.

Kamii, C., & DeVries, R. (1977). Piaget for early education. In M. C. Day & R. Parker (Eds.), *The preschool in action: Exploring early childhood programs* (pp. 363-420). Boston: Allyn & Bacon.

Karnes, M. B., Schwedel, A. M., & Williams, M. B. (1983). A comparison of five approaches for educating young children from low-income homes. *As the twig is bent: Lasting effects of preschool programs* (pp. 133-170). Hillsdale, NJ: Lawrence Erlbaum Associates.

Karnes, M. B., Zehrbach, R., & Teska, J. (1977). Conceptualization of the GOAL (Game-Oriented Activities for Learning) curriculum. In M. C. Day & R. Parker (Eds.), *The preschool in action: Exploring early childhood programs* (pp. 253-288). Boston: Allyn & Bacon.

Kessler, S., & Swadner, B. (Eds.). (1992). *Reconceptualizing the early childhood curriculum: Beginning the dialogue*. New York: Teachers College Press.

Kohn, A. (1997, February). How not to teach values: A critical look at character education. *Phi Delta Kappan*.

Kuhn, T. S. (1970). *The structure of scientific revolutions*. Chicago: Chicago University Press.

Langer, J. (1969). *Theories of development*. New York: Holt, Rinehart & Winston.

Lavatelli, C. S. (1973). *Piaget's theory applied to an early childhood curriculum*. Boston: Center for Media Development.

Lazar, I., & Darlington, R. (1982). Lasting effects of early education: A report from the Consortium for Longitudinal Studies. *Monographs of the Society for Research in Child Development, Serial #195*, 47 (Nos. 2-3).

Lerner, R. M. (1998). *The handbook of child psychology: Vol. 1. Theoretical models of human development* (5th ed., pp. 1-24). New York: Wiley.

Lubek, S. (1996). Deconstructing "child development knowledge" and "teacher preparation." *Early Childhood Research Quarterly, 11(2)*, 147-167.

Marcon, R. A. (1999). Differential impact of preschool models on development and early learning of inner-city children: A three cohort study. *Developmental Psychology, 35(2)*, 358-375.

McGilly, K. (Ed.). (1997). *Classroom lessons: Integrating cognitive theory and classroom practice*. Cambridge, MA: Bradford/MIT Press.

McLoyd, V. (1998). Children in poverty: Development, public policy, and practice. In W. Damon (Ed.), *Handbook of child psychology* (Vol. 4, pp. 135-210). New York: John Wiley & Sons.

Miller, L. B. (1979). Development of curriculum models in Head Start. In E. Zigler & J. Valentine (Eds.), *Project Head Start: A legacy of the War on Poverty* (pp. 195-200). New York: The Free Press.

Miller, L. B., & Bizzell, R. (1983a). The Louisville experiment: A comparison of four programs. *As the twig is bent: Lasting effects of preschool programs* (pp. 171-200). Hillsdale, NJ: Lawrence Erlbaum Associates.

Miller, L. B., & Bizzell, R. (1983b). Long term effects of four preschool programs: Sixth, seventh and eighth grades. *Child Development, 54*, 727-741.

Miller, L. B., & Dyer, J. (1975). Four preschool programs: Their dimensions and effects. *Monographs of the Society for Research in Child Development, Serial No. 162, Vol. 40, Nos. 5-6*.

Mussen, P. (Ed.). (1970). *Carmichael's manual of child psychology*. New York: Wiley.

Newman, S., Copple, C., & Bredekamp, S. (2000). *Learning to read and write: Developmentally appropriate practices for young children*. Washington, DC: National Association for the Education of Young Children.

O'Donnell, A. M., & King, A. (Eds.). (1999). *Cognitive perspectives on peer learning*. Mahwah, NJ: Lawrence Erlbaum Associates.

Overton, W. F. (1984). World views and their influences on psychological theory and research: Kuhn-Lakatos-Lauden. In H. W. Reese (Ed.), *Advances in child development and behavior* (Vol. 18, pp. 191-226). New York: Academic Press.

Peters, D. (1977). Early childhood education: An overview and evaluation. In H. L. Hom, Jr., & P. A. Robinson (Eds.), *Psychological processes in early education* (pp. 1-21). New York: Academic Press.

Peters, D. L., Neisworth, J. T., & Yawkey, T. (1985). *Early education: From theory to practice*. Monterey, CA: Brooks/Cole.

Pianta, R. C. (1999). *Enhancing relationships between children and teachers*. Washington, DC: American Psychological Association.

Powell, D. (1987). Comparing preschool curricula and practices: The state of the research. In S. Kagan & E. Zigler (Eds.), *Early schooling: The national debate* (pp. 190-211). New Haven, CT: Yale University Press.

Raver, C. C., & Zigler, E. (1997). Social competence: An untapped dimension in evaluating Head Start's success. *Early Childhood Research Quarterly, 12*, 363-385.

Reese, H. W., & Overton, W. F. (1970). Models of development and theories of development. In L. R. Goulet & P. B. Baltes (Eds.), *Life-span developmental psychology: Research and theory* (pp. 115-145). New York: Academic Press.

Rescorla, L., Hyson, M. C., & Hirsch-Pasek, K. (Eds.). (1991). Academic instruction in early childhood: Challenge or pressure? In *New directions for child development* (No. 53). San Francisco: Jossey-Bass.

Rogoff, B. (1990). *Apprenticeship in thinking: Cognitive development in social context*. New York: Oxford University Press.

Rogoff, B. (1998). *Handbook of child psychology* (Vol. 2, 5th ed., pp. 679-744). New York: John Wiley.

Sales, J. (1979). Implementation of a Head Start preschool education program: Los Angeles, 1965-1967. In E. Zigler & J. Valentine (Eds.), *Project Head Start: A legacy of the War on Poverty* (pp. 175-194). New York: The Free Press.

Scholnick, E., Nelson, K., Gelman, S., & Miller, P. (1999). *Conceptual development: Piaget's legacy*. Mahway, NJ: Lawrence Erlbaum Associates.

Schulman, K., Blank, H., & Ewen, D. (1999). State prekindergarten initiatives: A varied picture of states' decisions affecting availability, quality and access. *Young Children, 54*(6), 38-41.

Schweinhart, L., & Weikart, D. J. (1980). *Young children grow up: The effects of the Perry Preschool Program on youths through age 15*. (Monographs of the High/Scope Educational Research Foundation, 7). Ypsilanti, MI: High/Scope Press.

Schweinhart, L., & Weikart, D. (1997). The High/Scope preschool curriculum comparison study through age 23. *Early Childhood Research Quarterly, 12*(2), 117-144.

Schweinhart, L., Weikart, D., & Larner, M. (1986a). Child initiated activities in early childhood programs may help prevent delinquency. *Early Childhood Research Quarterly, 1*, 303-312.

Schweinhart, L., Weikart, D., & Larner, M. (1986b). Consequences of three preschool curriculum models through age 15. *Early Childhood Research Quarterly, 1*, 15-45.

Short, R. J., & Talley, R. C. (1997). Rethinking psychology and the schools: Implications of recent national policy. *American Psychologist, 52*(3), 234-240.

Sigel, I. (1987). Early childhood education: Developmental enhancement or developmental acceleration? In S. Kagan & E. Zigler (Eds.), *Early schooling: The national debate* (pp. 129-150). New Haven, CT: Yale University Press.

Spodek, B., & Brown, P. C. (1993). Curriculum alternatives in early childhood education. In B. Spodek (Ed.), *Handbook of research on the education of young children* (pp. 91-104). New York: Macmillan.

Stallings, J. A. (1975). Implementations and child effects of teaching practices in Follow Through classrooms. *Monographs of the Society for Research in Child Development, 40* (7-8).

Stallings, J. A., & Stipek, D. (1986). Research on early childhood and elementary school teaching programs. In M. Wittrock (Ed.), *Handbook of research on teaching* (3rd ed., pp. 727-753). New York: Macmillan.

Stipek, D. (1991). Characterizing early childhood education programs. In L. Rescorla, M. C. Hyson & K. Hirsch-Pasek (Eds.), *Academic instruction in early childhood: Challenge or pressure?* San Francisco: Jossey-Bass.

Stipek, D. (1993). Is child centered early childhood education really better? In S. Reifel (Ed.), *Perspectives in developmentally appropriate practice: Advances in early education and day care* (Vol. 5, pp. 29-52). Greenwich, CT: JAI Press.

Stipek, D., Daniels, D., Galluzzo, D., & Millburn, D. (1992). Characterizing early childhood education programs for poor and middle-class children. *Early Childhood Research Quarterly, 7,* 1-19.

Stipek, D. J., Feiler, R., Byler, P., Ryan, R., Millburn, S., & Salmon, J. M. (1998). Good beginnings: What difference does the program make in preparing young children for school. *Journal of Applied Developmental Psychology, 19*(1), 41-66.

Stipek, D., Feiler, R., Daniels, D., & Millburn, S. (1995). Effects of different instructional approaches on young children's achievement and motivation. *Child Development, 66,* 209-223.

Veras, Raymundo. (1975). *Children or dreams, children of hope.* Chicago: H. Regnery Co.

Wardle, F. (1999). In praise of developmentally appropriate practice. *Young Children, 54*(6), 4-12.

Weikart, D. P., Epstein, A. S., Schweinhart, L., & Bond, J. (1978). The Ypsilanti Preschool Curriculum Demonstration Project: Preschool years and longitudinal results. *Monographs of the High/Scope Educational Research Foundation, (4).* Ypsilanti: High/Scope Educational Research Foundation.

Weikart, D. P., Rogers, L., Adcock, C., & McClelland, D. (1971). *The cognitively oriented curriculum.* Urbana, IL: University of Illinois Press.

Zigler, E., & Valentine, J. (Eds.). (1979). *Project Head Start: A legacy of the War on Poverty.* New York: The Free Press.

II

PRACTICE OF PEDAGOGY IN EARLY EDUCATION

2

SOCIOECONOMIC DIFFERENCES IN CHILDREN'S EARLY COGNITIVE DEVELOPMENT AND THEIR READINESS FOR SCHOOLING

Robbie Case
Stanford University

Sharon Griffin
Clark University

Wendy M. Kelly
Trent University

As society becomes increasingly complex, access to high-level occupations is becoming increasingly dependent on a high level of education. This simple fact has created a profound dilemma that all modern democracies are beginning to recognize. On the one hand, equality of opportunity is a major cornerstone of their political philosophy. On the other hand, opportunities for success in the public school system are clearly *not* equal. Indeed, one of the most robust findings of modern educational sociology is that children's success in the public schools is a function of the level of educational attainment of their parents. This generalization holds true no matter what school subject or what country one looks at. Figure 2.1 displays the scores of young adults in the age range from 18 to 25 in several different countries as calculated from the International Adult Literacy Survey (Wilms, 1999). As may be seen, for all countries, the reading levels that young people attain in the present generation are a function of the years of schooling that their parents received in the previous generation. As may also be seen, the size of this effect-which is reflected in the slope of the Socioeconomic Status (SES) gradient-varies considerably from one country to the next.

The pattern of achievement in reading is not identical to that in other subject areas, but it is quite similar. Figure 2.2 displays children's achievement in science at Grade 8. Similar patterns have been reported at the same grade level for mathematics: Parents' years of schooling predict children's achievement in all countries, but the size of the gradient in the United States is quite steep relative to that of most other countries (Case, Griffin, & Kelly, 1999).

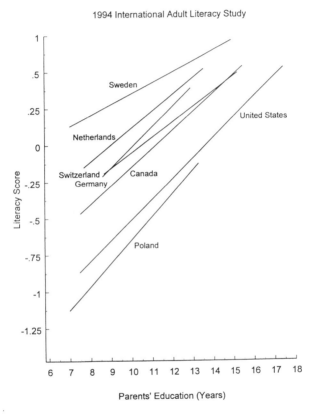

FIG. 2.1. Socioeconomic gradients for youth in seven OECD countries (calculated from the International Literacy Survey).

The most obvious interpretation of these gradients is that children from high-income homes receive better education than children from low-income homes. Although this may be part of the explanation, it is unlikely to constitute the whole story. The fact is that gradients of similar magnitude are also obtained before children ever enter school. They are present in their preschool tests of verbal and nonverbal ability, in tests of early subject matter concepts, and in teachers' ranking of school readiness in kindergarten (Duncan, Brooks-

Gunn, & Klebanov, 1994; Case, Griffin, & Kelly, 1999; Ginsburg et al., 1992; Fuchs & Reklis, 1997; Griffin, Case, & Siegler, 1994). Any full account of the pattern must therefore take account of the fact that children from different educational and socioeconomic backgrounds come to school differentially prepared for the experience that they encounter there.

In the present chapter, we take these general findings as our starting point. The questions we ask are: (a) What does "school readiness" consist of from a cognitive point of view? (b) How does this readiness develop? and (c)

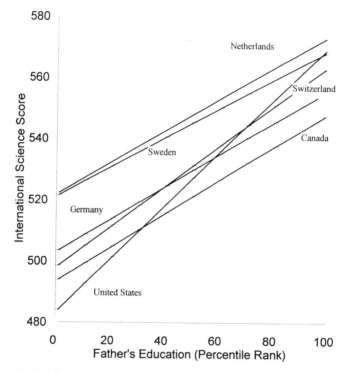

FIG. 2.2. Socioeconomic gradients for youth in six OECD countries (calculated from the International Mathematics and Science Survey).

Can anything be done to foster this readiness in children for whom it does not emerge spontaneously? Before attempting to answer these questions, we first review the different general classes of answer that have been offered in the past and the types of early intervention to which they have led.

RIVAL TRADITIONS IN THE STUDY OF YOUNG CHILDREN'S THINKING AND THEIR INTERPRETATION OF THE READINESS PROBLEM

Past research on children's thinking and learning has been conducted within three separate traditions: each with its own epistemology, its own pioneers, and its own history of progressive inquiry.

The Empiricist (Learning Theory) Perspective

The epistemological roots of the first tradition lie in British empiricism, as articulated by Locke (1696/1989) and Hume (1748/1955). According to the empiricist view, knowledge of the world is acquired by a process in which the sensory organs first detect stimuli in the external world, and the mind then detects the customary patterns or conjunctions in stimuli that are contiguous in space and/or time. Students of young children's learning who have been influenced by this view have tended to view the goal of developmental psychology as being to describe: (a) the process by which new stimuli are discriminated and encoded (perceptual learning), (b) the way in which correlations or associations among these stimuli are detected (cognitive learning), and (c) the process by which new knowledge is accessed, tested, and/or used in other contexts (transfer).

When this perspective has been applied to the problems faced by children from low-SES homes, a common interpretation has been as follows: Low-SES children are at a disadvantage compared to high-SES children because their homes offer fewer opportunities for the sort of stimulation that is essential for school success (Bereiter & Engleman, 1966; Stodolsky, 1965; Strodtbeck, 1965). What children from these backgrounds need, therefore, is a good program of early stimulation and direct instruction. Such a program should be based on a careful task analysis of the knowledge that is necessary for early school success--that is, an analysis which breaks up knowledge that is prerequisite for learning school subjects (reading, writing, arithmetic, etc.) into its component elements and subelements. With such a task analysis in hand, curriculum designers should then organize these elements and subelements into a carefully planned curriculum sequence and present the sequence using attractive and carefully designed curriculum materials. The goal of such curricula is to move children from the lower order associations and connections that are foundational to any discipline (e.g., the sounds of letter, the names for numbers) to the higher order skills, rules, and concepts that formal instruction in academic subjects requires.

The Rationalist (Constructivist) Perspective

A second theoretical tradition in which young children's thinking has been studied is quite different from the first and has been associated with a different set of educational programs. This tradition has drawn its inspiration from continental rationalism and its further development by Kant in his Transcendental Philosophy. As the reader will no doubt be aware, Kant (1961/1796) suggested that knowledge is acquired by a process in which organization is imposed by the human mind on the data that the senses provide, not merely registered as the empiricists had suggested. Examples of mental concepts that played this organizational role in Kant's system were space, time, causality, and number. Kant argued that, without some preexisting concept in each of these categories, it would be impossible to make any sense of the data of sensory experience: that is, to see events as taking place in space, as unfolding through time, or as exerting a causal influence on each other. Therefore, he believed that these categories must exist in some a priori form, rather than being induced from experience via association.

Developmental psychologists who were influenced by Kant's view tended to see the study of children's cognitive development differently from those influenced by empiricism. They presumed that one should begin by exploring the foundational organizing frameworks (structures or schemes) with which children come equipped at birth. They went on to document any change that may take place in these concepts with age. The best known theorist who applied this strategy was Piaget. Using evolutionary biology as his model of a mature science (not physics, which had been the predominant model for empiricists), he developed a set of methods designed to chart the full range of competencies that children develop at each major stage of their lives in each of Kant's categories and the general organizing frameworks or structures that underpin them. The theory he ended up with was one in which high-level structures were seen as being constructed by the differentiation and coordination of two or more lower level structures via a process in which children's own independent mental activity (not association and not direct instruction) played the major role. Forms of independent mental activity that he saw as being particularly crucial were those involved in independent exploration, play, problem solving, and reflection (Piaget, 1970).

When developmentalists in the constructivist tradition were confronted with socioeconomic differences of the sort indicated in the first two figures, they were quick to point out that-on their tests of cognitive development-children from low-SES homes went through the same general stages and demonstrated the same underlying mental structures as did high-SES children (Ginsburg & Russell, 1981). Thus, there was no reason to presume that their thinking processes were inferior or that they were missing certain essential prerequisites. When it was pointed out that the rate of progress through these stages was considerably slower (Gaudia, 1972), they countered that the solution for this was not an analysis of knowledge into little bits and pieces followed by an intense program of didactic instruction. Rather, the solution was exposure to a richer set of opportunities for play, exploration, and reflection (Ginsburg & Tang, 1997; Kamii & DeVries, 1977).

The Sociohistoric (Social Constructivist) Perspective

The third tradition within which children's early cognitive development has been studied has its roots in the sociohistoric interpretation of Hegel's epistemology, as developed by Marx and further expanded on by modern continental philosophers (Kaufmann, 1980). According to the sociohistoric view, conceptual knowledge does not have its primary origin in the structure of the objective world (as empiricist philosophers suggested). Nor does it have its origin in the structures of the subject and his or her spontaneous cogitation (as rationalist philosophers suggested). It does not even have its primary origin in the interaction between the structures of the subject and the structure of the objective world (as Piaget maintained). Rather, it has its primary origin in the social and material history of the culture of which the subject is a part and the tools, concepts, and symbol systems that the culture has developed for interacting with its environment. Developmental psychologists who were influenced by the sociohistoric perspective viewed the study of children's cognitive development in a different fashion from learning theorists or constructivists. They believed that one should begin by analyzing the social, cultural, and physical contexts in which human societies find themselves, the technology and practices that they have developed for dealing with these contexts, and the conceptual frameworks, forms of discourse, and symbol systems that support these practices. One should then proceed to examine the way in which these practices and conceptual tools are passed on from one generation to the next.

The best known of the early sociohistoric theories was Vygotsky's (1934/1962). According to his theory, children's thought must be seen in a context that includes both its biological and cultural evolution, and the study of this thought might combine the sorts of ethnographic methods used by anthropologists with those used by physicists and evolutionary biologists. According to Vygotsky, three of the most important features of human beings, as a species, are that they (a) have developed language, (b) fashion their own tools, and (c) transmit the discoveries and inventions of one generation to the next, via cultural institutions such as schooling. From the perspective of Vygotsky's theory, then, the most important aspect of children's development is neither their exposure to the stimulation that the world provides or their construction of universal mental structures for organizing that experience via independent exploration, play, and reflection. Rather, it is their acquisition of language (circa 2 years of age) for the purpose of mastering the conceptual frameworks, forms of discourse, and higher order symbol systems that are embodied in and transmitted by cultural institutions such as the modern school.

Given the emphasis on culture and cultural institutions, it was natural that research in this tradition would draw heavily on methods developed in anthropology and attempt to explore aspects of children's growth that were unique to particular contexts, not just those that were universal. It was also natural that researchers would focus on such variables as language, schooling, literacy, and other forms of symbolic and/or conceptual representation (Cole, 1991; Greenfield, 1989, 1994, 1995; Olson, 1994; Rogoff, 1990). Finally, it was natural that their analysis of socioeconomic gradients in school achievement would be different. For sociohistoric theorists, the origin of achievement gradients in modern society were seen as lying in the structure of this society, and the differential access that it provides to knowledge, and to the forms of technology and discourse that are associated with the creation, representation, and transformation of knowledge (Bernstein, 1983; Cole, Gay, Glick, & Sharp, 1971). The programs that were proposed to level these gradients were ones that were designed to open up access to high-level forms of knowledge acquisition (e.g., scientific inquiry) and the forms of discourse associated with those activities to children from all social classes (Bereiter & Scardamalia, 1987; Brown & Campione, 1994). An important caveat was also added by certain theorists--namely, that such programs might more appropriately be vested in and controlled by community organizations than schools because schools are institutions that actually transmit and preserve current patterns of inequality (Cole, 1997; M. Cole, personal communication; Pence, 1999).

Comparison of the Three Traditions

The main message we have attempted to convey so far is a simple one. Each of the three major traditions in developmental psychology has a different implicit model of cognitive development, and thus sees the readiness problem faced by children from low socioeconomic backgrounds in a different fashion. For empiricists, the essential motor of cognitive development is cumulative learning, which is seen as having a strong associative and/or didactic component. For constructivists, the essential motor of cognitive development is children's autonomous mental activity. Independent exploration, play, and reflection are particularly important forms of this activity because they promote the differentiation and coordination of the general mental structures for understanding time, space, number, and causality. For the sociohistoric theorists, the essential motor of cognitive development is initiation into a community in which knowledge is accessed, created, and shared via particular forms of technology and discourse.

Our own view of the matter is that no one of these three classical traditions offers the best analysis of children's cognitive development. By the same token, no one of the three traditions offers the most complete analysis of social class gradients in cognitive development or the best way to create a level playing field in the early years for children from different SES backgrounds. Rather, what we think is necessary is a view of cognitive development that combines elements from all three traditions, and that permits the gradient problem to be tackled in a broadly based, coherent fashion.

In the next section, we outline a view of children's early cognitive development that we believe has this sort of integrative potential. We then go on to describe the way in which that framework has been applied to level the SES gradient in preschool mathematics.

A MODEL OF CHILDREN'S EARLY COGNITIVE DEVELOPMENT THAT DRAWS ON INSIGHTS FROM ALL THREE TRADITIONS

The best way to introduce the model is to begin with an example of children's intellectual development in a specific content area and then examine the way in which all three types of developmental processes (learning of particular elements and associations, general differentiation and coordination of general structures, and mastery of class-specific forms of language and discourse) can make an impact on the way in which development in this context takes place.

Children's Early Understanding of Numbers, and its Development

By the age of 4, middle-class children in industrial and postindustrial economies have developed two basic competencies; these are illustrated in Figure 2.3. The top panel of the figure illustrates a competence that has to do with counting. By the age of 4 to 5, most preschoolers can count a small set of objects without error. They no longer miss items in the string of counting words (e.g., 1-2-3-4-6), and they no longer miss or double count items in the array that they are asked to count. Although their counting is much slower and more effortful than that of adults, they tag each object once and only once and cite the last number counted as the one that answers the question "How many things are there here?" (Gelman, 1978).

Children's ability to make relative judgments of numeriosity, without counting, is also quite well developed by this age. From birth, children show a predisposition to orient to the number of objects in a small array regardless of the spatial distribution of these objects (Starkey, 1992; see also Wynn, 1992). By the age of 4 years, not only can they make such judgments for a larger number of objects, but they can also make verbal predictions about changes in

A: Counting Schema

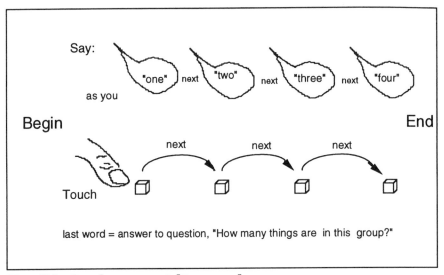

B: Global quantity schema
(Add/ subtract compare)

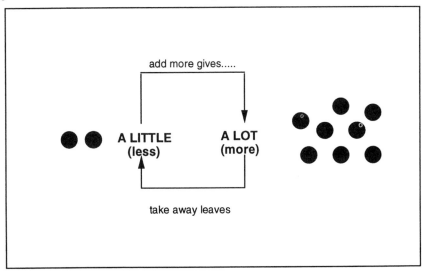

FIG. 2.3. Preschoolers schemas for counting (top panel) and for global quantity (bottom panel).

numerosity as a function of the sort of transformation that is made to the objects (addition, subtraction, etc.). Their nonverbal quantification scheme is represented visually in the bottom panel of the same figure.

Several changes take place in the counting schema and the global quantity schema as children enter the elementary school years. The most obvious change is in their counting. Children learn more words in the number sequence. Typically they can now count from 1 to 20 (and often on to 100) instead of just 1 to 5. A less obvious change--and one that is a great help to them when they encounter subtraction problems in first grade--is that they learn to count backward, at least for small numbers. This new counting knowledge is indicated in the top panel of Figure 2.4. Note that the diagram includes a more detailed set of verbal labels for the connections among elements as well as more elements.

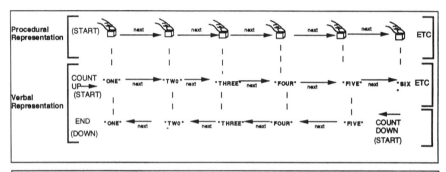

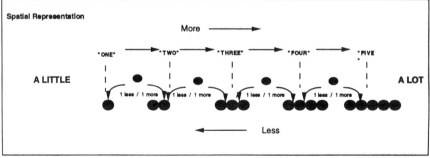

FIG. 2.4. Further developments in young children's schemas for counting (top panel) and for nonverbal quantification (bottom panel).

During the same time period, children's schema for nonverbal quantification also becomes more elaborated and differentiated. As children make the transition to formal schooling, they begin to distinguish between adding and taking away--global operations--and additions and subtractions that have a particular magnitude associated with them. Four and five not only become numbers that are associated with particular perceptual appearances, but they also become set sizes that can be derived from each other. Five can be derived from four by adding one unit while four can be derived from five by taking away one unit. The bottom panel of Figure 2.5 is intended to illustrate the complexity of the new knowledge that children acquire in this area in the same fashion as the top panel indicates the increased complexity of their knowledge about counting.

A third change that takes place during the same age range is that the two representations are gradually integrated into a single knowledge network of the sort indicated in Figure 2.5 (Griffin & Case, 1996, 1998). Because this network plays such a foundational role in children's subsequent learning of mathematics, it is worthwhile to say a word or two about its basic components and the way they are represented in the figure. The top two rows of the figure represent children's increasingly elaborate and bidirectional counting competence. The bottom two rows of the figure represent children's increasingly elaborate and bidirectional (nonverbal) magnitude knowledge and its representation by second order symbols. The polar words (*longer*, *taller*, etc.) at the edge of the figure represent children's ability to take this structure and use it to make a variety of dimensional judgments. Finally, the vertical lines in the figure represent the fact that all these various types of knowledge have become tightly linked to each other in a relationship of one-to-one correspondence.

C: Mental Counting Line

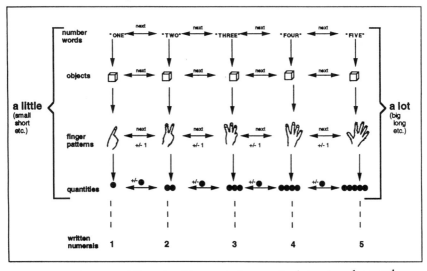

FIG. 2.5. The Mental Counting Line central conceptual structure for number.

There is one final element in Figure 2.5 that has not yet been mentioned. In the middle row is a representation of the standard way in which North American children represent quantities with their fingers. These representations have been placed in the middle because we see them as playing a central role in integrating the two precursor representations that have already been mentioned and that appear in the rows above and below. The advantage of the fingers is not just that they are universal and highly portable. It is that they can be used for two distinct purposes: (a) counting (by moving one finger at a time in sequence), and (b) indicating a set size (by forming the standard finger pattern for a particular number). We believe that they play a foundational role in children's early mathematics learning because they serve this integrative function.

The fingers may support the integration process in other more subtle ways. First, they may provide a pointer to, and hence carry with them, the child's first kinesthetic/ motoric representation of counting, thus permitting the intuitions developed when counting in this fashion to be integrated with the more abstract insights, intuitions, and symbolism being developed as children make the transition to formal schooling. Second, they may allow children to play events backward and forward, thus reviewing them and reflecting on their relationship. Finally, they may help children link numerical transformation processes as well as representations of numerical quantity per se. That is to say, they may help them realize that the verbal act of accessing the next word in the number sequence is equivalent to the nonverbal act of adding a single object to an existing array. This is the crucial insight on which all *mental math* depends, as well as most of the tasks that are taught in first-grade arithmetic.

Before proceeding, it is perhaps worthwhile to be more explicit about the way in which the prior characterization of children's numerical understanding, its schemas, and their development incorporates insights from the three traditions mentioned in the introductory section. The elements that are drawn from the constructivist tradition are perhaps the most obvious. Like Piaget's operative structures, the structures in the figure are seen as general conceptual frameworks that play a foundational role in organizing children's experience of numbers across a wide range of problem types and content domains. They are also seen as having different characteristic forms at different points in children's development. Finally, they are conceived as being formed by a similar process to the one Piaget described: one that involves the differentiation of previous structures, the construction of an integrated "superordinate" structure via active mental processes, and the processes of the sort that accompany such activities as play, problem solving, and reflection.

Because the conceptual structures we have hypothesized are similar to Piaget's in so many ways, it is important to stress that they are not identical. In contrast to Piaget's structures, the structures we have described contain content that is semantic, not syntactic. Stated differently, they are structures that represent the meaning of numbers, not just reversible operations or logic. A second way in which the structures differ from Piaget's is that their content is symbolic and represents the product of centuries of cultural learning. It may be that humans have been sensitive to quantities and counted objects of significance in their environment from time immemorial. However, it is not the case that they have always labeled them in the fashion indicated or utilized the correspondence between addition and forward counting to mentally count objects in their heads (for evidence on this point, see Saxe, 1995). Different cultures do not even use the fingers in the same fashion. The general point is a simple but important one. The semantic/procedural structures that we have analyzed have a strong cultural component: that is, a component that depends on being initiated into a particular set of ways for thinking about, talking about, and acting on the world, and one that our data suggest is strongly class-linked (Griffin & Case, 1998; Okamoto, Case, Henderson, McKeough, & Bleiker, 1996). For this reason, they might best be labeled *cultural/semantic structures*.

A final difference between the present model and Piaget's lies in the characterization of structural change and the roles of learning and practice. In Piaget's theory, change was seen as taking place centrally and as involving a process that Piaget labeled *reflective abstraction* rather than just simple maturation or experience. Increasingly, as children grew older, their reflective processes were viewed as becoming conscious in nature and as operating in a general rather than a specific manner. In the present model, conscious central processes are also assigned great importance. However, by contrast, equal importance is assigned to (a) socially mediated processes of discourse (as stressed by sociohistoric theorists), and (b) associative processes that connect the various elements in an overall structure (as suggested by learning theorists). These associative processes increase the strength of the links in the figure, thus enabling the overall structure to be applied and used in a fluent fashion. In this regard, it is important to mention that the general structure is also represented in a fashion that does contain a large number of little bits and pieces of knowledge, which is another central axiom of learning theory. It's just that these little bits and pieces form a coherent whole and are created by active reflection as well as associative and socially mediated learning.

It is because our model contains elements from all three traditions that we see it as having the power to integrate--not just the differing views of cognitive development that have been proposed in the past--but the differing analyses of socioeconomic gradients, and the different approaches to create a more level playing field in the early years.

USING THE MODEL TO FACILITATE CHILDREN'S READINESS FOR MATHEMATICS LEARNING ACROSS THE FULL SOCIOECONOMIC SPECTRUM

Assess Children's Knowledge in Different Socioeconomic Groups

Although most preschoolers come to school with the network indicated in Figure 2.5 already in place, there are always some who do not. Indeed, if one uses tests that are designed to assess the presence of the network with different socioeconomic groups, one finds that gradients of the same general magnitude as those indicated in Figure 2.2 are already present before children ever enter school. In one set of studies, for example, we found that 75% of the children in an upper middle-class school possessed the entire network of knowledge indicated in Figure 2.5, whereas the corresponding percentage in certain lower class schools was only 7%. When we calibrated the difference in terms of mental age, it turned out that the high-SES students were a full year and a half ahead of their low-SES peers in terms of the knowledge that is prerequisite for success in first-grade math. Very similar results have been found using much larger samples by Ginsburg and by Griffin (Griffin, Case, & Siegler, 1994; Ginsburg, Choi, Loez, Netley & Chao-Yuan, 1992).

Of course, the absence of the knowledge in Figure 2.5 does not mean that children from low-SES homes are less competent or less intelligent than those from upper middle-class homes. Nor does it mean that they are incapable of achieving these understandings and constructing such a structure. It simply means that their early home environment has not been one in which numbers are used and talked about the way they are in middle-class homes. One advantage of the analysis in the figure, then, is that it permits one to achieve a goal that often has been articulated by learning theorists; namely: (a) to state what knowledge is most crucial for early success in mathematics, and (b) to conduct an objective assessment to determine where any given population stands with regard to this knowledge. We would hasten to add, however (or to reiterate), that the knowledge in question is not restricted to the sort that has been most typically described by learning theorists. Nor are the techniques for fostering its development restricted to careful sequencing of materials and direct instruction.

Designing Preschool Programs Tailored to Children's Knowledge at School Entry

In the context of a math readiness program called Number Worlds (formerly Rightstart), Case and Griffin tried to use insights and techniques from all three traditions to foster the development of the structure illustrated in Figure 2.5 among low-SES populations. At the time that their study was designed, several early math programs already existed that were intended to teach children all the prerequisite skills and concepts that they need to succeed in first grade. A detailed analysis of these programs is available elsewhere (Case & Garrett, 1992). For the present purpose, what is important is the way in which the new program was different from those available at the time of its creation. Among the most important features were as follows.

1. *Presence of Additional Elements in the Curriculum.* First, the Number World program included elements that these other programs were missing, because it was based on a more detailed analysis of what the cognitive requirements for early mathematics success actually are. For example, most programs that were already in existence taught children the string of number words in the forward direction only (Figure 2.5: Row 1). They taught children to map these onto objects (Fig. 2.5: Row 2) in a one-to-one fashion. They also gave children worksheets where they had to match different numerals with different cardinal values (Fig. 2.5: Rows 4/5). By contrast, the Number Worlds program made provision for children to acquire the entire network of elements and relations indicated in the figure, which meant a much stronger emphasis on (a) learning to count backward as well as forward, (b) learning the conventional labels for referring to the relations in each row (next, up, etc.), as well as the elements themselves, (c) learning the increment (plus one) and decrement (minus one) rules, (d) learning that movement forward and backward in the number string could be treated as a reliable guide to movement forward and backward in the sequence of cardinal values, and (e) learning that the entire sequence could be used as a basis for making dimensional judgments.

2. *Stronger and more explicit developmental emphasis.* A second way in which the program differed from other programs that were already in existence was that it had a much stronger developmental emphasis--both in the sense that activities were sequenced in a developmental fashion and that teachers were provided with benchmark assessment devices for determining where any individual student was situated with regard to the general organizing structures on which successful development depends. Once again, this permitted a much finer grained intervention--one that could be adapted to the general knowledge or meanings that any particular school, neighborhood, or community brought to learning situations.

3. *Mix of didactic and exploratory methods.* A third difference between the Number Worlds program and others is in the pedagogical methods that are employed. At the time, most kindergarten and Grade 1 math programs were of two varieties: those that used classical didactic methods (exposition, followed by drill and practice) and those that concentrated on providing hands-on activities that encouraged children to construct their own mathematical meanings

and insights.   The Number Worlds program drew on both these general approaches. The materials were always ones that children could manipulate on their own. Moreover, the children were always given the time and opportunity to do so. At the same time, however, teachers were encouraged to ask children carefully targeted questions as they participated in these activities and to reformulate and reinforce the insights that they created for others to share. In effect, then, the program was both child and teacher centered.

4. *Transition from teacher-led to student-led language and activity.* Fourth, the asking of these questions, the assumption of "expert roles" in regard to the running of the game, and the summarization of existing knowledge was always in the end turned over to the children. Thus, the children thus got an opportunity to set the agenda and maintain the group on task--an experience that in our view, is much more frequently encountered by high- than by low-SES children under existing school conditions and is critical in shaping the metaposition that children learn to take with regard to their own knowledge and their own learning (see Bereiter & Scardamalia, 1987; Brown & Campione, 1994; Rogoff, 1990). They also received the opportunity to use mathematical language in an authentic context and authoritative manner.

5. *Heavy emphasis on mathematical games and language.* A final way in which the program differed from other programs that were already in existence was that it included a heavy emphasis on affectively involving games and the mathematical language that such games elicit. For example, in one game, there are three players, each of whom is trying to progress down his or her own row of squares, to reach a common square at the end. This latter square is the home of a mythical dragon, and the first player who reaches this square gets to put out the dragon's fire and save the city that the dragon is terrorizing. Children role a die and count the number of dots that it displays. They then count out the corresponding number of chips and place them one by one along the line. As they do, the teacher asks questions about who is closest to the dragon, how many more chips they need to reach the dragon, and so on.

Evaluating the Success of the New Program

The Number Worlds program has now been tried out in several different communities, both in Canada and the United States, in a fashion that engages teachers and parents as allies in support of children's learning. Several different forms of evaluation have also been conducted. In the first, children who participated in the Number Worlds program were simply compared with matched controls who had received a readiness program of a different sort. On tests of mathematical knowledge, on a set of more general developmental measures, and on a set of experimental measures of learning potential, children in the experimental program were consistently shown to be superior to those in the control groups (Case & Sandieson, 1988; Griffin, Case, & Sandieson, 1992; Griffin, Case, & Siegler, 1994). In a second type of study, children who had had the experimental program were followed up 1 year later, and evaluated on a variety of mathematical and scientific tests using a double-blind procedure. Once again, those who had had the experimental program were found to be superior on virtually all measures, including teacher evaluations of general number sense (Griffin & Case, 1996). In a third type of study, Number World graduates were compared with graduates of programs designed to improve children's readiness in the area of language arts. In this case, the Number World graduates showed the same degree of superiority in the area of first-grade mathematical concepts as they had in other studies, whereas those who had had the other training showed a parallel advance in the language arts area (Case, Okamoto, Henderson, & McKeough, 1993; Griffin, Case, & Capodilupo, 1995).

Although all these studies were important, the most impressive results were obtained from a longitudinal study by Griffin in which graduates of the program were followed over a three-year period and given a follow-up program based on the same general principles (Number Worlds for the first and second grades). At the beginning of the study and at the end of each year, the treatment children were compared with two other groups: (a) a second low-SES group that was originally tested as having superior achievement to the experimental group in mathematics, and (b) a mixed-SES (largely middle-class) group that also showed a higher level of performance at the outset and that then attended a magnet school with a special mathematics coordinator and an enriched mathematics program. As may be seen from Figure 2.6, the low-SES group that received the experimental program across the 3-year period gradually outstripped both other groups. They also compared favorably with high-SES groups from China and Japan that were tested on the same measures (Griffin & Case, 1998; Griffin, in press).

ANALYZING AND FOSTERING CHILDREN'S READINESS FOR SCHOOLING IN OTHER CONTENT AREA

Space does not permit a detailed analysis of the other strands of preschool development that are crucial for success in the elementary school years. Still it is worthwhile to consider the general outlines of the pattern in two other domains: social and spatial cognition.

Central Conceptual Structures Underlying Children's Social Thought

A great deal of research has been conducted in recent years on preschoolers' "theory of mind." What this work has shown is that preschoolers possess some

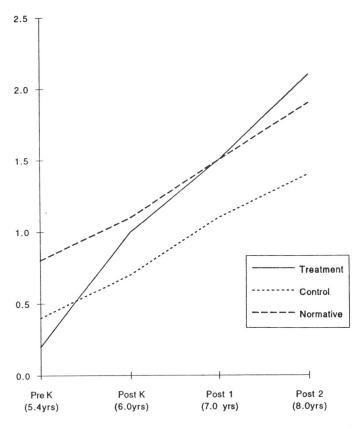

FIG. 2.6. Mean development level scores on number knowledge test for treatment group and two comparison groups at four time periods.

rudimentary understanding that people have minds by the age of about 3 years, and that they understand the way in which mental states can be modified by external events by the age of 4 to 5 years (Astington, Harris, & Olson, 1989; Astington, 1994). Another understanding that is in place by this age is that of scripts: Four- to 5-year-old children understand how familiar sequences of events unfold and the way in which one event can cause or prepare the way for the one that follows it. They can also describe these familiar scripts in language (Nelson, 1978; for a visual depiction of the content in each of these two schemas, see Case & Okamato, 1996).

    Although 4-year-olds are quite skilled at operating within each of these knowledge domains, they are much less skilled at moving across the two. Thus, for example, if asked why a mother performs some particular action in a familiar action sequence, they have no trouble referring to the key element in the previous event in the sequence that causes her to do so, or extrapolating forward, and predicting what event will come next. Even if probed with further questions, they do not spontaneously shift their focus and refer to the role of the mother's internal state in motivating her action (Goldberg-Reitman, 1992). As was the case with numerical understanding, one could say that children of this age have their knowledge of familiar scripts and their knowledge of familiar mental states stored in separate files, which they have great difficulty merging. Between the ages of 5 and 6 years, children become capable of answering such questions in an intentional fashion. Therefore, one can suggest that they have now merged the two original files and have formed a superordinate structure (for a visual depiction of the content of this structure, see Case & Okamoto, 1996). As a result, children can now think of any familiar human activity as a coordinated sequence of events involving two components: a *landscape of action*, which is the behavioral component of any event sequence, and a *landscape of consciousness*, which is the internal or intentional component (Bruner, 1986). If one thinks of the core numerical structure at this age as being something like a mental numberline or mental counting line, then this core social structure might be termed a *mental storyline*. Use of this structure actively directs children toward motivational explanations for interesting social events and--once assembled--produces a change in the way in which children perform a wide range of social activities and tasks. In school, it produces a change in children's understanding of the stories that they encounter in their reading lessons, as well as those that they encounter in their religious and historical education. Because the age at which the structure is assembled (and certain aspects of its content) is strongly linked to SES (Lillard, 1999; Okamato, Case, Bleiker, & Henderson, 1996), we have another example of a fundamental cognitive structure that mediates between children's home experience and their school learning and that can be impacted by early intervention programs (Case, Okamoto, Henderson, & McKeough, 1993; McKeough, 1992).

Central Conceptual Structures Underlying Children's Spatial Thought

A similar progression also takes place in children's spatial cognition during the same time period. By the age of 4 years, most children (or at least most Western, middle-class children) have developed a general schema for representing familiar three-dimensional objects on a two-dimensional surface. This representation correctly captures the shape of these objects, as well as the shape of their most salient component parts and the adjacency and inclusion relations that obtain among them. Thus, a tree is typically represented as a circle (for the branches and the leaves) with a line extending downward from the bottom (for the trunk). Similarly, the human figure is typically represented as a circle for the body, with two dots and a semicircle inside for the eyes and mouth and two straight lines extending downwards from the circle for the legs (Kellogg, 1969; Luquet, 1927; for a visual depiction of the content of this schema, see Case & Okamoto, 1996).

At the same age, children also learn to represent the location of any familiar three-dimensional object on a two-dimensional surface by noting its position vis-a-vis the scene of which it is a part. As this knowledge develops, they become capable of reproducing the position of a single dot that is placed on a 3 x 3 grid (Crammond, 1992) or a line of dots that goes along some particular edge (Halford & McDonald, 1977). They also became capable of placing predrawn stick figures in the correct position in a scene and of locating objects in a three-dimensional room by noting the position of these objects as depicted in a two-dimensional photograph or drawing (DeLoache, 1989). The emergence of these competencies suggests that children are simultaneously acquiring a primitive object-location or map schema, which is distinct from their object representation schema. (For a visual depiction of the object location schemes, see Case & Okamoto, 1996.)

Once again, although preschool children possess both these sorts of knowledge, they have great difficulty integrating the two in any systematic fashion. Thus, if asked to draw a picture of two people standing side by side on the grass, they tend to reproduce the internal relations of each individual correctly, but ignore the relations that obtain between these individuals and their general environment (Dennis, 1992). By the age of 6 years, this task poses little problem. Therefore, one may therefore infer that children have merged the two lower order structures into a superordinate structure in which each individual object can simultaneously be seen as a configuration of two-dimensional shapes with its own internal structure and as one component in a broader spatial field in which each object's position is referenced to a common ground line or reference axis. This structure, too, is foundational for a wide range of tasks, including those in art, map reading, and elementary geometry. (For a visual depiction of the content of this superordinate structure, see Case & Okamoto, 1996; for a description of an early intervention program see Case, Stephenson, Bleiker, & Okamoto, 1996.)

Parallels in Central Conceptual Structures Across Domains

As will hopefully be apparent, there is a strong similarity in the general form of children's numerical, social (narrative), and spatial development--or at least in our models of this development--between the ages of 4 and 6 years. In each domain, 4-year-olds appear to possess two separate structures, each of which represents a set of first-order symbolic relations. These two original structures become more elaborate and differentiated as children make the transition to the school years. They also gradually become integrated or merged, with the result that children begin to construct a system of second-order symbolic relations.

Finally, in each domain, the new structure serves as the foundation for some form of school learning.

There is one other parallel that deserves mention. In each domain, preliminary studies suggest that programs which draw on young children's natural love of play and problem solving, and which build bridges between the two existing schemas that are separate, can do a great deal toward fostering the development of central conceptual structures for children from the full range of socioeconomic backgrounds (Case, Okamoto, Henderson, & McKeough, 1993; Case, Stephenson, Bleiker, & Okamoto, 1996). The possibility exists, then, that one might combine these various programs into an overall program that would serve to facilitate cognitive development across the full range of domains that our culture values and in which early school success depends.

PLACING EARLY CHILDHOOD EDUCATION IN A BROADER SOCIAL CONTEXT

One of the central dilemmas of postindustrial society is that it is highly differentiated, with different subcultural and socioeconomic groups living in different microworlds, engaging in different practices, and having differential access to knowledge that is useful and increasingly vital to economic success. Yet it also has an ideology that is egalitarian and a public school system that is supposed to provide equal opportunity to children from all circumstances. If there were many other routes to economic success, the problems faced by the public school system would perhaps not be so serious. However, as society becomes more dependent on knowledge for its daily operation, school increasingly becomes the dominant--if not the only--route that low-SES and/or disenfranchised groups can utilize to improve their socioeconomic circumstances in the next generation.

The difficulties that this dilemma poses are perhaps nowhere seen more clearly than in the United States. Compared with many other countries, the United States has a great deal of economic and social diversity. It also has a history of immigration and a public school system that is designed to play a role in permitting upward mobility of newly arrived and/or disenfranchised groups. Yet as was illustrated in the first few figures, it also has an SES gradient in educational achievement that is among the steepest in the world. Moreover, this gradient is clearly not just a function of the resources that different schools have access to. It is a function of the fact that children arrive at these schools so differently prepared for the challenges that school presents. In this chapter, we described three different interpretations of SES gradients that have been offered in the past and the sorts of programs that have been created to make them less steep. In the first (empiricist) view, children from low-SES backgrounds are missing certain vital prerequisite skills that high-SES children possess and that all children should be directly taught. In the second (constructivist) view, children from low-SES homes have not had the opportunity for the same sort of educationally focused play, problem solving, and reflection that high-SES children have had. They should be offered the opportunity to encounter these experiences--very probably in the sort of child-centered environment that high-SES children encounter in nursery school--so that their foundational structures in such areas as number and causality will be adequate to the test to which they will be put once formal schooling is encountered. In the third (sociohistorical) view, children from low-SES homes have not had the chance to participate in the sort of knowledge-centered activities and discourse that are typical in middle-class homes and that they need to be exposed to if they are to play the role of intellectual leaders rather than just followers in their school and social lives. Ideally these opportunities should be presented in a community rather than (or perhaps in addition to) a school context.

The model of early development and school readiness proposed in the present chapter is one that incorporates elements from all three of these classic viewpoints. According to the model, there are certain general conceptual structures that children from different backgrounds have differential exposure and that underpin early school success. The elements of these structures, in effect, constitute the sets of concepts and skills that are most essential for school success. The elements cannot simply be taught in isolation, however. Rather, they must be assembled by children in a context that includes play, problem solving, and reflection, because these processes are the ones that ensure the structures will undergo the processes of differentiation, elaboration, and integration on which their smooth functioning and application as wholes depends. Finally, because the structures contain a good deal of content that is cultural and/or linguistic, and because their application and use are also deeply culturally rooted, they must be assembled in a context that provides rich opportunities for discourse, as well as participation structures where children move from a position where they are novices and learners to one where they are experts who take a role of leadership in facilitating the play (and learning) of others.

In several different experimental projects, we have shown that programs based on this sort of model can produce excellent results. Before concluding, however, it is important to point out that the contexts in which these curricula have been tried out have been isolated ones, in which the considerable resources of the university have been made available to local school boards, teachers, and parents who were interested in taking advantage of them and who were prepared to come together for that purpose. As a demonstration that socioeconomic gradients can be leveled when the social forces are appropriately aligned, such programs serve an important function. However, they leave unanswered the question of how to find the necessary resources and/or to achieve the same consensus at a broader societal level. We do not claim to have the answer for how to achieve this latter feat. However, we would like to conclude with a reminder that the three academic traditions described in the present chapter are rooted in different philosophies of human knowledge and its acquisition by individuals and social groups. Not coincidentally, we believe these same views-- or at least variants of them--also tend to underpin different political philosophies as well. Conservatives tend to favor the careful specifications of basic knowledge skills and values and their transmission via direct instruction. Liberals tend to emphasize a child-centered approach that encourages autonomy and individual reflection. Reformers on the Left tend to emphasize restructuring of power relations in classrooms and/or community context. Therefore, we predict that issues similar to those that have been argued back and forth between the various academic traditions will have to be argued back and forth more in the broader society at large, and that--if a strong coalition is to be found--it will have to incorporate at least some elements from each.

What is it that young children need? Is it specific training to standards that society agrees on? Is it guided discovery and play in an enriched context? Is it the change to participate in a community of learners where knowledge is actually created and not just received? How can communities be empowered to offer their children access to opportunities that they themselves have not experienced? As we move toward a knowledge society and become increasingly aware of the crucial importance of early childhood education, these are only some of the questions we will have to confront. Moreover, the solutions that we find may well have to entail a new balance among the three institutions that are responsible for children's early development: the family, the community, and the public school system.

As we grope our way toward new answers to these questions--ones that will honor our unique cultural history and balance our respect for individual liberty with our concern for justice and equity--the solutions that we evolve may well vary from one region of the country or one community within a region to the next. Whatever shape they take, however, we suspect that they will contain a number of common features. These will stem from the nature of the problem, on the one hand, to the contrasting ways that problem is perceived from different philosophic, scientific, and ideological viewpoints, on the other. Among the common features, our guess is that several will stand out as particularly salient. Most successful programs will be likely to include (a) some way to offer all preschoolers--not just those from high-SES homes--active exposure to, and experience with, the sorts of intellectual activities and materials that are crucial for early success in reading, writing, and mathematics; (b) some way to honor and mobilize the natural love of play, problem solving, and reflection that preschool children in all cultures and economic groups share; and (c) some way to permit local communities--not just to implement programs that have been designed elsewhere--but to create programs that are tailored to their own unique needs, values, and aspirations within the broader social context.

REFERENCES

Astington, J. W. (1994). *The child's discovery of mind.* New York: Cambridge University Press.

Astington, J. W., Harris, P. L., & Olson, D. R. (1989). *Developing theories of mind.* New York: Cambridge University Press.

Bereiter, C., & Engleman, S. (1966). *Teaching disadvantaged children in the preschool.* Englewood Cliffs, NJ: Prentice-Hall.

Bereiter, C., & Scardamalia, M. (1987). *The psychology of written composition.* Hillsdale, NJ: Lawrence Erlbaum Associates.

Bernstein, R. I. (1983). *Beyond objectivism and relativism.* Philadelphia: University of Pennsylvania Press.

Bronfenbrenner, U. (1992). Child care in the Anglo Saxon Mode. In M. Lamb, K. Sternberg, C. Hwang, & A. Broberg (Eds.), *Child care in context: Cross cultural perspectives* (pp. 281-291). Hillsdale, NJ: Lawrence Erlbaum Associates.

Brown, A. L., & Campione, J. C. (1994). Guided discovery in a community of learners. In K. McGilly (Ed.), *Classroom lessons* (pp. 229-272). Cambridge, MA: MIT Press.

Bruner, J. S. (1986). *Actual minds, possible worlds.* Cambridge, MA: Harvard University Press.

Case, R., & Garrett, N. B. (1992). New approaches to the teaching of mathematics and the role of the Rightstart program in laying an appropriate foundation for them. In S. Griffin & R. Case (Eds.), *Teaching number sense, Year 1 Report to the James S. McDonnell Foundation* (pp. 98-127). (Available from J. Griffin, Clark University.)

Case, R., Griffin, S., & Kelly, W. M. (1999). Socioeconomic gradients in mathematical ability and their responsiveness to intervention during early childhood. In D. Keating & C. Hertzman (Eds.), *Developmental health and the wealth of nations* (pp. 125-149). New York: Guilford.

Case, R., & Okamoto, Y. (Eds.). (1996). The role of central conceptual structures in the development of children's thought. *Monographs of the Society for Research in Child Development, 61(1-2),* 83-102, Serial 246.

Case, R., Okamoto, Y., Henderson, B., & McKeough, A. (1993). Individual variability and consistency in cognitive development: New evidence of the existence of central conceptual structures. In R. Case & W. Edelstein (Eds.), *The new structuralism of developmental theory and research: Analysis of individual developmental pathways* (pp. 71-100). Basel: S. Karger.

Case, R., & Sandieson, R. (1988). A developmental approach to the identification and teaching of central conceptual structures in middle school science and mathematics. In M. Behr & J. Hiebart (Eds.), *Research agenda in mathematics education: Number concepts and operations in the middle grades* (pp. 236-270). Hillsdale, NJ: Lawrence Erlbaum Associates.

Case, R., Stephenson, K. M., Bleiker, C., & Okamoto, Y. (1996). Central spatial structures and their development. In R. Case & Y. Okamoto (Eds.), The role of central conceptual structures in the development of children's thought. *Monographs of the Society for Research in Child Development, 61(1-2),* 83-102, Serial 246.

Cole, M. (1991). Cognitive development and formal schooling: The evidence from cross cultural research. In L. C. Moll (Ed.), *Vygotsky and education: Instructional implications and applications of sociohistorical psychology* (pp. 89-110). New York: Cambridge University Press.

Cole, M. (1997). *Cultural psychology.* Cambridge, MA: Harvard University Press.

Cole, M., Gay, J., Glick, J. A., & Sharp, D. D. (1971). *The cultural context of learning and thinking.* New York: Basic Books.

Crammond, J. (1992). Analyzing the basic developmental processes of children with different types of learning disability. In R. Case (Ed.), *The mind's staircase: Exploring the conceptual underpinnings of children's thought and knowledge* (pp. 285-302). Hillsdale, NJ: Lawrence Erlbaum Associates.

DeLoache, J. S. (1989). Children's pattern construction as a function of age and complexity. In H. W. Reese (Ed.), *Advances in child development and behavior, 22*. New York: Academic Press.

Dennis, S. (1992). Stage and structure in the development of children's spatial representations. In R. Case (Ed.), *The mind's staircase: Exploring the conceptual underpinnings of children's thought and knowledge* (pp. 229-245). Hillsdale, NJ: Lawrence Erlbaum Associates.

Duncan, G., Brooks-Gunn, J., & Klebanov, P. K. (1994). Economic deprivation and early-childhood development. *Child Development, 65*, 296-318.

Fuchs, V. R., & Reklis, D. (1997). Mathematical achievement in eighth grade. *Jobs and Capitals, 6(3)*, 27-29.

Gaudia, G. (1972). Race, social class, and age of achievement of conservation of Piaget's task. *Developmental Psychology, 6*, 158-165.

Gelman, R. (1978). Counting in the preschooler: What does and what does not develop? In R. Siegler (Ed.), *Children's thinking: What develops?* (pp. 213-242). Hillsdale, NJ: Lawrence Erlbaum Associates.

Ginsburg, H. P., & Tang, E. P. (1997). How can cognitive science help to inform the primary school mathematics curriculum? *Issues in Education, 3(1)*, 81-91.

Ginsburg, H. P., Choi, E., Loez, L. S., Netley, R., & Chao-Yuan, C. (1992). *Happy birthday to you: The roles of nationality, ethnicity, social class and schooling in the early mathematical thinking of Asian, South American and U. S. children*. Unpublished manuscript, Columbia University, New York.

Ginsburg, H. P., & Russell, R. (1981). Social class and racial influence on early mathematical thinking. *Monographs of the Society for Research in Child Development, 46* (Serial No. 193).

Goldberg-Reitman, J. R. (1992). Children's conception of their mother's role: A neo-structural analysis. In R. Case (Ed.), *The mind's staircase: Exploring the conceptual underpinnings of children's thought and knowledge* (pp. 135-152). Hillsdale, NJ: Lawrence Erlbaum Associate.s

Greenfield, P. M. (1995, June). *Development evolution and culture*. Paper presented at the annual meeting of the Jean Piaget Society, Berkeley, CA.

Greenfield, P. M. (Ed.). (1994). Effects of interactive entertainment technologies on development. *Journal of Applied Developmental Psychology, 15*, 1-139.

Greenfield, P. M. (1989). From birth to maturity in Zinacantan: Ontogenesis in cultural context. In V. Brinker & G. Gossen (Eds.), *Ethnographic encounters in southern Mesoamerica: Celebratory essays in honor of Evon Z. Vogt*. Albany, NY: Institute of Mesoamerican Studies, State, University of New York.

Griffin, S. A. (in press). Evaluation of a program designed to teach number sense to children at risk for school failure. *Journal of Research in Mathematics Education*.

Griffin, S. A., & Case, R. (1996). Evaluating the breadth and depth of training effects, when central conceptual structures are taught. In R. Case & Y. Okamoto (Eds.), The role of central conceptual structures in the development of children's thought. *Monographs of the Society for Research in Child Development, 61(1-2)*, 83-102, Serial No. 246.

Griffin, S. A., & Case, R. (1998). Re-thinking the primary school math curriculum: An approach based on cognitive science. *Issues in Education, 4(1)*, 1-51.

Griffin, S. A., Case, R., & Sandieson, R. (1992). Synchrony and asychrony in the acquisition of children's everyday mathematical knowledge. In R. Case (Ed.), *The mind's staircase: Exploring the conceptual underpinnings of children's thought and knowledge* (pp. 75-98). Hillsdale, NJ: Lawrence Erlbaum Associates.

Griffin, S. A., Case, R., & Siegler, R. S. (1994). Rightstart: Providing the central conceptual prerequisites for first formal learning of arithmetic to students at risk for school failure. In K. McGilly (Ed.), *Classroom lessons: Integrating cognitive theory and classroom practice* (pp. 1-50). Cambridge, MA: MIT Press/Bradford Books.

Griffin, S., Case, R., & Capodilupo, A. (1995). Teaching for understanding: The importance of the control conceptual structures in the elementary mathematics curriculum. In A. McKeough, J. Lupont, and A. Marini (Eds.), *Teaching for transfer*. NJ: Lawrence Erlbaum Associates.

Halford, G. S., & McDonald, C. (1977). Children's pattern construction as a function of age and complexity. *Child Development, 48*, 1096-1100.

Hume, D. (1955). *An inquiry concerning human understanding*. New York: Bobbs Merrill. (Original work published in 1748)

Kamii, C., & DeVries, R. (1977). Piaget for early education. In M. C. Day & R. K. Parker (Eds.), *The preschool in action* (pp. 421-460). Boston: Allyn & Bacon.

Kant, I. (1961). *Critique of pure reason*. New York: Doubleday Anchor. (Original work published in 1796)

Kaufmann, W. (1980). *Discovering the mind: Goethe, Kant and Hegel*. New York: McGraw-Hill.

Kellogg, R. (1969). *Analyzing children's art*. Palo Alto, CA: National Press.

Lillard, A. S. (1999). Developing a cultural theory of mind: The CIAO approach. *Current Directions in Psychological Science, 8*, 57-61.

Locke, J. (1989). *Essay concerning human understanding*. London: Clarendon Press. (Original work published in 1696)

Luquet, G. H. (1927). *Le dessin enfantin* [Children's drawing]. Paris: Alcan.

McKeough, A. (1992). Testing for the presence of a central conceptual structure: Use of the transfer paradigm. In R. Case (Ed.), *The mind's staircase: Exploring the conceptual underpinnings of children's thought and knowledge* (pp. 189-206). Hillsdale, NJ: Lawrence Erlbaum Associates.

Nelson, K. (1978). How children represent their knowledge of the world in an out of language: A preliminary report. In R. S. Siegler (Ed.), *Children's thinking: What develops?* (pp. 255-274). Hillsdale, NJ: Lawrence Erlbaum Associates.

Okamoto, Y., Case, R., Henderson, B., McKeough, A., & Bleiker, C. (1996). Cross-cultural investigations. In R. Case & Y. Okamoto (Eds.), The role of central conceptual structures in the development of children's thought. *Monographs of the Society for Research in Child Development, 61(1-2)*, 131-155.

Olson, D. R. (1994). *The world on paper: The conceptual and cognitive implications of writing and reading*. New York: Cambridge University Press.

Pence, A. R. (1999). It takes a village, and new roads to get there. In D. P. Keating & C. Hertzman (Eds.), *Developmental health and the wealth of nations: Social, biological and educational dynamics* (pp. 322-326). New York: Guilford.

Piaget, J. (1970). Piaget's theory. In P. H. Mussen (Ed.), *Carmichael's handbook of child development* (pp. 703-732). New York: Wiley.

Rogoff, B. (1990). *Apprenticeship in thinking: Cognitive development in social context*. Cambridge, MA: Oxford University Press.

Saxe, G. B. (1995, June). *Culture, changes in social practices, and cognitive development*. Paper presented at the annual meeting of the Jean Piaget Society, Berkeley, CA.

Starkey, P. (1992). The early development of numerical reasoning. *Cognition and Instruction, 43*, 93-126.

Stodolsky, S. M. (1965). *Maternal behavior and language concept formation in Negro preschool children: An inquiry into process*. Unpublished doctoral dissertation, University of Chicago.

Strodtbeck, F. L. (1965). The hidden curriculum in the middle class home. In J. D. Krumholtz (Ed.), *Learning and the educational process*. New York: Rand McNally.

Vygotsky, L. S. (1962). *Thought and language* (E. Hanfmann & G. Vaker, Trans.). Cambridge, MA: MIT Press. (Original work published in 1934)

Wilms, D. (1999). Socioeconomic gradients in literacy. In D. Keating & C. Hertzman (Eds.), *The developmental health and wealth of nations: Social, biological and educational dynamics*. New York: Guilford.

Wynn, K. (1992). Addition and subtraction by human infants. *Nature, 358*, 709-750.

3

ACHIEVEMENT MOTIVATION IN EARLY CHILDHOOD: CAUSE FOR CONCERN OR CELEBRATION?

Deborah J. Stipek
Stanford School of Education

Joelle K. Greene
Pomona College
Department of Psychology

Many researchers, including the first author of this chapter, have portrayed preschool and kindergarten children as being at little risk for achievement-motivation problems. This conclusion has been based primarily on findings that young children have high, often exaggerated perceptions of their abilities and expectations for success, which they maintain even after they experience failure. The absence of performance decrements following failure also suggests considerable resiliency. In brief, the findings of many studies suggest that it is difficult to discourage young children.

Behavioral indexes of motivation, however, suggest the possibility that motivation-related problems emerge as early as infancy. Because motivation in infancy and the preschool years have heretofore remained fairly disconnected domains of research, there has been little discussion of potential links between the two. The purpose of this chapter is to provide a more comprehensive account of children's motivational strengths and areas of vulnerability by assembling various strands of achievement-motivation research on young children. Our ultimate goal is to determine how motivation problems might manifest themselves in the early years, and what parents, day-care workers, and preschool or kindergarten teachers should monitor to identify emerging problems that might be ameliorated with intervention. We begin with a brief discussion of what we mean by *achievement motivation*.

WHAT IS ACHIEVEMENT MOTIVATION?

Achievement situations exist when there is a goal and some standard against which performance can be measured, thus offering an opportunity to succeed or fail. For young children, success may be defined as writing their name, identifying a few letters, completing a puzzle, or even getting one puzzle piece to fit. For an infant, success may be defined as persisting at achieving almost any self-directed, sensorimotor goal. Theorists and researchers have conceptualized and operationalized motivation in several different ways, which have implications for how motivational problems might be identified in young children.

White (1959) proposed that from birth humans are prewired with a motive to practice and develop their ability to affect or master their environment. He suggested that such a motive (which he referred to interchangeably as an *effectance* or *mastery* motive) was necessary for survival. To support his claim, he described infants' propensity to explore and manipulate their environment and the pleasure they express when they are successful. Most researchers that have based their work on White's proposal have, accordingly, operationalized motivation in terms of exploration, manipulation, persistence (especially in overcoming barriers to achieve a goal), and pleasure in mastery-related behaviors and achievements.

Inspired to a substantial degree by White's concept of a natural, inborn need to develop competencies and master the environment (as well as related proposals made by Piaget, 1952), intrinsic motivation theorists have examined another set of behaviors as evidence of motivation. They focus primarily on evidence that individuals engage in an activity because they want to, not because they are trying to avoid punishment or achieve extrinsic rewards. Here the measurement emphasis is on choice (does the person choose to do an activity in the absence of any pressure or reward for doing it) and self-reported pleasure or enjoyment. Other potential indexes of intrinsic motivation might be level of engagement (e.g., working half-heartedly vs. intensely), spontaneous expressions of enthusiasm, and resistance when asked to stop working on a task.

Building on McClelland's work, Atkinson (1964) focused researchers' attention on the underlying cognitive and affective causes of achievement-related behaviors, especially expectations for success and achievement-related values, which he operationalized narrowly as anticipated emotional reactions to success (pride) and failure (shame).[1] Cognitions and affective experiences expected in

---

[1]In this chapter, we do not discuss work based on McClelland's psychoanalysis theory of achievement motivation because both the theory and measurement have been criticized. Also there has been little research with young children that is based directly on McClelland's conceptualization of achievement motivation for several decades.

achievement contexts are, in turn, assumed in the theory to affect such things as effort, attention, independence, level of difficulty of the tasks chosen, problem-solving approaches, and persistence. Many studies have examined young children's expectations for success and their perceptions of their competencies (on which expectancies are partly based). Affective reactions to achievement outcomes are less well studied.[2]

In the next sections, we provide an overview of findings of studies that have assessed different aspects of achievement motivation in young children. Throughout we stress both strengths that appear to be associated with this developmental period and potential areas of vulnerability.

INDIVIDUAL DIFFERENCES IN ACHIEVEMENT MOTIVATION

Achievement-Related Cognitions

One method of assessing achievement motivation is to ask children to rate their competence and report their expectancies for success. To assess perceptions of competence, children are typically shown some kind of representation of a Likert scale (e.g., a bar graph with five bars of increasing height; a page with five pictures of faces on it, beginning with a big frown on the far left and gradually changing to a big smile on the far right). They are then asked to point to the representation that shows how *smart* they are or how good they are at a particular activity (e.g., letters, numbers). Expectancy measures usually ask children specific questions (e.g., How many of these puzzles will you be able to do? How high will your tower be?).

This line of research has contributed substantially to the picture of young children as motivationally robust. For example, a number of studies have shown that young children's ratings of their competence are consistently close to the top of the scale. In Stipek's recent studies, preschoolers and kindergartners always scored above 4.5 on a scale of 1 to 5 (Stipek et al., 1998; Stipek, Feiler, Daniels, & Milburn, 1995) or above 15 on a scale of 1 to 20 (Stipek & Daniels, 1988); (see also Eshel & Klein, 1981; Marsh, Barnes, Cairns, & Tidman, 1984; Nicholls, 1978, 1979; Ruble, Grosovsky, Frey, & Cohen, 1992, Stipek, 1984a; Stipek & Mac Iver, 1989).

---

[2]Many studies of children's perceptions of their control over achievement outcomes (referred to as *locus of control*), and their perceptions of the cause of achievement outcomes (referred to as *attributions*) have been conducted with older children, but only a few with preschool-age children. Consequently, these motivation-related cognitions are not reviewed.

Expectancy studies have yielded a similarly optimistic and positive picture of children's motivation. When shown six levels of task difficulty in Stipek's studies, children typically expected to complete the fifth level of difficulty (Stipek et al., 1995, 1998), (see also Clifford, 1975; Entwisle & Hayduk, 1978; Parsons & Ruble, 1977; Yussen & Berman, 1981; reviews by Stipek, 1984a, 1984b; Stipek & Mac Iver, 1989). Studies of the effects of failure on expectations suggest that young children's beliefs about their ability to achieve success are not easily discouraged. In a study by Stipek and Hoffman (1980), for example, children were asked to predict how high (on a 0 to 100 scale) they would be able to raise a platform on a tower without the ball on the platform falling off. Even after four failure experiences (never passing a score of 20), 3- and 4-year-olds predicted very high performance (over 90) for the fifth trial (see also Entwisle & Hayduk, 1978; Parsons & Ruble, 1977; Stipek, Roberts, & Sanborn, 1984).

These positive beliefs are short-lived, however. Children's achievement-related ratings begin to decline even before they enter elementary school, and they continue to decline over the elementary grades. In a cross-sectional study, Stipek and Tannatt (1984) found that children's ratings of their *smartness* declined from about 4.9 (on a 5-point scale) in preschool, to about 4.7 in kindergarten and Grade 1, and then to about 4.2 in second and third grade. Wigfield et al. (1997) found consistent declines from first to third grade in children's judgments of their competencies in a variety of domains. In the Stipek and Hoffman (1980) study using the tower balance task mentioned earlier, children's predictions after failure for their performance fell substantially, from over 90 on a 0 to 100 scale at ages 3 and 4 years to about 80 at ages 5 and 6, and about 60 at ages 7 and 8 (see also studies by Benenson & Dweck, 1986; Eshel & Klein, 1981; Nicholls, 1978, 1979; Pintrich & Blumenfeld, 1985).

Although there is not much variation in young children's achievement-related cognitions, there is considerable variation in the rate and extent of the declines over the first few years of elementary school. It is possible that seeds for the more precipitous declines in beliefs about competencies and expectations for success may be in place before seriously negative judgments are manifested. Therefore, we look to other indexes of motivation for possible precursors to later motivational problems

Achievement-Related Behavior

Most research on young children's behavior in achievement contexts is rooted in White's (1959) description of the mastery motive. Although White stressed the universality and adaptive qualities of the mastery motive, Harter (1978) proposed that the physical and social context might affect its strength. She suggested that another innate need, for social approval, renders humans susceptible to the effects of adult social reinforcement. For example, praise, provides an incentive to engage in behaviors as well as information regarding what is considered mastery or success. Therefore, Harter contended that adults shape the content, frequency, and intensity of children's independent mastery attempts by providing contingent reinforcement. Ultimately children internalize the once external reward system into a self-reward system, which presumably continues to reinforce mastery efforts in particular domains.

If Harter's analysis is correct, young children should exhibit different levels (frequency and intensity) of the behaviors that White (1959) brought under the conceptual umbrella of effectance motivation--including exploration, manipulation of objects, and other attempts to affect and ultimately master the environment. Furthermore, these differences should be associated with differences in children's physical and social environments. Following is a summary of research that shows systematic individual differences in mastery behavior in infants and preschoolers; it provides some suggestions regarding the social and physical contexts that produce these differences.

A number of researchers, most prominently Yarrow and his colleagues, have documented differences in mastery-related behaviors of children as young as 6 months (see MacTurk & Morgan, 1995; Morgan & Harmon, 1984, for reviews). Most of the studies conducted involve direct observations of young children engaged in a standardized task situation. Other measurement strategies include parent and teacher ratings and observations of children engaged in free play (see MacTurk, Morgan, & Jennings, 1995).

The Yarrow group was among the first to operationalize the concept of effectance motivation into a set of well-specified, measurable behaviors. Behaviors often recorded are (a) latency to involvement with materials provided, (b) visual attention to the materials, (c) exploratory behavior, (d) persistence in goal-directed behavior, (e) off-task behavior, and (f) positive affect.

With the exception of positive affect, the behaviors have cohered fairly well in studies of both 6- and 12-month infants, although there is also evidence of the multidimensionality of the mastery motivation. Stott and Sharp (1976) reported coherence among a similar set of behaviors rated by teachers (e.g., exploration, effecting change, completion) for 4-year-olds. Evidence for some stability in individual differences has been found from 6- to 12 months (Yarrow et al., 1983), 12 to 24 months (Power, Chapieski, & McGrath, 1985), 3 1/2 to 4 1/2 years (Jennings, Connors, & Stegman, 1988), and infancy to age 8 (Pedlow, Sanson, Prior, & Oberklaid, 1993). Other studies have found stability in some of these mastery behaviors across testing situations (Power, Chapieski, & McGrath, 1985; Yarrow, Morgan, Jennings, Harmon, & Gaiter, 1982) and between observations in experimental task situations and mothers' and preschool teachers' ratings of behavior at home and at preschool (see Morgan & Harmon, 1984; Sigman et al., 1987).

Ego-resiliency is another construct, similar to the construct of mastery motivation, that has been studied in young children (Block & Block, 1980). The concept is defined as the ability to respond flexibly, persistently, and resourcefully, especially in problem situations. A child very low in ego-resilience is inflexible, unable to respond to changing requirements of a situation, and may become disorganized in novel or stressful situations.

There is evidence for associations between ego-resiliency and mastery motivation as well as for stability in ego-resilience. Arend, Gove, and Sroufe (1979) reported significant correlations between ego-resiliency scores for children and behaviors similar to those assessed by Yarrow and colleagues, including exploration and the manipulation of objects. Block and Block (1980) found some stability in ego-resiliency for children between the ages of 3 and 7 using both laboratory observations and Q-sorts. Arend et al. (1979) found significant associations between a composite of scores assessing positive affect, enthusiasm, responsiveness, and compliance at age 2 years, and ego-resiliency scores at age 4.

Another construct related to mastery motivation is temperament. Temperament researchers have assessed behaviors that are very similar to those assessed by mastery motivation researchers. Latency to play with unfamiliar objects (Kagan, Reznick, & Snidman, 1987), persistence (engaging in an activity for a relatively long period of time), completing tasks (Pedlow, Sanson, Prior, & Oberklaid, 1993), activity level (Emde et al., 1992), and attention (McCall & Carriger, 1993) are all variables studied in the temperament literature that are either included in some assessments of mastery motivation or should affect infants' mastery behavior. For example, high activity levels and low levels of sustained attention may interfere with children's ability to persist to complete a difficult task.

Therefore, it is possible that the individual differences seen in young children's persistence and possibly other mastery behaviors reflect differences in temperament, which research suggests are, in part, biologically based (Vondra, 1995). Most likely temperament only affects mastery behavior directly in infancy. Later effects may be explained, using a transactional framework for development, by infant behavior affecting adult reactions, which in turn affect infants' future behavior. The early individual differences found in temperament may evolve into motivational problems that look quite different. Assume, for example, that persistence promotes cognitive competencies. It is clear from research that actual competence is a strong predictor of perceptions of competence (see Stipek, 1998). Thus, persistence in infancy could indirectly affect perceived competence much later.

Mastery Behavior and Cognitive Development

A number of studies have found associations between infants' behavior on various mastery motivation tasks (especially persistence) and indexes of cognitive development, such as Bayley Scores (Sigman, et al., 1987; Yarrow et al., 1982, 1983; Yarrow & Pedersen, 1976; see also Stott & Sharp, 1976) and memory (Colombo, Mitchell, Dodd, & Coldren, 1989).

The direction of causality, however, is unclear. Cognitive competencies have been shown to predict later mastery behavior, suggesting that mastery behavior may reflect cognitive competencies. However, some mastery behaviors have also been shown to predict later scores on cognitive development assessments (Messer et al., 1986; Yarrow, Klein, Lomonaco, & Morgan, 1975; Yarrow et al., 1983) even with previous cognitive levels covaried (Sigman et al., 1987), suggesting that mastery behavior may affect cognitive competencies. The association between mastery-related behaviors and cognitive development is all the more difficult to untangle because performance on a cognitive task in a testing situation is probably affected by motivation-related behaviors.

The causal relationship is most likely reciprocal, with a propensity for high levels of mastery motivation fostering cognitive development and cognitive development contributing to some kinds of mastery behavior. Whatever the nature of the connection, studies showing that the association between persistence and cognitive measures decreased with age suggest that indexes of mastery motivation reflect or affect cognitive development more in early infancy than in later infancy or early childhood (Redding, Morgan, & Harmon, 1988; Yarrow et al., 1982).

Summary

The research reviewed previously indicates that the concept of mastery motivation can be translated into reliable and valid measures, and it is related to other constructs such as ego-resiliency and temperament. We also know that there are stable individual differences in some mastery behaviors at least through preschool. Studies indicating that stable individual differences in mastery behavior emerge early in children's lives suggest that these behaviors merit consideration as potential early indexes of motivational patterns.

We do not know, however, whether mastery behavior in early childhood is in any way associated with achievement-related behaviors, cognitions, or emotions after children enter school. Do the infants who are not prone to explore and manipulate objects and who give up easily when they encounter difficulties become the elementary school-age children who avoid challenging tasks, give up easily, or who have low perceptions of their competence and low expectations for success? What is needed are longitudinal studies that follow children from infancy to toddlerhood to after the transition to school and that measure motivation, at least in the older children, in both behavioral and cognitive domains.

ACHIEVEMENT-RELATED EMOTIONS

Measures of pleasure children expressed while working on mastery tasks or after task completion have been included in many mastery motivation studies, but the incidence is low until age 2 or 3 and affective displays are not usually associated with behavioral indexes of mastery motivation (MacTurk, Morgan, & Jennings, 1995). The meaning of affective displays in infancy is also unclear. Children who are highly engaged in goal-directed behavior may express positive affect relatively little because they are concentrating on completing the task at hand, or they may express relatively more positive affect because they care more about the outcome. Affective displays also probably have a social component that cannot be disentangled from pure mastery motivation.

Emotions in preschool-age children are less ambiguous and easier to assess. One strategy that has been used is asking children to report on how much they like achievement-related contexts. Most young children give very positive reports. In Stipek's studies, kindergarten subscores on a school enjoyment scale averaged between 4.30 and 4.59 on a 5-point scale (Stipek et al., 1995, 1998). In contrast to these positive motivational dimensions, children's self-reported worries about school are typically low (1.94 and 2.03 on a 5-point scale; Stipek et al., 1995, 1998).

Again, however, these positive feelings are short lived for many children. As was found for achievement-related cognitions, studies show that, on average, children express increasingly negative attitudes toward academic work over the first few grades of school (Kush & Watkins, 1996; Wigfield et al., 1997), especially if they are doing poorly academically (McKenna, Kear, & Ellsworth, 1995).

LEARNED HELPLESSNESS

In studies of children's reactions to failure, Dweck and her colleagues have examined a broad set of negative cognitions, behaviors, and emotional variables, which they refer to as *learned helplessness*. They have observed that some preschool-age children are more impaired by failure than would be expected given the strong positive bias seen in research on achievement-related cognitions.

Learned helplessness following failure in achievement contexts was first identified by Diener and Dweck (1978, 1980) in their studies of elementary school-age children. It is manifested in displays of negative affect, challenge avoidance, and low expectancies for future success. In addition, helpless children tend to attribute failure to low ability or intelligence and success to luck or chance, both variables over which they may believe they have little control (Diener & Dweck, 1980).

Early research on preschool-age children suggested that they are not as vulnerable to learned helplessness as are older children. Rholes, Blackwell, Jordan, and Walters (1980), for example, found that kindergarten-age children persisted at a hidden figures task the same amount of time after experiencing failure that they persisted after experiencing success. In contrast, fifth graders, persisted far less time, on average, on the same and on a generalization task if they had previously experienced failure than if they had previously experienced success.

Findings of preschool invulnerability to helplessness were initially found to be consistent with classic learned helplessness theory because preschoolers were believed to lack the cognitively advanced reasoning skills necessary for the attributions that lead to helpless feelings.[3]   Dweck and her colleagues hypothesized that the helpless patterns of behavior they observed in young children might be related to more global concepts of self-worth, such as *goodness/badness*, and therefore might not require the cognitive skills required by helplessness theory. Thus, for example, if young children fail or are criticized, they may see themselves as bad, in a moral sense, and therefore withdraw. They also questioned the age-appropriateness of the tasks used in previous work, commenting that the failure experience may not have been salient enough and the wording of questions may have been too abstract for young children (Burhans & Dweck, 1995). Thus, Dweck and her colleagues turned to a familiar preschool task with salient outcomes-- wooden jigsaw puzzles--and asked specific and concrete achievement-related questions to explore individual differences in achievement-related cognitions, affect, and behavior.

Three studies from Dweck and her colleagues have demonstrated that preschool-age children do exhibit learned helplessness in achievement-related contexts: Cain and Dweck (1995), Hebert and Dweck (cited in Dweck, 1991), and Smiley and Dweck (1994). The basic methodology of these studies was similar: Children were presented with four puzzles of popular cartoon characters--three solvable and one unsolvable. The three unsolvable puzzles created a failure experience; the fourth puzzle was always solvable, and children were given sufficient time to complete the puzzle.

Following completion of the fourth puzzle, children were presented with all four puzzles they had worked on in the session (three unsolvable and one

---

[3]Learned helpless theory applied to older children assumes that helpless behavior is primarily a consequence of low perceptions of competence or control and low expectations for success.

solvable) and were asked to choose a puzzle to work on again. Children who chose to work on an unfinished (unsolvable) puzzle were categorized as *persisters*, whereas those who chose the completed (solvable) puzzle were categorized as *nonpersisters*. The reasons children gave for their puzzle choices were used to verify their categorization into these two groups. Thus, children were considered helpless nonpersisters only if they chose one of the completed puzzles and explained their choice of the completed task in terms of challenge avoidance (e.g., "That one was too hard") or task ease (e.g., "He was the easiest"). Expectancy for future success was assessed by asking children a forced-choice question ("Are you good or not-so-good at puzzles?") following completion of all four (three unsolvable, one solvable) puzzles. Finally, children were asked to rate their affect using a 5-point scale consisting of simple smiley faces ranging from *very sad* to *very happy*. Affective ratings were taken for each of the three unsolvable puzzles. Children were also asked to talk aloud as they worked on the puzzles. Their spontaneous utterances were then transcribed and coded to assess problem-solving strategies.

Across these three studies, from 36% to 51% of children were classified as *nonpersisters*. Puzzle choice (completed or noncompleted), however, was not the only variable that differentiated these two groups. Children's answers to a series of questions revealed that nonpersisters, compared with persisters, also: (a) were less confident about future success (they were more likely to say they could not finish any of the puzzles even if given more time or if they put forth more effort), (b) reported more negative affect on the smiley-face scale (only nonpersisters reported *very sad* affect), and (c) made more negative assessments of their own ability following failure (were more likely to say they were "not-so-good" at puzzles despite that they had said they were "good at" puzzles prior to failure. The spontaneous utterances of the two groups also differed. Nonpersisters were more likely than persisters to make negative evaluations of their own ability (I'm not good at this kind), make off-task comments (I'm having a birthday party), and express performance concerns (Did Mikey get this one?). These differences were found even though the two groups did not differ in a pretest of their puzzle-solving ability, in the number of pieces they fit into unsolvable puzzles, or in post failure puzzle-solving ability.

Differences in children's behavior are not limited to situations in which failure was just experienced. Smiley and Dweck (1994) also reported that nonpersisters set lower goals on a task unrelated to the puzzle task, which was administered in a session prior to any failure experience with the experimenter. Children were presented with a set of 25 blocks and were given six attempts to build a tower. Prior to each attempt, children were asked to estimate how tall a tower they would build. Although initial goals for tower height did not vary for the two groups, the two groups approached the task very differently: Across the next five trials, children who were later found to be persisters set much lower goals than nonpersisters. Although nonpersisters averaged an increase of about one block across the five trials, persisters averaged an increase of about four blocks.

There is also some evidence for stability in children's reactions to failure. Fifty of the preschoolers from the Smiley and Dweck (1994) study were reassessed (this time using an anagrams rather than a puzzle task) during the third and fourth grades (Smiley, Coffman, & Greene, 1994). The persistent elementary-age students (those who chose to work on the puzzle they had previously failed rather than one they had successfully completed) had higher expectations for success and rated their ability higher following failure as preschoolers than had nonpersistent elementary-age students (those who chose to work on the completed anagrams).

Dweck and her colleagues have also found helplesslike effects when children are given hypothetical vignettes. Heyman, Dweck, and Cain (1992) examined helplessness in young children in response to hypothetical criticism. Children were presented with a defective drawing or set of written numbers from 1 to 10, and were asked to pretend they had made this to give to their teacher. The experimenter pointed out the defect in the product (e.g., they forgot to put windows in a block-house, forgot to add feet to a painting of a family, or skipped the number 8 when writing the numbers 1 to 10) and then asked them to rate the quality of the product. Nearly all (94%) of all children gave their hypothetical products high ratings (5 or 6 on a scale of 1 to 6), although the defect had been pointed out to them. The experimenter, assuming the role of the child's teacher, then criticized the defective product.

Following the experimenter's (hypothetical teacher's) criticism, only 61% of children maintained high ratings of the product (high product raters); the remaining 39% lowered their rating from a mean of 5.57 to a mean of 3.36 in response to the criticism (low product raters). The two groups also differed in their cognitive and affective response to the teacher's criticism. Pretending to be the child who produced the product, low product raters rated their feelings about the criticism as more negative than high product raters. Low product raters also gave lower ratings when asked about their skill related to the task, their general intelligence, how good they were, and even how nice they were when given forced-choice options. Low product raters were also less persistent in that they were less willing to draw another picture or write more numbers following criticism than high product raters. Finally, when asked to role-play endings to the stories, high product raters were more likely to suggest endings that resulted in an improved product (e.g., take the picture home and finish it for homework) than were low product raters, who were more likely to suggest endings that did not result in an improved product (e.g., throwing away the numbers).

Although Dweck and her colleagues' studies have shown that some preschool-age children are negatively affected by failure in some ways, none of their studies have shown the performance decrements (e.g., using ineffective strategies) in preschool-age children following failure that are typically seen in studies of older children and adults. For example, in the Smiley and Dweck (1994) study, although nonpersisters generally felt *bad* after failing to solve three puzzles, their performance (e.g., time to completion) on the fourth (solvable) puzzle was not different from the time persisters took to complete the fourth puzzle or from the puzzle they had completed before they were given the failure experience. This finding is consistent with the unimpaired levels of persistence found in the Rholes et al. (1980) study mentioned earlier. Thus, although some preschool-age children experience the emotions and cognitions typically associated with helplessness in older children and adults, their performance suggests considerable resilience in problem-solving behavior. Young children appear to bounce back, at least in terms of performance, when presented with a solvable task.[4]

At first glance, their findings seem to contradict those of robust perceptions of competence and expectations for success reviewed earlier. However, a more careful analysis reveals similarities. Other studies of children's perceptions of their competencies and expectations for success have compared different age groups. Although they have found that young children were less affected by failure than older children, previous studies have also shown that even preschool-age children's competency-related judgments are at least modestly affected by failure experiences. For example, in the Stipek and Hoffman (1980) study, preschool-age children differentiated their expectations for success as a function of whether they previously succeeded or failed, although much less than older children. In the Stipek et al. (1985) study, 4-year-old children's expectations declined after each failure experience. Neither of these studies examined individual differences within age groups. It is possible that the modest decrease seen on average reflects some children who did not lower their expectations at all, and others lowered their expectations substantially. Together the research suggests that although young children are less vulnerable than older children, they are vulnerable.

What Dweck and her colleagues have done, that other researchers have not, is examine a broad spectrum of behaviors, cognitions, and affective reactions to failure. This approach reveals a coherent pattern of reactions that varies systematically among children as young as 4 years. These differences

---

[4]It is important to note that the expectancies for future success and emotion rating questions were asked after completion of the final, solvable puzzle. Therefore, nonpersisters reported that they felt bad and had low expectancies for success, although they had just experienced a salient success.

may have important implications for children's learning and motivation now as well as later on.

SUMMARY

In summary, stable individual differences have been found in infants and young children's achievement-related cognitions, behaviors, and affect associated with achievement contexts. These differences may be important because they most likely influence the development of cognitive competencies when they are young. Although longitudinal studies have not assessed associations between the motivational differences found in early childhood and motivational differences found in elementary school-age children, negative cognitions, affect, and behaviors seen in early childhood may portend future motivation-related problems.

Further evidence of variability and potential vulnerability in young children's motivation comes from studies demonstrating that aspects of parent interactions and the educational context in preschool and kindergarten affect children's motivation on a variety of dimensions. We turn now to these lines of research.

CONTEXT EFFECTS OF YOUNG CHILDREN'S ACHIEVEMENT MOTIVATION

There is some evidence supporting Harter's (1978) claim that differences in young children's mastery behavior are associated with differences in their social environments, particularly parents' behavior in task situations. Studies have also found systematic effects of the instructional and social climate of early childhood education programs on a variety of motivation-related variables. We discuss some of these findings next.

Physical and Social Environment in Infancy

Studies have shown positive associations between infants' mastery motivation and: (a) the number of toys in the home that are responsive to infants' manipulations and maternal kinesthetic and auditory stimulation (Busch-Rossnagel, Knauf-Jensen, & DesRosiers, 1995; Yarrow et al., 1982), (b) focusing infants' attention to objects (Yarrow et al., 1984), (c) positive parent affective exchanges with infants (Morgan et al., 1993), and (d) support for autonomy in task situations (i.e., nonintrusive assistance and encouragement; Frodi, Bridges, & Grolnick, 1985; Grolnick, Frodi, & Bridges, 1984). Parent's intrusiveness was negatively associated with infants' mastery behavior (Yarrow, Morgan, Jennings, Harmon, & Gaiter, 1982).

Somewhat different parent behaviors have been examined in studies of toddlers and preschool-age children. These studies report positive effects of (a) praise (Fagot, 1973; Hauser-Cram, 1996; Krantz & Scarth, 1979), (b) prompting (asking questions, offering suggestions; Henderson, 1984), and (c) adult involvement (e.g., demonstrating, giving information; Hauser-Cram, 1996; Krantz & Scarth, 1979). As was found for infants, studies of toddlers and preschool-age children suggest that intrusive behavior on the part of teachers or experimenters (Farnham-Diggory & Ramsey, 1971; Hamilton & Gordon, 1978) and criticism and directive comments (Fagot, 1973) negatively affect children's mastery behavior.

In most of the studies mentioned herein, adult behaviors were assessed in the same task situation that children's persistence and other mastery behaviors were assessed. Consequently, we do not know whether adult behavior in one situation (or an accumulation of situations) affects children's behavior in new situations.

There is also evidence suggesting that children's affective reactions in achievement contexts are associated with parenting style. For example, Lutkenhaus (1984) found that mother's behavior in a task situation was highly predictive of 3-year-old children's smiles, self-evaluations, and withdrawal from a task. Mothers' praise and promptness in responding to children's requests for help were associated with positive affect and persistence; mothers' intrusive behavior such as pushing the child's hand in a direction or taking an object from the child and negative remarks (e.g., ridicule) were associated with negative affective reactions, including withdrawal. Stipek, Recchia, and McClintic (1992) also found that the more mothers praised toddlers (13-39 months) while they worked on a task, the more their children spontaneously expressed pride (smiling, calling attention to their accomplishments) immediately after they completed a task or some part of a task. This was true even when the children completed a task for which they received no praise. Alessandri and Lewis (1993) did not find associations between parents' positive evaluative statements and pride reactions to success in 3-year-olds, but positive statements were associated with less evidence of shame in failure and negative statements were associated with more shame. They also found that girls received more negative evaluative statements from parents than boys (see also Lewis, Alessandri, & Sullivan, 1992).

In summary, studies of young children's behavior in achievement contexts and emotional reactions to achievement outcomes show variability that is systematically associated with parents' behavior in the task situation. What is not known is whether the parent effect transcends the particular situation in which parent behavior is assessed.

Classrooms

Although Stipek's and her colleagues' early childhood classroom studies found modest variation in children's cognitions about achievement outcomes, the variance they found, as well as variance on other motivation measures, was systematically associated with the classroom context. Their findings therefore indicate that some contexts may support and some may undermine achievement motivation. In the following discussion, we differentiate between the effects of the broader instructional and social climate of the classroom and the experiences of individual children. This is an important distinction because the experiences of children within the same classroom vary substantially, in part because of their own competencies and behavior and in part because of teachers' biases or preferences.

Between Classrooms. A number of studies have shown classroom effects on children's motivation (see e.g., Burts, Hart, Charlesworth, & Kirk, 1990; Burts, Hart, Charlesworth, Fleege, Mosley, & Thomasson, 1992; Charlesworth, Hart, Burts, & DeWolf, 1993). We describe next three studies that demonstrate the potentially depressing effects of some classroom contexts.

The first study focused on the nature and salience of evaluation in the classroom (Stipek & Daniels, 1988). The study was designed to explore the possibility that young children's positive perceptions of their ability and the development of more negative judgments in later grades could be explained in part by systematic, grade-related differences in the nature of instruction and evaluation. In preschool and kindergarten classrooms, children generally do not have available to them as much or as salient information about how well they perform relative to classmates as do children in the later elementary grades. The younger children are less likely to be grouped for ability or to be given grades or scores that facilitate social comparisons. Having all students work on the same task, in which performance outcomes can be easily ascertained (e.g., number correct), is also less prevalent in preschool and kindergarten than in the later grades. Bulletin boards with all children's products are likely to be seen in preschool and kindergarten classrooms, in contrast to the common practice in the later grades of displaying only the best work (see Stipek and Mac Iver, 1989, for a review of research on typical changes in classrooms that are associated with grade).

We reasoned that if the classroom context contributed to kindergarten-age children's typically positive perceptions of their competence, then competence ratings would be lower in kindergarten classrooms that looked more like upper elementary classrooms-with more frequent and more salient external, normative evaluation. Similarly, older elementary students' perceptions of competence might be higher if they were in classroom environments that are more typical of kindergartners, in which external, normative evaluation is deemphasized. Accordingly, we compared kindergartners' and fourth graders' perceptions of competence in kindergartenlike and fourth gradelike classrooms. Our hypothesis was partially supported. Kindergartners in fourth-gradelike classrooms (with normative information about their performance readily available) rated their academic competence roughly the same as the fourth graders (mean of 15.1 and 14.8 on a 20-point scale, respectively) and significantly lower than the kindergartners in more typical kindergarten classrooms (18.8). However, the classroom context had no effect on fourth graders' judgments of their competence (14.8 for salient normative information classrooms, 15.5 for low salient, more kindergartenlike classrooms). This interaction effect suggests that the judgments of younger children may have been more malleable or responsive to the evaluative context than the judgments of the older children, reminding us that similar treatments can have different effects on children at different ages. Nevertheless, the study does support the notion that kindergarten children's high perceptions of their competence may be partially explained by the typically low emphasis on performance outcomes and low amount of information available on their performance related to peers. It also shows that it is possible to create classroom contexts that lower those perceptions, indicating again that young children are not completely invulnerable.

Findings from a second classroom study provide additional support for the hypothesis that young children's motivation can be depressed under some classroom circumstances (Stipek, Feiler, Daniels, & Milburn, 1995). In this study, we compared preschoolers' and kindergartners' motivation on a variety of dimensions in two different kinds of classroom settings.

There were 32 classrooms altogether. In the classrooms that we refer to as *child centered* teachers did not stress basic academic skills; to the degree that basic skills were included in the curriculum, children had a great deal of discretion and initiated many of their own activities. The teacher often connected instruction to children's own experiences and interests, and there was little pressure to perform and very little negative evaluation of their work. Students were encouraged to work with peers, and the distinction between work and play was subtle. In *didactic* classrooms, teachers stressed academic performance and regularly gave tasks to the whole class for which performance was clearly defined and comparable (e.g., worksheets). Teachers chose and controlled most activities, making clear distinctions between work and play times, and children were not encouraged to work collaboratively as much as in the child-centered classrooms. In addition to the different instructional emphases, the teachers were generally less nurturing and attentive to individual student needs in the didactic classrooms.

The findings suggest that the more didactic, performance-oriented approach had negative effects on children's motivation. Compared with children in child-centered classrooms, children in didactic classrooms rated their academic competencies lower, selected an easier task when given an option, predicted lower performance on both a maze and a puzzle task, and were less likely to smile spontaneously when they completed a task (e.g., a puzzle, a sticker picture) or to draw the experimenter's attention to their achievement. They also showed more dependency on the experimenter (requesting permission, opinions, or approval) and claimed to worry more about school.

Despite the apparent costs to motivation, benefits to the didactic approach were found for basic skill acquisition. Both preschoolers and kindergartners in the didactic classrooms scored higher on a traditional test of literacy-related skills (e.g., letter and word recognition), although not on a test of math-related skills.

A follow-up study compared 42 classrooms varying in the same ways as the study described earlier but in this study, children's behavior in the regular classroom was observed (Stipek et al., 1998). As in the first study, most of the significant differences favored the child-centered instructional approach and social environment. The kindergarten children in the more didactic, teacher-controlled classrooms showed more evidence of stress (e.g., nail biting, frowning, turning away from a task) during daily classroom activities. Both preschoolers and kindergartners in the more didactic classrooms were more likely than children in the child-centered classrooms to request the teacher's permission or approval while they were engaged in activities. They were also less compliant and more likely to be disciplined, and they expressed more negative affect.

In contrast to the motivation variables, the effects of the program type on achievement outcomes varied depending on whether children were in preschool or kindergarten. Kindergarten children's gains on both literacy and mathematics achievement tests were higher in the didactic, performance-oriented classrooms than in the child-centered classrooms. Thus, despite some negative effects on motivation, kindergarten children learned basic skills better in a more academic, performance-oriented program. The reverse was found for children in preschool. They performed better on the basic skills tests if they were in classrooms that were more child-centered and less basic skills oriented. Children in child-centered preschools performed better although the tests assessed skills (e.g., counting, recognizing letters) that were stressed in the didactic instructional programs.

Overall, the findings in these three studies suggest possible trade-offs at least for kindergartners. Short-term motivational effects must be weighed against achievement effects. Longitudinal research is needed to determine whether the motivational costs take a toll on children's learning in later grades. It is possible that the depressing effects on motivation of a highly academic, skill-oriented, didactic approach puts children on a trajectory that spirals into more serious motivational problems that ultimately undermine their academic achievement.

One confounding factor in the two classroom studies described earlier was the social context. The teachers in the didactic programs tended to be less nurturing and responsive to children's individual social needs than were the teachers in the child-centered programs. It was impossible to separate the type of instructional program from the social context because these two dimensions were highly correlated to each other (see also Stipek, Daniels, Galluzzo, & Milburn, 1992). The motivational costs may have been a consequence of the social as much as the academic context. Perhaps stressing academic skills and performance would not undermine motivation in a more nurturing, child-sensitive social context, although this appears to be a rare combination in the real world of preschools and kindergartens in the United States.

Within Classrooms. Although most of Stipek's studies have examined classroom effects on children--as if all children experience the classroom in the same way--it is clear that children's experience within a classroom varies. For example, even a teacher who is, overall, sensitive and responsive to individual children's needs might vary in her responsiveness to particular children.

Stipek and her colleagues have just begun to examine these intraclassroom variations in a longitudinal study of very low-income kindergarten and first-grade children in three different geographical areas of the United States. Teachers in 171 classrooms were asked to rate their relationship with 276 study children (typically not more than 3 in any classroom). We used two subscales of the Student-Teacher Relationship Scale (STRS) developed by Pianta and his associates (Pianta, Nimetz, & Bennett, 1997; Pianta & Steinberg, 1992), which assesses teachers' perceptions of their relationship with particular students. The two subscales asked teachers to rate, on a 1 to 5 scale (*definitely not* to *definitely*), the degree to which they felt they had a close relationship with a particular study child (e.g., "I share an affectionate, warm relationship with this child") and the degree to which they had a conflictual relationship (e.g., "This child and I always seem to be struggling with each other"). Children rated their competencies in mathematics and literacy and their feelings about school.

Analyses revealed that children with whom teachers claimed to have a close relationship rated their math competencies higher and had more positive feelings about school than did children with whom teachers claimed to have a less close relationship. Thus, children's relationship with their teacher was associated with these two motivation variables.

Birch and Ladd (1996) reported further that children's relationships with their teachers are predictive of kindergarten children's attitudes toward school. For example, children who had conflictual relationships with their teachers claimed to like school less than children with less conflictual relationships. Moreover, in a follow-up study, they found, moreover, that relationships with teachers in kindergarten predicted relationships with teachers in first grade and changes in children's behavior (Birch & Ladd, 1998). For example, the children who had the most conflict with teachers in kindergarten declined the most in their relative social skills by first grade. Taken together, the findings suggest the importance of considering the classroom context as it is experienced by individual children.

Summary

Previous research suggests that various aspects of achievement motivation are affected by adult behavior in a task situation. Although preschool and kindergarten children's achievement-related cognitions are typically high, these, as well as other motivational variables, are systematically and predictably associated with children's experiences in classrooms. In brief, studies of social interactions in task contexts suggest that children's mastery behavior can be undermined by intrusive, directive, critical parental behavior. Studies of classroom environments suggest that didactic and performance-oriented instruction, in which information about relative performance is salient, combined with low levels of nurturing and responsiveness to children can depress preschoolers' and kindergartners' motivation.

CULTURAL CONTEXT

All of the studies reported here were carried out in the United States. The findings may not apply to other cultures, particularly cultures in which more didactic teaching methods are normative at home and at school. It is highly likely that children's experiences in their homes and their expectations about what learning environments should look like mediate the effects of learning environments on their motivation and learning.

Huntsinger, Jose, and Larson (1998) provided data that illustrate the importance of culture. The findings reveal that, compared to EuroAmerican parents, Chinese-American (immigrant) parents used more formal, didactic approaches (e.g., flashcards, memorization of math facts) to teach their first- and second-grade children. EuroAmerican parents used methods embedded in context (e.g., real-life situations and games) like those used by the child-centered teachers in Stipek's and her colleagues' studies. Huntsinger et al. reported that Chinese-American children outperformed Euro-American children on a mathematics test by a considerable margin. There were no differences between the two groups on teachers' ratings of social problems and contrary to what would be expected from the classroom research reported in this chapter, Euro-American children who received more child-centered instruction at home were rated higher on anxiety and depression by teachers.

The findings in the studies reported in this chapter may not apply equally well to different subgroups within the United States. Delpit (1995) suggested for example, that low-income, African-American children are accustomed to a more direct approach in making requests ("sit down") and may not understand a teacher's more subtle approach to directing behavior ("its circle time"). Furthermore, teachers may interpret a child's confusion about the cultural conventions of the classroom as disobedience or low motivation. Clearly cultural norms need to be considered in making judgments about what is an appropriate learning environment for young children.

CONCLUSIONS

Are Young Children Vulnerable to Achievement-Motivation Problems?

Overall the findings of the various lines of research reviewed in this chapter provide cause for both celebration and concern. Most young children have very positive and relatively robust achievement-related cognitions. They have confidence in their competencies, high expectations for success, positive attitudes toward achievement contexts, and they are less affected by failure than older children.

Nevertheless, there are also indicators of problems. As early as infancy, there are stable differences in how children deal with opportunities to explore and manipulate objects and the degree to which they persist in goal-directed behavior when they encounter obstacles. Some infants are less inclined than others to manipulate and explore objects and to persist when they encounter obstacles to their goal. According to studies conducted by Dweck and her colleagues, some preschool-age children develop a maladaptive pattern of behavioral, cognitive, and emotional reactions to failure.

Sources of Early Emerging Motivation Problems

It is likely that the kinds of systematic and somewhat stable behavioral differences observed in infancy reflect differences in temperament and cognitive competencies, which are to some degree biologically based. Biological explanations, however, most likely account for a decreasing proportion of the variance in children's achievement-related behavior as they become older.

The associations between mastery behavior in early and late infancy or toddlerhood most likely do not reflect a simple unfolding of a set of prewired dispositions. Individual differences observed after early infancy are probably best explained by transactional effects of early, perhaps biologically based predispositions and variations in social and physical environments. Infants' temperaments may affect caregivers' interactions, which then reinforce or even amplify initial differences. For example, parents may provide more stimulating toys for infants who are more prone to manipulate and explore objects. Early problems may also evolve into later problems that look very different. For example, infants who seek novelty, explore materials fully, and persist in overcoming obstacles to their goals may develop relatively better cognitive skills than children who are less mastery oriented. Later, when they can reflect on and compare their skills to their age mates, their relatively high levels of competence should lead to more positive judgments of their achievement-related competencies. There is also substantial evidence for physical, social, and instructional context effects on preschool-age children's motivation, suggesting that the environment also has important direct and independent effects that may not be mediated by early behavioral differences in children's approaches to task situations.

What Behaviors Should be Monitored?

Table 3.1 provides a summary of measures of young children's motivation that have been used in research. There is evidence for stability or environmental affects on most of these indexes. Practitioners could assess any of these behaviors to identify children with achievement-motivation problems that might have long-term effects on their learning and that might predict future motivation-related problems. The assessment can be very informal, with the practitioner simply paying attention to a child's behavior, spontaneous comments, or affective displays during regular classroom activities. Assessment could also be more systematic. For example, observers could use a checklist to record, over a period of time, incidences of some subset of the indicators of achievement motivation listed.

Although there is almost no evidence that behaviors, cognitions, and affective experiences observed in early childhood predict motivational problems in elementary school and beyond, previous research suggests the particular importance of reactions to difficulty or failure. Studies of individual differences in mastery behaviors indicate some stability in persistence, and studies of children's reactions to failure suggest that persistence is related to a host of other motivation-related variables. Persistence has also been found to predict cognitive competencies.

Persistence and other reactions to failure cannot be assessed easily by observing children in natural settings because children's behavior is substantially influenced by the nature and difficulty of the tasks that are available and that children choose to do. This limitation could be addressed by using a quasistructured approach, in which the observer encourages a child to engage in tasks that are moderately challenging (for the child being observed). Moderate difficulty is necessary because children have no need to persist on easy tasks, and persistence can be maladaptive on impossibly difficult tasks.

Assessing reactions to failure may require a preplanned, unsolvable task that gives the impression of being solvable--with considerable attention given to making sure that the child leaves the situation feeling successful and confident.

TABLE 3.1
Possible Measures of Motivation in Early Childhood

Behaviors

- Choice--to engage in intellectual tasks or other activities
(for an infant, may be exploration and manipulation of objects)
- Level of difficulty selected
- Level of engagement/attentiveness
- Resistance to stopping
- Flexibility and resourcefulness in novel or problem situations
- Resourcefulness in problem solving
- Persistence in the face of obstacles or difficulties
- Dependency (e.g., requests for permission, approval, opinions
- Expectations for success, generally and after a failure experience
- Self-evaluations of competencies (asked directly or spontaneous comments while working on a task
- Perceptions of control
- Attributions for success and failure

Affect

- Self-reported worrying
- Stress (e.g., nail biting, frowning, turning away from tasks)
- Pleasure in mastery striving and goal attainment
- Spontaneous pride or shame reactions to success or failure
- Enjoyment in process of working on task (asked directly or observed)

We do not recommend global ratings of children. Rating scales that include the behavioral components of mastery motivation that Yarrow and colleagues have studied have been created for both infants and preschool-age children (e.g., Morgan et al., 1993). However, ratings by adults who know a child well are likely to be influenced by other qualities of the child or the nature of their relationship with the child. Specific behavioral ratings in circumscribed situations are less vulnerable to such biases (although not altogether).

IMPLICATIONS FOR PRACTICE

Heretofore we have discussed strategies for identifying young children who might have motivation problems that are already or may in the future undermine their learning, as well as their comfort in and enjoyment of academic settings. Remedying problems identified is another issue. It is important, however; as difficult as the task may be in early childhood, it becomes harder as children's motivation-related beliefs become more consolidated over the first few grades of elementary school.

Some strategies are suggested by the research reviewed earlier on parents' and preschool teachers' practices that are associated with relatively high motivation levels. The research reviewed in the chapter suggests the value of providing infants objects to manipulate, encouraging exploration without being directive, guiding activity (e.g., by asking questions) while supporting autonomy, and creating a child-centered instructional environment for preschoolers. There is too little space remaining to treat such an important topic fully. In the following, we add to what has been said to be a few principals supported by research on motivation (see Stipek, 1998, for an in-depth review):

1. Create a safe environment for children, where right answers are not prized and mistakes are not viewed as something to be avoided-- where initial failure is treated as a natural part of learning.
2. Provide challenging tasks--manageable but requiring some effort--to give children experience having to overcome initial obstacles.
3. Encourage children to persist directly ("I know you can do it, try it another way") and indirectly (e.g., by praising them specifically for taking on challenging tasks and for exerting effort and persistence).
4. Do not give false praise or try to artificially raise their perceptions of their competence or their expectations for success. The best way to make children feel competent is to help them be competent.
5. Give substantive critical feedback that provides information that the child can use to guide subsequent efforts.
6. Provide diverse tasks that are connected to children's own lives and

interests.

7. Give children opportunities to select tasks and strategies for completing tasks; encourage creativity.

8. Develop and maintain a caring relationship with each child that is not contingent upon the child's behavior or performance.

These principles apply to the entire class. Indeed, it is not possible to remedy individual children's problems if the classroom context does not support high motivation. However, accommodations may be needed for children who show signs of distress (as opposed to mild frustration) about his difficulties. The most effective strategy for increasing the motivation of children whose motivation problems are coupled with relatively poor skills is to help them increase their skills. Thus, special attention may need to be given to these children in class, and parents may need guidance in how they can support children's learning environment at home.

Special efforts to maintain children's optimism and enthusiasm can make a valuable contribution to children's learning, immediately and long into the future. In addition to assessing children's skills frequently, to adjust their educational program to meet students' learning needs, teachers need to watch carefully for early emerging motivational problems--to catch and remedy them before they become more serious and resistant to intervention.

REFERENCES

Alessandri, S., & Lewis, M. (1993). Parental evaluation and its relation to shame and pride in young children. *Sex Roles, 29*, 335-343.

Arend, R., Gove, F., & Sroufe, A. (1979). Continuity of individual adaptation from infancy to kindergarten: A predictive study of ego-resiliency and curiosity in preschoolers. *Child Development, 50*, 950-959.

Atkinson, J. (1964). *An introduction to motivation.* Princeton, NJ: Van Nostrand.

Benenson, J. F., & Dweck, C. S. (1986). The development of trait explanations and self evaluations in the academic and social domains. *Child Development, 57*, 1179-1187.

Birch, S., & Ladd, G. (1996). Interpersonal relationships in the school environment and children's early school adjustment: The role of teachers and peers. In N. K. Wentzel & J. Juvonen (Eds.), *Social motivation: Understanding children's school adjustment* (pp. 199-225). New York: Cambridge University Press.

Birch, S., & Ladd, G. (1998). Children's interpersonal behaviors and the teacher-child relationship. *Developmental Psychology, 34*, 934-946.

Block, J. H., & Block, J. (1980). The role of ego-control and ego-resiliency in the organization of behavior. In W. A. Collins (Ed.), *Minnesota symposia on child psychology* (Vol. 13, pp. 39-101). Hillsdale, NJ: Lawrence Erlbaum Associates.

Burhans, K. K., & Dweck, C. S. (1995). Helplessness in early childhood: The role of contingent worth. *Child Development, 66*, 1719-1739.

Burts, D., Hart, C., Charlesworth, R., Fleege, P., Mosley, J., & Thomasson, R. (1992). Observed activities and stress behaviors of children in developmentally appropriate and inappropriate kindergarten classrooms. *Early Childhood Research Quarterly, 7,* 297-318.

Burts, D., Hart, C., Charlesworth, R., & Kirk, L. (1990). A comparison of frequencies of stress behaviors observed in kindergarten children in classrooms with developmentally appropriate versus developmentally inappropriate instructional practices. *Early Childhood Research Quarterly, 5,* 407-423.

Busch-Rossnagel, N. A., Knauf-Jensen, D., & DesRosiers, F. (1995). Mothers and others: The role of the socializing environment in the development of mastery motivation. In R. MacTurk & G. Morgan (Eds.), *Mastery motivation: Origins, conceptualizations, and applications: Advances in applied developmental psychology* (Vol. 12, pp. 117-146). Norwood, NJ: Ablex.

Cain, K. M., & Dweck, C. (1995). The relation between motivational patterns and achievement cognitions through the elementary school years. *Merrill-Palmer Quarterly, 41,* 25-52.

Charlesworth, R., Hart, C., Burts, D., & DeWolf, M. (1993). The LSU studies: Building a research base for developmentally appropriate practice. In S. Reifel (Ed.), *Advances in early education and day care: Perspectives on developmentally appropriate practice* (Vol. 5, pp. 3-28). Greenwich, CT: JAI.

Clifford, M. (1975). Validity of expectation: A developmental function. *Alberta Journal of Educational Research, 48,* 220-226.

Colombo, J., Mitchell, D. W., Dodd, J., & Coldren, J. T. (1989). Longitudinal correlates of infant attention in the paired-comparison paradigm. *Intelligence, 13*(1), 33-42.

Delpit, L. (1995). *Other people's children: Cultural conflict in the classroom.* New York: New Press.

Diener, C. I., & Dweck, C. S. (1978). An analysis of learned helplessness: Continuous changes in performance, strategy, and achievement cognitions following failure. *Journal of Personality and Social Psychology, 36,* 451-462.

Diener, C. I., & Dweck, C. S. (1980). An analysis of learned helplessness: II. The processing of success. *Journal of Personality and Social Psychology, 39,* 940-952.

Dweck, C. S. (1991). Self-theories and goals: Their role in motivation, personality and development. In R. Dienstbier (Ed.), *Nebraska symposium on motivation, 1990* (Vol. 36, pp. 199-235). Lincoln, NE: University of Nebraska Press.

Emde, R., Plomin, R., Robinson, J., Corley, R., DeFries, J., Fulker, D., Reznick, J., Campos, J., Kagan, J., & Zahn-Waxler, C. (1992). Temperament, emotion, and cognition at fourteen months: The MacArthur longitudinal twin study. *Child Development, 63,* 1437-1455.

Entwisle, D., & Hayduk, L. (1978). *Too great expectations: Young children's academic outlook.* Baltimore, MD: Johns Hopkins University Press.

Eshel, Y., & Klein, Z. (1981). Development of academic self-concept of lower-class and middle-class primary school children. *Journal of Educational Psychology, 73,* 287-293.

Fagot, B. (1973). Influence of teacher behavior in the preschool. *Developmental Psychology, 9,* 198-206.

Farnham-Diggory, S., & Ramsey, B. (1971). Play persistence: Some effects of interruption, social reinforcement, and defective toys. *Developmental Psychology, 4,* 297-298.

Frodi, A., Bridges, L., & Grolnick, W. (1985). Correlates of mastery-related behavior: A short-term longitudinal study of infants in their second year. *Child Development, 56,* 1291-1298.

Grolnick, W., Frodi, A., & Bridges, L. (1984). Maternal control style and the mastery motivation of one-year-olds. *Infant Mental Health Journal, 5,* 5, 72-82.

Hamilton, H., & Gordon, D. (1978). Teacher-child interactions in preschool and task persistence. *American Educational Research Journal, 15,* 459-466.

Harter, S. (1978). Effectance motivation reconsidered: Toward a developmental model. *Human Development, 21,* 34-64.

Hauser-Cram, P. (1996). Mastery motivation in toddlers with developmental disabilities. *Child Development, 67,* 236-248.

Henderson, B. (1984). Parents and exploration: The effect of context on individual differences in exploratory behavior. *Child Development, 55*, 1237-1245.

Heyman, G. D., Dweck, C. S., & Cain, K. M. (1992). Young children's vulnerability to self-blame and helplessness: Relationship to beliefs about goodness. *Child Development, 63*, 401-415.

Huntsinger, C., Jose, P., & Larson, S. (1998). Do parent practices to encourage academic competence influence the social adjustment of young European American and Chinese American Children? *Developmental Psychology, 34*, 747-756.

Jennings, K., Connors, R., & Stegman, C. (1988). Does a physical handicap alter the development of mastery motivation during the preschool years? *Journal of the American Academy of Child and Adolescent Psychiatry, 27*, 312-317.

Jennings, K., Harmon, R., Morgan, G., Gaiter, J., & Yarrow, L. (1979). Exploratory play as an index of mastery motivation: Relationships to persistence, cognitive functioning, and environmental measures. *Developmental Psychology, 15*, 386-394.

Krantz, M., & Scarth, L. (1979). Task persistence and adult assistance in the preschool. *Child Development, 50*, 578-581.

Kush, J. C., & Watkins, M. W. (1996). Long-term stability of children's attitudes toward reading. *Journal of Educational Research, 89*(5), 315-319.

Lewis, M., Alessandri, S., & Sullivan, M. (1992). Differences in shame and pride as a function of children's gender and task difficulty. *Child Development, 63*, 630-638.

Lutkenhaus, P. (1984). Pleasure derived from mastery in three-year-olds: Its function for persistence and the influence of maternal behavior. *International Journal of Behavioral Development, 7*, 343-358.

MacTurk, R., & Morgan, G. (Eds.). (1995). *Mastery motivation: Origins, conceptualizations, and applications: Advances in applied developmental psychology* (Vol. 12). Norwood, NJ: Ablex.

MacTurk, R., Morgan, G., & Jennings, K. (1995). The assessment of mastery motivation in infants and young children. In R. MacTurk & G. Morgan (Eds.), *Mastery motivation: Origins, conceptualizations, and applications: Advances in applied developmental psychology* (Vol. 12, pp. 19-56). Norwood, NJ: Ablex.

McCall, R., & Carriger, M. (1993). Infant habituation and recognition memory performance as predictors of later IQ: A review and conceptual analysis. *Child Development, 64*, 5-79.

Marsh, H., Barnes, J., Cairns, L., & Tidman, M. (1984). Self-description questionnaire: Age and sex effects in the structure and level of self-concept for preadolescent children. *Journal of Educational Psychology, 76*, 581-596.

McKenna, M. C., Kear, D. J., & Ellsworth, R. A. (1995). Children's attitudes toward reading: A national survey. *Reading Research Quarterly, 30*(4), 934-956.

Messer, D., McCarthy, M., McQuiston, S., MacTurk, R., Yarrow, L., & Vietze, P. (1986). Relation between mastery behavior in infancy and competence in early childhood. *Developmental Psychology, 22*(3), 366-372.

Morgan, G., & Harmon, R. (1984). Developmental transformations in mastery motivation. In R. Emde & R. Harmon (Eds.), *Continuities and discontinuities in development*. New York: Plenum.

Morgan, G., Harmon, R., Maslin-Cole, C., Busch-Rossnagel, N., Jennings, K., Hauser-Cram, P., & Brockman, L. (1993). Parent and teacher perceptions of young children's mastery motivation: Assessment and review of research. In D. Messer (Ed.), *Mastery motivation in early childhood: Development, measurement, and social processes* (pp. 109-131). London: Routledge.

Nicholls, J. (1978). The development of the concepts of effort and ability, perceptions of academic attainment and the understanding that difficult tasks require more ability. *Child Development, 49*, 800-814.

Nicholls, J. (1979). The development of perceptions of own attainment and causal attributions for success and failure in reading. *Journal of Educational Psychology, 71*, 94-99.

Parsons, J., & Ruble, D. (1977). The development of achievement-related expectancies. *Child Development, 48*, 1975-1979.

Pedlow, R., Sandon, A., Prior, M., & Oberklaid, F. (1993). Stability of maternally reported temperament from infancy to 8 years. *Developmental Psychology, 29*(6), 998-1007.

Piaget, J. (1952). *The origins of intelligence in children.* New York: Norton.

Pianta, R., Nimetz, S., & Bennett, E. (1997). Mother-child relationships, teacher-child relationships, and school outcomes in preschool and kindergarten. *Early Childhood Research Quarterly, 12*, 263-280.

Pianta, R., & Steinberg, M. (1992). Teacher-child relationships and the process of adjusting to school. *New Directions for Child Development, 57*, 61-80.

Pintrich, P., & Blumenfeld, P. (1985). Classroom experience and children's self-perceptions of ability, effort, and conduct. *Journal of Educational Psychology, 77*, 646-657.

Power, T., Chapieski, L., & McGrath, M. (1985). Assessment of individual differences in infant exploration and play. *Developmental Psychology, 21*, 974-981.

Redding, R. E., Morgan, G., & Harmon, R. J. (1988). Mastery motivation in infants and toddlers: Is it greatest when tasks are moderately challenging? *Infant Behavior & Development, 11*(4), 419-430.

Rholes, W., Blackwell, J., Jordan, C., & Walters, C. (1980). A developmental study of learned helplessness. *Developmental Psychology, 16*, 616-624.

Ruble, D. N., Grosovsky, E., Frey, K., & Cohen, R. (1992). Developmental changes in competence assessment. In A. Boggiano & T. Pittman (Eds.), *Achievement motivation: A social-developmental perspective* (pp. 138-164). New York: Cambridge University Press.

Sigman, M., Cohen, S. E., Beckwith, L., & Topinka, C. (1987). Task persistence in 2-year-old preterm infants in relation to subsequent attentiveness and intelligence. *Infant Behavior & Development, 10*(3), 295-305.

Smiley, P. A., Coffman, J., & Greene, J. (1994). *Achievement goals: Stability and relation to achievement beliefs.* Poster presented at the annual meeting of the American Psychological Association, Los Angeles, CA.

Smiley, P. A., & Dweck, C. S. (1994). Individual differences in achievement goals among young children. *Child Development, 65*, 1723-1743.

Stipek, D. (1984a). The development of achievement motivation. In R. Ames & C. Ames (Eds.), *Research on motivation in education: Student motivation* (Vol. 1, pp. 145-174). New York: Academic press.

Stipek, D. (1984b). Young children's performance expectations: Logical analysis or wishful thinking? In J. Nicolls (Ed.), *Advances in motivation and achievement: The development of achievement motivation* (Vol. 3, pp. 33-56). Greenwich, CT: JAI.

Stipek, D. (1998). *Motivation to learn: From theory to practice.* Needham Heights, MA: Allyn & Bacon.

Stipek, D., & Daniels, D. (1988). Declining perceptions of competence: A consequence of changes in the child or the educational environment? *Journal of Educational Psychology, 80*, 352-356.

Stipek, D., Daniels, D., Galluzzo, D., & Milburn, S. (1992). Characterizing early childhood education programs for poor and middle-class children. *Early Childhood Quarterly, 7*, 1-19.

Stipek, D., Feiler, R., Byler, P., Ryan, R., Milburn, S., & Salmon, S. (1998). Good beginnings: What difference does the program make in preparing young children for school? *Journal of Applied Developmental Psychology, 19*, 41-66.

Stipek, D., Feiler, R., Daniels, D., & Milburn, S. (1995). Effects of different instructional approaches on young children's achievement and motivation. *Child Development, 66*, 209-223.

Stipek, D., & Hoffman, J. (1980). Development of children's performance-related judgments. *Child Development, 5*, 92-94.

Stipek, D., & Mac Iver, D. (1989). Developmental change in children's assessment of intellectual competence. *Child Development, 60*, 521-538.

Stipek, D., Recchia, S., & McClintic, S. (1992). Self-evaluation in young children. *Monographs of the Society for Research in Child Development, 57*(1), Serial No. 226.

Stipek, D., Roberts, T., & Sanborn, M. (1984). Preschool-age children's performance expectations for themselves and another child as a function of the incentive value of success and the salience of past performance. *Child Development, 55*, 1983-1989.

Stipek, D., & Tannatt, L. (1984). Children's judgments of their own and their peers' academic competence. *Journal of Educational Psychology, 76*, 75-84.

Stott, D., & Sharp, J. (1976). Effectiveness-motivation in pre-school children. *Educational Research, 18*, 117-125.

Vondra, J. (1995). Contributions and confounds from biology and genetics. In R. MacTurk & G. Morgan (Eds.), *Mastery motivation: Origins, conceptualizations, and applications: Advances in applied developmental psychology* (Vol. 12, pp. 165-200). Norwood, NJ: Ablex.

White, R. (1959). Motivation reconsidered: The concept of competence. *Psychological Review, 66*, 297-333.

Wigfield, A., Eccles, J., Yoon, K., Harold, R., Arbreton, A., Freedman-Dona, C., & Blumenfeld, P. (1997). Change in children's competence beliefs and subjective task values across the elementary school years: A 3-year study. *Journal of Educational Psychology, 89*, 451-469.

Yarrow, L., Klein, R., Lomonaco, S., & Morgan, G. (1975). Cognitive and motivational development in early childhood. In B. Z. Friedlander, G. Sterritt, & G. Kirk (Eds.), *Exceptional infant: Assessment and intervention* (pp. 491-502). New York: Bruner/Mazel.

Yarrow, L., McQuiston, S., MacTurk, R., McCarthy, M., Klein, R., & Vietze, P. (1983). Assessment of mastery motivation during the first year of life: Contemporaries and cross-age relationships. *Developmental Psychology, 19*, 159-171.

Yarrow, L., Morgan, G., Jennings, K., Harmon, R., & Gaiter, J. (1982). Infants' persistence at tasks: Relationships to cognitive functioning and early experience. *Infant Behavior and Development, 5*, 131-141.

Yarrow, L., & Pedersen, F. (1976). The interplay between cognition and motivation in infancy. In M. Lewis (Eds.), *Origins of intelligence*. New York: Plenum.

Yussen, S., & Berman, L. (1981). Memory predictions for recall and recognition in first-, third-, and fifth-grade children. *Developmental Psychology, 17*, 224-229.

4

LEARNING, ATTENTION, AND PLAY

Lorraine Mccune
Mary B. Zanes
Rutgers - The State University of New Jersey

How does the child's ability to pay attention impact on learning? Is there a role for play at school? Few would disagree with the notion that the primary goal of schooling is child learning. We as teachers (preschool through the college years) bear responsibly the burden of deciding what and how to teach, of packaging the wisdom of our culture appropriately for delivery to young minds. In return, we expect students to learn. The question addressed here is: How can our knowledge of the developmental abilities, tendencies, and learning capacities of young children help in the process of packaging and delivering information for learning? Children are designed to learn: The more we can learn about and use the child's own design features, including the role of attention and play in their learning, the more effective will be our instruction.

Thinking in evolutionary terms, it is important to remember that Nature takes no chances. Our long period of immaturity and dependence offers both the opportunity and necessity for new members of our species to learn from adults. Humans and other primates are born with strong sucking and rooting reflexes that ensure early nourishment. Small mammals such as kittens, blind and mobile at birth, are further provided with a tropic tendency to seek warmth, thus ensuring their ability to locate the mother animal (Freeman & Rosenblatt, 1978). So it is with learning. It is no accident, but a design of Nature. For example, newborn infants fixate their eyes at about an eight-inch distance and greatly prefer the visual configurations of the face to any other (Fantz, 1963). These tendencies ensure that the nursling will lock onto the mother's eyes, thus ensuring her of her importance to the newborn and her beauty in that baby's eyes. Preference for the mother's face and voice is the earliest learning (Brown, 1979; Maurer & Salapatek, 1976; Watson, Hayes, Vietze, & Becker, 1979). This preference guides the baby in maintaining eye contact with mother while deepening mother's commitment to someone who deems her so very special.

Many studies have documented parents' support for their baby's learning (e.g., Matas, Arend, & Sroufe, 1978; Slade, 1987). Although baby cannot yet remain easily upright, but loves to explore the world visually, mother and father hold baby to their shoulder or facing outward on a lap as the world goes by. Parents are alert to babies' expanding interests, offering toys, books, rough and tumble games, or merely quiet company as their children develop the skills of independent manual exploration, crawling, and walking. Surprisingly, parent behavior reflects and predicts the level of the baby's and later the child's learning (McCune, DiPane, Firevoid, & Fleck, 1994). Thus, parents increase the complexity of the language they use with their children just as the children's own language makes developmental shifts (Snow, 1972).

McCune's original work on the development of play (McCune, 1984, 1995; Nicolich, 1977) focused on learning what 1- and 2-year-olds were likely to do when provided with a bucket of toys placed on the floor and a mother sitting nearby. In those days of reel-to-reel video, tapes were 30 minutes long and there was no simple way to locate a precise spot on the tape where one session ended and the next began. Thus, it was simplest to use a whole tape for each child even if 30 minutes was too long a time for play to continue. As the camera began running, awareness grew that the success of the research depended entirely on the spontaneous behavior of 1-year-old babies. Suppose the brief attention span of young children led to a paucity of data: Any anxiety was short-lived because that baby and the other four girls comprising that initial sample did play, and over the course of the year, they fulfilled expectations for unfolding levels of development--if each in her own way.

We would like to highlight here that they and those in the 1995 study focused on the toys and interacted with their mothers for the full 30 minutes, month after month across the second year of life. What of the short attention span attributed to young children? It was not apparent in these sessions. For the most part in this early study, children began the sessions by removing objects one by one from the bucket in which they were presented. They might fiddle with an object, examine it, or use it appropriately (e.g., pretend to sip from a toy cup). They might show or pass objects to mother. Early in the first year, they would be attracted to a toy in view, perhaps a clear bottle full of small objects, and by themselves or engaging mother explore its potential. Mothers reacted, demonstrated, and occasionally instructed. By 18 to 20 months of age, the children had favorite games and often went quickly through the bucket looking for the props of choice. For example, one baby whose father had a hair salon used brush, comb, and mirror--along with plastic pliers as scissors--to minister to dolls and mother. Another went immediately to the puzzle and, with mother, repeatedly completed and dissembled it often as many as six to eight times in a row.

The mothers' role was key to the maintenance of attention and play in these young children. If mother was called to the phone, it was best to stop the tape because the baby was likely to follow her or sit staring vacantly until she returned. When mothers commented on and extended their children's ongoing activities, children's enthusiasm increased. Their bouts of play on a given theme lengthened and the interaction seemed suffused with joy. When mothers tried to shift babies to new activities, the results were less positive. It might be difficult for a mother's attention span to continue through completing the same puzzle six or eight times, but attempts to remove a toy when the child was not finished playing often resulted in the child's persistent return to the toy or tears and distress if that was not permitted. Sometimes mothers would prematurely up the ante--one mother persistently asked what the child was feeding the doll-- and was consistently ignored. Interestingly, we noticed that although babies seemed somewhat impervious to mothers' suggestions, if mother touched or readjusted a toy, baby would soon select that toy for play. In short, babies were exquisitely aware of mother's presence, subtly monitoring her attention to their play and engaging socially with her whenever her interventions could be incorporated into their own activities.

Examination of this early period--the cradle of play and attention-- infancy--can inform the continued interplay of the relationships among play, attention, and learning throughout the school years. Why could these babies attend for 30 minutes to these self-selected tasks greatly benefit from their mothers' presence, yet fail to respond to her well-meant interventions? The answers to these questions provide the key to using the design features of children to structure their learning.

First, it should be obvious that 1- to 2-year-olds have incredible amounts of perceptual and motor information to acquire, so Nature's plan is to engage their attention in activities of interest that promote this acquisition. Second, the presence and support of a familiar adult is known to contribute to affective regulation in young children, helping them to maintain the calm frame of mind necessary for processing the information gained from their interaction with objects (Ainsworth, Blehar, Waters, & Wall, 1978; Ainsworth & Bell, 1970). Finally, recent research has demonstrated severe limitations in young children's voluntary control of attention. Once they are engaged in a particular activity, they have a tendency to continue it until information processing is complete (Johnson, Posner, & Rothbart, 1991; Tennes, Emde, Kisley, & Metcalf, 1972). If information from a given activity is not capable of being processed, either because it is too familiar or too extremely novel, the activity simply fails to engage a young child's attention (Haith & Campos, 1977; Piaget & Inhelder, 1969).

In the first 3 years, activities with a bit of structure, but lots of opportunity for the play of young minds, is the best route to children's learning. Young children are simply not very good at following an adult agenda too remote from their own "natural" interests. In young infants, learning is completely "self-regulated" in a biological sense--not under the infant's voluntary control or that of adults (Smith, Quittner, Osberger, & Miyamoto, 1998).

With increasing development, the young child becomes more capable of directing his or her own learning and more capable of benefiting from direct adult guidance. Throughout the toddler period and continuous into the early elementary years, children grow in their ability to benefit from explicit instruction (Piaget & Inhelder, 1969; Vygotsky, 1978). By age 7 or 8, in the primary grades, teachers recognize children's ability to control attention voluntarily, and schools routinely expect them to follow the agenda educators have planned for them. However, the same internal processes underlying learning continue. The need to ensure that their attention is engaged remains critical to ensuring that they are learning. Play can be a key element in this process.

Play is sometimes described as opposed to learning. We *take a play break* at recess. It is probably more useful to think of play, along with focused exploration, as the linked poles of learning. Across the animal and human literature, play is recognized as including some level of self-determination, repetition with variation, and neutral to positive affect. Between birth and 8 years of age--the current definition in U.S. education of *early childhood*--successful learning by children depends upon adult monitoring of the child's attention to relevant activities and the design of activities that attract the child's attention.

FOCUSED ATTENTION AND LEARNING

It seems reasonable that attention to a task would enhance learning. Current research shows evidence of young children's enhanced performance during periods of attending (Golbeck, Rand, & Soundy, 1986; Ruff & Rothbart, 1996). When asked to name objects that had been shown to them and then placed in a box out of sight, preschoolers were most successful at recalling the object previously noted as their favorite, suggesting that enhanced attention to that object when in view may have enhanced their memory (Renninger & Wozniak, 1985). In a task measuring reaction times to a same/different judgment, Morrison (1982) found that 5-year-olds took longer to achieve maximum alertness than adults and maintained alertness poorly. However, during their period of maximum alertness, they were as successful as adults in the task. This points up both the fragility of young children's attention and the critical role of attention in successful performance. The message: Curricular goals must yield to the capacities of individual children for attending to and learning the material. Without attention, no learning occurs; with attention, children may accelerate and learn more rapidly than curricular plans anticipate. Time is not lost by suiting activities to children's levels. Time naturally stretches and shrinks as children are engaged in learning.

HOW FOCUSED ATTENTION WORKS

Attention has been most carefully studied in infants and is considered to involve several phases defined by heart rate (HR) characteristics (Richards & Casey, 1992). There is always a certain amount of environmental monitoring going on. When the infant is not engaged in focal attention, a reflexive peripheral eye system attracts visual looking to transient changes in the environment (e.g., a new stimulus). This system, termed *preattention*, is in place from birth. At 2 to 3 months, attention becomes capable of affecting a brain pathway that controls frontal targeted eye movements (Lewis, Maurer, & Brent, 1989). Engagement of this pathway inhibits the reflexive pathway that usually allows stimulus orienting. That is, once orienting to one event begins, it becomes difficult for the child to notice and shift attention to new stimuli. This second system reaches adult characteristics by 5 to 6 months. During visual orienting, the actively controlled visual system is engaged and HR decelerates during a period of 5 or more seconds. The depth of the deceleration depends on the extent of novelty of the new object or event (Richards, 1997). If the object or event is sufficiently engaging, the child will enter sustained attention. Heart rate remains low during sustained attention. The infant is not easily distracted during this phase (Richards & Gibson, 1997).

For the first time, at 6 months of age, the infant is able to control attention, monitoring an environmental event until it is processed. Individual differences are found here in both the amount of slowing of HR and the length of time the infant remains attentive (Ruff, Lawson, Parrinello, & Weissberg, 1990). The next phase, preattention termination (the time between HR beginning to rise and returning to its original level) is transitional between focused attention and attention termination. Active disengagement of the stimulus seems to be required on the part of the child. When a new stimulus is detected, the infant locates the stimulus, but the HR response is much less than that in the previous bout of sustained attention. Ruff and Saltarelli (1993) used 8-to-10-ten-month old children's focused looking and other examining (e.g., active mouthing, alternating mouthing and looking) as indexes of focused attention and found the same resistance to distraction during exploration as Richards noted during lower HR phase of visual attention in 8-to-26-month-olds. This means that observing a child's behaviors can provide strong clues that the underlying physiological processes of attention are activated.

Several important points can be drawn from the sequential nature of focused attention phases. First, this is a natural system designed to direct the child to environmentally relevant stimuli that are then attended until available information has been sufficiently processed. During this period, the child is relatively impervious to distraction (Lansink & Richards, 1997). Although a child can be engaged in a new bout of focused attention once attention termination is reached, this second bout will not be as concentrated or as lengthy as the first bout (Richards & Casey, 1992). The implication of this situation is the critical importance of maximizing use of the child's bouts of focused attention. This suggests respect for individual children's rate of processing information. If a child is fully engaged in one task, it may be difficult for him or her to shift attention to a new one. Furthermore, once that shift is made, the new bout of attention may be brief and less fruitful than the original bout.

In the early years, whole-group activities are particularly challenging. How likely is it that an entire group maintains attention for exactly the same time period? Advance warnings of the need to shift attention can encourage voluntary shifts of attention. Suzuki and Cavanagh (1997) found that voluntary rather than cue-induced attention was longer lasting.

Research suggests that until ages 8 or 9, there are severe limits on children's capacity to control attention and direct attention voluntarily to complex and unfamiliar activities (Miller, 1993; Vurpillot & Ball, 1979; Tennes, Emde, Kisley, & Metcalf, 1972). Children's strategies for attending to objects become more efficient over time. They only slowly develop the capacity to voluntarily direct attention to tasks that do not spontaneously engage their interest.

When children's capacities for attending to a televised puppet show, free play, or a task that required pressing a button when a rabbit appeared on a video screen were compared, developmental differences were immediately apparent. Children extended the time they attended to the puppet show and the free play from age 2 1/2 to 3 1/2, whereas the ability to attend and perform accurately on the button press task (experimenter designed and rather boring) did not increase until 4 1/2. By this age, children have some capacity to follow an adult's agenda for brief periods, even if the task is uninteresting (Ruff, Capozzoli, & Weissberg, 1998). When a more complex task was devised (pressing a button when the digit 9 appeared, only if the 9 followed the digit 1), a major developmental change in accuracy of performance was noted between ages 7 and 9 years, suggesting that the capacity to direct attention to tasks demanded by others is still growing at this age (Smith, Quittner, Osberger, & Miyamota, 1998). Furthermore, children in these studies participated individually with an adult experimenter seated near them.

In the typical classroom, children between ages 6 and 8 years may be asked to maintain attention to paper-and-pencil tasks on their own for 15 to 30 minutes or longer, with periodic monitoring by teachers. Children may have limited capacity to do this, so devising playful child--child interactive approaches that engage children's natural interests can provide a valuable counterpoint.

Cooperative learning can provide such an approach and has been shown to increase learning awareness and performance (Kumar & Harizuka, 1998).

PLAY IN THE PROCESS OF LEARNING

Although we commonly think of play as *fun* and *recreation*, analyses by Piaget (1962) and McCune (1998) demonstrated that play can also be a method for children to take into themselves important aspects of new experiences. It would be wonderful for teachers if the *empty bucket* theory of learning were correct. By this theory, instruction is accomplished by exposing students to important educational material--filling the bucket! This we do every day in school, yet the results vary by child and lesson. Of course, this is because young learners are not empty buckets to be filled with knowledge, but active, committed learners with agendas of their own--agendas driven by the natural need to learn. The challenge for teachers is to get our material onto the children's agenda and somehow ensure that they have ways of making that learning their own. According to Piaget, play is the child's method of making novel information and experience part of a growing internal knowledge bank. Simply put, it is virtually impossible for teachers to package material so that it will be perfectly adaptable to all of their students' learning. Rather teachers need to expose new learning in ways that arouse the children's natural interest, engage their attention, and provide opportunities for them to make the new knowledge and skills their own.

One of the ways in which teachers can help children make new material their own is to give them a chance to play with it. They enter a learning and play cycle that spirals as they make new material their own. This spiral typically begins with some environmental event that brings about an initial orienting to the situation, possibly followed by a bout of focused attention, the length of which is determined by the child's processing of new material.

Learning requires an interactive balance of assimilation to the self (making material one's own) and accommodation to reality (gaining the facts and skills required by our culture). This is most easily demonstrated in the simple behaviors of infancy, but readily translates to school learning in older children. We see that at every level reality intrudes on play. Hence, from the early months of life, children's activity includes both efforts to understand the world through reality-directed action and playful enactment expressing that understanding. These interrelated functions of child action can be understood with some attention to temporal changes in the form of that activity in the course of a given episode as well as over developmental time.

An example can illustrate the coordination of the self-dominant and reality-dominant poles in learning in an activity that might appear as play to an observer. A major challenge of infancy is to be able to manipulate the environment (i.e., reliably cause objects to move, obeying our intentions). For example, a 6-month-old child might accidentally brush a toy hung over the crib with a waving arm, making it swing. To repeat this interesting effect, the child must target his or her action precisely to the position of the toy. The child must take account of external reality in relation to visual experience, tactile experience, and motor control of the arm (self-dominated reality). The next movement must be controlled in relation to external reality (accommodated) to make the toy swing. The exact position of the toy, for example, must be reached. This control is possible because the experience of external reality affects the child's internal system for guiding such actions by what Piaget termed *assimilation*. In neurological terms, we can think of the detailed calibration of motor control in relation to ongoing afferent feedback from movement (Evarts, 1982). This example should make it clear that accommodation and assimilation need to be in balance for learning to occur.

What of play? Once the child is able to make the toy swing reliably, because of these periods of struggle that involve integration of self-action with external reality, he or she keeps up the activity for fun.

"In a word he repeats the behavior, not in any effort to further learn or to investigate, but for the sheer joy of mastering it and showing off to himself his own power of subduing reality." Assimilation is dissociated from accommodation by subordinating it and tending to function by itself, and from then on play occurs. (Piaget, 1962, p. 162). This spontaneous play has the effect of *locking in* the new learning. A more extended example illustrates the juxtaposition of play and learning in physical activity.

A 9-month-old boy given a bell to ring (a novelty) at first banged it rhythmically on the table. Noting that the noise continued between contacts with the table, he eventually took some swings in the air that seemed clumsy in relation to the rapid bangs on the table. He may have needed to inhibit the downward motion to avoid hitting the table. Eventually his bellringing seemed more masterful, and he continued quite joyfully. Investigation for learning and play were thus interwoven in this episode. He began with an assimilation predominant mode, mainly playfully banging. However, because the bell was a new object, there was some quality of investigation in his action, and he noted the continued sound in the air that needed to be accommodated into his knowledge of this object. He also noted the visual qualities of the object, turning and looking into it. Eventually swinging the bell to ring it became at least partially playful. He also learned what a bell was for and in future encounters would ring one for fun, enjoying a sense of mastery.

With a small toy car, somewhat similar to objects at home, he gave a couple of light bangs at first, exercising his favorite scheme for pleasure, but quickly began experimenting with moving the car on the surface, wheels down, in a way that was at first clumsy, mixed with an occasional bang, and eventually with a smooth swiping back-and-forth motion. His activity still did not resemble those of a child who knows exactly what a toy car is for. Rather he accommodated his arm movements to the properties of the car, assimilated the experience with the car to his own schemes for action, and ended up with a repeatable horizontal swipe against the table that did not look very much like his banging motion. The entire experience was a mixture of investigation for learning and pleasure in exercising a new function.

This description provides an example of three interrelated activities, two of which are partially accommodated to the particular objects encountered. Banging is a well-learned action pattern continually exercised for pleasure in play. When an aspect of reality (interaction with a particular object) presents interesting responses to his activity, the child begins modifying the activity to learn more about the object. Although his initial rhythmic banging is almost purely egocentric or assimilatory, his response to the bell shows how accommodatory activity can arise in response to an interesting experience of the world. He continues banging, alternating with swinging and examining, and eventually masters swinging, continuing for pleasure. Similarly with the car, banging yields to examining and swiping on a surface. As the child applies an expanding repertoire of schemes, suiting them to object properties, the child will gain information that allow him to sort objects into categories (e.g., things that make a banging sound; things that move in an interesting way). Thus, categorical learning will occur.

Not all activities are equally suited to all objects. We see in the prior examples a general scheme-- banging--that is applied indiscriminately. As the child gains more information about the objects, we see the emergence of two more specific schemes: one potentially defining "things that make noise when swung" and, in the case of the car, "things that move smoothly on a surface." This type of knowledge, emerging from physical activity play, contributes to early object meaning and later to the child's transition into the developmental period of simple representational play and language. Byers and Walker (1995) demonstrated that play in the young of various nonhuman animals is confined to the period of maximal brain development, suggesting a critical interaction between the evolution of play and the evolution of the capacity to transform neurological structures through environmental action.

Play is a facet of developing motor skills in the preschool years. Consider the 4-year-old enduring a bowling lesson. As the family began bowling, she protested and cried, refusing to take her turn, but eventually relented and studiously aimed the ball. After a couple of gutter balls, she began to strike a pin or two. The transformation was immediate--the lesson was transformed to play as she eagerly awaited her turn, rolling each ball with a bit of aim and quite delighted to hit any number of pins at all, experiencing the joy of mastery. The peak of physical exercise play at 4 or 5, the age by which children perfect such skills as running, skipping, and jumping, suggests that the playful occurrence of these activities is related to their recent or ongoing mastery. Subsequently, these actions are incorporated into everyday life--hurrying to keep up with mom, jumping over a puddle--and into organized physical sports.

Children may experience group care from an early age, and these examples from infancy provide clues on promoting learning in infancy and the early preschool years. How can these same principles apply to more typical school learning? In academic settings, activities directed at learning can be effectively interweaved with play, just as they naturally are in the child's investigation of objects during the first year of life. Teachers can function as facilitators of learning, the role previously taken by parents. Either by their presence or their assistance when requested, they can help their students work towards skill mastery.

Examples of children's games that incorporate newly learned concepts frequently occur in the classroom setting. Students engage teachers to react, demonstrate, and instruct as infants did their mothers in the play study. An example was seen in a class for 5- and 6-year-old students with learning disabilities. The children had been introduced to writing the numeral 5. In addition to writing the number, they were taught to use the verbal mediator, "Five, down, around and put a hat on it." During the play period that followed the lesson, several children went to the chalkboard making efforts to write the numeral 5. Each of the three children was doing this in a different way. We can see the teacher-as-parent serving the children in different roles using the child's lead. Her presence increases the likelihood of children approaching the task, encourages children to continue the task, and provides assistance to the child who is learning the task.

The first child simply wrote the numeral. After she had completed this, she asked the teacher to watch while she wrote the number several more times. Then she began writing other numbers. The second child wrote the number 5 much more slowly saying "Five, down, around and put a hat on it" as he wrote. The third child after one or two unsuccessful attempts asked the teacher to write the numeral. He then traced it.

The attention of the teacher to such tasks served to maintain the student's attention longer and ensured the likelihood that this behavior was repeated over other play periods. In this example, teacher attention also motivated other students to join the practice play session. Although the teacher never told other children to play or told the children playing to play longer, the practice sessions increased in duration and included more students although not all students played for the entire period nor did they play every day. Some students did not play at all. However, on some days, it was necessary to ration board space so that all students could have a turn.

Opportunities of this sort require flexibility in scheduling the transition from one activity to the next. Children may need some time to translate knowledge from a lesson into play. Then it will be important to let them keep at it until their attention begins to wander. This wandering of attention, like the HR changes in 6-month-olds, indicates attention termination and readiness for a transitional activity and a new task. If the play activity is terminated prematurely the benefit of locking in learning will be lost, and the child may not be ready to redirect attention to the next curricular item on the classroom agenda.

Another academic task incorporated into play activity is counting. Counting is seen in many of the play centers. Children count blocks in the building center, cups and saucers in the kitchen area, toy money at the play store, and even other children as they go to lunch or get into a line. We observed a teacher capitalizing on this love of counting and naming by having children count the number of letters in each child's name and then writing the number (see Ginsburg, et al., chap. 8, this volume).

Examples of reading/writing practice can be seen in the playground activities of this same class. During free time, students were allowed to choose their playground toys. Some chose the thick playground chalk sticks. Their first efforts were writing letters of the alphabet or numerals or scribbling on the playground blacktop. This progressed to writing upper case letters, particularly those letters associated with their names or the names of classmates. The child who was writing might say, "S. S for Sarah, that's my letter." This would continue as they wrote M for their friend Mark, A for Anthony, and so on. Besides writing letters of the alphabet, the children would also write numerals 1 to 10 throughout the playground creating a chain of digits (see Morrow, chap. 10, this volume).

During the school years, playtime fulfills two needs related to children's learning. First, it provides opportunities for playful repetition and social games that rework curricular information. This provides the opportunity for children to assimilate the information to make it their own. Just as the mother of a 2-year-old is bored by repeating a picture puzzle long before the baby is finished, the teacher may be done with a math lesson at a point where children still need opportunities to play together and with the teacher in games that incorporate the newly learned concept. The classroom pointer is a prop that encourages practice efforts. Students will pretend to be the teacher, pointing to a letter of the alphabet and asking a playmate, "What is this letter?" After the student responds, they praise or correct the answer. The teacher would then point to colors, numerals, days of the week, or names of other students, asking the student for a correct response.

Cooperative learning offers an example of a playlike practice environment in which students can assimilate new learning. Through discussion, explanation, and recording, students can master the material. Again the teacher is required to react, demonstrate, and instruct so that the process continues effectively.

Play was used in a class for children with communication difficulties to encourage nonverbal children-- children with speech and language delays--to communicate with each other, reinforcing the work of both the teacher and the speech therapist. The desire to play with a friend became a strong incentive to speak. On the playground, children who were barely audible in the classroom setting would shout to their friends or engage in loud arguments over who had a toy first.

A second role for play is that of freshening up the child's mental energy. This essential renewal is necessary at the physiological level (Richards & Casey, 1992). This need for freshening up grows as students progress through the grade levels. Each higher grade requires more and more prolonged periods of attention for students. An example of freshening up can be seen in this example from a class for students with learning disabilities. These students were given two play breaks during their academic day. Each period was 15 minutes in length, and whenever possible, students who wished to go outdoors were allowed to do so with adult supervision. As in the case with the younger students, these 12-to-13-year-olds asked for teacher attention and occasional participation in their games. Although 4 students in this class of 12 were labeled as *hyperactive* or having attention deficit disorder (ADD), there were rarely instances of inattention, out-of-seat behavior, or excessive talking during instruction after the freshening up period. In addition to the freshening up for students who are fatigued from learning activities, this teacher noted that the period also served as waking up for hypoactive children. By encouraging them to play, their activity level in general is raised and they enter the learning task with greater attention and alertness.

The freshening up effect was seen with a group of 10-to-13-year-old students with neurological impairment. Eight of these 11 boys were considered hyperactive and distractible. As a motivator for homework completion, students were given 15 minutes to play basketball outdoors at the beginning of the day if they handed in homework assignments. Students then completed a 90-minute work period and then were allowed free play if all work was completed. The hyperactive and oppositional behavior previously reported by other teachers was considerably reduced in this class. Although the behavior modification program was of great importance to this decrease in negative behavior, the opportunity for frequent play breaks was probably a significant factor. Although not formally measured, teacher and paraprofessional in this class felt that students were less able to concentrate on learning tasks when the weather prohibited outdoor play. This freshening up is consistent with Pellegrini's (1998) work on recess.

Throughout the elementary school years, voluntarily directing attention to the teacher's agendas remains difficult for all children, some more than others. By allowing time when children follow their own focus and take a break from the effort of directing attention, the very capacity for learning is renewed.

REFERENCES

Ainsworth, M. D. S., Blehar, M. C., Waters, E., & Wall, S. (1978). Patterns of attachment: *A psychological study of the strange situation*. Hillsdale, NJ: Lawrence Erlbaum Associates.

Ainsworth, M. D. S., & Bell, S. M. (1970). Attachment, exploration, and separation: Illustrated by the behavior of one-year-olds in a strange situation. *Child Development, 41*, 49-67.

Brown, C. (1979). Reaction of infants to their parents voices. *Infant Behavior and Development, 2*, 295-303.

Byers, J. A., & Walker, C. (1995). Refining the motor hypothesis for the evolution of play. *The American Naturalist, 146*, 25-40.

Evarts, E. V. (1982). Analogies between central motor programs for speech and for limb movements. In S. Grillner, B. Lindblom, J. Lubker, & A. Persson (Eds.), *Speech motor control* (pp. 19-41). Oxford: Pergamon.

Fantz, R. L. (1963). Pattern vision in newborn infants. *Science, 140*, 296-297.

Freeman, N. C. G., & Rosenblatt, J. S. (1978). The interrelationship between thermal and olfactory stimulation in the development of home orientation in newborn kittens. *Developmental Psychobiology, 11*, 437-457.

Golbeck, S. L., Rand, M., & Soundy, C. (1986). Constructing a model of a large-scale space with the space in view: Effects on preschoolers of guidance and cognitive restructuring. *Merrill-Palmer Quarterly, 32*, 187-203.

Haith, M. H., & Campos, J. J. (1977). Human infancy. *Annual Review of Psychology, 28*, 251-293.

Johnson, M. H., Posner, M. I., & Rothbart, M. K. (1991). Components of visual orienting in early infancy: Contingency learning, anticipatory looking and disengaging. *Journal of Cognitive Neuroscience, 3*, 335-344.

Kumar, S., & Harizuka, S. (1998). Cooperative learning-based approach and development of learning awareness and achievement in mathematics in elementary schools. *Psychological Reports, 82*, 587-591.

Lansink, J. M., & Richards, J. E. (1997). Heart-rate and behavioral measures of attention in six-, nine-, and twelve-month-old infants during object exploration. *Child Development, 68*, 610-620.

Lewis, T. L., Maurer, D., & Brent, H. P. (1989). Optokinetic nystagmus in normal and visually deprived children: Implications for cortical development. *Canadian Journal of Psychology, 42*, 121-140.

Maurer, D., & Salapatek, P. (1976). Developmental changes in the scanning of faces of young infants. *Child Development, 47*, 523-527.

Matas, L., Arend, R., & Sroufe, A. (1978). Continuity of adaptation in the second year: The relationship between quality of attachment and later competence. *Child Development, 49*, 547-556.

McCune, L. (1995). A normative study of representational play at the transition to language. *Developmental Psychology, 31*, 198-206.

McCune, L. (1998). Immediate and ultimate functions of physical activity play. *Child Development, 69*, 601-603.

McCune, L., Dipane, D., Fireoved, R., & Fleck, M. (1994). Play: A context for mutual regulation with mother-child interaction. In A. Slade & D. P. Wolf (Eds.), *Children at play:*

Clinical and developmental approaches to meaning and representation (pp. 148-166). New York: Oxford University Press.

Miller, P. H. (1993). *Theories of developmental psychology* (pp. 355-361). New York: Freeman.

Morrison, F. J. (1982). The development of alertness. *Journal of Experimental Child Psychology, 34*, 187-189.

Nicolich, L. (1977). Beyond sensorimotor intelligence: Assessment of symbolic maturity through analysis of pretend play. *Merrill-Palmer Quarterly, 23*, 89-99.

Pelligrini, A., & Smith, P. (1998). Physical activity play: The nature and function of a neglected aspect of play. *Child Development, 69*, 577-598.

Piaget, J. (1962). *Play, dreams and imitation.* New York: Norton.

Piaget, J., & Inhelder, B. (1969). *The psychology of the child.* New York: Basic Books.

Renninger, K. A., & Wozniak, R. H. (1985). Effect of interest on attentional shift, recognition and recall in young children. *Developmental Psychology, 21*, 624-632.

Richards, J. E. (1997). Effects of attention on infants' preference for briefly exposed visual stimuli in the paired-comparison recognition-memory paradigm. *Developmental Psychology, 33*, 22-31.

Richards, J. E., & Gibson, T. L. (1997). Extended visual fixation in young infants: Look distributions, heart rate changes, and attention. *Child Development, 68*, 1041-1056.

Richards, J. E., & Casey, B. J. (1992). Development of sustained visual attention in the human infant. In B. Cambell, H. Hayne, & R. Richardson (Eds.), *Attention and information processing in infants and adults* (pp. 30-60). Hillsdale, NJ: Lawrence Erlbaum Associates.

Ruff, H. A., Capozzoli, M., & Weissberg, R. (1998). Age, individuality, and context as factors in sustained visual attention during the preschool years. *Developmental Psychology, 34*, 454-464.

Ruff, H. A., & Rothbart, M. (1996). *Development of attention in infants and children.* New York: Oxford University Press.

Ruff, H. A., & Saltarelli, F. (1993). Exploratory play with objects: Basic cognitive processes and individual differences. In M. H. Bornstein & A. W. O'Reilly (Eds.), *The role of play in the development of thought* (pp. 5-16). San Francisco: Jossey-Bass.

Ruff, H. A., Lawson, K. R., Parrinello, R., & Weissberg, R. (1990). Long-term stability of individual differences in sustained attention in the early years. *Child Development, 61*, 60-75.

Slade, A. (1987). A longitudinal study of maternal involvement and symbolic play during the toddler period. *Child Development, 58*, 367-375.

Smith, L. B., Quittner, A. L., Osberger, M., & Miyamoto, R. (1998). Audition and visual attention: The developmental trajectory in deaf and hearing populations. *Developmental Psychology, 34*, 840-850.

Snow, C. E. (1972). Mothers speech to children learning language. *Child Development, 43*, 549-565.

Suzuki, S., & Cavanagh, P. (1997). Focused attention distorts visual space: An attention repulsion effect, *Journal of Experimental Psychology--Human Perception & Performance, 23*, 443-463.

Tennes, K., Emde, R., Kisley, A., & Metcalf, D. (1972). The stimulus barrier in early infancy. *Psychosomatic Medicine, 35*, 206-234.

Vurpillot, E., & Ball, W. A. (1979). The concept of identity and children's selective attention. In G. Hale & M. Lewis (Eds.), *Attention and cognitive development.* New York: Plenum.

Vygotsky, L. S. (1978). *Mind in society--The development of higher psychological processes.* Cambridge, MA: Harvard University Press.

Watson, J. S., Hayes, L. A., Vietz, P., & Becker, J. (1979). Discriminating infant smiling to orientations of talking faces of mother and stranger. *Journal of Experimental Child Psychology, 28*, 92-99.

5

LEARNING THROUGH FEELING: CHILDREN'S DEVELOPMENT, TEACHERS' BELIEFS AND RELATIONSHIPS, AND CLASSROOM PRACTICES

Marion C. Hyson
Jennifer Molinaro
University of Delaware

The kindergarten children are seated on the rug for story time. Ms. Barber waits quietly for the children to settle down and then begins her lesson. "Today we're going to read a new book (holding it up). Who knows what this book might be about?"

Four children wave their hands. "I know!" Avram exclaims. "It's about a lion!"

"Lions roar," adds Tyrone, growling realistically. "They roar and they *attack*!" (reaching over to grab Paulina's arm). Paulina shrinks back and covers her face.

"Let's look at the first page," Ms. Barber continues, ignoring the lion play. "Who can tell me what might be happening?" More hands wave. "I see a mother lion and a baby lion," says Lorraine.

"They miss the daddy." She tips her head to the side, looking sad.

"I have a daddy," Tyrone says. "But he lives in New York. Hey--I'm gonna go there next week and play basketball at the park. My daddy knows how to play basketball. He's the best player."

"He is not," says Avram. "Michael Jordan is the best player. Your daddy is a dumb player." Avram smiles the smile of superior knowledge. The children snicker.

"Now, class," Ms. Barber interrupts. "We're not talking about basketball, are we? We are talking about lions. Let's read the book, together. What letter do you think lion begins with?"

Ms. Barber continues reading the story. When the story is finished she dismisses the children to tables to write in their journals. Some

children do pretend "scribble writing," while others carefully print letters and words. Lorraine uses markers to draw a picture of a mother lion and her baby. She calls Ms. Barber to look at her work. Ms. Barber leans over and places her hand on Lorraine's shoulder.
"Lorraine, look at that mother and baby! You have really worked hard on that picture. Can you write something about the mother and baby?" Lorraine chews her lip, thinking.
"How about I write 'This is a mother lion. She loves the baby?'" asks Lorraine?
"Good thinking, Lorraine," says Ms. Barber.
"Can you help me?" asks Lorraine.
"In a minute," Ms. Barber responds. "I want to see how Paulina is doing."
Paulina is on the floor, leaning against a cushion. She looks away as Ms. Barber approaches, putting her blank piece of paper behind her. "Paulina!" Ms. Barber exclaims. "You haven't even started your story, and it is almost time to clean up for recess. If you don't get that story done, you may have to stay in and work on it with me." Paulina looks at the floor as Ms. Barber returns to Lorraine's table.

This is much more than an example of literacy instruction in kindergarten. Even without the benefit of direct observation or videotape, one can see that the entire episode is embedded within emotions and relationships. Interest, surprise, shyness, fear, affection, anger, and pride are as much a part of the curriculum as phonemes and inventive spelling. The children in Ms. Barber's class are learning about books, story structure, letter-sound correspondences, and so on. They are writing, talking, and working on academic skills, but they are doing so within a complex matrix of feelings and relationships. As 5 and 6-year-olds, they have a lot in common, but they also have individual styles of expressing emotions and of connecting with others. Like the children, Ms. Barber, too, has her own style of emotion expression and her own relationship style. The ideas she has about emotions and the emotional context of her work as a teacher come from many sources--her temperament and personality, her experiences, her beliefs about children's development, and about her role as their teacher. Although she may not be aware of it, Ms. Barber is an important contributor to the children's emotional development and to their ability to use emotions in the service of learning.

CHAPTER PREVIEW

In this chapter, we explore the ways in which teachers' emotion-related beliefs, representations, and classroom practices may influence young children's learning and development. The study of human emotions is one of the most influential areas in contemporary psychology. We know that development is enhanced and learning is supported when young children have secure, emotionally positive relationships with adults and when adults provide the scaffolding needed for appropriate regulation and understanding of emotions. However, most research has been conducted within families rather than with teachers in classroom environments. We are just beginning to understand how the classroom teacher serves as an essential catalyst for early emotional development and how that emotion-related involvement may influence young children's learning and cognitive development.

The chapter begins with a brief overview of the intense burst of theory and research on young children's emotional development and its links to learning (see Lewis & Haviland, 1993, for an edited volume representing much of this body of work). We then describe what is known about the role of adults in children's emotional development, noting the scarcity of research about the role of nonparental adults (teachers and other caregivers) in supporting the emotional development of young children.

To illustrate these points, we raise three critical questions that have been addressed in recent research by the authors and others:

1. How can teachers' emotional involvement in young children's activities sustain their involvement in learning?
2. What do teachers believe about children's emotional development and about adults' influence on that development?
3. Why do teachers' emotion-related beliefs, styles, and practices emotions vary, and what does this mean for early education?

After describing research directed toward each of these questions, we will conclude by discussing the implications of this research for personnel preparation in early childhood education, and for the design and evaluation of learning environments for young children.

EMOTIONAL DEVELOPMENT AND EARLY CHILDHOOD EDUCATION

Developmental research emphasizes the value of early nurturance from warm, sensitive caregivers in families and in out-of-home care (Ainsworth, Blehar, Waters, & Wall, 1978; Bretherton & Waters, 1985). Yet national studies have found that 35% of family child-care homes, 40% of child-care center infant programs, and 10% of child-care classrooms serving preschoolers were of notably poor quality, with insensitive, harsh, or detached caregiving practices (Cost, Quality, and Child Outcomes Study Team, 1995; Kontos, Howes, Shinn,

& Galinsky, 1994). Participant observers in early childhood programs (Suransky, 1982) including infant/toddler programs (Leavitt & Power, 1989) have described how often teachers ignored or denied young children's feelings or manipulated those feelings to serve predetermined needs. Observations of programs for 3- 5-year-olds revealed that teachers rarely talked about feelings or labeled children's feelings for them (Hyson, Hirsh-Pasek, & Rescorla, 1990). Early interventionists who work with young children with disabilities are also unlikely to help children identify and regulate their emotional states (Frede, Barnett, & Lupo, chap. 12, this volume). In the primary grades, too, educational researchers have noted little adult involvement in helping children understand or express emotions (Goodlad, 1984).

In 1989, Jessica Cone and this chapter's first author published an article in the *Journal of Applied Developmental Psychology*, called "Giving Form to Feeling: Emotions Research and Early Childhood Education" (Hyson & Cone, 1989). At the time, our goal was to introduce early childhood educators and others interested in young children's learning to the rapidly growing field of emotions theory and research. Preparing this chapter, we reread that article and were struck both by some of the positive changes and also by some continuing concerns since that article was written.

On the one hand, the domain of early emotional development is, if anything, an even livelier area of theory and research than in the late 1980s. The continuing interest in neuroscience and in (as early childhood education calls it) the *new brain research* (Kolb, 1993; Shore, 1997), coupled with a growing interest in relationships as contexts for early development and learning, have fed this interest on the part of practitioners as well as researchers. Interest in the function of emotions in early learning has been heightened by the dismal results of national studies of child-care programs, documenting the emotionally incompetent interactions of many child-care providers. Of special concern are patterns of insensitive or detached caregiving among those who care for infants and toddlers, our most developmentally vulnerable group of children. Along with Gardner's broadened view of intelligence to include *interpersonal intelligence* (Gardner, 1983), the concept of *emotional intelligence* (Goleman, 1995; Salovey & Sluyter, 1997) has come into the popular lexicon and has informed a number of educational programs. Finally, growing concerns about violence in schools, including children's murderous attacks on their classmates, have further highlighted the need to understand the roots of later development in early emotional experiences and in early, affectively laden relationships.

Despite these reasons for an upsurge of interest in emotions on the part of educators, other factors have created an emotional backlash that, in some settings, has diminished interest in this aspect of development as an important influence on early education. Continuing a trend begun in the 1980s, the education reform movement continues to lean heavily on upgrading academic content standards while, in some states at least, diminishing attention to motivational and relationship issues. These trends are most evident in K to 12 education, but, as at other times, have trickled down to influence preschool and child-care programs that are supposed to get children ready for formal education. Even the influential report of the National Academy of Sciences, *Preventing Reading Difficulties in Young Children* (Snow, Burns, & Griffin, 1998), may have already created some unintended shifts in emphasis. The report's description of typical 4-year-olds knowing 10 letters of the alphabet was incorporated into Congressional language reauthorizing Head Start, and it has now been viewed by many Head Start programs as a pedagogical mandate (abandon the formerly used curriculum in favor of alphabet drills). Although early childhood programs have been justly criticized for an overemphasis on child development (interpreted solely as socioemotional development) to the detriment of cognitive and language development, educators may be throwing the affective baby out with the bath water.

Many of today's critical issues in early childhood education can benefit from the perspective of developmental studies of emotional development and, especially, of teachers' potential influence on that development. The following brief outline, adapted from Hyson (1994), describes some areas of knowledge from emotions theory and research that may be useful to the early childhood field.

The Adaptive Function of Human Emotions

Although an adaptive or evolutionary perspective on emotions can be traced to Darwin (1872), this perspective has reemerged as a dominant force in developmental psychology in the 1980s and 1990s. According to many theorists and researchers, an organized system of human emotions guides and motivates behavior from infancy throughout life (e.g., Campos, Barrett, Lamb, Goldsmith, & Stenberg, 1983; Izard, 1991; Saarni, Mumme, & Campos, 1997; Sroufe, 1996). Although different scholars would classify them in various ways, the emotions included in the human lexicon may include, among others, anger, sadness, joy, interest, fear, surprise, shame, empathy, guilt, and pride. Scholars vary in their beliefs about the extent to which these emotions are innate or learned in the course of development, although most agree that a basic set of emotions is universal and wired in.

In the view of most emotions researchers, each of these emotions (and combinations of emotions) serves a particular adaptive or motivational function in human development and behavior. Using the example at the beginning of this chapter, Avram's interest and joy motivate him to attend to his teacher and volunteer information about the book's cover. Paulina's feelings of sadness and fear contribute to her helpless, avoidant behavior in the face of the writing task.

Through their expression in her face and body, these feelings also communicate her sadness and fear to others, including her teacher.

The Pathways of Emotional Development

Besides describing the essential functions of human emotions, recent developmental research has outlined the processes by which basic feelings emerge, change, and become connected with other aspects of children's development. A compelling set of theories or models have emerged, each of which gives a somewhat different story about how emotional development occurs, what stages (if any) characterize this process, and what new skills or competencies may be expected at various points in children's development (e.g., Denham, 1998; Fischer, Shaver, & Carnochan, 1990; Greenspan & Greenspan, 1985; Sroufe, 1996). Although differing in specifics, these writers tend to find similar developmental trends over the years of infancy, toddlerhood, and early and middle childhood.

Briefly, when children are developing well,

- their emotional relationships become wider and more complex;
- they are able to express their feelings in more varied, flexible ways;
- they can coordinate, control, or regulate their emotions in socially approved and adaptive ways;
- they become better able to think about and understand their own and others' emotions;
- they are able to represent feelings symbolically through play and language;
- they can connect individual emotions (such as interest) to skills and standards that their culture values; and
- they gain a sense of self that is connected emotionally to others but is also autonomous.

Influences on Emotional Development

This developmental process does not happen automatically. Even those theorists who emphasize the innate, biological foundations of human emotions (e.g., Izard, 1991) acknowledge the powerful role of family, culture, and other contexts in the dynamic story of emotional development. In brief, these factors surely include at least five groups of influences: neurobiological processes, individual differences in temperament, skills and limitations in other developmental areas, family environment and relationships, and cultural influences (Hyson, 1994). All of these, of course, interact with one another, and all are relevant for early childhood educators.

We have known for some time that the maturation of the brain and the central nervous system (CNS) helps children express and regulate emotions. Recent research in neuroscience has moved us away from this maturational view to emphasize the active contribution of parents and teachers in the actual process of brain development (Greenberg & Snell, 1997). This so-called "new" brain research supports the importance of warm, stimulating relationships with adults in early childhood, viewing these relationships as important contributors to how the brain organizes itself and as buffers of stress in young children's lives (Greenspan, 1997; Gunnar, 1998; Kolb, 1993; Kraemer, 1992; Shore, 1997). Caregivers who are *in tune* may perhaps stimulate brain development; caregivers who are not in tune--who are overstimulating, understimulating, or inconsistent-- may have negative effects on later development (Sroufe, 1996).

Temperament also plays a part in emotional development. Although the basic themes and trends in children's emotional development may be universal, parents and teachers know that each child also displays a unique, seemingly constitutional, style of behavior. The characteristics usually referred to as *temperament* are closely connected to individual emotion styles: (a) the slow to warm up, inhibited, or fearful child; (b) the emotionally intense child who is described as feisty or temperamentally difficult; and (c) the emotionally smooth or easy child. Appearing early in life, these individual differences usually persist over time and may have a hereditary basis (Plomin, Chipauer, & Loehlin, 1990; Saudino & Eaton, 1991). Besides influencing how children express and regulate their emotions and how they respond to challenging academic tasks (Stipek & Greene, chap. 3, this volume), temperament also influences how adults and peers respond to children, setting up yet another complex feedback loop.

Children's emotional development is also influenced by development in other domains. Cognitive growth allows children to symbolize their fears and understand the causes of others' emotions. Similarly, children's limited understanding (of why lions roar, for example) may cause them to fear things that adults find trivial or humorous. The development of language skills creates another channel for the communication of feelings and, therefore, for emotion regulation. Finally, children's growing social worlds (such as the world of kindergarten) offer new contexts in which they can try out various ways of expressing emotions and in which they can come to understand how others feel and behave.

Culture is increasingly recognized as a significant influence on emotion expression and emotional development. Cultures differ greatly in their tolerance for various forms of emotion expression, either by children or adults (Gordon, 1989). The Korean culture discourages open displays of emotion and has an expression (*myu-po-jung*) that refers approvingly to a blank, expressionless face (Lynch & Hansen, 1992). In schools as well as families, culture influences teachers' beliefs and decisions about emotion expression within the classroom. Lewis (1988) observed Japanese preschool teachers who routinely allowed children to express anger physically in ways that most U.S. teachers would reject. The underlying cultural belief--that children's intense quarrels reflected a growing interest in others--influenced the Japanese teachers' reactions to aggression among peers. Adults in different cultures, and in different ethnic groups, often have very different ideas about what emotions are important to encourage and what is appropriate to expect of children at different points in their development.

Finally, the influence of adults--parents and teachers alike--plays a considerable part in children's emotional development. Ideally, adults can support emotional development in at least six ways (Hyson, 1994): They can create a secure emotional environment, help children understand emotions, model appropriate emotional responses, support children's regulation of emotions, recognize and respect children's individual emotion styles, and connect children's learning with positive emotions. The next section of this chapter describes some of these functions in more detail. This section also discusses what may influence adults' success in building positive relationships with children and effectively guiding children's emotional development.

WHAT DO ADULTS DO? RELATIONSHIPS IN EARLY CHILDHOOD

Relationships with adults are the cornerstone of emotional development in early childhood. Young children learn about themselves and the world around them through interactions with others; these early relationships form the basis for later relationships and development (Bretherton & Waters, 1985; Raikes, 1996). Early childhood programs are an important context for children's emotional development, and it is teachers who create the emotional climate and regulate the emotional experiences of the children in their care (Hyson, 1994). The NAEYC guidelines for developmentally appropriate practice stress the importance of warm, sensitive, and responsive interactions between children and their teachers (Bredekamp & Copple, 1997).

Because many preschool children today spend a considerable amount of time in some form of out-of-home care, teachers play an increasingly important role in children's development. One significant aspect of young children's emotional development is the forming of attachment relationships. Although parents are the most important attachment figures for most children, teacher-child relationships also serve many attachment functions. They provide physical and emotional care, act as a secure base for exploration, and serve as a safe haven when children are frightened or distressed. Children form secure attachment relationships with teachers from whom they have received consistent, responsive, and sensitive care (Howes, Phillips, & Whitebook, 1992; van IJzendoorn, Sagi, & Lambermom, 1992). In turn, positive teacher-child relationships have also been linked to other aspects of later development, including children's social development and peer relations (Elicker & Fortner-Wood, 1995; Howes & Matheson, 1992; Kontos & Wilcox-Herzog, 1997; Pianta, 1992). Positive relationships between teachers and children may assist those children whose relationships with their own parents is insecure or troubled (Copeland-Mitchell, Denham, & DeMulder, 1997). Finally, positive teacher-child relationships have been associated with later school competence (Pianta, 1992; Pianta, Nimetz, & Bennett, 1997; Pianta & Walsh, 1996; Stipek & Greene, chap. 3, this volume).

Adults also influence young children's ability to understand and express emotions. Thompson (1994) claimed that key developmental tasks in early childhood are the understanding, expression, and control of emotions. Children use adults as mirrors; they learn from watching others. In early childhood, they also rely on adults to scaffold their own control or regulation of emotions. Adults assist in emotion regulation by reading children's often subtle cues to their emotional state, using these cues to respond, model, and reinforce children's emotional behaviors and expressions. Teachers manage and guide children's emotions through relieving distress and modeling positive emotional expression (Thompson, 1994). As Stipek and Greene (chap. 3, this volume) described, teachers also create environments that can support or undermine early achievement-related emotions, such as persistence, anxiety, and feelings about one's own competence.

Many factors may influence the quality and nature of teacher-child relationships. Children's own individual characteristics--temperament, gender, disability status, and so on--may contribute to the quality of teacher-child relationships just as these characteristics contribute to attachment relationships within the family. Teachers' characteristics, too--their training, education, experience, personal history, and beliefs about children--have an influence on the relationship. Finally, a variety of contextual factors such as teacher-child ratios, group size, classroom environment, and cultural norms provide another set of variables that may impact the nature of the relationship that develops between teachers and children.

We certainly know a great deal about general processes of emotional development and about adult-child relationships as contexts for that development. However, many of our ideas about teachers' roles are rather speculative, based on analogies to parents rather than on research in the distinctive settings of early childhood programs. The research that we conducted at the University of Delaware is aimed at filling in some of these blanks. In the next sections, we describe three recent studies that have tried to answer the questions posed at the beginning of this chapter.

HOW CAN TEACHERS' EMOTIONAL INVOLVEMENT IN YOUNG CHILDREN'S ACTIVITIES SUSTAIN THEIR ENGAGEMENT IN LEARNING?

Teachers want to help children become deeply involved in productive learning activities. How might their emotional relationship with children influence this process? In a recent study, Ann Dilcher Figueroa asked how young children's engagement in learning activities may be helped or hindered by the emotional climate created by teachers (Hyson, Figueroa, & Hallam, 1999). She also asked what effect the learning activities had on children's level of engagement.

As Stipek and Greene (chap. 3, this volume) pointed out, it is difficult in "real life" to disentangle the effects of classroom emotional climate from those of the instructional approach. In Stipek's work (Stipek, Daniels, Galluzzo, & Milburn, 1992) and in our earlier classroom observations (Hyson et al., 1990), child-focused or developmentally appropriate classrooms had more affectively positive climates. In contrast, more didactic or developmentally inappropriate classrooms were less emotionally positive. DeVries, (DeVries, chap. 7, this volume; DeVries & Zan, 1994) has also found that child-focused constructivist classrooms are characterized by more friendly, collegial, and responsive climates--qualities that have an emotional as well as an interpersonal tone.

In our study (Hyson et al., 1999), we attempted to disentangle emotion from curriculum by creating a set of experimental conditions that mirrored some of the kinds of events that may happen in early childhood classrooms. We know that teachers vary in the amount and kind of emotional involvement they have with children. Some teachers prefer a relatively disengaged or detached style, whereas others prefer to be affectively closer to the children they teach. What might be the effect of these varying emotional climates? We asked our experimenters to assume each of these roles (emotionally positive vs. detached) at different points in a series of play sessions. In the emotionally positive condition the experimenter used the child's name, used a warm tone of voice, responded to the child's initiations in a personal manner, commented on the child's activity, and so on. In the detached condition, the experimenter worked on a clipboard, did not use the child's name, and responded only minimally to the child's questions or comments.

Besides varying the emotional quality of the "teacher's" interaction, we also wished to look at variations in the activities offered to the children. We know that early childhood teachers differ in the kinds of learning activities they offer to children, with variations in developmental appropriateness being the most frequently discussed. In a simple way, we tried to examine this variable as well. We created two versions of the same activity: one that was (by NAEYC guidelines at least) more developmentally appropriate, and one that was less appropriate for the 3- and 4-year-olds in our study. For example, we had two versions of a Lego activity. In the first version (more appropriate), the child was given a box of Legos and invited to play with them for a while, using them any way she or he chose. In the second version, the child was given the Legos, but was also presented with a picture to copy. Although one could productively debate whether the model-copying task is equally inappropriate for all children, we felt that the tasks captured the general parameters of the developmental appropriateness (DAP) debate.

As noted earlier, we were interested in children's *engagement* as an outcome of variations in adult involvement and of variations in the appropriateness of the activities. Engagement has, especially in the early intervention literature, been viewed as an important marker of learning opportunities for children. Engagement is conceptually related to, but not identical with, the motivational constructs described by Stipek and Greene (chap. 3, this volume), including effectance, intrinsic motivation, mastery behavior, and persistence. Without sustained, effortful engagement, children cannot learn. In other words, engagement is a necessary but not sufficient component of early learning and development. By coding amount, types, and levels of engagement with the activities and with the adult, we hoped to get a better sense of young children's responses to adult emotion and activity type.

The 41 children participating in this study were 3- and 4-year-olds from area early childhood programs. Eighteen of the children had identified disabilities, mostly developmental delays. The reason for this feature of the study was that we also wanted to see whether teachers' emotional involvement (as well as the type of activities) had different effects on children with and without disabilities.

The results of the study show effects for both activity appropriateness and teachers' emotional involvement. Because the latter is the special focus of this chapter and because the results were actually more powerful for the emotion manipulation, we concentrate on that. Children with and without disabilities were more engaged with the adult in the emotionally positive climate. All children showed significantly more nonengaged behavior (not involved with the learning materials) when the adult was detached. In general, children were more engaged in learning activities of all kinds when the adults were emotionally warm, personal, and involved (note that in this study, *involved* does not mean helping the child or doing the activity with the child). This effect, however, was especially pronounced in the case of children with disabilities. Children with disabilities had the lowest frequency of constructive play (building with materials, making something) and the highest level of nonengaged behavior during periods when the adult was emotionally detached and the materials were less developmentally appropriate. Thus, those children who have disabilities seem to have the greatest need for emotionally positive adult involvement. Yet many early childhood programs may fail to provide this component of effective classroom practice (Frede, Barnett, & Lupo, chap. 12, this volume).

WHAT DO TEACHERS BELIEVE ABOUT CHILDREN'S EMOTIONAL DEVELOPMENT AND ABOUT THEIR ROLE IN THAT DEVELOPMENT

The study just described did not involve real teachers. We deliberately manipulated variations in adult behavior to duplicate, in a crude way, the range of emotion styles that might characterize early childhood practitioners. In real life, variations in the emotional climates and socialization practices of early childhood programs may depend, in part, on teachers' underlying beliefs about emotions and emotional development. Many studies have examined parents' belief systems about children's learning (e.g., Miller, 1988; Sigel, McGillicuddy-DeLisi, & Goodnow, 1992), but virtually no attention has been paid to adults' beliefs about emotions. Because beliefs do influence behavior (although they certainly do not determine behavior), it seems important to have a better idea of what teachers think about emotional issues in early development and education.

A few years ago we (Hyson & Lee, 1996) tried to develop a way to assess these emotion-related beliefs by developing a self-report measure and administering it to early childhood teachers from two cultural groups: American and Korean. The Caregivers' Beliefs About Feelings (CBAF) measure contained 40 items that tapped teachers' emotion beliefs in 10 areas or domains. These domains were selected because of their importance in contemporary emotions research and because both developmental psychologists and teachers may have varying points of view about these domains. Each domain was represented by a set of four statements. Respondents used a 6-point Likert scale to indicate their level of agreement with each statement. After some preliminary psychometric work on the measure, we revised it to include a smaller set of 23 items grouped into six areas:

1. Belief in the importance of affectionate bonds with children (e.g., "Children need to feel emotionally close to their teachers").
2. Belief in the open expression of positive and negative feelings (e.g., "It's good for a teacher to let children know when she is feeling angry").

3. Belief in teaching or modeling how children should express feelings (e.g., "I think it's better for children to figure out how to express their feelings on their own, instead of having the teacher show them how" [reverse scored]),

4. Belief in talking about and labeling feelings for children (e.g., "I often label children's feelings for them, such as 'You seem worried about our trip to the swimming pool'").

5. Belief that young children should be protected from strong emotions (e.g., "If a class pet died, I would not tell the children because they might become too upset").

6. Belief that children should learn "display rules" and control of emotion expression (e.g., "As a teacher, it's important for me to teach children socially acceptable ways of expressing their feelings").

Our analysis of data from 279 U.S. early childhood teachers showed that some beliefs were widely shared. As a group, teachers believed strongly in expressing physical affection to children. They also agreed, almost unanimously, that children need to feel emotionally close to their teachers. Teachers also believed strongly that children learn about emotions from seeing how adults behave, and they found it especially important to teach children socially acceptable ways of expressing feelings.

These general patterns have been replicated in Molinaro's (Hyson & Molinaro, 1999) research, in which she administered the measure to a group of 59 family child-care providers. Items that elicited the strongest levels of agreement and disagreement among providers were almost identical to those found for the American teachers in Hyson and Lee's (1996) study. The results of this study show that items about the importance of emotional bonds had particularly strong levels of agreement, indicating that providers tend to agree that this is an important role of teachers in early care and education. Given current concerns about sexual abuse accusations in child-care settings, this commitment to adult-child affection is in some ways surprising. However, it is also consistent with an experimental study by Hyson, Whitehead, and Prudhoe (1988), in which early childhood practitioners were more likely than either parents or college students to approve of videotaped scenes in which teachers showed normal physical affection toward young children.

Despite these areas of agreement, there was also wide variability on most items, showing that teachers do not have uniform beliefs about emotional development and its relation to early education. Molinaro's sample of family child-care providers (Hyson & Molinaro, 1999) showed considerable variability in their responses to questions regarding their role in teaching children about emotions. They also differed in their beliefs about the importance of teacher modeling of emotions. The statement "I believe some teachers spend too much time talking to children about their feelings" also elicited widely varying levels of agreement. These variations are consistent with the results of prior studies of teacher beliefs in other areas (Hyson et al., 1990; Smith & Shepard, 1988), which have shown similar variability in ideas about academic instruction, school readiness, and other developmental and educational issues.

In a way, beliefs about emotions seem similar to other kinds of personal theories that teachers build up from their own experience (Ross, Cornett, & McCutcheon, 1992). Our research has begun to show general trends and variations in the intensity with which early childhood teachers hold certain beliefs about emotions. The next step is to engage in further exploration of the underlying reasons for those beliefs and to look at the effect they may have on actual classroom practices.

WHY DO TEACHERS' EMOTION-RELATED BELIEFS, STYLES, AND PRACTICES EMOTIONS VARY, AND WHAT DOES THIS MEAN FOR EARLY EDUCATION?

What are the sources of differences in teachers' emotion-related characteristics? Besides examining the content of teachers' beliefs about emotions, we have also investigated influences on those beliefs, including teachers' education and training, cultural background, and relationship styles or working models of attainment. Although the research is exploratory, we have been particularly interested in how teachers' relationship styles might influence their ability to provide positive emotional experiences for children--experiences that may support children's emerging cognitive and social competence.

Education and Training

We expected that professional preparation would influence emotion beliefs, perhaps creating more awareness of the characteristics of young children's emotion system. In the Hyson and Lee (1996) study, we found that there were some connections between patterns of emotion beliefs and teachers' levels of education. In this study, teachers' education ranged from a high school education or less (23%) to a college degree. For example, those with higher levels of education were significantly more likely to agree that it is important to form strong emotional bonds with children. Compared with less educated teachers, those with higher levels of education were also more likely to believe that children are, in fact, able to control their displays of emotion, and those teachers were less likely to try to shelter children from unpleasant emotional experiences. Teachers with early childhood degrees were especially likely to believe that teachers should be emotionally expressive, but also to believe that children should be able to display their feelings in acceptable ways. In general, education seems to bring emotions to teachers' consciousness, making emotion issues part of the teacher's role to a greater extent than for early childhood teachers with lower levels of education.

Culture

Cultural beliefs, values, and customs play a role in childrearing practices, caregiving routines, and beliefs about child development, including beliefs about emotions (Saarni, 1998). In Hyson and Lee's (1996) research, the same emotion beliefs measure that had been administered to American teachers was given to a group of 175 Korean teachers of 5-to-6-year-olds. A comparison of their responses showed some interesting patterns. The two groups had significantly different emotion beliefs on 37 of the 40 items on the original scale, and they had notably wide discrepancies (with one cultural group strongly agreeing and the other strongly disagreeing) on 12 items. As compared with American teachers who work with children of the same ages (4-to-6-year-olds), Korean teachers were much more likely to believe that teachers should avoid being emotionally demonstrative. They also believed strongly that children need protection from emotionally upsetting events (such as a pet dying or a scary story). The Korean teachers were also much less likely to endorse children's open expression of feelings or frequent displays of affection. These kinds of differences in emotion beliefs have also been investigated among U.S. ethnic groups (Harwood, Miller, & Izarry, 1995), although the focus remains more on parents than on teachers.

Adults' Attachment Representations and Relationship Styles

Although culture and education certainly shape early childhood teachers' ideas and practices, these ideas can be better understood in the context of teachers' own attachment representations--also known as working models or, in some research, as attachment styles (Becker, Billings, Evelenth, & Gilbert, 1997). A basic premise underlying research and theory in attachment across the life span is that internal working models of the self and others, based on early infant-caregivers interactions, remain relatively stable and are carried forth into subsequent relationships (Bretherton & Waters, 1985; Crandall, Fitzgerald, & Whipple, 1997; Main, Kaplan, & Cassidy, 1985; Mickelson, Kessler, & Shaver, 1997). This is not to say that these models determine later personality; a person classified as insecurely attached in childhood is not necessarily doomed to have insecure relationships later in life. However, once developed, working models, seem resistant to change.

Using a similar theoretical perspective, other researchers have examined the construct of attachment or relationship style in adult development. *Relationship style* can be defined as a characteristic manner in which an individual interacts in close relationships based on feelings about the self and others in relationships (Bartholomew, 1994). These generalized feelings about the self and others are thought to be based on one's experiences as a participant in relationships. We have become interested in how these related frameworks-- working models of attachment and attachment styles--may help us better understand emotion beliefs and relationships between early childhood teachers and young children. Cassidy (1994) suggested that people may regulate the emotional experiences of others based on their own adult attachment representations. If so, this would have great relevance in designing and evaluating growth-producing educational environments for young children.

In Molinaro's research (Hyson & Molinaro, 1999), she identified the attachment styles of a sample of family child-care providers using a self-report measure--the Attachment Style Scale (ASS; Becker et al., 1997). The ASS is designed to assess attachment styles within romantic and nonromantic relationships. Using a 6-point Likert scale, respondents are asked to give responses to 19 items measuring their typical style of interaction in relationships (e.g., "I find it difficult to trust others completely"; "I do not often worry about people letting me down"; "I find that others are not willing to get as close to me as I would like)". They are then asked to read three short paragraphs about relationships and pick the one that is most like them. From the responses, participants can be classified into one of three groups: secure, fearful, or preoccupied. These classifications are conceptually linked to the classifications used in the Adult Attachment Interview (AAI; Main et al., 1985), although the measure has not yet been validated against the AAI. Scores on each of the three scales (secure/fearful/preoccupied) or on secure/insecure may also be used in analyses. In Molinaro's sample of family child-care providers, the proportions of participants who were classified as Secure ($\underline{n}=37$; 63%), Detached ($\underline{n}=18$; 31%), and Preoccupied ($\underline{n}=4$; 6%) were similar to those found in studies of college students and other adults.

Although it should be regarded as a pilot study, Molinaro's study suggests some interesting patterns. When family child-care providers' attachment style scores were correlated with their emotion beliefs as measured by the Caregivers' Beliefs About Feelings measure (Hyson & Lee, 1996), the results showed that more secure caregivers were significantly more likely to believe in the importance of close affectionate bonds between teachers and children than caregivers with a less secure attachment style. In contrast, those with high scores on the ASS fearful and preoccupied subscales were significantly less likely to believe that teachers should encourage emotionally close relationships with young children. Considering the potential importance of caregiver-child relationships in early brain development and in buffering stress reactions (Greenberg & Snell, 1997; Gunnar, 1998), these beliefs--and their links with individual differences in adult attachment styles--seem critically important.

A small subscale of 12 providers was observed during interactions with children in their family child-care homes. Observers rated providers' sensitivity, harshness, and detachment during interactions with children using the Arnett (1989) scale. We predicted that more secure caregivers would display more sensitive patterns of interaction. However, the data did not support this prediction. No differences were found in interaction patterns as a function of adult attachment style. However, sample characteristics may have influenced this finding: The sample was better educated than the larger sample and, as a group, displayed higher levels of sensitivity and lower harshness than family child-care providers in a national study (Kontos, Howes, Shinn, & Galinsky, 1994). The lack of variability in this group of providers made it difficult to identify meaningful patterns. However, case examples suggest some directions for future research with larger, more diverse groups.

"EMOTIONAL EDUCATION REFORM": IMPLICATIONS FOR RESEARCH AND PRACTICE

Research on emotional development and early adult-child relationships has broad implications for the field of early childhood education. Teachers of young children need to understand the impact that early experiences may have on brain development and on children's later learning. They need to be especially sensitive to children's emotional cues and engage children in emotionally rich interactions and stimulating activities. They also need to be sensitive to their own relationship styles and how those styles may influence how they think about and respond to children's feelings. Secure, intimate, growth-promoting relationships with every child should be the primary goal of early childhood programs. These relationships lay the foundation for motivation, learning, and competence across all domains of development.

The kind of research described in this chapter is just a first look at the important role of early childhood teachers in the emotional development of young children. If, as we now know, early relationships have both physiological and psychological effects on later development, then even greater attention needs to be paid to how we recruit, train, and evaluate early childhood teachers--not just as instructors, but as significant partners in children's emotional development.

Emotions need to become part of the educational reform agenda. Just as it is generally acknowledged that reforms are needed to create challenging content standards, we need equally challenging standards or desired outcomes for children's emotional development. We also need to recognize that helping children become effective learners of content will not be possible without equally rigorous, research-based attention to the emotional and motivational underpinnings of that learning.

As in other areas of educational reform, teachers are the key to success. However, in the domain of emotional development as well as in other domains, we know that current practices often fall short of what is needed. Two simultaneous initiatives will help to move this reform agenda forward--one focusing on research and the other on teacher preparation and renewal.

Calls for more research are typical of chapters like this, and with the outpouring of research on early emotional development and adult-child relationships, one might wonder why more is needed. Although the work described in this chapter is useful to the profession, much of it has been laboratory-based or conducted in homes rather than in schools and child-care settings. In studying adults' beliefs about and relationships with young children, the focus is still primarily on parents, not teachers. A few questions that would help us bring research closer to educational practice include:

- How do teachers' beliefs about emotions and about the connections between emotions and learning change over time, and why? Here we need to go beyond correlations with years of experience to look closely at processes of change.

- How are classroom practices influenced by (and how do they, in turn, influence) teachers' ideas about emotions and emotional development? As seen in our own research, the connections are seldom simple. Teachers are not the only ones who, at times, fail to practice what they preach. As Eheart and Leavitt (1989) observed in their study of family child care providers, teachers' stated intentions and their actual behavior are often inconsistent. Although almost all of the providers in their study felt that their primary role was to provide love and care, observers saw many instances of harshness, favoritism and punishment. The careful qualitative analysis done by Carol Ann Wien (1996) in her book *Developmentally Appropriate Practice in "Real Life"* is an excellent model for the kind of work that is needed to uncover the reasons for these inconsistencies.

- What effect does the teacher's emotion-toned relationship with young children have on their development of both socioemotional and academic skills? The quality of this relationship is a hidden variable in much research on educational effectiveness; we need to know a great deal more.

- What kinds of preservice and inservice professional development can be most effective in providing teachers with research-based tools to use in building young children's emotional competence and using that competence in the service of academic success?

No matter how much research is conducted, children will not benefit without high-quality professional development. Salovey and Sluyter's (1997) edited volume focusing on elementary education contains useful ideas, but at present there are few examples of professional development around emotion issues especially for early childhood practitioners. Knowledge about the importance of emotional development and affective relationships between teachers and children needs to be infused into the higher education curriculum, into community-based child-care training, and into inservice programs for public school kindergarten-primary teachers. In doing this, however, we need to heed the research on effective professional development. Professional development in this and other domains must be research based, ongoing, linked with opportunities to practice new skills, and relevant to teachers' daily concerns. A coaching process rather than a one-time workshop will have a much higher probability of being effective.

Although it was originally intended for teachers of first and second graders, a program developed in Delaware is being adapted to the needs of teachers of younger children as well. The program, "Helping Children Understand and Manage Emotions" (Izard & Bear, 1999), was designed by faculty at the University of Delaware, with the support of the State Department of Education, the College of Arts and Science, and the College of Human Resources, Education, and Public Policy. The program aims to introduce teachers to six socioemotional competencies based on theory and research in emotional development:

1. Recognizing and understanding emotions of self and others.
2. Understanding that emotions, thoughts, and behaviors are closely related.
3. Knowing how to regulate one's emotions.
4. Deciding what is fair and just when evaluating emotion-action sequences.
5. Communicating feelings in healthy ways.
6. Resolving interpersonal, emotion-laden conflicts.

By helping teachers build these competencies in children, the program hopes to facilitate the development of adaptive social behavior, prevent personal and social adjustment problems, and improve classroom climate, to promote concentration, learning, and safety for all children. Teachers in first- and second-grade classrooms have participated in a series of staff development meetings to introduce them to core concepts derived from theory and research on emotional development. Optionally, teachers may take a graduate course designed to provide theoretical background and specific techniques for program implementation. With this foundation, they receive materials that include at least 30 core lessons and other suggested activities to help children recognize and respond appropriately to their own feelings and those of their peers. The lessons feature training in empathy and prosocial behavior, but they also include discussion and exercises for dealing with the emotions and social conflict involved in teasing, bullying, lying, and stealing.

Healthy emotion management and social problem solving are central components of the program. Teachers are encouraged to enhance friendly peer interactions, take individual differences seriously, and foster empathy in the classroom. Some of the material is presented to children in interactive stand-alone lessons specifically designed for this purpose. However, the teachers' manual also includes many suggestions about how to increase the emotion-related content of other parts of the curriculum (e.g., using story reading to engender a discussion around emotion issues or adapting a social studies unit to emphasize conflict management). Teachers--both program participants and others--play a role in designing these materials. Finally, the program stresses the affective quality of the teacher's relationship with the children and highlights the importance of that relationship in creating a secure base for learning.

The program was implemented on a pilot basis in 1998 to 1999. The program's effectiveness is being evaluated using multiple measures of children's behavior and emotion understanding. Comparisons will be made with classrooms with similar demographic characteristics, in which the intervention has not yet been tested. As mentioned above, the program is also being adapted for use with teachers of younger children.

Although professional development holds promise as a tool to create a clearer emotion focus in teachers' beliefs and practices, we need to begin by recruiting into the profession only those people who have the potential to be positive emotion models and guides for children. We have always had a kind of gut feeling that these emotion-related characteristics were important although difficult to quantify and assess. Now we have clear evidence that the affective quality of teachers' relationships with children does a lot more than just put smiles on children's faces. It is true that adults can change their beliefs and actions on the basis of new knowledge, but the potential for change has limits. There are people who, for emotional reasons, should probably not be teachers of young children and should not be encouraged to enter the profession.

Finally, we need to place this issue in a broader societal context. Until teachers are more valued and, especially in child care, much better compensated, we will continue to have high turnover. This means that we will continue to be forced to hire people who have little real commitment to the profession, who are unlikely to profit from even the best training, and who may be more likely to take out their resentment on the young children they teach. The emotional and intellectual cost to children--and to the society they will enter as adults--will be high. To support young children's emotional development and, by doing so, to support their academic success, a broad-based agenda of research, professional preparation, and social change is essential.

REFERENCES

Ainsworth, M. D. S., Blehar, M., Waters, E., Wall, S. (1978). *Patterns of achievement*. Hillsdale, NJ: Lawrence Erlbaum Associates.

Arnett, J. (1989). Caregivers in child care centers: Does training matter? *Journal of Applied Developmental Psychology, 10*, 23-67.

Bartholomew, K. (1994). Assessment of individual differences in adult attachment. *Psychological Inquiry, 5* (1), 23-67.

Becker, T. E., Billings, R. S., Evelenth, D. M., & Gilbert, N. W. (1997). Validity of scores on three adult attachment style scales: Exploratory and confirmatory evidence. *Educational and Psychological Measurement, 57* (3), 477-493.

Bredekamp, S., & Copple, C. (1997). *Developmentally appropriate practice in early childhood programs* (rev. ed.). Washington, DC: NAEYC.

Bretherton, I., & Waters, E. (Eds.). (1985). Growing pains of attachment theory and research. *Monographs of the Society for Research in Child Development, 50* (1-2), Serial No. 209.

Campos, J. J., Barrett, K. C., Lamb, M. E., Goldsmith, H. H., & Stenberg, C. (1983). Socioemotional development. In M. Haith & J. J. Campos (Eds.), P. H. Mussen (Series Ed.), *Handbook of child psychology: Vol. 2. Infancy and developmental psychobiology* (pp. 783-795). New York: Wiley.

Cassidy, J. (1994). Emotion regulation: Influences of attachment relationships. In N. Fox (Ed.), *The development of emotion regulation: Biological and behavioral considerations. Monographs of the Society for Research in Child Development, 59* (2-3), No. 240, 228-249.

Copeland-Mitchell, J., Denham, S. A., & DeMulder, E. K. (1997). Q-sort assessment of teacher child attachment relationships and social competence in the preschool. *Early Education and Development, 8* (1), 222-239.

Cost, Quality, and Child Outcomes Study Team. (1995). *Cost, quality, and child outcomes in child care centers*. Denver: University of Colorado at Denver.

Crandall, L. E., Fitzgerald, H. E., & Whipple, E. (1997). Dyadic synchrony in parent-child interactions: A link with maternal representations of attachment relationships. *Infant Mental Health Journal, 18* (3), 200-211.

Darwin, C. (1872). *The expression of emotion in man and animals*. London: John Murray.

Denham, S. (1998). *Emotional development in young children*. New York: Guilford.

DeVries, R., & Zan, B. S. (1994). *Moral classrooms, moral children: Creating a constructivist atmosphere in early education*. New York: Teachers College Press.

Eheart, B. K., & Leavitt, R. L. (1989). Family day care: Discrepancies between intended and observed caregiving practices. *Early Childhood Research Quarterly, 4*, 145-162.

Elicker, J., & Fortner-Wood, C. (1995). Research in review: Adult-child relationships in early childhood settings. *Young Children, 51* (1), 69-78.

Fischer, K. W., Shaver, P. R., & Carnachon, P. (1990). How emotions develop and how they organize development. *Cognition and Emotion, 4*, 81-127.

Gardner, H. (1983). *Frames of mind: The theory of multiple intelligences.* New York: Basic Books.

Goodlad, J. I. (1984). *A place called school: Prospects for the future.* New York: McGraw-Hill.

Gordon, S. L. (1989). The socialization of children's emotions: Emotional culture, competence, and exposure. In C. Saarni & P. L. Harris (Eds.), *Children's understanding of emotion* (pp. 319-340). New York: Cambridge University Press.

Greenberg, M. T., & Snell, J. L. (1997). Brain development and emotional development: The role of teaching in organizing the frontal lobe. In P. Salovey & D. J. Sluyter (Eds.), *Emotional development and emotional intelligence: Educational implications* (pp. 93-126). New York: Basic Books.

Greenspan, S. I. (1997). A developmental approach to intelligence. In S. I. Greenspan & B. I. Benderly (Eds.), *The growth of the mind and the endangered origins of intelligence.* Reading, MA: Addison-Wesley.

Greenspan, S. I., & Greenspan, N. T. (1985). *First feelings: Milestones in the emotional development of your baby and child.* New York: Viking.

Gunnar, M. R. (1998). Quality of early care and buffering of neuroendocrine reactions: Potential effects on the developing human. *Preventive Medicine, 27* (2), 208-211.

Harwood, R. L., Miller, J. G., & Izarry, N. L. (1995). *Culture and attachment: Perceptions of the child in context.* New York: Guilford.

Howes, C., & Matheson, C. (1992). Sequences in the development of competent play with peers: Social and social preferential play. *Developmental Psychology, 28*, 961-974.

Howes, C., Phillips, D., & Whitebook, M. (1992). Thresholds of quality: Children's social development in center based child care. *Child Development, 63*, 449-460.

Hyson, M. C. (1994). *The emotional development of young children: Building an emotion-centered curriculum.* New York: Teachers College Press.

Hyson, M. C., & Cone, J. (1989). Giving form to feeling: Emotions research and early childhood education. *Journal of Applied Developmental Psychology, 10*, 375-399.

Hyson, M. C., Figueroa, A. D., & Hallam, R. (1999). *Keeping them involved: The effects of developmental appropriateness and adults' emotional involvement on young children's activity engagement.* Manuscript submitted for publication.

Hyson, M. C., Hirsh-Pasek, K., & Rescorla, L. (1990). The classroom practices inventory: An observation instrument based on NAEYC's guidelines for developmentally appropriate practice. *Early Childhood Research Quarterly, 5*, 475-494.

Hyson, M. C., & lee, K. M. (1996). Assessing early childhood teachers' beliefs about emotions: Content, context, and implications for practice. *Early Education and Development, 7*, 59-78.

Hyson, M. C., & Molinaro, J. (1999, April). *Adult attachment in child care contexts: Child care providers' attachment styles, emotion beliefs, and behaviors with children.* Paper presented at biennial conference of the Society for Research in Child Development, Albuquerque, NM.

Hyson, M. C., Whitehead, L. C., & Prudhoe, C. (1988). Influences on attitudes toward physical affection between adults and children. *Early Childhood Research Quarterly, 3*, 55-75.

Izard, C. E. (1991). *The psychology of emotions.* New York: Plenum.

Izard, C. E., & Bear, G. (1999). *Helping children understand and manage emotions.* Unpublished manuscript. Newark, DE: University of Delaware.

Kolb, B. (1993). Brain development, plasticity, and behavior. *American Psychologist, 44*, 1203-1212.

Kontos, S., Howes, C., Shinn, B., & Galinsky, E. (1994). *Quality in child care and relative care.* New York: Teachers College Press.

Kontos, S., & Wilcox-Herzog, A. (1997). Teachers' interactions with children: Why are they so important? *Young Children, 52*, 4-12.

Kraemer, G. W. (1992). A psychobiological theory of attachment. *Behavioral and Brain Sciences, 15* (3), 494-511.

Leavitt, R. I., & Power, M. B. (1989). Emotion socialization in the postmodern era: Children and day care. *Social Psychology Quarterly, 52*, 35-43.

Lewis, C. C. (1988). Cooperation and control in Japanese nursery schools. In G. Handel (Ed.), *Childhood socialization* (pp. 125-142). New York: Aldine deGruyter.

Lewis, M., & Haviland, J. M. (Eds.). (1993). *Handbook of emotions.* New York: Guilford Press.

Lynch, E. W., & Hansen, M. J. (1992). *Developing cross-cultural competence: A guide for working with young children and their families.* Baltimore: Paul H. Brookes.

Main, M., Kaplan, N., & Cassidy, J. (1985). Security in infancy, childhood and adulthood: A move to the level of representation. In I. Bretherton & E. Waters (Eds.), *Growing points of attachment theory and research. Monographs of the Society for Research in Child Development, 50* (1-2), Serial No. 209, 66-104.

Mickelson, K. D., Kessler, R. C., & Shaver, P. R. (1997). Adult attachment in a nationally representative sample. *Journal of Personality and Social Psychology, 73*, 1092-1106.

Miller, S. A. (1988). Parents' beliefs about children's cognitive development. *Child Development, 59*, 259-295.

Pianta, R. C. (Ed.). (1992). *Beyond the parent: The role of other adults in children's lives. New directions in child development.* San Francisco: Jossey-Bass.

Pianta, R. C., Nimetz, S. L., & Bennett, E. (1997). Mother-child relationships, teacher-child relationships, and school outcomes in preschool and kindergarten. *Early Childhood Research Quarterly, 12*, 263-280.

Pianta, R. C., & Walsh, D. J. (1996). *High-risk children in schools: Constructing sustaining relationships.* New York: Routledge.

Plomin, R., Chipauer, H. M., & Loehlin, J. C. (1990). Behavior genetics and personality. In L. A. Pervin (Ed.), *Handbook of personality theory and research* (pp. 225-243). New York: Guilford.

Raikes, H. (1996). A secure base for babies: Applying attachment concepts to the infant care setting. *Young Children*, pp. 59-67.

Ross, E. W., Cornett, J. W., & McCutcheon, G. (Eds.). (1992). *Teacher personal theorizing: Connecting curriculum practice, theory, and research.* Albany: State University of New York Press.

Saarni, C. (1998). Issues of cultural meaningfulness in emotional development. *Developmental Psychology, 34* (4), 647-658.

Saarni, C., Mumme, D. L., & Campos, J. J. (1997). Emotional development: Action, communication, and understanding. In N. Eisenberg (Ed.), *Handbook of child psychology. Fifth edition: Vol. 3. Social, emotional, and personality development.* New York: Wiley.

Salovey, P., & Sluyter, D. J. (Eds.). (1997). *Emotional development and emotional intelligence: Educational implications.* New York: Basic Books.

Saudino, K., & Eaton, W. O. (1991). Infant temperament and genetics: An objective twin study. *Child Development, 62*, 1167-1174.

Shore, R. (1997). *Rethinking the brain: New insights into early development.* New York: Families and Work Institute.

Sigel, I. E., McGillicuddy-DeLisi, A. V., & Goodnow, J. J. (Eds.). (1992). *Parental belief systems: The psychological consequences for children* (2nd ed.). Hillsdale, NJ: Lawrence Erlbaum Associates.

Smith, M. L., & Shepard, L. A. (1988). Kindergarten readiness and retention: A qualitative study of teachers' beliefs and practices. *American Educational Research Journal, 25*, 307-333.

Snow, C., Burns, M. S., & Griffin, P. (Eds.). (1998). *Preventing reading difficulties in young children.* Washington, DC: National Academy Press.

Sroufe, L. A. (1996). *Emotional development: The organization of emotional life in the early years.* New York: Cambridge University Press.

Stipek, D., Daniels, D., Galluzzo, D., & Milburn, S. (1992). Characterizing early childhood programs for poor and middle-class children. *Early Childhood Research Quarterly, 7*, 1-19.

Suransky, V. P. (1982). *The erosion of childhood.* Chicago: University of Chicago Press.

Thompson, R. A. (1994). Emotion regulation: A theme in search of a definition. In N. Fox (Ed.), *The development of emotion regulation: Biological and behavioral considerations. Monographs of the Society for Research in Child Development, 59* (2-3), Serial No. 240, 25-52.

Van IJzendoorn, M. H., Sagi, A., & Lambermom, M. W. E. (1992). The multiple caregiver paradox: Data from Holland and Israel. In R. C. Pianta (Ed.), *Beyond the parent: The role of other adults in children's lives. New Directions in Child Development* (pp. 5-24). San Francisco: Jossey-Bass.

Wien, C. A. (1996). *Developmentally appropriate practice in "real life."* New York: Teachers College Press.

6

CHILDREN'S PERSPECTIVES ON THEIR EXPERIENCES IN EARLY EDUCATION AND CHILD-CARE SETTINGS

Elisa L. Klein
University of Maryland, College Park

Children's entry into out-of-home educational settings such as child care or preschool often constitutes their first experience in the larger social context. They move from the relatively self-contained circle of home, family, and neighborhood to the broader world of school, with teachers, peers, and new activities, events, and expectations. Research on young children's early school and child-care experiences has primarily focused on curricular innovations, instructional strategies, or learning outcomes, with less attention paid to children's perspectives on school.[1] How do young children come to understand the roles of peers and teachers, the rules for behavior and social interaction, and the expectations and obligations for learning? Although previous research has helped us learn about the quality of children's experiences through assessing cognitive or social processes on a wide variety of measures, we can develop a deeper understanding of life in early childhood settings, and children's cognitions of these experiences, by observing and asking children to share their perspectives on the daily events of school.

---

[1]The terms *school, preschool, child care, day care,* and *nursery school,* for the purposes of this chapter, are all considered to refer to the same first center-based, out of home educational experience for young children. While some literature draws a distinction between early education and child care, more recent work, as well as the general consensus in the field, views these activities as synonymous with the possible exception of the number of hours spent in the center. In this chapter, *early childhood education, school,* and *child care* will be used interchangeably. Some family child care settings share many similar characteristics with center-based child care; however, unless specifically indicated, the work cited and research described here does not include family child care settings.

Children's views of their surrounding social milieu are an important, albeit overlooked, vehicle for understanding how they come to make sense of and participate in and with the people and experiences that make up their world. In school, the role of the student is communicated to children in a variety of subtle ways. Messages are transmitted through the physical environment of the classroom, the curriculum, and the actions of individuals within that structure. What teachers say, and often what they don't say, tells children much about what is expected of them as learners and participants in the school culture. Yet we know very little about how children interpret these messages, how they decide what becoming a *student* is all about, and how they construct an understanding of a new and important context called school, where they will spend much of the next two decades of their life (Klein, Kantor, & Fernie, 1988).

There is a growing body of research on children's perceptions of their school and child-care experiences. This work includes children's understanding of the structural events of school (e.g., Fivush, 1984; Nelson & Gruendel, 1986; Reifel, Briley, & Garza, 1986). It also addresses children's views on the process of instruction and of themselves as learners (e.g., Stipek, Feiler, Daniels, & Milburn, 1995); their goals and motivation for learning (Stipek & Greene, chap. 3, this volume), the functions of and relationships among major actors within the setting such as teachers (e.g., Bigler & Paris, 1994; Klein, 1988; Pianta, 1992, 1997, 1999). Children's preferences and attitudes about daily events, their categorization of activities as work or play (e.g., Hennessey & Berger, 1993; King, 1979; Wiltz & Klein, 1994; Zhang & Sigel, 1994), and children's evaluations of the quality of their experience (e.g., Wiltz, 1997) have also been studied. Additionally, researchers have explored children's understanding and perceptions of critical school passages, such as the transition from preschool to kindergarten (Murphy, 1999), noting that children's views may be very different from the perspectives of others, such as their parents (e.g., Graue, 1993).

The purpose of this chapter is to discuss the importance of children's views of their early childhood experiences and to argue that the applications of dimensions of psychological theory to early childhood practice will benefit from a consideration of the child's perspective. Beginning with a brief overview of theoretical approaches and methodological issues, research on children's perceptions of school is reviewed. The chapter closes with a description of two recent studies that provide a unique look at the interplay between contextual variation on dimensions of quality and developmental appropriateness and children's perceptions. Using a mixed methods approach, one study examines the influence of program quality on children's views of school and the other explores the relationship between children's experience with different curricula and their understanding of the transition from preschool to kindergarten.

SOCIAL COGNITION AND CHILDREN'S PERSPECTIVES ON SELF AND OTHERS

Children's growing abilities to conceptualize, reason, and act on their social world have been studied from a social cognitive perspective (e.g., Shantz, 1975, 1983). Within this framework, the relationship between children's social behavior and their cognitive development has been examined. Primarily drawing on the developmental theories of Piaget (1970; Piaget & Inhelder, 1969) and Vygotsky (Cole & Scribner, 1974; Corsaro, 1985; Rogoff, 1990), and the social interactionist theories of Mead (1934), Taguiri (1969), Kelly (1955), and others, a wide range of children's relationships with self, other people, groups, and social institutions has been examined.

Central to most of this research is an examination of the process by which children become aware of the distinctions between self and others and their growing ability to take on the perspectives and roles of different people (Mead, 1934). This development is influenced not only by the setting but the information children bring to the setting, and by the social reality that participants construct (Corsaro, 1985; Klein, 1988), as well as their growing cognitive abilities (Piaget, 1952; Shantz, 1983; Youniss, 1975). Children must learn how to develop systems for identifying and classifying themselves and others (e.g., Dubin & Dubin, 1965; Livesley & Bromley, 1973; Yarrow & Campbell, 1963); make inferences about people's thoughts, feelings, and intentions (e.g., Peevers & Secord, 1973); understand rules and values that determine right and wrong (Damon, 1977, 1983; Turiel, 1983); and define the roles and expectations of institutions such as the family, neighborhoods, and schools (Furth, 1980). Within a constructivist perspective, these processes develop as part of a dynamic interaction between the self and the larger context, as children negotiate their relationships with peers and adults in an ever-widening array of settings. Based on a year-long ethnography of the development of a peer culture in a preschool, Corsaro suggested that there is a need for the integration of information on children's *life worlds* (Corsaro, 1985, p. 73) with the interactionist or constructivist theories of Piaget, Mead, and Vygotsky. If children construct social knowledge and acquire interactive skills by acting on the environment, then there is a need to examine these actions within their social context (i.e., within the life worlds of children).

INTO THE WORLD OF SCHOOL AND CHILD CARE

The social perimeters of the world begin to expand as children move out of the home and into the domain of school and child care. With the numbers of women working outside of the home continuing to increase over the last two decades, children begin to experience additional contexts for development beyond the family fairly quickly. Recent figures place almost 13 million children under the age of 6 in child care and education settings with adults other than parents (West, Wright, & Hausken, 1996), with at least 30% in some type of group care and over 21% in out-of-home family child care (Casper, 1996; West et al., 1996). The percentage of children in nonparental care and education increases with age, with 78% of 4-year-olds and 84% of 5-year-olds participating (West et al., 1996).

As increasing numbers of young children spend a large part of their day outside of the home, it is important to expand our understanding about what happens to them in these new settings and how they view their experiences. There are a variety of unique components to school that are very different from home life. For example, children must learn to navigate through the structure of the school day, negotiate choices and fulfill expectations within particular activities, develop new relationships with peers, and bid for limited resources such as teacher attention. These events must be studied within context, necessitating a departure from traditional experimental methods that remove children from the natural settings of school and child care.

Methodological Issues in Studying Children's Understanding of School

Observation, interviews, and simulations have been the primary methods for studying children's understanding of social phenomena. Traditional studies of children's social cognitive processes have used interviews in which children might be asked to identify certain components of the school day, highlight preferences for particular activities, or describe the functions of teachers or students (e.g., Furth, 1980). In simulations, children might be asked to pretend they are in a particular social situation and solve an equity problem or distribute limited goods (e.g., Damon, 1977). Observations have been based on *a priori* coding systems that formally structure the way in which the researcher enters the setting and determines what to observe. Other techniques such as forced-or free-choice picture sorting (Klein, 1988; Murphy, 1999), model construction (Armstrong & Sugawara, 1989; Murphy, 1999), or even projective measures (Bigler & Paris, 1994) have been used to gain access to children's ways of thinking about school and school-related events. These are also structured by the researcher to a certain extent.

Traditional methods have been augmented, enhanced or sometimes replaced with approaches that emphasize an active, interpretive means of understanding children's views of social events and interactions, as described by Walsh, Tobin, and Graue (1993):

"Interpretive inquiry compels both researcher and researched to see themselves in a new way. At the heart of interpretive inquiry is a passion to understand the meaning that people are constructing in their everyday situated actions, that is, actions 'situated in a cultural setting, and in the mutually interacting intentional states of the participants' (Bruner, 1990, p. 19)." (p. 465)

These interpretive techniques range from script analysis (e.g., Fivush & Hudson, 1990; Hudson, Shapiro, & Sosa, 1995; Mandler, 1983; Nelson & Gruendel, 1986), in which children are asked to recount the order of events that make up a particular part of their school day (e.g., Garza, Briley, & Reifel, 1985), to various types of participant observation, in which researchers actively participate in the life of the school (e.g., Corsaro, 1985; Fernie, Kantor, Klein, Meyer, & Elgas, 1988; Wiltz, 1997). In addition to providing important information through formal and informal interviews, children can also validate information (as a triangulation source) gained through observation or other strategies (Corsaro, 1985; Corsaro & Streeck, 1986; Hatch, 1990). Corsaro and Streeck (1986) noted that these approaches allow us to more accurately consider children's development in situ:

the larger number of research studies in children's language and social cognition that have been conducted over the last several years show a noticeable movement away from strict experimental and hypothesis-testing methods to more naturalistic and interpretive approaches. However, this shift is not only the result of the discovery of limitations of traditional methods when studying young children (most especially experiments, cf. Bronfenbrenner, 1979), but also reflects a recognition of our lack of knowledge of children's worlds and peer cultures. Children are not passive receivers, processors, and storers of social and linguistic information but use their growing mastery of language and interactional strategies to actively construct a social world around themselves. Children's worlds are endowed with their own rules, rituals, and principles of conflict resolution and, depending upon the roles children are given within a society, not always easily accessible to adults. (p. 15)

More recently, a number of studies have attempted to use a mixed methodological approach, combining important measurement techniques from both quantitative/experimental and qualitative/interpretive perspectives to gain a more complete picture of children's social worlds. Combining the two approaches can substantially broaden and deepen our knowledge of phenomena (Goodwin & Goodwin, 1996). Whereas Walsh, Tobin, and Graue (1993) argued that qualitative methods are sometimes relegated to a minor role in mixed methods studies, there is ample evidence that this is a genuine and growing approach to gain a comprehensive, indepth view of children's lived experiences in various social milieu. Creswell (1994), Miles and Huberman (1994), and Patton (1990), for example, provided specific techniques that identify several different strategies for combining the two methods (Goodwin & Goodwin, 1996). In the last two sections of this chapter, two examples of studies which combine methodologies are presented.

Children's Views of the School Day

Learning the role of student involves understanding many things, including the curricular events that make up the school day. Studies of children's understanding of the routine activities of school are based on the belief that children, like adults, mentally organize, remember, and understand their daily experiences in terms of the predictable aspects of the events within them. For instance, children might remember a field trip such as going to a pumpkin farm in terms of the actors (the bus driver who takes you there, the hay ride attendant, the farmer who shows the pumpkins), the activities (riding on the bus and the hay wagon, picking out a pumpkin, tasting pumpkin bread, petting farm animals), or the objects (pumpkins, hay, scarecrows). These aspects become a *script*, or set of expectations for other similar activities, which helps us anticipate and understand recurring events in our world (Shank & Abelson, 1977).

Children's scripts reveal a developmental progression. Children's ability to report the events in their daily routine improves with age (Nelson & Gruendel, 1979, 1986). Even very young children show an understanding of the structure of events in their day, including activities such as how to bake cookies (Fivush, 1984) or how to go to the beach (Hudson et al., 1995), and they can demonstrate an ability to plan for experiences with which they are familiar (Hudson et al., 1995).

Children's understanding of the structure of the school day is evident in the scripts they use to describe these activities. As early as the second day of school, children are able to provide consistent reporting of the traditional school activities such as group time, snack, clean up, outdoor play, and so on (Fivush, 1984; Reifel, Briley, & Garza, 1986). Wiltz and Klein (1994, 1995, 1996) asked 3-, 4- and 5-year-old children what they did at school. Activities reported were consistent with previous research, and two distinct categories-- structured and unstructured--were identified. Structured activities involved teacher-controlled curricular activities that were related to the more academic areas of school, functional activities that involved routine tasks, and construction activities that were primarily teacher directed. These were mentioned more often by older children than by younger children. Unstructured activities, including play with toys, and creative play were mentioned most often by younger children and decreased significantly with age.

Other researchers have also interviewed children about their knowledge of the school day (e.g., Armstrong & Sugawara, 1989; Bigler & Paris, 1994) and have made cross-cultural comparisons which indicate that young children's perceptions of school are heavily influenced by the expectations for learning that are predominant in the culture (e.g., Zhang & Sigel, 1994). There is a general agreement that first school settings provide an initial introduction to the expectations of schooling in general and that at least part of the time is spent in learning how to *do* school and become a student (e.g., Fernie, Kantor, Klein, Meyer, & Elgas, 1988; Gracey, 1975; LeCompte, 1980).

What Is it Children Do in School? Distinctions Between Work and Play

In the course of interviews about school, a question commonly asked by researchers is, "What do children do in school?" Children make interesting distinctions between what they consider to be work and what they consider to be play within the school setting. There appears to be a general consensus that play is freely chosen, child controlled, and something in which teachers are rarely involved (e.g., Fein, 1985; King, 1979; LeCompte, 1980). In contrast, work is something that teachers expect you to do, even if it is a pleasurable activity (Hennessey & Berger, 1993). As such, what children say about play and work within the preschool setting provides a way to understand how they view their life in school. In LeCompte's (1980) study, children told her, "Play is at a different time; it is easy. Play is fun. Play is not working" (p. 123). Once again, cultural differences emerge when children are asked about their work and play activities in school. Zhang and Sigel (1994) found that American children in kindergarten emphasized the importance of having fun in school, whereas Chinese children clearly indicated that learning was the main focus of their kindergarten. It is interesting, and a little disconcerting, to note that even at a very young age the notion that learning and play are two distinct and primarily incompatible processes appears to be firmly in place. Despite the widespread call for developmentally appropriate practices, which emphasize play and autonomy as being of paramount importance in early childhood, children themselves make distinctions among learning, work, and play that may be reflective of cultural and community assumptions about the nature of learning as well as children's own growing understanding of these concepts (Elgas, Klein, Kantor, & Fernie, 1988; King, 1979; Marshall, 1990, 1994; Wiltz & Klein, 1995).

Views of the Teacher

Teachers play an important role in children's views about school. They are often the first adults outside of family members who have direct and sustained contact with the child. Few researchers, however, have explored children's perspectives on what teachers do and their relationships with these new adults. Teachers' roles include not only the overt functional characteristics that may be directly observable to the child, but also the more subtle components that are revealed through the underlying philosophy of the setting and the ways in which teachers interact with parents, administrators, other teachers, and the larger community.

There is a large body of research on the effects of teaching style on student performance (e.g., Weinstein, 1983). However, there are dimensions of the relationship between teacher and child that extend beyond the effects of instructional strategy on achievement and that may influence peer competencies and overall classroom adjustment (Pianta, 1999). Most of the descriptions of teacher-child relationships have been from the teacher's perspective, as Pianta (1999) noted. An alternative perspective may be acquired by looking at children's understanding and perceptions of teachers' roles. Furth (1980) asked children to describe the *world of grown-ups*, including what it means to be a teacher. He found that 5- and 6-year-olds confuse the broad societal requirements of the teacher's role with the more individual and idiosyncratic factors that may be part of a personal relationship with an individual teacher. Children may view all teachers as having the same characteristics as their own teacher, and thus respond to questions about the general characteristics of teachers with specific behaviors particular to one teacher ("She always gives you hot cocoa when it's cold outside"). This is consistent with the likelihood that the young child has insufficient experience with teachers to know in what ways teachers are alike and what ways they are not. Watson and Fischer (1980) found that understanding multiple social roles (e.g., that a woman can be both a teacher and a mother) emerges over time. Takanishi and Spitzer (1980) found that children make distinctions among the abilities of individual teachers to meet particular needs. In classrooms with more than one teacher, children were able to identify particular teachers they would turn to for differing needs (instructional questions vs. emotional needs).

For young children, the most obvious comparison for the teacher role is with the mother role. In a series of studies with children in preschool, child-care and kindergarten settings, Klein (1978, 1983, 1988) explored their perceptions of teachers and mothers. Children's views of the roles of mothers and female teachers were fairly stereotypic. Mothers were almost exclusively involved in the care of children, whereas teachers were often overly didactic, giving even preschoolers "homework." As might be expected, children's perceptions of the role of the teacher changed from preschool to kindergarten to include more instructional behaviors such as writing on the blackboard. The type of curriculum, however, was a more significant factor than the child's age or grade level. Children in more child-centered programs tended to view the teacher as a warm, nurturant person who is also a good play partner. Children in more traditional, academic settings described teachers almost exclusively in instructional terms. As is noted in a later section, this influence of the contextual frame, defined by setting parameters such as overall quality and curricular focus, appears to be related to children's perspectives about different components of school.

RECENT RESEARCH ON CHILDREN'S UNDERSTANDING OF SCHOOL

The influence of the context of early childhood education on children's perceptions of their experiences has not been adequately explored. Although Corsaro (1985) and others (e.g., Fernie, Kantor, Klein, Meyer, & Elgas, 1988) have looked at children within preschool/child-care settings, the setting characteristics have not been sufficiently examined. Do differences in the type of setting have any impact on how children understand school and the perspective they have on school-related events or issues? For instance, is experience in a high-quality center predictive of more positive views of school? Do children from centers with child-centered curricula have a different notion of what future school experiences will be like than children from centers with an overt academic orientation? Two recent studies, both of which employed a multiple methods approach, were designed to begin to answer these questions.

Quality of Care and Children's Perceptions of Setting

Wiltz (1997; Wiltz & Klein, 1997) examined 4-year-old children's perceptions of their daily child-care experiences in centers evaluated for quality of care and developmental appropriateness of the curriculum. Although there have been a number of recent studies on the influence of structural variables (such as child-staff ratio, classroom size and cleanliness, etc.) and on overall child-care quality (see, e.g., the Cost, Quality and Child Outcomes Study in Helburn et al., 1995), less attention has been paid to the relationships among these structures and the processes (such as curricular philosophy, peer interactions, teacher engagement) within the setting. One way to determine outcomes of differential quality is to examine whether it has an impact on children's daily experiences. If children's descriptions of their life in school differ by child-care setting (high vs. low quality), evidence for an interaction between structure and the intimate processes of children's lives would be supported. In addition, an alternative indicator of quality, coming directly from children's own experiences, would be identified. Eight childcare centers (four of high quality and four of low quality) were identified from an initial pool of 15 using a measure of overall structural quality, the Early Childhood Environment Rating Scale (ECERS; Harms & Clifford, 1980), and a measure of general classroom developmental appropriateness--the Classroom Practices Inventory (CPI; Hyson, Hirsh-Pasek, & Rescorla, 1990). Classrooms were observed using both of these measures by trained research assistants. Overall scores (combined ECERS plus CPI) for the centers ranged from 176 to 376 (out of a possible 389). The four low-quality centers had scores between 176 and 204; the high-quality centers had scores between 333 and 376. Of the centers rated as being low in quality, one was NAEYC accredited; of the centers rated as being high in quality, three were NAEYC accredited. There were no significant differences between the centers on a variety of demographic measures, including parent income level and mother's educational level (Wiltz, 1997).

In the second phase of the study, Wiltz (1997) combined participant observation, structured and informal interviews, drawings, and storytelling with photographs as multiple means to gain access to children's views of their child-care experience. Children were asked about their life in school--what they liked and did not like, what made them happy and unhappy about school. They also were asked to draw pictures about their school and to describe generic photographs of children in group settings and pick the ones that looked most like their own school experiences. In addition, parents completed the Parent Educational Attitude Scale (PEAS; Rescorla, Hyson, Hirsh-Pasek, & Cone, 1990), which is designed to identify parental attitudes about child development and education. Teachers completed the preschool version of the Charlesworth Teacher Questionnaire (Hart et al. 1990), which measures beliefs about developmentally appropriate practices. (It is beyond the scope of this chapter to report the adult data; interested readers are referred to Wiltz, 1997, for a presentation of these results.)

With some important exceptions discussed later, children's everyday actions, their discussions during interviews, and their responses to the photographs and story-drawing activities did not differ across high- and low-quality centers. Children were generally positive about their experiences and seemingly found ways to engage in the important activities of their day, regardless of the setting characteristics. However, there were subtle differences that suggest experience may vary across environment.

First, children were quite knowledgeable about the structure and activities of their child-care experience. Examining the structure of the discourse with which children shared this knowledge revealed variations on traditional scripts previously discussed. Children in the lower-quality centers described their days in fairly spare, sequential terms, listing activities with little elaboration. For example, when Brent, a child at a low-quality center, described his day, this was his dictated story:

School By Brent

This is a story about school. We play and then we do
circle. And then we do art. And then we do Spanish.
And then we go outside and play. Then we come inside
and take a nap. And we eat lunch before we take a nap.
Then we wake up again. Then we play again. Then
we have snack and then we play again. And then go
outside again. And then, at last, our mommies pick
us up. The end. (Wiltz, 1997, p 111)

Contrast this with a conversation, in response to the same question,
with several children about their day at a high-quality center:

Randi: That's dramatic play (pointing to each center)
that's blocks that Chuck's doing. That's play dough.
Allison: And this is the writing center.
Researcher: What do you do at writing center?
Randi: We write! And then stamp and then
Allison: And we have art things (pointing to the shelves where art
supplies are used at the children's discretion), to stick on with glue.
Randi: And we have paper, and play dough, and computers
(pointing to where these things are located).
Allison: And envelopes like I'm using.
Bob: And we have green paper like I'm using.
Randi: the covers are over there (continues pointing to areas in the
room). Books are over there. And listening center. And the art table
is over there. It's the dolphin table.
Bob: And those are our art folders (points to the wall).
Allison: On the wall. Right. (Wiltz, 1997, p. 112)

This distinction between *listening* and *describing* was consistent. Wiltz
found that children in low-quality centers tended to emphasize teacher-directed
activities and the repetitive nature of the schedule with little elaboration.
Children in the high-quality centers, in contrast, used detail to outline the
complexity of the activities and focused much less on the actual order of the
schedule.

Second, children's determination to play was paramount. Even in
centers where play was either highly structured or not particularly supported by
teachers, children's need and desire to play resounded through their descriptions
of their day. There was a slightly higher frequency of play-related descriptions

in high-quality centers, but the difference was not significant.

Third, each center had a clear, distinctive character above and beyond the overall level of quality. This character was a combination of program philosophy, the attitudes of the caregivers, and the children's personalities. It was only after extended observation that this character emerged, which indicates that brief observations, with or without reliable measures, may not fully reveal the true nature of the center environment.

Finally, observations and interviews with children consistently revealed the resilience and optimistic attitude with which they approached their daily lives in school settings. Regardless of the measured quality of the center and the attitudes of the caregivers, which in some cases were distinctly negative and unpleasant, children continued to express their overall pleasure for their surroundings. Although they did comment about teachers who were mean, peers who were difficult to get along with, and activities that they regarded with displeasure because they interrupted their freely chosen play times, children were nonetheless basically positive about their lives in school.

These findings provide cause for both relief and concern. On the positive side, there was support for the strong resilience and general optimism of children who found pleasure in much of what they did and who were able to create play opportunities in even less than ideal conditions. On the negative side, it is possible that this resilience on the part of children might be used to excuse low-quality child-care environments. There were some centers where teachers were observed engaged in what could be considered verbally abusive behaviors, yet children indicated general happiness. These findings might be considered from the same perspective as the phenomenon of children who wish to be with abusive parents--the need for contact and affiliation may supersede negative interactions. Obviously, early childhood educators should never use children's positive comments as validation for these type of experiences.

It is important to note again the limited richness and complexity with which children in low-quality centers described their days compared with children in high-quality centers. Although children in all settings are able to adequately identify the formal structural events of the settings, the depth of description by children in the high-quality centers is clearly preferable. The ability to provide such rich description may have long-term effects related to school outcome measures--an area of potential research. These findings should be considered together with Stipek and Greene's review (chap. 3, this volume) of the potentially depressive effects of didactic and performance-oriented instruction on young children's motivation, and should support future research that examines relationships between contextual variation and young children's attitudes and motivations in school settings.

Relationships Between Curricular Philosophy, Conceptions of Preschool and Expectations for Kindergarten

Although previous research has focused on children's understanding of the role of student, and even on their expectations for later school experiences (e.g., Summers, Stroud, Stroud, & Heaston, 1991), how children view the transition from preschool to kindergarten has not been examined. The beginning of kindergarten is seen as a major life event in American culture. Riding the yellow school bus, being part of a school with *big kids*, and even, in some cases, dealing with homework or eating in the cafeteria are viewed as signifiers of growing up and moving into the larger spheres of influence of community, school, and peers. Research on parental and community attitudes about readiness (Graue, 1993) reveal that this concept is constructed differently based on beliefs and attitudes about the nature of schooling, the expectations for success, and the demands of the larger society. Children may enter the same kindergarten in a community from preschool and child-care settings with very different philosophies and with differing amounts of knowledge and preparation for this new and exciting place called school.

Murphy (1999; Murphy & Klein, 1999) explored children's conceptions of the transition from preschool to kindergarten at the beginning and end of the preschool year. This was part of a larger research project that also included case studies of individual children in programs with differing educational philosophies and interviews with parents. Eighty-five children in three academically oriented and two child-centered child-care programs were observed over the course of a school year. Children were interviewed about their perceptions of their current setting as well as their beliefs and expectations regarding kindergarten in the fall and the spring of the year prior to kindergarten entry.

First, 13 centers were assessed for curricular philosophy by trained research assistants using the Classroom Practices Inventory (CPI; Hyson et al., 1990; Rescorla et al., 1990). With a score range of 26 to 130, centers with scores above 110 were considered to reflect a child-centered philosophy, whereas those with scores below 70 were considered to reflect an academic orientation. The two child-centered classrooms had scores of 128 and 129, and the three academic classrooms had scores between 39 and 59.

In the second part of the study, a card-sort task designed to explore conceptions of preschool and expectations for kindergarten was administered. Similar to a technique developed by Klein (1988), children were asked to sort 20 drawings--10 of which reflected activities consistent with a child-centered focus and 10 of which reflected activities consistent with an academic focus--on two separate occasions at the beginning and the end of the school year. First, children were asked to select those pictures that were most similar to "their school.". Several days later, they were asked to select the pictures that were like things they would probably do in kindergarten. At the time of the spring card sort, children were asked if they had visited their prospective kindergarten classroom and whether there was anything they needed to know or be able to do before they could go to kindergarten. Several individual children were observed and interviewed more extensively, as were their parents, for a case study analysis, which is not discussed here (see Murphy, 1999, for a discussion of these data). More global observations of the classroom environment, with a focus on how the student role was communicated to children as well as ways in which current activities or interactions might influence later school expectations (e.g., ways in which teacher or child talk about kindergarten were present in the classroom), were noted for qualitative analysis.

Differences across curricula were evident in the way in which children viewed their present and future school experiences. Those in academic preschool classrooms reported more academic activities and fewer child-centered activities in their classroom than did children in child-centered classrooms, and these differences increased over time. At the beginning of the school year, children in both types of curricula expected kindergarten to be more academic than their current classroom. This trend continued at the time of the spring assessment. Children in both types of centers expected more academic activities in kindergarten. In addition, children in the child centered classrooms expected kindergarten to be less child centered than preschool at both points in the year. Between group differences were found only for the mean number of academic activities expected in kindergarten, which were significantly higher for academic classrooms during the spring assessment.

Analysis of the interview question, "Is there anything you have to know or be able to do before you go to kindergarten?" yielded intriguing differences between children in classrooms with different curricular philosophies. Children in the child-centered classrooms were more likely (24%) to indicate that there was nothing they needed to know or be able to do to go to kindergarten than children in the academic-oriented classrooms (12%). Conversely, children in the academic programs indicated that academic skills (e.g., "learn to spell," "read," "do homework") were required before going to kindergarten more often (20%) than those in the child-centered settings (13%). Practical skills such as knowing how to put on your shoes or brush your teeth were mentioned more frequently (16%) by children in child-centered settings than those in academic settings (6%). Finally, traditional preparation activities (get shots, visit the kindergarten, say goodbye to your old school) were mentioned more often by children in academic classrooms (18%) than those in child-centered classrooms (8%). Children from the academic programs thus appear to have a distinct notion of kindergarten requiring more specific academic skills and the completion of a series of advance preparation activities, whereas children in the child-centered settings show an awareness of maturational skills and expectations for independence that might accompany the move to kindergarten.

Several implications for children's understanding of the transition from preschool to kindergarten emerge from these findings. First, children's expectations for kindergarten are similar regardless of their preschool setting, but still reflect the curricular focus of these settings in important ways. Although all of the children expected more academic activities in kindergarten, children in academic preschools expected significantly more of these than their peers in child-centered programs. The differences accurately reflect the experiences children have had in their preschools.

However, the similar trend in reporting an increase in academic expectations for kindergarten also reflects something else that goes beyond classroom experience. The cultural archetype about kindergarten--the formal entry into school and all of the stereotypes that go with it--(e.g., desks in rows, basal readers, teachers with glasses and hair in buns)--are rife in the media (in children's books and TV shows, movies, commercials) and passed along through older siblings and other family members (Murphy, 1999). Children inculcate these stereotypes at the same time that they participate in school experiences that may or may not be similar. Somehow they find a way to reconcile what may be contradictory messages.

Finally, this research demonstrates stability in children's conceptions of kindergarten over time. The trends reported here were significant as well as stable over the course of the school year, supporting the notion that even young children are reliable sources of information about their understanding of school events and that their reporting is accurate and reflects the reality of their classroom environment.

CONCLUSION

In this chapter, the contributions of children's perspectives on their school experiences to our understanding of early childhood education were examined. A small but growing body of research that explores the ways in which children come to understand and develop strategies for making sense of and participating in the everyday events of school has contributed a beginning knowledge of children's views of their lives in this important social context. Combined with previous work on social cognitive processes and script analysis, the recent research, which often integrates qualitative methods with more traditional approaches to access children's construction of certain aspects of their life in school, gives us a fuller picture of the events and activities that children engage in on an ongoing basis.

Although the influence of differences in the contextual frame (e.g., the curricular orientation or the overall quality of the program) is beginning to be explored, much remains to be done to gain a deeper understanding of the impact of these important variations. The recent research on the long-term influence of quality child care on school performance well into elementary school (Peisner-Feinberg et al., 1999) demonstrates that the structural variables that are essential to quality care do make a substantial difference in child outcomes for many years beyond the early education/care setting. Focused work on the process variables (such as curricular variation and teacher-child interaction differences) not always included in research on quality may yield a more fine-grained analysis of the specific patterns of influence on children's understanding, attitudes, and motivation about school and school-based activities.

ACKNOWLEDGMENT

The author would like to acknowledge the assistance of Nancy Wiltz and Karen Murphy, who generously provided pertinent information in the preparation of this chapter.

REFERENCES

Armstrong, J., & Sugawara, A. I. (1989). Children's perceptions of their day care experience. *Early Child Development and Care, 49,* 1-15.

Bigler, K., & Paris, R. D. (1994, April). *Children's emerging theories about school.* Paper presented at the Annual Meeting of the American Educational Research Association, New Orleans, LA.

Bronfenbrenner, U. (1979). *The ecology of human development: Experiments by nature and design.* Cambridge, MA: Harvard University Press.

Casper, L. (1996). *Who's minding our preschoolers? (P7-053) Washington, DC: U.S. Department of Commerce, Bureau of the Census.*

Cole, M., & Scribner, S. (1974). *Culture and society.* New York: Wiley.

Corsaro, W. A., & Streeck, J. (1986). Studying children's worlds: Methodological issues (pp. 13-35). In J. Cook-Gumperz, W. Corsaro, & J. Steeck (Eds.), *Children's worlds and children's language.* Berlin: Mouton de Grayter.

Creswell, J. W. (1994). *Research design: Qualitative and quantitative approaches.* Thousand Oaks, CA: Sage.

Damon, W. (1977). *The social world of the child.* San Francisco, CA: Jossey-Bass.

Damon, W. (1983). The nature of social-cognitive change in the developing child. In W. Overton (Eds.), *The relationship between social and cognitive development.* Hillsdale, NJ: Lawrence Erlbaum Associates.

Dubin, R., & Dubin, E. (1965). Children's social perceptions: A review of research. *Child Development, 36,* 809-837.

Elgas, P., Klein, E., Kantor, R., & Fernie, D. (1988). Play and the peer culture: Play styles and object use. *Journal of Research in Childhood Education, 3* (2), 142-153.

Fein, G. G. (1985). Learning in play: Surface of thinking and feeling. In J. L. Frost & S. Sunderlin (Eds.), *When children play* (pp. 45-53). Wheaton, MD: Association for Childhood Education International.

Fernie, D. E. (1988). Becoming a student: Messages from first settings. *Theory Into Practice, 27* (1), 3-10.

Fernie, D., Kantor, R., Klein, E., Meyer, C., & Elgas, P. (1988). Becoming students and becoming ethnographers in a preschool. *Journal of Research in Childhood Education, 3,* 132-141.

Fivush, R. (1984). Learning about school: The development of kindergartners' school scripts. *Child Development, 55* (5), 1697-1709.

Fivush, R., & Hudson, J. A. (Eds.). (1990). *Knowing and remembering in young children.* Cambridge, England: Cambridge University Press.

Furth, H. (1980). *The world of grownups.* New York: Elsevier.

Garza, M., Briley, S., & Reifel, S. (1985). Children's views of play. In J. L. Frost & S. Sunderlin (Eds.), *When children play* (pp. 31-37). Wheaton, MD: ACEI.

Goodwin, W. L., & Goodwin, L. D. (1996). *Understanding quantitative and qualitative research in early childhood education.* New York: Teachers College Press.

Gracey, H. L. (1975). Learning the student role: Kindergarten as academic boot camp. In H. R. Stub (Ed.), *The sociology of education: A sourcebook* (3rd ed., pp. 83-95). Homewood, IL: Dorsey.

Graue, M. E. (1993). Expectations and ideas coming to school. *Early Childhood Research Quarterly, 8,* 53-75.

Harms, T., & Clifford, R. M. (1980). *Early childhood environments rating scale.* New York: Teachers College Press.

Hart, C., Burts, D., Charlesworth, R., Fleege, P., Ickes, M., & Durland, M. (1990). *The teacher questionnaire: Preschool version.* Baton Rouge, LA: Louisiana State University, School of Human Ecology.

Hatch, J. A. (1990). Young children as informants in classroom studies. *Early Childhood Research Quarterly, 5,* 251-264.

Helburn, S., Culkin, M., Morris, J., Mocan, N., Howes, C., Phillipsen, L., Bryant, D., Clifford, R., Cryer, D., Peisner-Feinberg, E., Burchinal, M., Kagan, S., & Rustici, J. (1995). *Cost, quality and child outcomes in child care centers.* Denver, CO: University of Colorado at Denver.

Hennessey, B. A., & Berger, A. R. (1993, April). *Children's conceptions of work and play: Exploring an alternative to the discounting principle.* Paper presented at the Biennial Meeting, Society for Research in Child Development, New Orleans.

Hudson, J. A., Shapiro, L. R., & Sosa, B. B. (1995). Planning in the real world: Preschool children's scripts and plans for familiar events. *Child Development, 66* (4), 984-998.

Hyson, M., Hirsh-Pasek, K., & Rescorla, L. (1990). The classroom practices inventory: An observation instrument based on NAEYC's guidelines for developmentally appropriate practices for 4- and 5-year-old children. *Early Childhood Research Quarterly, 5,* 474-494.

Kelly, G. (1955). *The psychology of personal constructs.* New York: Norton.

King, N. R. (1979). Play: The kindergartner's perspective. *The Elementary School Journal, 80* (2), 81-87.

Klein, E. L. (1978, June). *Teachers and parents: Young children's perceptions of functional roles of adults.* Paper presented at the eighth Annual Symposium of the Jean Piaget Society, Philadelphia.

Klein, E. L. (1983, April). *When is a teacher different than a mother? The influence of early child care experience on children's perceptions of functional social roles of mothers and female teachers.* Paper presented at the annual meeting, American Educational Research Association, Montreal.

Klein, E. L. (1988). How is a teacher different from a mother? Young children's perceptions of the social roles of significant adults. *Theory Into Practice, 27* (1), 36-41.

Klein, E. L., Kantor, R., & Fernie, D. E. (1988). What do young children know about school? *Young Children, 43* (5), 32-39.

LeCompte, M. D. (1980). The civilizing of children: How young children learn to become students. *Journal of Thought, 15* (3), 105-127.

Livesley, W., & Bromley, O. (1973). *Person perception in childhood and adolescence.* London: Wiley.

Mandler, J. E. (1983). Structural invariants in development. In L. S. Liben (Ed.), *Piaget and the foundations of knowledge.* Hillsdale, NJ: Lawrence Erlbaum Associates.

Marshall, H. H. (1990). Beyond the workplace metaphor: The classroom as a learning setting. *Theory Into Practice, 19,* 94-101.

Marshall, H. H. (1994). Children's understanding of academic tasks: Work, play, or learning. *Journal of Research in Childhood Education, 9* (1), 35-46.

Mead, G. H. (1934). *Mind, self and society.* Chicago: University of Chicago Press.

Miles, M., & Huberman, A. M. (1994). *Qualitative data analysis* (2nd ed.). Thousand Oaks, CA: Sage.

Murphy, K. L. (1999). *Children's conceptions of the preschool-kindergarten transition.* Unpublished dissertation, University of Maryland.

Murphy, K. L., & Klein, E. (1999). *Changes over time in children's conceptions of preschool and expectations for kindergarten in academically oriented and child centered early childhood programs.* Paper presented at the annual meeting of the American Educational Research Association, Montreal.

Nelson, K., & Gruendel, J. (1979). At morning it's lunchtime: A scriptal view of children's dialogues. *Discourse Processes, 2,* 73-94.

Nelson, K., & Gruendel, J. (1986). Children's scripts. In K. Nelson (Ed.), *Event knowledge: Structure and function in development.* Hillsdale, NJ: Lawrence Erlbaum Associates.

Patton, M. Q. (1990). *Qualitative evaluations and research methods* (2nd ed.). Thousand Oaks, CA: Sage.

Peisner-Feinberg, E. S., Burchinal, M. R., Clifford, R. M., Culkin, M. L., Howes, C., Kagan, S. L., Yazejian, N., Byler, P., Rustici, J., & Zelazo, J. (1999). *The children of the cost, quality and outcomes study go to school: Technical report.* Chapel Hill, NC: University of North Carolina at Chapel Hill, Frank Porter Graham Child Development Center.

Piaget, J. (1952). *The language and thought of the child.* London: Routledge & Kegan Paul.

Piaget, J. (1970). Piaget's theory. In P. Mussen (Ed.), *Carmichael's manual of child psychology* (Vol. 1, 3rd ed.). New York: Wiley.

Piaget, J., & Inhelder, B. (1969). *The psychology of the child.* London: Routledge & Kegan Paul.

Pianta, R. C. (1992). *New directions in child development: Vol. 57. Beyond the parent: The role of other adults in children's lives.* San Francisco, CA: Jossey-Bass.

Pianta, R. C. (1997). Adult-child relationship processes and early schooling. *Early Education and Development, 8,* 11-26.

Pianta, R. C. (1999). *Enhancing relationships between children and teachers.* Washington, DC: American Psychological Association.

Reifel, S., Briley, S., & Garza, M. (1986). Play at child care: Event knowledge at ages three to six. In K. Blanchard (Ed.), *The many faces of play* (Vol. 9, pp. 80-91). Champaign, IL: Human Kinetics.

Rescorla, L., Hyson, M., Hirsh-Pasek, K., & Cone, J. (1990). Academic expectations in mothers of preschool children: A psychometric study of the educational attitude scale. *Early Education and Development, 1* (3), 165-184.

Rogoff, B. (1990). *Apprenticeship in thinking.* Oxford: Oxford University Press.

Shank, R., & Abelson, R. (1977). *Scripts, plans, goals and understanding.* Hillsdale, NJ: Lawrence Erlbaum Associates.

Shantz, C. U. (1975). The development of social cognition. In E. M. Hetherington (Ed.), *Review of child development research* (Vol. 5, pp. 257-323). Chicago: University of Chicago Press.

Shantz, C. U. (1983). Social cognition. In P. Mussen (Ed.), *Handbook of child psychology* (Vol. 3, pp. 495-555). New York: Wiley.

Stipek, D., Feiler, R., Daniels, D., & Milburn, S. (1995). Effects of different instructional approaches on young children's achievement motivation. *Child Development, 66* (1), 209-223.

Summers, M., Stroud, J., Stroud, J., & Heaston, A. (1991). Preschoolers' perceptions of teacher role and importance. *Early Child Development and Care, 68,* 125-131.

Taguiri, R. (1969). Person perception. In G. Lindzey & E. Aronson (Eds.), *The handbook of social psychology* (Vol. 3). Reading, MA: Addison Wesley.

Takanishi, R., & Spitzer, S. (1980). Children's perceptions of human resources in team-teaching classrooms. *The Elementary School Journal, 80* (4), 203-212.

Turiel, E. (1983). Domains and categories in social-cognitive development. In W. Overton (Eds.), *The relationship between social and cognitive development.* Hillsdale, NJ: Lawrence Erlbaum Associates.

Watson, M. W., & Fischer, K. W. (1980). Development of social roles in clinical and spontaneous behavior during the preschool years. *Developmental Psychology, 16,* 483-494.

Walsh, D., Tobin, J., & Graue, M. (1993). The interpretive voice: Qualitative research in early childhood education. In B. Spodek (Ed.), *Handbook of research on the education of young children* (pp. 464-476). New York: Macmillan.

Weinstein, R. (1983). Student perceptions of schooling. *Elementary School Journal, 83* (4), 287-312.

West, J., Wright, D., & Hausken, E. G. (1996). *Child care and early education program participation in infants, toddlers, and preschoolers.* Washington, DC: U.S. Department of Education, National Center for Education Statistics.

Wiltz, N. (1997). *Four year-olds' perceptions of their experiences in high and low quality child care.* Unpublished doctoral dissertation, University of Maryland at College Park.

Wiltz, N., & Klein, E. (1995, March). *Young children's perceptions of activities in child care.* Paper presented at the Biennial meeting, Society for Research in Child Development, Indianapolis.

Wiltz, N., & Klein, E. (1996, June). *Children's understanding of the structure of activities in child care settings.* Poster presented at Head Start's Third National Research Conference, Washington, DC.

Wiltz, N., & Klein, E. (1997, March). *Four year olds' perceptions of day care in developmentally appropriate and inappropriate child care centers.* Paper presented at the annual meeting of the American Educational Research Association, Chicago.

Yarrow, M. R., & Campbell, J. D. (1963). Person perception in children. *Merrill-Palmer Quarterly, 9,* 57-72.

Youniss, J. (1975). Another perspective on social cognition. In A. Pick (Ed.), *Minnesota symposia on child psychology* (Vol. 9). Minneapolis: University of Minnesota Press.

Zhang, X., & Sigel, I. (1994, April). *Two kindergarten programs and children's perceptions of school--A cross-cultural study.* Paper presented at the annual meeting, American Educational Research Association, New Orleans.

I

FOUNDATIONS FOR INSTRUCTION

AND PEDAGOGY

7

CONSTRUCTIVIST EDUCATION IN PRESCHOOL AND ELEMENTARY SCHOOL: THE SOCIOMORAL ATMOSPHERE AS THE FIRST EDUCATIONAL GOAL

Rheta DeVries
University of Northern Iowa

If we follow John Dewey (1916/1944) and Jean Piaget (1948/1973) in taking development as the aim of education, then our operationalization of this aim demands a description of experiences that optimally promote the child's development--physical, social, moral, and affective, as well as intellectual. However, as Dewey (1916/1944) pointed out, "education as such has no aims. Only persons, parents, and teachers, etc., have aims" (p. 107). Extending this to children, Dewey emphasized that, "An educational aim must be founded upon the intrinsic activities and needs of the given individual to be educated" (pp. 107-108). Dewey and Piaget converged in their emphasis on education that realizes the aim of development by capitalizing on children's interests and cooperating with children rather than coercing them.

Over more than 29 years, my colleagues and I have worked to articulate the aims of both teachers and children in education prompted by the goal of development. Inspired especially by Piaget's insight that development occurs through an active process of construction, we have called this *constructivist education* (DeVries & Kohlberg, 1987/1990; DeVries & Zan, 1994). Piaget's work has inspired us to articulate a general view of classroom experiences (Kamii & DeVries, 1975/1977), including traditional pretend play, block building, art, music, woodworking, and stories, as well as adding to these traditional activities new types of activities such as arithmetic debates (Kamii, 1985, 1989, 1993), group games (Kamii & DeVries, 1980), physical-knowledge activities (Kamii & DeVries, 1978/1993), and social and moral discussions (DeVries & Zan, 1994). The teaching of literacy follows a whole language emergent literacy approach. Subject matter goals are approached through an integrated curriculum organized around projects and themes such as making paper and simple machines (also see Morrow, chap. 10, this volume).

In recent work, we point out, however, that it is possible for a teacher to conduct physical knowledge activities and group games and use all the other activities mentioned above without implementing constructivist education in its most essential aspect. Activities, materials, and classroom organization by themselves are not the essence of this educational approach. Rather, the *first principle of constructivist education is to cultivate a sociomoral atmosphere in which respect is continually practiced*. By *sociomoral atmosphere*, I refer to the entire network of interpersonal relations in a classroom. These pervade every aspect of the child's experience in schools. Adults determine the nature of the sociomoral atmosphere in which the young child lives through daily interactions. The child's sociomoral atmosphere is made up, in large part, of the countless adult actions and reactions to the child that form the adult-child relationship. Peer relations also contribute to the sociomoral atmosphere, but the adult often establishes the framework of limits and possibilities of peer relations. The principle of mutual respect leads teachers and children to value fairness and cooperative methods of resolving social and moral conflicts in a community characterized by caring relationships. The principle of mutual respect also leads to democratic processes. This sociomoral atmosphere also may be viewed as an intellectual atmosphere in which the teacher's respect for children leads to valuing their discovery, invention, debate about ideas, and especially their wrong ideas and reasoning. Therefore, the conditions that promote sociomoral development are the same conditions that promote intellectual development. This sociomoral atmosphere must be the first principle because it is a necessary context for children's optimal development in all domains.

THE FOUNDATION IN PIAGET'S THEORY

Piaget pointed out that constructive activity flourishes best in a particular kind of relationship with adults. To understand this point, it is necessary to go back to Piaget's (1932/1965) book *The Moral Judgment of the Child*. In constructivist education, the conception of the teacher-child relationship is based on Piaget's (1932/1965) distinction between two types of morality and two types of adult-child relationships: one that promotes development and one that retards it.

Two Types of Morality

The first type of morality is a morality of obedience. Piaget called this *heteronomous*. The word *heteronomous* comes from roots meaning "regulation by others." Therefore, the individual who is heteronomously moral follows moral rules given by others out of obedience to authority having coercive power. Heteronomous morality is conformity to external rules that are simply accepted and followed without questions.

The second type of morality is autonomous. The word *autonomous* comes from roots meaning "self-regulation." By autonomy, Piaget did not mean simply *independence* in doing things for oneself without help. Rather, the individual who is autonomously moral follows moral rules of the self. These have a feeling of personal necessity. Autonomous morality is following internal convictions about the necessity of respect for persons.

Two Types of Adult-Child Relationships

These two types of morality correspond to two types of adult-child relationships. The first is coercive and promotes heteronomous morality. In this relation, the adult prescribes what the child must do by giving ready-made rules and specific instructions for behavior. In this relation, respect is a one-way affair. That is, the child is expected to respect the adult, and the adult uses authority to socialize and instruct the child. The adult controls the child's behavior. The child's reason for behaving is therefore external to her own reasoning and system of personal interests and values.

Certainly, the young child's relations to adults are necessarily and largely heteronomous. That is, for reasons of health and safety, as well as reasons stemming from practical and psychological pressures on the adult, parents and teachers must regulate children externally in many ways. The child is forced to submit to a whole set of rules whose reasons are incomprehensible to him. The obligations to eat certain foods at certain times, not touch certain delicate or important objects, and so on, can only be felt by the child as external because these obligations cannot be felt from within. When governed continually by the values, beliefs, and ideas of others, the child practices a submission that can lead to mindless conformity in both moral and intellectual spheres. In other words, so long as adults keep the child occupied with learning what adults want him to do and with obeying their rules, he will not be motivated to question, analyze, or examine his own convictions and construct his own reasons for following rules. In Piaget's view, following the rules of others through a morality of obedience will never lead to the kind of reflection necessary for commitment to a set of internal or autonomous principles of moral judgment. Piaget warned that coercion socialized only the surface of behavior and actually reinforces the child's tendency to rely on purely external regulation.

The teacher whose objective is obedience must be coercive, even if he or she attempts to foster obedience through positive means such as coaxing or bribing. Certainly heteronomous practices can be discussed as a continuum from outright hostile and punitive methods to sugar-coated coercion. What these all have in common is emphasis on obedient behavior. The teacher is clearly the authority, and children's behavior is regulated by what the teacher wants.

Piaget noted that extensive coercion can produce three unfortunate reactions: rebellion, mindless conformity, or calculation. When children are governed continually by the values, beliefs, and ideas of others, they practice a submission that can lead to mindless conformity in both moral and intellectual life. Such an individual may be easily led by any authority. Because of failure to develop a personal feeling about the necessity of moral rules, the obedient child may eventually rebel, openly or privately. By *calculation*, I refer to the child who follows adult rules only so long as under surveillance.

Piaget contrasts the heteronomous adult-child relationship with a second type that is characterized by mutual respect and cooperation. The adult returns the child's respect by giving him the possibility to regulate his behavior voluntarily. Piaget called this type of relation *autonomous* and *cooperative*. He argued that it is only by refraining from exercising authority that the adult opens the way for the child to develop a mind capable of thinking independently and creatively, to construct a decentered personality, and to develop moral feelings and convictions that take into account the best interests of all parties. By insisting that the child only follow rules, values, and guidelines given ready-made by others, the adult contributes to the development of an individual with a conformist mind, personality, and morality--an individual capable only of following the will of others. Tragically, obedience-based schools simply perpetuate qualities needed for submission.

Basically, what we are talking about is power. Kipnis (1976) has written a book called *The Powerholders* in which he emphasized that no one wants to be powerless. We all know about the use of power of men over women, by women who dominate men, or executives or political leaders who exercise raw power over people. Kipnis wrote about adults, but I would like to direct your attention to the issue of power in the classroom and especially to what happens when authoritarian teachers control children. As we look at some of Kipnis's research with adults, think about parallels in the teacher-child relationship.

One solid finding from the work of Kipnis and his colleagues is that when powerholders are successful in coercing others with strong tactics such as ordering, threatening, and getting angry, the belief of the powerholders is strengthened that he or she controls the other person. The powerholder demands. The other obeys. A second finding, is that to the extent powerholders believe they control others, they devalue those they believe they control. This sets the stage for exploitation of the less powerful. Do even well-meaning adults exploit children?

Heteronomy is a relation of unequal power in which the adult has it all. Cooperation is a relation in which power is equalized. Obviously, children and adults are not equals. However, when the adult is able to respect the child as a person with a right to exercise his will, one can speak about a certain psychological equality in the relationship. Piaget, of course, was not advocating complete freedom, and neither am I. Rather, the suggestion is that coercion is minimized to the extent possible and practical, and that what is most desirable is a mixture increasingly in favor of the child's regulation of his own behavior.

The method by which the autonomous relationship operates is that of cooperation. *Cooperating* means coordinating one's own feelings and perspective with a consciousness of another's feelings and point of view. The motive for such decentering and reciprocity begins in feelings of mutual affection and mutual trust, which become elaborated into feelings of sympathy and consciousness of intentions of others. The constructivist teacher appeals to cooperation rather than obedience by asking rather than telling, suggesting rather than demanding, and persuading rather than controlling (see also Hyson, this volume, for further discussion of the power of emotions in early development and education).

To clarify, it is important to say that heteronomy is often appropriate and certainly sometimes unavoidable in adult-child interactions. However, when it is necessary to coerce a child, it is important how one does so. The adult can be disrespectful by saying, "Do it because I say so," or respectful, by explaining why something is required in a way the child can understand.

When we talk about decentering, autonomy, and cooperation, we are talking about processes that are simultaneously cognitive and emotional. Adult coercion produces a constriction of children's minds, personalities, and feelings. Adult cooperation produces a liberation of children's possibilities for construction of their intelligence, their personalities, and their moral and social feelings (see also Stipek & Greene, chap. 3, this volume, for discussion of the potential impact of emotions on achievement).

The reader may rightly protest that no child's life is totally coercive or totally cooperative. I agree. The focus here is on how a predominance of coercion or cooperation influences children's development. However, each child presents a unique history of coercive and cooperative experiences. We are convinced that no child has experienced so much coercion that a cooperative teacher cannot ameliorate, at least to some extent, the effects of heteronomy. Each classroom, too, will provide a mixture of coercive and cooperative experiences. Again, our stance is optimistic. I believe that moral classrooms will promote moral development in children--as well as emotional, social, and intellectual development.

Peer Relations

According to Piaget, peer interactions are crucial to the child's construction of social and moral feelings, values, and social and intellectual competence. As suggested by the prior discussion of teacher-child relationships, I do not agree with those who interpret Piaget as saying that it is *only* in relations with peers that autonomous morality and intelligence develop.

However, peer relations are especially conducive to social, moral, and intellectual development for two reasons. The first is that peer relations are often characterized by an equality that can never be achieved in adult-child relations, no matter how hard that adult tries to minimize heteronomy. Peer relations can lead to recognition of the reciprocity implicit in relations of equality. This reciprocity can provide the psychological foundation for decentering and perspective-taking. However, autonomy can be violated in child-child interactions as well as in interactions with adults.

The second reason peer relations provide a good context for development is that seeing other children as like themselves results in a special feeling of interest that motivates peer contacts. These contacts are social, moral, and intellectual endeavors. In the course of peer interaction, children construct consciousness and differentiation of self and others, schemes of social reaction, and cooperation in thought and action. Conflict situations, discussed later, provide a special context in which children construct social and moral convictions.

The cooperative teacher-child relation is realized in part when the teacher engages with children as a peer. For example, in a board game, the teacher can take the role of a player alongside children. As a player, the teacher must also agree with children on the rules, abide by the rules, and accept their consequences. By giving up authority in this situation, the teacher promotes child autonomy. As a player, the teacher can ask direction from children and give them the instructional role. As a loser, the teacher can model an attitude of good sportsmanship, share feelings of disappointment, and demonstrate methods of coping with defeat.

THE SOCIOMORAL ATMOSPHERE IN PRACTICE

In our book *Moral Classrooms, Moral Children: Creating a Constructivist Atmosphere in Early Education* (DeVries & Zan, 1994), Betty Zan and I operationalized our definition of the sociomoral atmosphere by focusing on every aspect of the constructivist program. Let me outline some of the principal ways in which we think it is possible for a teacher to promote children's development by practicing mutual respect.

Conflict Resolution

Conflicts are inevitable in an active classroom where free social interaction occurs. In Piaget's theory, conflict plays a special role, serving to motivate reorganization of knowledge into more adequate forms. Piaget (1975/1985) stated that intraindividual conflict is the most influential factor in acquisition of new knowledge structures. Intraindividual conflict can be prompted in the case of interindividual conflict. Children's conflicts may thus be viewed as a possible source of progress in social, moral, and intellectual development.

In the face of a conflict between children, the constructivist teacher recognizes that the conflict belongs to the children and believes in the children's ability to solve their conflicts. The teacher takes conflicts seriously and devotes the necessary time to helping children work through to a solution satisfactory to both. The teacher's role may be described in 14 principles of teaching (see DeVries & Zan, 1994), including helping children talk and listen to each other, giving them the opportunity to suggest solutions, upholding the value of mutual agreement, giving children the opportunity to reject proposed solutions, and helping children repair their relationship.

Rule Making and Decision Making

A unique characteristic of constructivist education is that responsibility for much decision making is shared by everyone in the class community. Inviting children to make rules and decisions is one way the teacher can reduce heteronomy and promote autonomy.

Through reflecting on the problems of classroom life together, children can be led to realize that particular rules are necessary and why. For example, in one classroom of 5-year-olds, some children complained that others were mistreating the guinea pig. The teacher took the opportunity to suggest making rules. The following rules were made by the children:

*Ask Mrs. Wells before you get the guinea pig out.
*Be careful--no hurting the guinea pig.
*Don't squeeze, drop, or throw him. Hold him gently.
*Don't put him on the floor. Hold him.
*Don't pull his hair. Be gentle.
*Don't pull his hand or sit on him.
*Don't let him down in the house. Hold him in a blanket.
*Hold him like a baby.

This shows how the rules that make sense to children include many that adults would never think of proposing. Rules made by children are more powerful than rules given ready-made.

In guiding rule making by children, the constructivist teacher follows 10 principles of teaching (see DeVries & Zan, 1994). For example, he or she encourages children to discuss the reasons for the rules they propose; accepts children's ideas, words, and organization; cultivates the attitude that rules can be changed; and emphasizes that teachers must also follow rules. Rules made by children become a familiar part of the classroom culture. For example, rules can be written and posted on the wall or can be written and made into a book with children's illustrations. Such a book can be placed in the library as a resource to which children may add pages as the need arises for new rules. When children feel ownership of classroom rules, they also become concerned about rule breaking and remind each other of the rules.

Children can be involved in many other decisions besides rule making, including decisions about activities, classroom procedures, and special problems. The teacher should choose decision-making opportunities carefully, selecting those that are not too complex for children to deal with and those where the teacher will have no difficulty in accepting children's decisions. For example, a teacher of 4-year-olds asked them what they wanted to learn. Children suggested breaking glass, flower girls, and washing hands. The teacher then expanded the question about breaking glass into a unit on safety, in which she arranged a safe way in which children observe what happened when she broke glass (in a box covered with a towel). Children then learned why adults *freak out* and say to be careful with glass.

The question about flower girls was expanded into a focus on families, and a staff member who was planning her wedding was invited to talk about loving relationships, getting married, and starting a family. The group discussed the many different kinds of families represented in the class. They learned about family names and began to write initials of last names after first names. The dress-up center was equipped with lace, flowers, and fancy apparel, and the group decided there was no reason one could not have a flower boy, so both boys and girls enjoyed dressing up.

The question about washing hands came from a boy who was mystified as to why his parents and teachers told him to wash his hands so often. Because children cannot see germs, the teacher engaged the help of a microbiologist mother in making germs more visible. Petri dishes were prepared in systematic ways. For one, the teacher took fingernail clippings after children washed their hands. They passed around a dish on which everyone coughed, then another on which they coughed with hands over their mouths. One dish was merely exposed to air. When the mother brought the dishes back 2 days later, dramatic results were visible. One container had become so toxic that it had to be sealed and returned to the lab for disposal. Children discussed what they had done and saw what is meant by germs. This example illustrates how curriculum that stems from children's goals engages them more actively and results in more solid learning than curriculum stemming simply from the teacher's interests.

Children can be consulted about classroom procedures, such as how to regulate turns as Special Helper and sharing other responsibilities and privileges. In discussions about these decisions, the teacher must uphold values of fairness and equality.

Children can also be called on to make decisions about problems that arise in the classroom. For example, in a class of 5-year-olds, the school year began with problems at clean-up time. Some children were cleaning, but others were running around the class and playing. The children who cleaned complained about the children who did not clean, and no one was happy. At group time, the teacher asked what they should do about clean-up time. One of the children suggested having a circle before clean up. His idea was not clear, but in response to questions from the teacher, the idea was developed that children would then come to circle and choose which area to clean up. Another idea was that children who do not clean up sit out during activities the next day. They voted on these two options, and the clean-up circle got all but one vote. Eventually, the idea was elaborated into having the Special Helper take the responsibility of choosing who would clean up each area, and the children made necklaces with the names of the areas on them, which they wore during clean up. The clean-up circle solved the problem because it gave children a reason to stop their play and made easy the transition from activity time to clean-up time.

A teacher of 4-year-olds found a different kind of opportunity for children's decision making. She explained at group time that workers were on the playground with dangerous tools so that they could not go out there. She asked, "What should we do instead?" The children had many ideas and all were combined into an itinerary that took them on a shuttle bus ride across the university campus, then on a walk to see water fountains, to look for caterpillars and acorns, and finally to have a picnic lunch. Although the teacher could easily have planned an educational experience and presented it to the children, she preferred to give children the opportunity to take initiative, organize their experience together, and feel they had some control over their lives.

Voting

Voting is an integral part of the sociomoral atmosphere of the constructivist classroom. The rationale behind voting is threefold. First, voting is a process of self-regulation. When children exercise initiative to make group decisions, they feel in control of what happens in their classroom. They are motivated to formulate and express opinions. Through exchanging points of view, children may be persuaded to make new efforts to persuade others. Children have the opportunity to construct the idea of equality as they see that each person's opinion is valued and give equal weight in the decision-making process.

Second, children come to feel a sense of cooperative group purpose that transcends the needs and wants of the individual. Children can come to terms with the idea of majority rule yet develop sensitivity to minority positions.

Third, children have opportunities during voting to think about writing and number. Through conceptualizing and recording issues and votes, conviction is cultivated about the usefulness of written language. Similarly, as children count votes, decide which is more, and predict how many more votes are needed for a particular decision, they construct number in a personally meaningful context.

Certain precautions must be given about the use of voting. An issue should not be brought to vote if it is not of concern to children, if it concerns an individual rather than the entire class, or if a difference of opinion is not expected. It is important to conduct a thorough discussion of the pros and cons of the alternatives suggested. Children may need help in articulating an idea so that it is clear. If children do not understand what they are voting for, they will not make the connection between the process of voting as its result, and the outcome will seem arbitrary. We recommend against saying, "Raise your hands if" because young children experience too many problems with this procedure. They often vote more than once, responding simply to "Raise your hands," not understanding the mutual exclusiveness of the alternatives. When the teacher simply points and counts, children may not clearly realize their hand was counted. Better procedures include polling children by going around the circle and writing names of children (or slash marks) under the written option on the board or putting name cards in columns on the floor. Other issues with respect to voting are discussed in DeVries and Zan (1994).

Social and Moral Discussions

A moral dilemma is a situation in which competing claims, rights, or points of view can be identified. There is no clear right or wrong solution to a dilemma. Dilemmas for discussion can be hypothetical or real-life dilemmas from children's own experiences. Both types are useful because each has its strengths and weaknesses with respect to promoting children's development of sociomoral judgment.

Hypothetical dilemmas are not as emotionally laden as real-life dilemmas because children are not personally involved in the issue. There is some emotional distance between the children and the story. No one stands before the class angry, hurt, or bleeding. Impersonal issues can often be discussed more rationally, and it is safer to express opinions when no one will react personally or suffer a real consequence. Children can engage in "What if" thinking, and they can discuss what is right or wrong without the risk of hurting someone's feelings by failing to take a particular side in the issue.

However, real-life dilemmas offer certain advantages for discussion as well. Because they occur spontaneously, the situations are intimately familiar to children. The actors involved are themselves and fellow classmates, and the situations usually bear directly on the life of the classroom so children feel genuine concern about what happens. They also offer the advantage of having consequences children can recognize and evaluate fairly easily.

Children's literature is one source of hypothetical social and moral dilemmas. However, many children's stories have moral lessons but not moral dilemmas. For example, the story of the boy who cried wolf may be a good story to read to children, but it is not a dilemma. We have published three storybooks with dilemmas drawn from real classroom experiences (Goolsby & DeVries, 1993a, 1993b, 1993c).[1]

One story, entitled *When a Friend Steals* (Goolsby & DeVries, 1993c), tells about a boy, Jack, who comes to school hungry every day because he does not get up in the morning early enough to eat breakfast. His solution is to take items of food from his classmate' lunches while they are outside playing. Eventually, the teacher discovers him stealing food, and he agrees to talk about the problem with the class. Children tell Jack that they do not like having their food taken. The teacher in the story asks the children if they can think of any solutions to Jack's problem.

In discussion with children about this story, they suggest numerous solutions. For example, Jack can get up earlier, he can get an alarm clock or a rooster to wake him up, and he can pack a breakfast to eat in the car on the way to school. They also suggest things that the entire class can do, such as bringing extra food for Jack to eat in the morning and writing a note to his parents asking them to pack him a breakfast to eat at school. This leads to a moral question. Should Jack be punished for taking the children's food or should the children try to help Jack? Among 5-year-olds, we found a difference of opinion. One child is very clear that Jack should be punished because, "He takes stuff out of people's lunches." Another child, however, disagrees. He thinks that the children should help Jack. When asked why, he explains, "Because then he'll stop doing it. If they punish him, then he might take *two* things out of people's lunches." We were amazed that a 5-year-old could understand that punishment is ineffective and that only cooperative methods really work. This reflects the kind of reasoning we hope to promote in children.

Guidelines for conducting social and moral dilemma discussions focus on helping children recognize opposing points of view and think about how to resolve issues in ways fair to everyone involved (see DeVries & Zan, 1994).

---

[1]Three illustrated moral dilemma story books that can be read to and discussed with children can be ordered from: Regents' Center for Early Developmental Education, 107 Schindler Education Center, University of Northern Iowa, Cedar Falls, IA 50614-0616.

COOPERATIVE ALTERNATIVES TO DISCIPLINE

Constructivist teachers do not discipline children in the sense of controlling and punishing to socialize children. We do not train children in obedient self-control. Autonomous self-regulation is our goal rather than obedience to authority.

Nevertheless, children in constructivist classrooms are not allowed to *run wild*. Teachers must develop strategies for managing a classroom of children and coping with inevitable breakdowns in cooperation. Constructivist teachers are highly active in their efforts to facilitate children's self-regulation. Their activity, however, does not take unilateral forms of commanding or punishing. Rather, it takes cooperative forms to enable children to construct convictions and follow their own social and moral rules independent of adult coercion.

What we mean by *discipline* through cooperation is that the teacher cooperates in terms of the child's point of view. That is, the teacher establishes an atmosphere in which children feel that the teacher cares for them, enjoys being with them, and respects them by taking their feelings, interests, and ideas into account.

The challenge of socializing children is to figure out how to help them control impulses, think beyond the here and now, and become able to reflect on consequences of their actions. This involves decentering to consider views and feelings of others.

Piaget's (1932/1965) distinction between expiatory and reciprocity sanctions provides the basis for planning general responses to misdeeds. Specifically, the criterion of reciprocity leads constructivist teachers to types of sanctions that emphasize the social bonds broken by children's misdeeds. (See DeVries & Zan, 1994, for nine guidelines on how to protect children's autonomy and promote development by reducing the possibility that children will experience consequences as arbitrary and punitive.)

ACADEMICS

One misconception about constructivist education is that, because it includes play, it does not include academics. On the contrary, constructivist educators are serious minded about children's literacy, number and arithmetic, science, social studies, and fine arts. However, the constructivist teacher believes that a cooperative sociomoral atmosphere is crucial for optimal learning of academics. In most schools, the priority is academics, and learning is considered a matter of direct transmission. With such a view, the teacher easily falls into a heteronomous relation to children. However, with development as the priority and with learning considered a matter of child's construction, a heteronomous relation is not possible. In constructivist classrooms, academics are pursued with three characteristics of constructivist education and four general principles of teaching in mind.

Three Characteristics of Constructivist Education

Respect for children leads to the definition of constructivist education as active. Specifically, constructivist education:
1. Engages in child's interest
2. Inspires active experimentation with all its necessary groping and error
3. Fosters cooperation between adults and children and among children

These points are elaborated next.

Engaging Interest. Interest in activity is at the heart of constructivist education. Both Dewey and Piaget recommended that we start from the active powers of children. Without interest, the child would never make the constructive effort to make sense out of experience. Without interest in what is new, the child would never modify reasoning or values. Thus, methods aimed at promoting the constructive process must arouse the child's spontaneous interest that is inherent in constructive activity.

Encouraging Experimentation. By experimentation, we refer to the child's actions on physical objects, together with observations of the reactions of the objects to these actions as well as new actions informed by previous observations. Freedom to experiment with objects is an important part of the constructivist sociomoral atmosphere because it reflects the teacher's general attitude toward the child's interests and ways of knowing. This includes recognition of the importance of children's errors to their construction of knowledge. Up to the age of about 7 years, child is dominated by the physical, material, observable aspects of experience. The child's main interest in objects is what happens when he or she acts on them. In infancy and early childhood, especially, children construct knowledge of the physical world by acting on it. In the course of experimenting, according to Piaget, the child constructs not only physical knowledge but also intellectual power or intelligence.

The reactions of adults to children's experimentation are crucial to the sociomoral atmosphere. If experimentation is viewed as misbehavior, it may be punished. It is easy to squelch a child's experimental attitude. The challenge for the constructivist teacher is now to foster it.

Promoting Cooperation. By cooperation, we refer to operating in relation to another's behaviors, desires, ideas, and other psychological states. Piaget talked about the cognitive and moral importance of decentering from awareness of a single perspective. Cooperation is not possible unless children decenter to think about the perspective of the other. Cooperation, with its implicit reciprocity, is critical to the sociomoral atmosphere.

Four Principles of Teaching

Although life in a moral classroom creates general conditions for intellectual development, it is possible to establish a cooperative atmosphere with inadequate attention to academics. The challenge for constructivist teachers is to incorporate academics into classroom life and integrate developmental and academic objectives. In fact, we argue that the best teaching of academics is rooted in knowledge of developmental transformations in children's conceptions of academic content. In contrast to the traditional approach to academics that is centered on subject matter, the constructivist approach is centered on children's construction of subject matter (see also Liben & Downs, chap. 9, this volume). We offer the following guidelines for constructivist academics.

Creative Active Situations Related to Children's Purposes. A general constructivist principle is that the intellect develops through its exercise. Therefore, constructivist teaching of academics aims to promote children's active reasoning about content. The constructivist teacher fosters an atmosphere of thinking. This is accomplished through activities that appeal to children's interests and to their own purposes for thinking about academic content. We agree with advocates of the Whole Language approach to teaching literacy that the best activities are authentic rather than contrived (Manning, Manning, & Long, 1989). For example, when a child's purpose is to play a board game, interest is spontaneous in written rules, counting and number, and writing words and numerals. When children want to cook, they are inspired to figure out what the recipe says. To ensure that his friend gets to do a water activity with him, 4-year-old Cory writes Andrew's name on the sign-up list, going to the Special Helper list six times to copy the spelling one letter at a time. Andrew, a 5-year-old, consults the numbered list of Special Helpers by counting to find out how to write "12" on the calendar. Children are also inspired by interest to attend to the writing in stories and song and fingerplay charts. Physical-knowledge activities involving the movement of objects (elementary physics, especially mechanics) and changes in objects (elementary chemistry) inspire children to construct knowledge about the physical world. For example, using a ball on a string (as a pendulum bob) to knock down a target inspires children to construct specific spatial and causal knowledge about the reactions of a pendulum. Experimenting with using different amounts of flour, water, and oil to make playdough inspires children to construct specific knowledge about the influences of each substance on the playdough's consistency.

Foster Social Interactions Centered on Academics. The study of academics in a constructivist classroom is a very social affair. The general atmosphere of vitality and energy invested in the experience of life together suffuses academics as well as all other aspects of the program. Needing a menu for their pretend restaurant, children write items and prices: "Pepsi 4, 1 pizza 6, 2 pies 2." They keep score in Uno and bowling. Five-year-olds are motivated to write and memorize phone numbers in order to know how to call each other. In the Piggy Bank card game, children figure out how to collect sets of cards that add up to 5 and, later, to 10.

Encourage Children's Reasoning. To encourage children's reasoning, the constructivist teacher begins with what children know, respects constructive error, and teaches in terms of the kind of knowledge involved.

With regard to the latter point, Piaget's (1964, 1969, 1970) distinction among three kinds of knowledge is useful to teachers in thinking about activity time. These are physical knowledge, logico-mathematical knowledge, and conventional arbitrary knowledge.

Physical knowledge is based on experiences of acting on objects and observing their reactions. This may be action simply to find out what will happen, with no preconceived ideas. For example, a child may drop an object in water to find out whether it sinks or floats. A second type of action is to find out whether the object will react as one predicts. An example is the child who expects an object to sink before dropping it in the water. The source of physical knowledge is therefore partly in observing properties of the object. The child cannot construct physical knowledge without getting information from the object's reaction to actions on it. However, physical knowledge cannot be elaborated without logical reasoning: Knowledge about floating requires observation of various kinds of objects and inferences drawn from these observations.

Logico-mathematical knowledge is the result of reflective mental actions on objects that introduce characteristics that objects do not have into the individual's ideas about those objects. For example, number is not a property of any group of objects. Rather, it is a system of relationships created by the knower. That is, the *twoness* of a book and a cup does not exist in either object but in the mind of the knower who gives the objects this numerical characteristic. The knower would not have to see the two objects as two, but could simply see them as a book and a cup. The source of logico-mathematical knowledge is therefore the knower's own constructive processes.

Logico-mathematical knowledge is particularly important because intelligence can be described as a framework of potential logico-mathematical relationships. In early education, constructivist teachers recognize that the young child is still dependent on contexts involving physical action for construction of logico-mathematical relationships that constitute both knowledge and developing reasoning. (See DeVries & Zan, 1994, for an extended example and discussion of the way in which children construct logico-mathematical knowledge in the course of physical-knowledge activities; also see Kamii & DeVries, 1978/1993, for more specifics on physical-knowledge activities, including principles of teaching and classroom examples.)

The third kind of knowledge, conventional arbitrary knowledge,[2] is arbitrary truth agreed on by convention (such as that December 25 is Christmas Day in the United States) and rules agreed on by coordination of points of view (such as the rule that cars stop when a traffic light is red). The source of arbitrary conventional knowledge is other people through various means of communication.

Having made these distinctions, Piaget quickly pointed out that it is difficult to conceive of pure physical or conventional knowledge. Virtually all knowledge involves logico-knowledge construction. For example, the child who knows the color blue knows it in a system of similarities and differences with other colors. A child who knows that Paris is the capital of France has constructed a relation of spatial and logical inclusion.

These distinctions are useful because the constructivist teacher realizes that young children construct logico-mathematical knowledge particularly in the course of physical-knowledge activities. This leads the teacher to plan activities in which children can act on objects and reason about the relationships embedded in thinking about their reactions.

Second, the constructivist teacher uses the distinction among three kinds of knowledge to think about what kind of knowledge is involved in curriculum topics. For example, a study of dinosaurs involves a lot of knowledge that is arbitrary conventional in nature, such as the names of dinosaurs and the class names of carnivore, herbivore, and omnivore. Children can construct knowledge of herbivores, carnivores, and omnivores only if the teacher explains the meaning of these words. Although the names are arbitrary conventions, the classification of dinosaurs is logico-mathematical. That is, children have the possibility to understand the mutually exclusive nature of the subcategories herbivore, carnivore, and omnivore and their hierarchical relation to the superordinate category *dinosaurs*. In contrast, in sinking-floating activities, children are motivated to construct logico-mathematical relations to understand why objects react as they do. Although the teacher would not hesitate to inform children of the definition of *herbivore*, he or she would not tell children about the principle of specific gravity. Therefore, the three kinds of knowledge therefore help the teacher make decisions about educational goals and about how to intervene in children's in activities.

---

[2]Elsewhere the term used is *social knowledge*. However, this term has created some confusion in that some interpret social knowledge as knowledge about social relations. The term *conventional, arbitrary knowledge* more clearly communicates the intended meaning.

OTHER PROGRAM ASPECTS

With a concern for the sociomoral atmosphere throughout the school day, the constructivist teacher plans and conducts activity time (at least 1 hour in the morning and another hour in the afternoon) in ways that promote children's development. Similarly, this focus leads to certain considerations for organizing lunch time and nap/rest time (see DeVries & Zan, 1994).

EXAMPLES OF MUTUAL RESPECT IN THE CLASSROOM

Now we turn to the practical meaning of these ideas. What does *mutual respect* look like in the classroom? Segments of interaction from Terry Anderson's Project Construct[3] classroom in Robinson School in Kirkwood, Missouri, illustrate this idea, including a bit from the first-grade year and then more of the same group that continues with Terry in second grade. These segments illustrate how Terry respects children by giving them choice, responsibility, and control. One way to express the idea of teachers respecting children is to say that it is a "way of being with" children. Notice the various ways in which Terry is a companion/guide who engages children's interests, consults them, helps them develop their own purposes, and generally minimizes her role as the authority while not being permissive. In the first segment, you will get a glimpse of Terry's class when they were first graders. It is March of that year. This is a small piece of the first group time of the morning when they discuss and list the many activities taking place in the classroom on that day. Terry called these *invitations*. A wide variety of invitations are available from which children can choose.

The overarching theme at this time is simple machines, and many of the activities link back in some way to this theme. The list includes:

Ramp letters (children are writing letters to inquire whether various public buildings have wheelchair accessibility);
Wheelchair (they are taking turns riding and pushing a wheelchair up and down a ramp in the hallway, finding out what it is like to use one);
Projects (many children are pursuing individual interests);
Games (they are experimenting and designing games that include inclines and ramps, and keeping scores in these games as part of their

---

[3]Constructivist education in Missouri is called Project Construct and is advocated by the State Department of Elementary and Secondary Education for prekindergarten through second grade (see Murphy & Goffin, 1992).

math time) (See Kamii & DeVries, 1980, for the rationale behind using group games in the constructivist curriculum);

Bicycle (they are taking a bicycle apart, examining its many parts, and one child had the idea of grouping like parts together in labeled envelopes);

Secret messages (they have books on codes, their own code, and a pulley strung across the room that they use to send secret messages to each other).

The following segment during the same group time illustrates Terry's respect for children's initiative:

Terry: Allison, tell me what it was that I was going to say. You guessed it. You read my mind.

A: Read with a friend.

Terry: Would you spend some time today, maybe about 15 minutes, sometime today when you take a break from what you're doing and read with a friend. And you and your friend decide what it is you want   to read. And a good idea might be to choose someone you could help   or who could help you, so you've got a good pair. Anything else?

Children: No.

Terry: I think we've got about everything that we can think of around the room.

Child: I've got one.

Terry: Oh, Allison has something.

A: Easel.

Terry: The easel. You know what? I think with everything else that's available, I think we'll leave the easel closed today. We've got so many things going on--or did you have something in mind that you needed for it?

A: Machine painting on the easel.

Terry: Machine painting?

A: Yeah.

Other children: Yeah!

Terry: OK, Cindy, would you open the easel? Some of the kids want to do that, so I'll put that up here (writes on the board).

Terry: Ok, does everybody have in their head, what they are going to be working on?

Children: Yeah.

This segment is a partial illustration of the constructivist sociomoral atmosphere. Terry's attitude is collegial with children. She communicates that the room and its activities belong to them and that they are responsible for organizing and making decisions about how they spend their time so they accomplish their work. When she gives an assignment, she presents it as a request--to read with a friend. She leaves children the choice of with whom to read, what to read, and when to read. Terry is responsive to children's ideas and suggestions. She acquiesces when Allison wants the easel to make a machine painting. She is respectful when one child expresses the concern that to write a sloppy copy before the final copy is a waster of paper. A child's suggestion to recycle seems to satisfy the objection. It is clear that Terry has confidence that children can and will take responsibility for their learning.

During the activity period, Terry circulates as the children go about their work. Some children bring their journals and read them to her, and she responds verbally and in writing. She helps one child with his report on rocks. She listens to children practicing the reading of a story so they can read it to the kindergarten children. She asks one child if she wants to ask another child to help with editing or whether she wants the teacher to help her. She occasionally asks questions such as, "Would you like to see *beaver* dictionary-style?" She asks permission from a child to make a correction on his paper. Children come to complain that Danny is not doing anything for their group project. Terry suggests they go to the Peace Table and figure out what can be done. Later the children come to share how they settled the problem. On the wall is a list entitled: "Things We Learned about Ramps and Rollers." This list reads as follows:

Crayons are faster than markers.
Small things are faster than big things.
A crayon is faster than the #13 big pool ball.
Things go down the ramp faster than they go up.
Things that have more weight go slower.
When the ramp is low, the heavier things go faster.
When the ramp is high, smaller things go faster.
When you have two ramps opposite each other and one
is high and one is low and you send a ball down the
higher ramp, it goes up the other ramp.
The higher it is, the farther up the ramp it goes.

As you see here, a constructivist curriculum contains many activities that are not unique, but nevertheless are important to constructivist education. These include an integrated curriculum in which academics are embedded in projects that children pursue out of their own interests and purposes, a whole language approach to literacy, science activities that include opportunities for experimentation, math experiences that are meaningful to children, and extensive opportunities for peer interaction.

The class meeting is an important time in which one child takes charge and the teacher sits with the group. "If you have something for class meeting, would you sign up?" Here is how it begins one day in December during the second-grade year.

Terry: Is there anybody else who has something for the class meeting-that they want to bring up? Did you, Blake? Kelly? Blake did? Do you want me to put your name on there? (When he nods, she adds his name to the list on the board).

Terry: (To Evan) You're in charge? Greg asked you to be in charge?

Evan: yeah.

Terry: OK. OK, I'm going to have a seat (unintelligible) (sits in the middle of the group) OK, Evan's in charge, so he's our leader for the meeting.

Allison: See, the bookshelf people are not ever taking care of the bookshelves. They're always like helping in the art center or they're helping in the writing center. They're never helping to rearrange the bookshelves.

Discussion ensues, and Evan writes suggestions about what to do and takes a vote. They decide to develop a book center as a place where they could leave books they are reading and come back to them. A committee later redesigns the whole center and writes rules for using it.

The sociomoral atmosphere of mutual respect provides the general context in which academic work occurs. Within the general context of building pyramids with sugar cubes, children calculate the number of cubes used in pyramids with bases of different sizes. Terry also focuses for brief periods on practice in calculation. She regularly engages small groups in mental math, which she organizes as an enjoyable social activity. Below is a segment in which a disagreement occurs, and children revise their calculations to resolve the contradiction.

Terry: Let's see. (Writes) $896 - 429 =$

Greg: Cool! I like this!

Children: (Reflect, then raise hands)

Terry: Oh, everybody has it. John?

John: 477

Greg, Les and Ian: Disagree!

Terry: OK, Greg.

Greg: 473

Lee, Ian, and John: Disagree!

Greg: (Changes his mind) 463

Terry: 463?
Greg: Yeah.
Terry: (Erases and changes) All right. Lee.
Lee: 473
Terry: Ian
Ian: Oh, I agree with Greg.
Terry: Who had the--John, you want to tell us how you did it?
John: I took that (400) from that (800).
Terry: (Writes) 800 - 400
Ian, Lee, and Greg: That's what I did.
John: Then I did 90 take away 20.
Chorus: That's what I did.
Terry: So that gives you--?
John: 70
Terry: OK.
John: Then 6 minus 9 - 3.
Greg: Negative 3.
John: No, 3--Oh, yeah, negative 3.
Terry: OK, negative 3, so that gives us--?
John: No, I think it's 467.
Ian: I think it's 460.
Terry: So you want to change yours to 467?
Ian: I want to -- 470.
Lee: 470.
Terry: Is this (473) yours?
Lee: Yeah.
Terry: You want yours 470. OK. So then we had 470. So let me
         write that and then a negative 3.
Ian: See, it's 473 with the negative 3.
Terry: See, if you look--
Ian: (Jumps up) OK, I agree with John?
Lee: (Jumps up) I agree with John. See, the minus is off of 70.
Greg: I agree with John.
Ian: I changed the 3 and the 7 around.
Lee: I just didn't see it right.
Terry: OK, are you sure?
Lee: I agree with him now.
Terry: Everybody agrees with this (467)?
All: Yeah.
Terry: Well, you know, it's OK because when we have to explain
         something, sometimes we find our own mistakes when we do
         that. That's why it's good to explain things. OK, let's try
         another.

Now let us take a look at a literacy activity during the first-grade year. The teacher has made a transparency of a page from the phone book. She has the overhead projector on the floor aimed at the wall.

Terry: Oh, that's a good idea. Yeah, great idea. Do you see some-- what does this look like to you?
Child: Lots of numbers.
Terry: Lots of numbers.
Child: Lots of words.
Terry: Lots of words. Have you ever seen anything like that before?
Child: No.
Carrie: Man.
Terry: What does it look like to you?
Kelly: Wow!
Kelly: All the S's and all the Rs.
Terry: Oh, look what Kelly noticed. She noticed a lot of Rs.
Ellen: And some Es.
Terry: And she notices a lot of S's.
Carrie: A lot of 7s.
(They talk for about 2 more minutes.)
Terry: What are those?
Ellen: Phone numbers.
Terry: Could these be phone numbers, do you think?
Ellen: Yeah.
Kelly: They are like (unintelligible).
Ellen: Eight, two, one, six--
Terry: Oh! So these might--
Ellen: Phone number.
Terry: These must be phone numbers. All right, so these must be phone numbers. So, what do you think this is?
Ellen: It's a--
Barry: Pho--oh, I know, I know.
Ellen: It's the--out of here (points to phone book)
Barry: Ah.
Terry: It's a page out of the phone book. You guessed it.
Ellen: I want to show you something.
Terry: Kelly even said that she saw schools. Show us the school word you noticed.
Kelly: School, school, school.
Terry: Look what she--Find another school and make it stand out a little bit, Kelly. Make--OK, find another school word. How about another one?
Kelly: (Laughs)

Ellen: I see one.
Barry: I see one, I think.
Terry: Look at that!
Ellen: I see one. It's right up there.
Terry: Ah, so, Kelly, how about if you take this pointer--
Ellen: I'll show you.
Terry: --and start at the top where the top school. And can you find a lot of schools?
Kelly: (Points to the words on the screen)
Terry: One, two--
Kelly: (Unintelligible)
Terry: We might. (To Ellen and Barry) Did you hear what Kelly just said? She said we might find our school in here...
Ellen: I see it! I see it!
Terry: Robinson School. Where could it be?
Ellen: (Comes closer to the screen)
Kelly: (Steps us to the screen and points) Right here.
Ellen: I'll show you.
Terry: You were close, you were close.
Kelly and Ellen: (Try to find)
Terry: Do you see it, Barry?
Barry: I see it, I see it, I saw it!
Terry: You found our school.
Barry: Robinson, Robinson, Robinson--
Terry: Look at that. It was the phone book. Did you know that our school was in the phone book?

The children notice the different words for elementary, high school, and junior high. They go on to find Saint John's Mercy Medical Center and the address and phone number where Kelly's mother works. One child says her mother is a dental hygienist and wants to find dentists. They know the yellow pages are organized differently than the white pages. They identify the words *carpet* and *auto*, and want to find their own names. They consult the alphabet trip on the board to figure out whether to go forward or backward in the book from one letter to another. Terry eventually leaves them to continue the exploration on their own. They spend 45 minutes in this activity. At the end of activity time, Terry returns:

Terry: I think we've got some kids who are really interested in this phone book. Can you believe all the--
Kelly: I love it. I love doing it.

DOES CONSTRUCTIVIST EDUCATION ATTAIN THE AIM OF DEVELOPMENT?

To begin to answer this question, I compared sociomoral atmosphere and sociomoral development in three 5-year-old public school classes in working-class neighborhoods in Houston, Texas. The three programs were constructivist, eclectic, and behaviorist. The behaviorist program was DISTAR, reflecting the assumption of knowledge as accumulated bits of information coming from outside the individual to the inside in unmodified form. The teacher followed programmed lessons with children in fast-paced drills. In contrast to the constructivist program, DISTAR education suppressed children's interests, taught right answers and rejected children's errors, maintained a heteronomous teacher-child relationship, and prohibited children's peer interaction in the classroom. The eclectic program shared some characteristics of both constructivist and behaviorist programs.

To assess sociomoral classroom atmosphere, the three teachers were videotaped for 2 entire days wearing a wireless microphone. To assess children's sociomoral development, they were observed in pairs in two seminaturalistic situations. The first involved playing a board game. Children in pairs were taught to play a homemade path game in which players took turns rolling a die and moving markers along a path to see who got to the end first. In the second situation, children divided a set of stickers, having only one that both children liked.

Using transcripts and videotapes, researchers coded teachers and children. Analysis of the large volume of data was guided by Selman's (1980; Selman & Schultz, 1990) work on the development of interpersonal understanding. He conceptualized two aspects of interpersonal understanding--negotiation strategies and shared experiences. Three levels of interpersonal understanding are based on Piaget's notion of perspective taking. A detailed coding manual defines categories of interaction at the three levels.

Negotiation strategies describe interaction when the interpersonal dynamic is in disequilibrium or tension. The tension may be mild, as when one asks another a question, or strong, as when one attacks another physically or verbally. Level 0 is unreflective, impulsive exercise or raw will or giving in to raw will. At this level, negotiation strategies are primarily physical actions to get what one wants or allow oneself to be overwhelmed by another's physical or verbal intimidation. Examples are grabbing the other or yelling to emotionally intimidate the other. Level 1 negotiation strategies are unilateral expressions of the self's needs or wishes. This is observable as verbal control of the other through communication of the self's own needs or wishes without consideration of the other's needs or wishes. Examples are assertions, demands, threats, test questions, and criticisms. Level 2 negotiation reflects consideration of an other's needs or wishes through an effort to coordinate these with one's own. Psychological influence is used to change the other's mind. This involves attending to the other's needs or wishes and trying to coordinate these with those of the self. At Level 2, the self is still trying to attain the Self's goals, however. Examples are making a suggestion, encouraging the other's self-regulation, explaining with reasons, and raising issues of fairness. Level 3 negotiation strives for mutual understanding through shared reflection. Here we have an exchange of points of view to collaboratively change both self's and other's wishes to pursuit of mutual goals. The general orientation is concern with maintaining a long-term relationship. Examples (not observed in the children) are encouraging children to discuss and resolve interpersonal conflicts, presenting a problem to the group of children for solution, stating different points of view, and encouraging fair processes.

One way to summarize these levels is to say that at Level 0, people are viewed as nonpsychological objects. At Level 1, people are to command or control. At Level 2, people are to persuade. At Level 3, people are to understand and be understood by.

Shared experiences describe interaction when an interpersonal dynamic is in equilibrium. Equilibrium is present when an interaction is characterized by an absence of tension, precluding the necessity for resolution through negotiation. The equilibrium may be weak, as when one briefly acknowledges the other, or strong, as when two laugh together at a shared secret. Level 0 shared experience is unreflective or impulsive and operates by a process of contagious enthusiasm. It is poorly regulated and can get out of hand. Examples are children having a burping contest or jumping together on a bed, higher and higher. Level 1 involves more conscious sharing, but remains unilateral as the other's perspective is not taken into account. It operates by a kind of expressive enthusiasm (e.g., "I want to play Superman!"). Level 2 involves reciprocal sharing of the other's perspectives with one's own. There is a conscious feeling of commonality with the other. For example, two children might reminisce over a past shared experience: "Remember when we saw the elephants at the zoo?" Level 3 involves mutual collaboration of the other's concerns that are considered as important as one's own in the context of long-term relationship. The self-disclosure in sharing life stories is an example.

These levels may be summarized by saying that Level 0 is contagion, Level 2 is reciprocal sharing and conscious commonality, and Level 3 is mutual sharing. The advantage of Selman's conceptualization is that it permits assessment of interpersonal understanding at the moment of interaction.

Analysis of the teachers' enacted interpersonal understanding showed that the three teachers created different sociomoral atmospheres in their classes. The constructivist teacher had a much higher percentage of overall shared experiences and much higher percentages of Levels 2 and 3 negotiations. The DISTAR teacher engaged with children almost totally at Level 1 Negotiation (telling, demanding, asking test questions, etc.). The picture of the eclectic teacher was in between that of the constructivist and DISTAR teachers. In general, the constructivist teacher was distinctly different from the other two teachers. She created a classroom atmosphere with a friendly social dynamic in which she shared experiences with children and negotiated with them in ways that reflected higher levels of perspective-taking (see DeVries, Haney, & Zan, 1991, for details of this study).

Statistically significant differences appeared in interpersonal understanding of the children in these three classrooms. Children from all three groups expressed their own desires and tried to control the other (Level 1). However, children from the constructivist classroom were more actively engaged with one another. They had more friendly, shared experiences with each other and not only negotiated more but negotiated more successfully. Constructivist children used a greater variety of different strategies and resolved more conflicts than children from the other two classrooms. DISTAR children tended to try to resolve conflicts by overwhelming the other physically or emotionally and, in general, related socially in less complex ways. Moreover, children from the constructivist classroom used significantly more strategies reflecting consideration for the other's point of view and efforts to achieve mutually satisfactory interaction (Level 2). Further, in harmonious shared experiences, children from the constructivist classroom were also more reciprocal (e.g., sharing secrets and recalling past shared experiences) than children from the other two classrooms (who engaged in much more impulsive silliness). It is clear that the leading edge in development of interpersonal understanding is more advanced among children from a constructivist program than among children from a DISTAR program. The constructivist group is also generally more advanced than children from an eclectic program whose development appears to be midway between that of constructivist and DISTAR groups (DeVries, Reese-Learned, & Morgan, 1991).

Another important study addressing the question of the effects of constructivist education was reported by Pfannenstiel (1997) and Pfannenstiel, Schattgen, and Zguta (1997). Their study of 40 constructivist and 40 traditional kindergarten classrooms showed, among other findings, that children in constructivist classrooms scored significantly higher on standardized mathematics tests, writing functions, and forms of reading. These results suggest that constructivist education does achieve its objective of promoting children's development and learning. When children experience on a regular basis an environment in which the teacher is predominantly unilateral (Level 1) and in which social interaction is discouraged, children's development and ability to enact a higher level of interpersonal understanding is more limited than when the children experience a cooperative environment in which they are interpersonally active. When children experience on a regular basis an environment in which the teacher practices cooperation (Levels 2 and 3 interpersonal understanding) and encourages both children's community and conflict resolution, children develop greater capacities for intimacy and negotiations with others.

CONCLUSION

The basic theme developed in this chapter is that an important part of creating an effective learning environment is the establishment of a cooperative sociomoral atmosphere. Piaget's constructivist theory suggests that this atmosphere is the best context for academic learning as well as for emotional, social, moral, intellectual, and personality development. The most essential aspect of the constructivist sociomoral atmosphere is a cooperative teacher-child relationship characterized by mutual affection and mutual respect. The constructivist teacher promotes children's development by engaging them in conflict resolution, rule and decision making, voting, and social and moral discussion.

Research is beginning to show that interpersonal development and school achievement are significantly more advanced in children from constructivist classrooms compared with children from traditional or didactic classrooms. These promising findings suggest that we need more research of this type to better understand the effects of constructivist early education.

REFERENCES

DeVries, R., Haney, J., & Zan, B. (1991). Sociomoral atmosphere in direct-instruction, eclectic, and constructivist kindergartens: A study of teacher' enacted interpersonal understanding. *Early Childhood Research Quarterly, 6,* 449-471.

DeVries, R., & Kohlberg, L. (1987/1990). *Constructivist early education: Overview and comparison with other programs.* Washington, DC: National Association for the Education of Young Children.

DeVries, R., Reese-Learned, H., & Morgan, P. (1991). Sociomoral development in direct-instruction, eclectic, and constructivist kindergartens: A study of children's enacted interpersonal understanding. *Early Childhood Research Quarterly, 6,* 474-517.

DeVries, R., & Zan, B. (1994). *Moral classrooms, moral children: Creating a constructivist atmosphere in early education.* New York: Teachers College Press.

Dewey, J. (1916/1944). *Democracy and education.* New York: Macmillan.

Goolsby, L., & DeVries, R. (1993a). *When a friend eats more than her share.* Cedar Falls, IA: Regents' Center for Early Developmental Education.

Goolsby, L., & DeVries, R. (1993b). *When a friend refuses to share.* Cedar Falls, IA: Regents' Centre for Early Developmental Education.

Goolsby, L., & DeVries, R. (1993c). *When a friend steals.* Cedar Falls, IA: Regents' Center for Early Developmental Education.

Kamii, C. (1985). *Young children reinvent arithmetic: Implications of Piaget's theory.* New York: Teachers College Press.

Kamii, C. (1989). *Young children continue to reinvent arithmetic: Second grade.* New York: Teachers College Press.

Kamii, C. (1993). *Young children continue to reinvent arithmetic: Third grade.* New York: Teachers College Press.

Kamii, C., & DeVries, R. (1975/1977). Piaget for early education. In M. Day & R. Parker (Eds.), *Preschool in action* (2nd ed., pp. 363-420). Boston: Allyn & Bacon.

Kamii, C., & DeVries, R. (1978/1993). *Physical knowledge in preschool education: Implications of Piaget's theory.* New York: Teachers College Press.

Kamii, C., & DeVries, R. (1980). *Group games in early education: Implications of Piaget's theory.* Washington, DC: National Association for the Education of Young Children.

Kipnis, D. (1976). *The powerholders.* Chicago: University of Chicago Press.

Manning, M., Manning, G., & Long, R. (1989). Authentic language arts activities and the construction of knowledge. In G. Manning & M. Manning (Eds.), *Whole language beliefs and practices, K-8* (pp. 93-97). Washington, DC: National Education Association.

Murphy, D., & Goffin, S. (1992). *Project Construct, a curriculum guide: Understanding the possibilities.* Jefferson City, MO: Missouri Department of Elementary and Secondary Education.

Pfannenstiel, J. (1997). *Executive summary, kindergarten learning environments and student achievement: A study of constructivist and traditional teaching practices.* Columbia, MO: Missouri Department of Elementary and Secondary Education and Project Construct National Center.

Pfannenstiel, J., Schattgen, S., & Zguta, N. (1997). *Evaluating the effects of pedagogy informed by constructivist theory: A comprehensive comparison of student achievement across different types of kindergarten classrooms.* Paper presented at the annual meeting of the National Association for the Education of Young Children, Anaheim, CA.

Piaget, J. (1932/1965). *The moral judgment of the child.* New York: The Free Press.

Piaget, J. (1948/1973). *To understand is to invent.* New York: Grossman. (First published in Prospects, UNESCO Quarterly Review of Education.)

Piaget, J. (1964). Development and learning. In R. Ripple & V. Rockcastle (Eds.), *Piaget rediscovered: A report of the conference on cognitive studies and curriculum development* (pp. 7-20). Ithaca, NY: Cornell University Press.

Piaget, J. (1969/1970). *Science of education and the psychology of the child.* New York: Viking Compass.

Piaget, J. (1975/1985). *The equilibrium of cognitive structures: The central problem of intellectual development.* Chicago: University of Chicago Press.

Selman, R. (1980). *The growth of interpersonal understanding.* New York: Academic press.

Selman, R., & Schultz, L. (1990). *Making a friend in youth.* Chicago: University of Chicago Press.

8

EVERYDAY MATHEMATICAL KNOWLEDGE: ASKING YOUNG CHILDREN WHAT IS DEVELOPMENTALLY APPROPRIATE

Herbert P. Ginsburg
Sandra Pappas
Kyoung-Hye Seo
Teachers College, Columbia University

What type of mathematics learning should preschool and kindergarten children engage in? What topics, if any, should young children be taught beyond simple counting and recognition of basic shapes like circles and squares? The basic issue is whether organized mathematics learning should be considered a key goal for early childhood education--a vital part of the preschool and kindergarten curriculum.

At present, there are few definitive answers to questions like these. In fact, in the recent past, there has been considerable controversy about what is "developmentally appropriate" for early mathematics education. There seem to be at least three points of view--what we call *play*, *drill*, and *challenge*. In the play group, so to speak, the belief is that *young children* (which is our shorthand for preschoolers and kindergartners) should not be exposed to academic subject matter, that cognitive immaturity places "barriers"[1] (Elkind, 1998) in the way of their learning mathematics, and that children's main concern during the preschool years (and early childhood educators' main focus) should be play and social-emotional development. The drill perspective, which seems

---

[1]For example, Elkind (1998) focused on "three major obstacles to effective math, science, and technology instruction in early childhood," including "the transductive nature of young children's thinking. These obstacles are not insurmountable but must be addressed to engage in meaningful and effective early childhood education" (pp. 12-13). The general tone of Elkind's paper involves reference to impediments to learning, not to opportunities for teaching. He largely ignored the very competent work in mathematics and science that children can demonstrate under facilitating conditions.

to be influential among parents of all social class groups anxious for their children to succeed at school, has produced scores of workbooks and drill sheets that can be purchased at K-Mart and similar educational concerns. The challenge group, in which we hereby disclose our membership, rejects the views of both the play group and the K-Mart drill team and asserts its belief that young children can learn, enjoy learning, do not need to be made ready to learn, and should learn a good deal more challenging mathematics than they do now.

As if this is not enough controversy to begin with, there is another long-standing dispute, namely, possible social class and ethnic differences in mathematical competence. We know that in elementary school and beyond, lower class children generally, and African Americans and Latinos in particular, demonstrate lower academic achievement than do their middle-class peers (Natriello, McDill, & Pallas, 1990; Oakes, 1990). Does a difference in basic mathematical competence manifest itself as early as the preschool and kindergarten years? If so, what is the nature of the difference? Does it indicate weakness, deficiency, or difference? Are poor children a little slower than their middle-class peers or do they suffer from some basic cognitive deficiencies? If there are differences, what causes them? Do poor children need special programs in preschool and kindergarten? Do they need extra help to prepare them for school? If so, what kind of help is developmentally appropriate?

Current psychological research on the development of children's mathematical thinking provides some useful information concerning these questions about developmentally appropriate mathematics learning and the competence of poor children. Consider first the issue of children's mathematical competence.

There is consensus, we think, on the proposition that, despite evident limitations, young children possess a relatively powerful informal mathematics (Ginsburg, Klein, & Starkey, 1998). Even babies possess an informal mathematics. They are born with some fundamental notions of quantity. They can see that there is more here than there or that this has the same amount as that. They realize that adding makes more and subtracting makes less. Although crude and effective only with very small numbers of objects, their judgments seem to be genuinely quantitative. Much of this occurs before the onset of language and extensive cultural transmission. Like crawling or perceiving, the fundamentals of mathematical cognition have a strong basis in human biological endowment (Dehaene, 1997).

The social environment provides young children in virtually all cultures with a rich counting system, which can serve as a basic tool for mathematical thinking. Children are active in making good use of this environment. They learn the counting words. More important, from the outset, children's counting employs mathematical principles of one-to-one correspondence, order, and cardinality (Gelman & Gallistel, 1978). To a large extent, early counting is an abstract, principled activity.

Before entering school, children spontaneously develop operational definitions of addition and subtraction (Ginsburg, 1989). Addition is combining sets and then counting the elements to get a sum; subtraction is taking away a subset from a larger set and then counting the elements to get a remainder. Of course there are important limitations to children's approach to addition and subtraction. They can deal only with small numbers and their methods are sometimes less than fully efficient (e.g., when they add by counting all rather than by counting on from the larger number). Nevertheless, over time, young children refine these strategies, making them more efficient and extending their use from concrete objects to imaginary ones.

Further, for young children, addition and subtraction are not simple mechanical routines or mindless algorithms. These operations make sense. Adding is interpreted in terms of increments and subtracting in terms of decrements (Brush, 1978). However, young children's reasoning about these operations suffers from some basic limitations. For example, they have difficulty understanding *reversibility* (Piaget, 1952)--the conceptual links between addition and subtraction. Nevertheless, their thinking incorporates the beginnings of what could be a sound understanding of basic mathematical ideas.

In brief, the acquisition of informal mathematics is a constructive process guided by biology, physical environment, and culture. Biology provides an elementary framework for appreciating number--for perceiving differences in quantity and even the effects of quantitative transformations. The physical world is replete with quantitative phenomena and events; these are so pervasive that they often go unnoticed (Ginsburg & Seo, 1999). The social environment provides children in all cultures with a basic tool for mathematical thinking--the system of counting words. Before entrance to school, children exploit the opportunities offered by the physical and social environments, constructing an informal mathematics. Children count and reason about number in their own principled ways that do not simply copy or mimic formal mathematics. At the same time, children's informal mathematics is not as sophisticated, powerful, or abstract as formal mathematics.

Although the research offers valuable insights into mathematical competence, it is incomplete. Despite some exceptions (see e.g., Hunting's [1999] work on sharing or Clements' [1999] work on geometry), much of the available psychological research on young children's mathematics is limited in focus, seldom straying beyond the three c's--conservation (and related Piagetian and neo-Piagetian investigations), counting, and calculation.[2] The research

---

[2]This is even true of the few studies investigating young children's mathematical competence in everyday contexts (Court, 1920; Saxe, Guberman, & Gearhart, 1987; Wagner & Walters, 1982). These studies mainly focus on the use of counting and calculation in everyday activities.

generally does not provide much information concerning the broad range of children's mathematical abilities, motivations, and interests. Why? With few exceptions, researchers have failed to employ naturalistic observation to investigate children's mathematical thinking. Without using some form of this method, one cannot learn a great deal about children's everyday, spontaneous mathematical interests, motivations, and competence. Of course information of this type would be enormously important for understanding what kind of mathematics education is developmentally appropriate for young children.

What does research have to say about the second claim often advanced in early childhood education--namely, that poor children suffer some kind of weakness in early mathematical thinking? Unfortunately, there has been relatively little research on social class and ethnic variation in young children's mathematical abilities, and the little research that does exist (e.g., Ginsburg & Russell, 1981; Hughes, 1986) does not tell a clear and consistent story.

Our own reading of the literature (Ginsburg et al., 1998) is that children in many different cultures and social circumstances possess the fundamentals of informal mathematics. Even when provided with little or no education, children in some cultures nevertheless invent useful strategies for dealing with everyday mathematical problems (e.g., those involving calculation with money, Carraher, Carraher, & Schliemann, 1985). We believe--and we are not sure that others would agree--that poor children possess the same basic, informal mathematical abilities as middle-class children. Yet many of these abilities, especially in the very poor seem to develop at a slower rate than in children from more economically advantaged groups. Although that is currently our view, we recognize that the evidence is incomplete and that we require a good deal more research to provide deeper understanding of possible social class and ethnic differences in mathematical thinking.

In brief, the research shows that young children exhibit a surprisingly powerful, yet limited, mathematical competence. At the same time, the research does not provide sufficient information concerning the broad range of children's mathematical abilities, motivations, and interests, and it does not provide consensus on the nature and extent of possible social class and ethnic differences in mathematical thinking.

In this chapter, we report research bearing on two key issues relevant for developing early childhood mathematics education. The first is the nature of children's everyday mathematical abilities, motivations, and interests; the second is the extent and nature of social class and ethnic group differences in early mathematical ability. We describe two types of research. The first involves naturalistic observation describing the mathematical activities spontaneously undertaken by 4- and 5-year-old children--African American, Latino, and White from lower, middle, and upper class groups--during their free play. This type of research allows us to determine the mathematical content of children's everyday activities and to identify possible social class, ethnic, and gender differences in everyday mathematical activity. In effect, this research allows us to ask children what kinds of mathematical activities they consider to be developmentally appropriate.

The second type of research we describe in this chapter involves intensive clinical interviews of basic mathematical concepts in the same groups of children described earlier. This research allows us to gain deeper insight than can be obtained by standardized testing or questioning into young children's mathematical competence. It allows us to make distinctions between competence and performance and to make careful assessments of possible social class and ethnic differences in mathematical competence as opposed to typical performance.

After describing our results, we return to the issue of whether and how to teach early mathematics, discussing whether to join the play group, enroll in the drill team, or accept the challenge of early childhood education.

BACKGROUND

It is important to note that, before beginning the focused research described next, we spent several years in the informal investigation of young children's behavior in a single day-care center. The Center is located in a low-income housing project in Manhattan, affiliated with the New York City Agency for Child Development, which operates facilities for some 50,000 preschoolers across the city. The center operates four classrooms serving 2-, 3-, 4-, and 5-year-olds, respectively, each run by two teachers and one aide. There are approximately 80 children in the center, and the number of children in the classrooms increases with age.

We tried to follow Labov's (1972) dictum that to study a phenomenon intelligently one has to have informal knowledge of its functioning within the local culture. Consequently, for some time, we acted like ethnographers and immersed ourselves in the everyday life of the Center, observing the daily activities of children in the classrooms and meeting with teachers and parents. We became quite familiar with the children, the teachers, how the center operated, its politics, the parents, the official rules and regulations, and the like. In the course of these observations, we became convinced of three things: First, poor African and Latino children seem to engage in interesting mathematical activities during free play. Second, at least some of these children seem to have advanced mathematical competence. A third was that their teachers had little to do with facilitating whatever competence these children possessed. The teachers seemed largely unaware of their students' mathematical abilities and did virtually nothing to foster them.

As a result of these observations, we decided to conduct two studies: one involving naturalistic observation and the other involving intensive clinical interviews, with low-, middle-, and upper class children.

NATURALISTIC OBSERVATION OF YOUNG CHILDREN'S EVERYDAY MATHEMATICS

Several basic questions framed our naturalistic observation study, influencing its design and the analysis of data:

. In what kinds of mathematical activities do young children engage during their free play?
. Does the everyday mathematics of low-class African-American and Latino children differ from that of middle-class African-American, Latino, and White children and from that of White upper class children?

METHOD

Design

The basic plan was to obtain videotapes of young children's everyday behavior during free play. Individual 4- and 5-year-old children from the various groups --lower class African American and Latino; middle-class African American, Latino, and White; upper class White--were taped during free play, which usually was scheduled for the morning. Anything a child did was recorded. Two types of analyses were then conducted--a *surface analysis* which involved coding all of the videotaped observations, and a *deep analysis*, which involved comprehensive interpretation of individual cases. Statistical analyses were performed on the coded material to compare the different ethnic and social class groups.

Participants

The participants were 80 children ranging in age from 4.17 to 6.00 years ($M = 4.97$, $SD = .48$) in four day-care centers located in Manhattan. We considered families to be *lower-class* if they qualified for subsidized daycare according to the Agency for Child Development guidelines. Most lower class children were from single-parent families. Families were considered *middle class* if they failed to qualify for such subsidy and if one or both parents were working. Families were *upper class* if they could afford to send their children to a very expensive preschool in one of the most affluent areas of New York City. One of the day-care centers contained all lower class children, two contained mixtures of low- and middle-class children, and one contained only upper class children. All of the day-care centers had roughly the same kinds of materials and room arrangement--block area, legos, and so on--although the more affluent centers had a greater variety and quantity of materials.

Of the 80 children, 30 were from lower class (LC) families (mean age = 4.92, $SD=.53$, range 4.17-5.92). The LC group consisted of 17 African Americans, 12 Latinos, and 1 mixed African American and Latino. The second group included 30 children from middle-class (MC) families (mean age = 4.86, $SD=.48$, range 4.08-6.00). The MC group consisted of 12 African Americans, 9 Latinos, 4 Whites, 2 mixed African American and Latino, and 5 Asians. The last group, which we call upper class (UC), consisted of 20 White children from affluent families ($M=5.20$, $SD=.29$, range 4.75-5.75).

Data Collection

Our investigation employed naturalistic observation to capture children's spontaneous mathematics in everyday activities. We began by introducing the video camera and cordless microphone to the children in the four day-care centers to make them comfortable with the equipment. When ready to begin the data gathering, we randomly selected a target child from the 4- and 5-year-old rooms in each of the day-care centers. We placed a cordless microphone on the target child and videotaped the target child's play for 15 minutes during the free play time, usually 8:30 a.m. to 9:00 a.m. and 10:00 a.m. to 11:00 a.m. Once videotaping began, we continued for 15 minutes without interruption. Eighty 15-minute episodes of children's play were collected.

Data Analysis

One of the biggest analytic challenges we faced was to reconcile an individual case's uniqueness with the need for more general understanding. To capture the uniqueness and richness of individual children's everyday mathematics, it seemed that each case must be understood in its own terms. Thus, an in-depth case study approach seemed to be needed. At the same time, we wanted to acquire a more general understanding about children's everyday mathematics. We wanted our findings about individual cases to generalize beyond these particular children. We also wanted to compare the everyday mathematics of young children from different social classes and ethnic groups. To do this, we needed a different type of analysis--one that would allow us to combine data so that we could generalize across subjects.

Consequently, we decided to conduct two different kinds of analysis: a deep analysis of the individual child's mathematical activity, and a surface analysis of children's explicit mathematical behaviors. We believe that these two levels of analysis provide a more comprehensive knowledge of young children's everyday mathematics than would either one alone.

Deep Analysis. The deep analysis aims to gain an in-depth understanding of the child's everyday mathematics that emerges as she engages in play. Perhaps no other child will behave precisely as she does. However, examination of her unique behavior provides us with invaluable insight into her individual intellectual competence. Further, such detailed case studies of individual children provide a kind of thick description (Geertz, 1973) that permits an in-depth interpretation taking into account the child's history, motives, intentions, physical settings, social discourse, interactions, cultural values, and the like. Thus, our deep analysis closely examines the dynamic interactions among individual, physical, and sociocultural factors and the mathematics that emerges from such interactions.

This interpretive approach, however, raises the issue of validity. Our conception of validity is based on the view that it involves convincing the community of scientists that our interpretations are rationally and sensibly derived from the weight of the evidence that we and others have collected (Ginsburg, 1997). We accomplished this by first viewing as a group the video segments of individual children's play. Next each of us presented our interpretations of the target child's mathematical activities with enough evidence to support the interpretations. Finally we established validity through hermeneutic debate, in which interpretations are grounded "not only in the textual and contextual evidence available, but also in a rational debate among the community of interpreters" (Moss, 1994, p. 7).

Surface Analysis. Although the deep analysis concerns the individual child's mathematical activity, the surface analysis focuses on the explicit mathematical behaviors children exhibit in their play. The surface analysis aims to identify patterns across individual's everyday mathematical activities and so gain generalizable findings about children's everyday mathematics.

We divided the videotaped episodes of each child's play into 15 one-minute segments and then coded each minute-long segment. The code was developed inductively. Instead of imposing conceptual categories derived from the literature, we tried to draw analytic constructs from our empirical data, explored many possible explanatory concepts, and looked for the best of several alternative accounts. Progressively new analytic schemes emerged as we went through lengthy and repetitive processes of coding, revising codes, and recoding.

The coding system used for this study involved mathematical content (whether the target child engages in mathematical activity and if so, what kind of mathematical activity she engages in), location (where the target child plays), play object (what kind of object the target child plays with), social interaction (whether and how the target child interacts with her peers), and play activity (in what type of play the target child engages). Pairs of independent raters coded the entire videotape (15 minutes each) of 30 children (out of 80), evenly distributed among the social class groups, and achieved satisfactory agreement in coding. Percent-perfect agreement for mathematical content was 89; for location, 92; for play object, 92; for social interaction, 87; and for play activity, 86.

The mathematical content codes are intended to analyze the kinds of mathematical activity that emerge in play. They involve the following categories:

- **Classification**: Systematic arrangement in groups according to established criteria
- **Dynamics**: Exploration of the process of change or transformation
- **Enumeration**: Numerical judgment or quantification
- **Magnitude comparison**: Comparison of two or more items to evaluate relative magnitude
- **Spatial Relations**: Exploration of positions, direction, and distances in space
- **Pattern and Shape**: Exploration of patterns and spatial forms

The context codes (location, play object, social interaction, and play activity) were intended to describe the environmental conditions under which children's everyday mathematical activities occur. Because the present chapter focuses on mathematical content, we do not describe the context codes in detail. (A detailed description of mathematical content codes is included in Appendix A.)

RESULTS

To provide a flavor of young children's everyday mathematics, we first present excerpts from our deep analysis of individual children's mathematical activities.

The Case of Matthew and Friends

How much is a lot? How little is little? Is a lot of these the same as a lot of these? Is one person's little the same as another's little? Children attempt to understand magnitude concepts like these from a very early age. These are the sorts of questions Matthew and his friends grappled with during free play. Matthew is 4.75 years old and from a lower class African-American family. Like other children chosen for deep analysis, Matthew engaged in at least 5 minutes of mathematical activities that were considered especially interesting by the consensus of our research group.

Jessica brings a book and reads it to Matthew and Ralph. She is actually making up a story based on pictures.

Jessica: So, daddy said, hey, nobody touch the pumpkin! That's mine. (short pause) He feels so bad.

Ralph: (with a doubtful voice) Who? No, he is happy.

Matthew: Can I see it? (Jessica shows the picture.)

Jessica: Then he said, somebody touches the pumpkin. (short pause) That's a lot.

Ralph: That's a lot.

Matthew: (spreading his arms) A lot like this? This much? (spreading his arms more widely) How about this? (again spreading his arms more widely) Like this?

Ralph: I want to have a big, big pumpkin (spreading his arms wider than Matthew did) like this large.

Jessica: Okay. (turning her eyes to the book) Daddy, look! It's dark.

Matthew: Oh, man, that's scary.

Jessica: No, this is cool.

Matthew: But, no it's scary.

Jessica: No, it's not scary.

Ralph: It's scary. Look, look at the face. (Both Ralph and Matthew curl up as if they are scared)

Jessica: No, it's cool. It's not scary. It's cool.

Matthew: A little bit scary (indicating a small amount with his thumb and index finger), tiny scary. I'm a little bit scary.

Ralph: I'm a lot scary (stretching his thumb and index finger to indicate a large amount)

Matthew Oh, my God (stretching his thumb and index finger), not this much scary (narrowing the distance between his thumb and index finger), just this much scary.

Jessica: (indicating a large amount with her thumb and index finger) I'm this much scary.

Matthew: I'm a little bit scary like this (making some distance between his thumb and index finger).

Ralph: That's big.

Matthew: This is tiny.

Ralph: No (narrowing his thumb and index finger), this
         is very little, like this (narrowing his thumb
         and index finger more closely).

As Jessica told a story, the three children spontaneously engaged in a
mathematical debate. As Jessica said "a lot," Matthew wondered how much was
a lot. He asked, "a lot like this?" showing his stretched arms. Then he spread
his arms more widely and widely, asking them how much was a lot. Jessica and
Ralph seemed to agree that all of those indicated a lot. Next, Matthew brought
up another relational term, *a little*. Three children started talking about how
much they were scary. They used their thumbs and index fingers (instead of
their arms) to indicate the magnitude--how much or how little. This time Ralph
disagreed with Matthew's *little*. When Matthew showed what a *little* is like
with his thumbs and index finger, Ralph said that it was *big*, not a *little*. Then
he showed what a little is a really like with his thumb and index finger, making
almost no distance between them.   Matthew did not disagree with him.
Apparently, his a *little* is bigger than Ralph's a *little*. In this way, they settled
the issue of how little is a little.
        This conversation was not unusual: We often found that in free play
children raise interesting and serious mathematical questions and spontaneously
engage in mathematical discussion. They have their own ways of dealing with
these questions and seek answers though they are often temporary.

Surface Analysis

We also employed surface analysis to examine patterns across individual
children's activities emerging in their free play. We examined the relative
frequency of different kinds of mathematical activity in the play of children from
different social class and ethnic groups.
        Frequency of Mathematical Activity.   When children engage in free
play, how much of their time is devoted to mathematical activities?   At the
outset, this might appear to be an absurd question. When children play, they
do not appear to be doing mathematics. However, our results show otherwise.
The percentage of minutes (15 minutes for each of 80 children, for 1,200
minutes) in which at least one mathematical activity occurs is 46.6.   In other
words, during free play, children engage in mathematical activity--of course, as
we define it--during about half of the minutes. This does not mean that half of
their time is spent in mathematics, but that in half of the minutes there is at least
some mathematical activity. On the face of it, this would appear to be a much
higher percentage of such cognition than one would expect.
        Consider next social class differences. Here we were interested in
knowing whether children from different social class groups engaged in different

amounts of mathematical activity. To answer this question, we performed an analysis of covariance, using age as the covariate,[3] to examine the effects of social class (low, medium, and high) on the average number of minutes (range from 0-15) in which at least one mathematical activity occurred. The results show that age is related to frequency of mathematical activity ($r=.37$), and that with age removed social class was not significantly related to frequency of mathematical activity, with lower and middle-class children showing virtually identical averages (44.0 and 44.5, respectively) and the somewhat older upper class children slightly more (53.7). In brief, we find a lack of social class differences in overall frequency of children's mathematical activity.

Next we considered ethnicity and social class within the LC and MC groups. We were limited to comparing low- and middle-class African-American and Latino children. There were no lower class Whites, not enough middle class Whites, and no upper class African American and Latino children. Such is the reality of demographics in New York City. Analysis of covariance (ANCOVA; with age as the covariate) showed no effects of either social class or ethnicity, although the trend is for Latino children (lower class mean = 54.4 and middle-class mean = 49.7) to show somewhat more activity than African Americans (lower class mean = 38.1 and middle-class mean = 36.1).

Finally, ANCOVA, with age as a covariate, shows that gender is not associated with overall frequency of mathematical activity, with boys showing 44.8% and girls 49.1% mathematical activity.

Different Types of Mathematical Activity. We also examined the relative frequency of different types of mathematical activity--specifically the average percentage of minutes during which a particular category of mathematical activity occurred (see Figure 8.1). The most frequently occurring mathematical activity was Pattern and Shape (an average of 25% of the 15 minutes), then Magnitude Comparison (13%), followed by Enumeration (12%), Dynamics (6%), Spatial Relations (5%), and Classification (2%). Clearly the Pattern and Shape, Magnitude Comparison, and Enumeration, each occurring a portion of the time. Figure 8.2 shows that a similar rank order was shown by all social groups.

We saw earlier that older children engage in more mathematical activity than younger. Consider next how age is related to specific types of mathematical activity. Correlational analyses show that there is a relation between age and two of the three most frequent sub-categories of mathematical

---

[3]We did this here and in other analysis because the frequencies of subjects were unequally distributed across the 4- and 5-year-old age groups, with some cells being unacceptably small for ANOVA. Hence, it is necessary to partial out age in this manner.

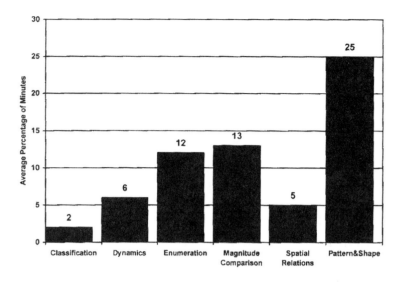

FIG. 8.1 Relative frequency of different types of mathematical activity.

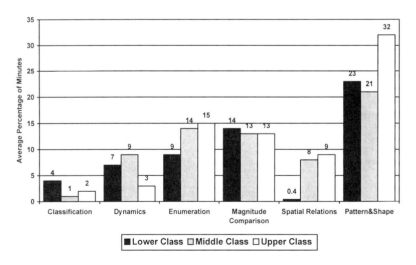

FIG. 8.2 Social class differences in relative frequency of different types of mathematical activity.

activity--Enumeration ($r=.29$) and Pattern and Shape ($r=.27$). Older children enumerate and deal with patterns and shapes to a slightly greater extent than do younger children. Perhaps the correlation between age and enumeration can be attributed to older children's ability to count higher than can younger children. The explanation of the correlation between age and Pattern and Shape is not evident. There is no correlation between age and magnitude comparison.

We also saw earlier that the social classes did not differ in overall levels of mathematical activity. Consider next whether and how the social class groups differed in the specific types of mathematical activity. ANCOVAs, with age as the covariate, and chi-square analyses (used because of insufficient variance in some cases) show that there is no relation between social class and any of the subcategories of mathematical activity, with the exception of Spatial Relations, which middle- and upper class children engage in to a small extent and lower class children not at all. This result should be evaluated with caution because the frequency of Spatial Relations was very small (5% overall).

Finally, what about gender differences in the specific types of mathematical activity? Again, ANOVAs and chi-square analyses show that boys and girls did not differ in mathematical activities except for Spatial Relations, where boys showed roughly four times as much of this activity as did girls. Again the results should be treated with caution because the frequencies were so low (8% on the average for boys and 2% for girls) and also because gender differences in spatial abilities have not been seen to emerge until adolescence (Leder, 1992).

In brief, our results show that frequency of overall and some specific mathematical activity is related to age, but not to social class, ethnicity, and gender. During free play, children engage in a significant amount of activity involving Pattern and Shape, Magnitude Comparison, and Enumeration.

One important caveat must be attached to these results. Our data do not yet include scores reflecting level of mathematical activity. It is possible, of course, that two children showing the same amounts of Magnitude Comparison, or any other category, could be engaged in different developmental levels of activity. Our results do not yet capture possible level or complexity differences of this type.

CLINICAL INTERVIEW INVESTIGATION OF MATHEMATICAL KNOWLEDGE

Our clinical interview research rose from the observation that the lower class preschool children with whom we interacted in ethnographic pilot work appeared to have a far greater understanding of mathematical concepts than the previous literature had indicated. This gap between what research said this particular group could do and what they appeared to be doing prompted us to look at how these earlier studies had assessed mathematical competence.

Closer examination revealed that, in general, the tasks employed in the previous research were highly structured and adult directed. Typically the individual child was asked by an unknown adult to engage in unfamiliar tasks in a standardized fashion. The examiner had little latitude in adapting the language of the task or the task itself to the needs of the young child. Aside from rather lame attempts to create rapport, the typical standardized procedure did not attempt to take into account the child's motivation or style. This kind of decontextualized, rigid social interaction is problematic in several ways. It is often not suitable for shy, young children, and particularly for minority children who speak nonstandard forms of English and who may be uncomfortable in a testing situation with an often nonminority adult. A structured, standardized method indeed may prevent them from using previous social experience to bring meaning to the task (Schubauer-Leoni & Perret-Clermont, 1997).

Our hypothesis is that commonly observed social class differences may result more from lack of sensitivity in standard tests than from genuine and substantial cognitive differences among the groups. Evidence supporting our interpretation can be seen in the fact that studies finding the largest social class differences used the most structured procedures (e.g., Kirk, Hunt, & Volkmar, 1975), whereas studies such as Ginsburg, Choi, Lopez, Netley, and Chi (1997), which utilized mathematical tasks embedded in meaningful contexts, found fewer consistent social class differences across task items.

Therefore, we decided to undertake a study that would make intensive use of the clinical interview method to investigate possible social class and ethnic differences in young children's mathematical competence. We believe that the clinical interview, because it can be sensitive to various psychological, social, and task factors affecting the child's performance, may be able to identify mathematical competence more accurately (i.e., with greater validity) than can standardized tests or structured assessments of one kind or another. The clinical interview can be a sound assessment technique, although of course like any other assessment method it can be used badly. In this chapter, we report on one part of our clinical interview study--namely, what it reveals about the underlying mathematical competence of the various groups.

Participants

The participants were 88 children ranging in age from 4.00 to 5.92 years ($M =$ 4.80, $SD = .50$) in the same four day-care centers described earlier. (Almost all of these children also participated in the naturalistic portion of the study; for various reasons, several of these children were not available for videotaping.)

Of the 88 children, 24 were from lower class families, with ages ranging from 4.00 to 5.42 years ($M=4.72$, $SD=.45$). This lower class (LC) group consisted of 12 African Americans, 11 Latinos, and 1 other. The second group included 35 children from middle-class families, with ages ranging from 4.00 to 5.92 years ($M=4.65$, $SD=.48$). This middle-class (MC) group consisted of 15 African Americans, 7 Latinos, 8 Whites, and 5 Asians. The last group consisted of 29 White children from upper class (UC) families, with ages ranging from 4.08 to 5.92 years ($M=5.03$, $SD=.50$).

Procedure

Each child was interviewed by one of seven different clinical interviewers, all graduate students at Teachers College, each of whom was carefully trained for this task. At any one of the four day-care centers, no more than half of the children might have been interviewed by one of the interviewers. The duration of each clinical interview was approximately 30 minutes. On entering the room, the child was made aware of the video camera and told that he or she was going to be asked some questions about numbers. Each interviewer was provided with a protocol that was to be used as a guide, although the actual questions could vary depending on the child's level of mathematical competence, linguistic understanding, motivation, and/or interests. As used in this study, the clinical interview is a deliberately nonstandardized method in which the researcher tailors each question to the individual, giving the child time to understand the situation and learn the rules of the game. The clinical interview focuses on dynamic processes involved in cognition, using probes to uncover reasons behind an answer (Ginsburg, 1997). The interviewer also utilizes hints of various sorts in an effort to learn about the child's developing intelligence in the zone of proximal development (Vygotsky, 1978).

Thus, we designed a protocol that would cover the mathematical concepts in which we were interested while simultaneously using the freedom of the clinical interview method to individualize the questions. We attempted to create an assessment procedure designed to sift out the grains of competence from the chaff of various interfering performance factors.

Tasks

Each child was first given a warm-up task, which consisted of sorting coins. This was intended to familiarize interviewer and child with each other and to engage the child in an easy and enjoyable activity. After that, each child participated in a series of tasks, examples of which include:

Addition. "Let's pretend you have X pennies in one hand and Y pennies in the other hand. How many pennies do you have altogether?"

Subtraction. "There are X children in the playground and Y children leave the playground to go home and do their homework. How many children are left in the playground?"

Reversibility. Initially the child was told that nine children were in the playground and two left to go home and do their homework. If the child answered the question correctly, the interviewer reversed the problem by saying: "The two children finish their homework and go back to the playground. How many children are in the playground now?" If the child immediately maintains, without calculation, that nine *must* now be on the playground, then he or she is assumed to have used the principle of reversibility.

Representation. The child was first asked to use paper and pencil to represent pennies placed in a line on at least two separate tasks. The interviewer then made paper and pencil available to the child for the solution of the next task: "Suppose we are having a party. At the party you get X presents. Then you get Y more presents. How many presents do you have altogether?"

(A full description of all the problems employed is presented in Appendix B.)

Data Analysis

Because of the individualized nature of the clinical interview, each interaction between researcher and child was likely to be different. We wanted both to preserve the rich data we obtained using such an in-depth research method and generalize across subjects and groups. Hence, as in our naturalistic research, we employed two levels of data analysis: one involving interpretation of individual cases, and the other employing common codes that could be used to make generalizations and comparisons between individuals and groups.

Interpretive Analysis. The goal of the interpretive analysis is a deep understanding of the mathematical competence of each individual child. This level avoids the use of generic codes and instead employs narrative prose. Interpretive analyses conducted in this manner are less like descriptions of activities and more like arguments for a particular point of view. The analyst uses evidence from the interview to support an argument for a particular interpretation in the hopes of convincing a reader or viewer of the videotape that the interpretation is correct. An interpretive analysis argues for plausible explanations, always citing evidence to support them. Subsequent discussion with and feedback from knowledgeable peers help the analyst revise and clarify the interpretation.

In this chapter, we present an example of such an interpretation. To portray the complexity of children's mathematical competence, we provide an excerpt from the interpretive analysis of an individual child.

Objective Analysis. Whereas the interpretive analysis attempted to provide unique accounts of each individual child's type and level of mathematical competence and cognitive performance, the objective analysis focused on a common set of mathematical strategies and concepts children might exhibit during the clinical interview. Independent judges, whose interrater reliability was ascertained, coded each section of the videotaped material according to categories that can be used to provide a common basis for comparison across all subjects. The coding scheme derived in part from categories commonly found in the research literature (e.g., tagging and counting all), and in part from an inductive analysis of the interviews of a group of pilot subjects. Two independent coders rated a sample of 12 children's addition, subtraction, and representation strategies and concepts, agreeing on 89% of their initial judgments. They then discussed and reached agreement on the coding of the remaining 11%.

RESULTS

Interviews with individual children revealed an interesting complexity of mathematical thought. Consider an interpretation of an interview with Tricia, a lower class Latino girl age 5 years and 4 months.

Tricia's Clinical Interview

Earlier in the interview, Tricia had solved some addition problems involving pennies. At this point, Amy Olt, the interviewer, wants to determine whether Tricia can perform addition with imaginary objects. She shows Tricia a paper with two, empty houses drawn on it.

> Amy: [She points to a house.] Okay, let's pretend
>   that in this house there are seven children.
> Tricia: All right.
> Amy: [She points to the adjacent house.] And in this
>   house there are two children. And they all go
>   outside to play [places her finger on an empty
>   space near the houses] on the playground. How many
>   children are there altogether in the playground?
> Tricia: [She extends one finger on her left hand.] Uhmm,
>   seven?
> Amy: [She points at the house.] Seven in this house.

Tricia: [She counts as she taps a finger on the table.]
One, two, three, four, five, six, seven, eight.
Amy: Eight?
Tricia: I can't count them because there's no children.

Tricia displays metacognitive awareness. She accurately describes her difficulty: Now that the problem does not involve concrete objects, she seems unable to employ her counting strategies. Why? Perhaps Tricia does not understand how using some form of representation--like making tallies for the imaginary children--might help her solve the problem. Perhaps she is not sure of the rules of the game. Previous problems had involved concrete objects. What has the game changed into at this point? In any event, Amy then provides a minimal scaffolding; she suggests the possibility of using pennies as a representational aid.

Amy: [She touches the pile of pennies.] You want to
use the pennies for children?
Tricia: Yeah.
Amy: Yeah, use the pennies.
Tricia: [As she counts the pennies, she places each of them
into a house.] One, two, three, four, five, six,
seven. [After placing the seventh penny into the
house, she grabs another penny, but hesitates for a
moment.]
Amy: [She points to the adjacent house.] Two in this house.
Tricia: [She lays two pennies on the adjacent hous.] One,
two.
Amy: [With a circular motion, she points at the playground
area.] They all go to the playground. How many do we
have in the playground all together?
Tricia: [As she counts, she points to the pennies.] One, two,
three, four, five, six, seven, eight, nine. Nine.
Amy: Nine children altogether. How did you know that?
Tricia: Because I was counting.

In brief, Tricia responds quickly to the interviewer's hint and is able to represent the absent children with pennies. She creates two groups of pennies, touching each carefully as she counts them, uses the strategy of counting all to get the sum, and repeats the last number in the sequence, apparently to indicate the cardinal value. She is also able to describe her strategy in words.

Amy: You were counting. Great. All right. [She slides the
pennies off the drawing into the center of the table.]

Well, all these children go back to their friends. [She points to the drawing of a house.] Now we have eight children in this house.

Tricia: [She extends fingers on her right hand.] Eight?

Amy: [She points to each house.] Eight in this house. And four children in this house.

Tricia: [She points to the house that was described by Amy as having eight children.] Four children in this house?

Amy: [She points to the previous house.] Eight children in this house.

Tricia: [She points to the adjacent house.] And four children in that house.

Amy: And four children in that one. Uhmmm. They all go to the playground.

Tricia: [She places seven pennies in one house. She counts them, adds a penny to the group, and counts and then recounts the quantity of pennies.] Okay and four.

Note the care with which Tricia performs the operation of counting.

Amy: Four. Good.

Tricia: [She places four pennies on the second house. She counts each one as she points to it.] One, two, three, four. [She scratches her head.]

Amy: All the children go to the playground to play. How many do we have altogether?

Tricia: [She points to each penny as she counts.] One, two, three, four. [She counts silently from five to twelve. Then she rubs her right eye.] Twelve.

Amy: Twelve altogether.

Tricia's counting is beginning to "go underground" as she is dealing with larger numbers. She does not need to say all of the numbers out loud. Next, although Tricia is beginning to get tired, Amy asks her to add 12 and 5, and Tricia succeeds, again using the same *counting all* strategy.

We see then that, in this sequence, Tricia initially failed at a simple task involving imaginary addition. She was aware of her difficulty and was able to express it. With a slight hint from the examiner, Tricia was able to employ pennies as simple representational aids; use the counting all strategy to solve problems as large as 12 + 5, carefully monitor her efforts at enumeration, and diligently executed the addition strategy.

Amy then continues with an even more difficult imaginary addition problem, this time not even involving a house which can provide a minimal context for the problem. Amy asks Tricia to imagine the following situation.

Amy: You get seven presents and then you get six more.
         [Tricia sits back in her chair with her arms folded.]
         How many presents do you get altogether?
Tricia: [She counts her fingers.] One, two, three, four
         five, six, seven, eight, nine. Nine.
Amy: Nine. Are you sure?
Tricia: Yeah.
Amy: Can you check to be sure? How can you check to be
         sure?
Tricia: Because I just know.
Amy: Uhhm.
Tricia: I'm very, very, very tired now.

In this sequence, given a new type of problem, Tricia tries a new strategy--counting on the fingers. However, that method is difficult to use when the problem involves a sum greater than 10. Tricia does not seem to know what to do or how to check. Moreover, she is "very, very, very tired." Clearly, Tricia seems to have had enough. In this situation, the interviewer needs to decide whether the child cannot continue or whether the apparent fatigue is a temporary response to a difficulty in dealing with the problem. Amy decides to continue; she does not believe that Tricia has yet revealed the full extent of her competence on this problem.

Amy: You're getting tired. Just a few more questions.
Tricia: [She stands up beside the table and extends the
         fingers in her right hand.] How many more?
Amy: Do you mind if I ask you a couple more? Well,
         how many presents do you have altogether?
Tricia: Altogether. [She uses the pencil to draw figures
         representing the presents.]

Perhaps surprisingly, Amy's persistence pays off. Tricia now initiates a new strategy--namely, representing the imaginary presents by means of schematic written figures. What stimulated her to do this? Immediately before Tricia expressed her fatigue, Amy turned over the paper with the houses drawn on it to expose a blank side. Perhaps this served as a very subtle hint that the paper could be used for making written representations. However, Amy said nothing specific about using paper and pencil.

Amy: At the party you get seven presents and then you
get six more.

Tricia: [She stops drawing.] At the party I get seven
presents.

Amy: Ahmmm.

Tricia: [She counts the shapes she has drawn.] One,
two, three. [She continues to count as she
draws.] Four, five, six, seven.

Amy: Okay. And then you get six more presents. How
many do you have altogether?

Tricia: [She continues to draw shapes.] Seven, eight,
nine, ten, eleven, twelve, thirteen.

Note that this is the first time she uses *counting on* as a strategy.

Amy: How many presents do you have altogether?

Tricia: [She points to each figure that she drew.] One,
two, three, four, five, six, seven, eight, nine,
ten, eleven, twelve, thirteen. [She taps on the
table with the pencil.]

Amy: Thirteen. Great job. How did you know that?

Tricia: [As she stretches, she speaks with a strained
voice.] Because I was counting them.

In brief, even after a long time in the interview and some tiredness,
Tricia manages to initiate some new strategies--namely, pictorial representation
and counting onto achieve success at a problem she had previously been unable
to solve. Amy's persistent use of clinical interview probes and scaffolds
manages to elicit from Tricia a level of competence that was not evident at the
outset--when she seemed confused about how to add in the absence of concrete
objects--and results in important insights into her abilities.

Objective Analysis

Consider next an objective analysis of the clinical interview data. In the course
of the interview, children were given a series of problems varying in level of
difficulty. In accordance with clinical interview procedure, each problem was
initially presented in the same way to all children. After that point, however,
the interviewer was free to restate the question, probe, ask questions, and, in
general, modify the procedure according to the individual child's needs.

The data concerning children's responses to the concrete and mental
addition problems described earlier were first analyzed according to use of

strategy and then understanding of principle. In solving the problems described previously, the children used a wide variety of strategies ranging from pushing objects aside to representing them symbolically. To obtain an index of children's performance, we developed a score depicting overall strategy level. This was done first by grouping strategies into four levels of developmental sophistication, in which lower levels represent a relatively concrete approach to the task and higher levels rely more heavily on relatively abstract reasoning. Thus, Level 1 includes strategies like counting all and quick guessing (usually incorrect). Level 2 includes tagging (e.g., while counting the child solving 3-11 touches each penny without moving it) and pictographic representation. Level 3 includes subitizing (seeing a number without counting), estimation, and matching (or use of one-to-one correspondence to determine equality and inequality of number). Last, Level 4 includes what we consider to be the most sophisticated, representational strategies--mental addition, quick recall, and iconic and symbolic representation. Strategies were coded and grouped in such a way as to produce an overall strategy score indicating degree of abstraction and ranging from 1 to 4. (Details of coding and derivation of the level scores are presented in Appendix C.)

Because analyses show that boys and girls did not differ on overall strategy level or in understanding of principle, gender was ignored in subsequent analyses, which focused on possible social class differences. The results show that average strategy level is associated with social class. An ANCOVA (which employed age as a covariate because the upper class group tended to be older than the others) showed that the main effect of social class is significant ($F = 7.65$, $df = 2, 84$, $p < .001$). However, the means were very close. Average strategy for lower class children was 1.78; for middle class children, 1.94; and for upper class, 2.11. Moreover, post hoc t tests show that lower and middle-class children's mean strategy levels differ from that of upper class children, but not from each other.

Table 8.1 presents details of strategy use in the various social class groups. The table shows that the distribution of strategy use is extremely similar in the three social class groups. About half of the children in all groups use Level 1 strategies, about a quarter use Level 2 strategies, and about a tenth use Level 3 strategies. The groups differ mainly in use of Level 4 strategies: Upper class children use about twice as many (.21) as low- (.09) and middle-class children (.13). Indeed, a notable aspect of these data is the strong similarity between low- and middle-class children. The two groups are almost identical in distribution of strategies across the different levels.

Level 4 strategies, as we have defined them, include both abstract procedures like written representation, as well as quick recall of number facts (which we interpret as mostly rote memory). Although the two types are very different, we included both in Level 4 because they are developmentally advanced. Proficiency in rote memory of number facts is correlated with use of more advanced strategies of calculation. Do the social classes differ in their use of these two very different procedures embedded within level 4? Table 8.2 shows different groups' use of Level 4 quick recall procedures and Level 4 representational procedures. The results show that upper-class children use quick recall slightly more often (.22) than the low- and middle-class children

TABLE 8.1

Percentage of Strategy Level Usage in Socioeconomic Groups

Strategy Level	Lower Class	Middle Class	Upper Class
1	52	47	46
2	28	27	21
3	11	13	12
4	9	13	21

TABLE 8.2

Number and Proportion (in Parentheses) of Quick Recall and Representational Level 4 Procedures

Socioeconomic Group	Level 4 Procedures		Total
	Quick Recall	Representational	
Lower class	23 (.15)	130 (.85)	153
Middle class	52 (.16)	264 (.84)	316
Upper class	101 (.22)	357 (.78)	458

(both around .15), and therefore the low- and middle-class children use representational strategies slightly more often (both around .85) than do upper class children (.78).

In brief, upper class children use more Level 4 strategies than the others (and therefore receive a significantly higher average strategy level score). At the same time, upper class children use slightly more rote memory within their Level 4 strategies than do the other children. Are these results paradoxical? We think they only indicate that, as children become more skilled in using various addition and subtraction strategies, they also tend to remember more facts. Perhaps those more skilled in strategy use have better memories than those less skilled. Perhaps practice with strategies helps produce quick recall. After all, it is boring to always count on and efficient to remember the results thus obtained. In any event, upper class children tend to employ more Level 4 strategies and hence more quick recall than low- and middle-class children.

The children's responses were also scored for understanding of a key principle--namely, reversibility. Because analysis showed that boys and girls did not differ on understanding of reversibility, gender was ignored in subsequent analyses, which focused on possible social class differences. The results (see Table 8.3) showed that understanding of reversibility was clearly linked to social class (chi-square = 15.7, $df=2$, $p < .001$). Almost all upper class children understood the concept, whereas most lower class children did not. Of course, success at reversibility was significantly and positively associated with age, which serves to confirm the validity of the measure. Nonetheless, it also clouds the analysis of social class. Because upper class children tended to be somewhat older than low- and middle-class children, the difference among the groups looks more extreme than it really is. In other words, some of the upper class children's superior performance must be associated with age. Nevertheless, the

TABLE 8.3

Understanding of Reversibility in Social Class Groups

Variable	Lower Class	Middle Class	Upper Class
No Understanding	15	14	3
Understanding	9	21	26

trend and the results are clear: There is a clear social class difference in the understanding of reversibility.

In summary, our objective analyses show that upperclass children use somewhat more advanced strategies and demonstrate greater understanding of a key mathematical principle than do the low- and middle-class children. However, all groups use similar strategies, and the low- and middle-class children show highly similar patterns of performance.

CONCLUSIONS

Our research has implications for understanding the nature of young children's mathematical thinking, social class differences, methods of research, and early childhood education.

Mathematical Thinking

Our naturalistic research shows that, in their free play, young children frequently engage in mathematical activities. They often explore patterns and shapes, compare magnitudes, and enumerate. Less frequently, they classify, explore dynamic change, and use spatial relations. In almost all cases, no one tells them to do these things; adults typically do not instruct them in the kinds of early mathematical activities exhibited in their free play. Instead, mathematical activities emerge in the content of young children's ordinary interactions with the everyday environment. Young children have widespread mathematical interests and choose to satisfy them in daily activity. Their mathematical interests clearly extend beyond the *three c's* common in research-- conservation, counting, and calculation. Further, the complexity of young children's activities can be surprising. They create block constructions symmetrical in three dimensions, and they employ elaborate rhythmic patterns.

Our clinical interview research confirms and extends what the literature (Ginsburg et al., 1998) has already shown--namely, that young children's mathematical thinking employs a wide range of strategies from the concrete to the representational. Clearly, before entrance to school, 4- and 5-year-old children know a good deal about addition and other elementary mathematical topics.

Social Class Differences

Our naturalistic research fails to uncover differences between low-, middle-, and upper class children's mathematical behavior in free play. Children from all of these groups display similar amounts and patterns of mathematical behavior.

(The same is true of boys and girls.) Although further research--which we are now conducting--is needed to examine possible social class differences in complexity of mathematical behavior, it is clear that lower class children engage in significant amounts of mathematical activity in free play, and that some lower class children have provided our most interesting and complex examples of everyday mathematical activity. Whatever may ultimately be found concerning social class differences in this area, our research shows that lower class children do not lack mathematical interests and do not fail to explore them in the preschool environment.

Our clinical interview research shows that upper class children exhibit a slightly higher level of strategic complexity in solving simple calculation problems than do lower and middle-class children, who perform at an equivalent level. All of the groups employ similar strategies, albeit with small differences in frequency. The research also reveals a positive association between social class and understanding of at least one basic mathematical principle (the inverse). In evaluating these results, it is important to recognize that the upper class children are highly selected, partly on the basis of IQ and other cognitive tests, for admission to their school. These children are not a random sample of upper class children. Further, leaving aside the issue of upper class children, the results as a whole suggest only minor differences in the mathematical abilities of lower and middle-class children. We believe that the clinical interview data support our hypothesis that flexible methods of testing are more sensitive than standard tests and more appropriate for revealing the competence of lower class children.

Methods

We began with the hypothesis that lower class children's knowledge about mathematics is more complex than indicated by traditional research methods, and that both naturalistic observation and clinical interview are necessary to uncover children's competence. Our research confirms this point of view concerning methods. Both naturalistic observation and clinical information provided extremely valuable information concerning children's mathematical thinking, interests, and motivations. Naturalistic observation allowed us to discover that children engage in a variety of mathematical activities that are not typically revealed by standard methods. As a result, we can broaden the scope of research beyond the three C's. Clinical interviewing allowed us to obtain a more accurate portrait of the competence of lowerclass children than usually emerges from standard methods. These children are more similar to their middle- and upper income peers than standard methods suggest. In brief, both naturalistic observation and clinical interviews illuminate aspects of mathematical thinking and social class differences--or rather the lack of them--more clearly than do standard methods.

Implications for Education

Our research was based on the assumption that if we hold in abeyance our traditional notions of what young children can and cannot do, look closely at the children, and listen carefully to what they tell us, then we may be in a position to acquire empirically based and theoretically sound knowledge of what is developmentally appropriate for early childhood education. Such knowledge can then guide the development of mathematics learning activities or curricula for young children that are at least partly child-determined and therefore developmentally appropriate.

What do we learn? Our research shows that informal mathematics is more fully developed and powerful than is often realized. Young children, including poor children, are often engaged in mathematical thinking and learning. In everyday play, they involve themselves in the spontaneous study of patterns and shapes, enumeration, and magnitude comparison. Early childhood educators need to appreciate the intellectual accomplishment that is young children's informal mathematics. Certainly it suffers from limitations and is not as sophisticated as adults'. Yet the striking fact is not young children's mathematical incompetence. Instead it is their ability to engage with interesting and serious mathematical questions. The research does not highlight barriers to mathematics learning.

Indeed, the psychological research points the way towards providing young children with challenges--with rich opportunities for learning mathematics. The research suggests that young children do not have to be protected from the study of mathematics or prepared to do it (Greenes, 1999). They are already interested in mathematics learning. Therefore, early childhood educators should not be afraid to engage young children in significant and challenging forms of mathematical thinking.

Clearly, these children deserve more than mindless drill or academic seatwork of the type that characterizes too many elementary school classrooms. Such activities would only serve to dampen children's interest in mathematics at an even earlier age than is unfortunately typical (around the third grade in schools employing such methods).

However, should the teacher do nothing but let the children play? After all, we have shown that their play is interesting and important. Although preferable to subjecting children to a mindless curriculum, a focus on play has the unfortunate result of neglecting many interesting opportunities for engaging children in creative learning. A little adult guidance can help young children learn even more than they manage to learn on their own, can help introduce them to introductory formalizations of the ideas and methods they are interested in, and can help them prepare for later learning in school.

Although such guided learning may not be essential for promoting the education of middle- and upper class children, it can be of special value for poor children who are at heightened risk of school failure and failing schools. Young children in poverty demonstrate more than adequate intellectual abilities. They are capable of learning mathematics and much else. Because of the hard road that lies ahead of them, they can benefit more than their middle- and upper class peers from educational challenge, help, and encouragement.

REFERENCES

Brush, L. W. (1978). Preschool children's knowledge of addition and subtraction. *Journal for Research in Mathematics Education, 9*, 44-54.

Carpenter, T. P., & Mozer, J. M. (1982). The development of addition and subtraction problem-solving skills. In T. P. Carpenter, J. M. Moser, & T. A. Romberg (Eds.), *Addition and subtraction: A cognitive perspective* (pp. 9-24). Hillsdale, NJ: Lawrence Erlbaum Associates.

Carraher, T. N., Carraher, D. W., & Schliemann, A. D. (1985). Mathematics in the streets and in schools. *British Journal of Developmental Psychology, 3*, 21-29.

Clements, D. (1999). Geometric and spatial thinking in young children. In J. Copley (Ed.), *Mathematics in the early years* (pp. 66-79). Reston, VA: National Council of Teachers of Mathematics.

Court, S. R. A. (1920). Numbers, time, and space in the first five years of a child's life. *Pedagogical Seminary, 27*, 71-89.

Dehaene, S. (1997). *The number sense: How the mind creates mathematics*. Oxford, England: Oxford University Press.

Elkind, D. (1998). Educating young children in math, science, and technology. In *The Forum on Early Childhood Science, Mathematics, and Technology Education*. Washington, DC: American Association for the Advancement of Science.

Geertz, C. (1973). *The interpretation of cultures*. New York: Basic Books.

Gelman, R., & Gallistel, C. R. (1978). *The child's understanding of number*. Cambridge, MA: Harvard University Press.

Ginsburg, H. P. (1989). *Children's arithmetic: How they learn it and how you teach it* (2nd ed.). Austin, TX: Pro Ed.

Ginsburg, H. P. (1997). *Entering the child's mind: The clinical interview in psychological research and practice*. New York: Cambridge University Press.

Ginsburg, H. P., Choi, Y. E., Lopez, L. S., Netley, R., & Chi, C.-Y. (1997). Happy birthday to you: Early mathematical thinking of Asian, South American, and U.S. children. In T. Nunes & P. Bryant (Eds.), *Learning and teaching mathematics: An international perspective* (pp. 163-207). East Sussex, England: Taylor & Francis.

Ginsburg, H. P., Klein, A., & Starkey, P. (1998). The development of children's mathematical thinking: Connecting research with practice. In I. Sigel & A. Renninger (Eds.), *Handbook of child psychology: Child psychology and practice* (Vol. 4, 5th ed., pp. 401-476). New York: Wiley.

Ginsburg, H. P., & Russell, R. L. (1981). Social class and racial influences on early mathematical thinking. *Monographs of the Society for Research in Child Development, 46* (Serial No. 193, No. 6).

Ginsburg, H. P., & Seo, K. H. (1999). The mathematics in children's thinking. *Mathematical Thinking and Learning, 1* (2), 113-129.

Greenes, C. (1999). Ready to learn: Developing young children's mathematical powers. In J. Copley (Ed.), *Mathematics in the early years* (pp. 39-47). Reston, VA: National Council of Teachers of Mathematics.

Hughes, M. (1986). *Children and number: Difficulties in learning mathematics.* Oxford, England: Basil Blackwell.

Hunting, R. (1999). Rational number learning in the early years: What is possible? In J. Copley (Ed.), *Mathematics in the early years* (pp. 80-87). Reston, VA: National Council of Teachers of Mathematics.

Kirk, G. E., Hunt, J. M., & Volkmar, F. (1975). Social class and preschool language skills: V. Cognitive and semantic mastery of number. *Genetic Psychology Monographs, 93*, 131-153.

Labov, W. (1972). *Language in the inner city.* Philadelphia: University of Pennsylvania Press.

Leder, G. C. (1992). Mathematics and gender: Changing perspectives. In D. A. Grouws (Ed.), *Handbook of research on mathematics teaching and learning: A project of the National Council of Teachers of Mathematics* (pp. 597-622). New York: Macmillan.

Moss, P. A. (1994). Can there be validity without reliability? *Educational Researcher, 23* (2), 5-12.

Natriello, G., McDill, E. L., & Pallas, A. M. (1990). *Schooling disadvantaged children: Racing against catastrophe.* New York: Teachers College Press.

Oakes, J. (1990). *Multiplying inequalities: The effects of race, social class, and tracking on opportunities to learn mathematics and science.* Santa Monica, CA: The RAND Corporation.

Piaget, J. (1952). *The child's conception of number* (C. Gattegno & F. M. Hodgson, Trans.). London: Routledge & Kegan Paul.

Saxe, G., Guberman, S. R., & Gearhart, M. (1987). Social processes in early number development. *Monographs of the Society for Research in Child Development, 52* (2), Serial No. 216.

Schubauer-Leoni, M. L., & Perret-Clermont, A. N. (1997). Social interactions and mathematics learning. In T. Nunes & P. Bryant (Eds.), *Learning and teaching mathematics: An international perspective* (pp. 265-283). Sussex, UK: Psychology Press.

Vygotsky, L. S. (1978). *Mind in society: The development of higher psychological processes.* Cambridge, MA: Harvard University Press.

Wagner, S. H., & Walters, J. (1982). A longitudinal analysis of early number concepts: From numbers to number. In G. E. Forman (Ed.), *Action and thought: From sensorimotor schemes to symbolic operations* (pp. 137-161). New York: Academic Press.

APPENDIX A: MATHEMATICAL CONTENT CODES

Classification

- Systematic arrangement in groups according to established criteria.
- It involves activities such as sorting, grouping, or categorizing.
- Examples: Jessica sorts the animal toys into two groups: babies and mommies. David cleans up the blocks on the rug. He picks out one block at a time and puts it into one of the boxes that contains the same size and shape of blocks as the one he picked up.

Dynamics

- Exploration of the process of change or transformation.
- It involves activities such as adding, subtracting, or exploration of motions like rotations, flips, or turns.
- Examples: Jessica takes away the buttons on the table one by one and holds them in her hand. When she takes away the last one, she says, "Now there's nothing." Jeff flips the symmetrical structure over and over saying, "I can flip this over like, this, this, this" He seems to enjoy the fact that the shape of a symmetrical object is kept unchanged when flipped over along its symmetrical axis.

Enumeration

- Numerical judgment or quantification.
- It involves activities such as one-to-one correspondence, counting, subitizing, or explicit use of number words.
- Examples: Briana counts the beads on the table, picking out one by one and uttering "one, two, three." Putting the last one in her hand, she says, "I have one hundred beads." Michael looks at the circles drawn on the paper and says, "There are three."

Magnitude Comparison

. Comparison of two or more items to evaluate relative
  magnitudes.
. It involves activities such as ordering by length, size,
  or weight, measuring, or comparing length, size, area,
  weight, height, depth, or volume.
. Examples: Briana and Michael set their Lego structures
  side by side and compare whose is taller, David brings
  a newspaper and puts it on the table. Jessica says to
  David, "This newspaper isn't big enough to cover the table."

Spatial Relations

. Exploration of positions, courses, and distances in space.
. It involves activities such as representing the locations of
  objects in space; telling directions like left, right, front,
  above, or behind; or drawing maps.
. Examples: When Briana places a puzzle on the table, David
  asks her where she found it. She tells him that it was in
  the cabinet. David goes to the cabinet and asks her again,
  "Where?" She replies, "Next to the tinker-toys, no, the
  left side." Jessica and Michael rearrange the furniture
  in the dollhouse. When Jessica puts a couch beside a
  window, Michael moves it to the center of the living room,
  saying "The couch should be in front of the TV."

Pattern and Shape

. Exploration of patterns and spatial forms.
. It involves activities such as detecting patterns, identifying
  shapes, exploring parts and attributes of shapes, drawing
  shapes, or creating patterns and shapes.
. Examples: Michael connects unifix cubes one by one, and
  makes a yellow-red-blue-yellow-red-blue cube string; Sean
  builds a monster house with wooden blocks. He picks up the
  same size of small rectangle blocks and lines them vertically
  at regular space. Placing five blocks in a line on the
  floor, he makes another line of five blocks parallel to the
  first one. Then he places three blocks between each end
  of the two lines of blocks and make a square-shaped house.

APPENDIX B: TASKS FOR THE CLINICAL INTERVIEW STUDY

Tasks

Each child first participated in a warm-up task that consisted of sorting coins. This was intended to familiarize interviewer and child with each other, and to engage the child in an easy and enjoyable activity. The following tasks were presented in order.

Addition 1. The interviewer said that she was going to ask the child some questions about numbers: "Let's pretend you have X pennies in one hand and Y pennies in the other hand. How many pennies do you have altogether?" The following problems were available to be used: 2 + 1, 3 + 2, 4 + 3, 6 + 2, 8 + 3, 7 + 5, 8 + 7, 11 + 5 and 13 + 8. Four-year-old children began with the first problem and 5-year-old children with the second. Problems were presented in sequence until the child exhibited difficulty in solving a task, at which time the interviewer would suggest using pennies as an aid to solving the problem.

Addition 2. Next, the interviewer told the child that together they were going to draw two houses and a playground on a piece of paper. Generally the interviewer drew a simple, schematic first house and a nearby playground, and the child drew the second house. The interviewer then stated: "In this house there are X children and in this house there are Y children. All the children go outside to the playground. How many children are in the playground altogether?" The interviewer began by presenting a task at a level that was easily solved by the child in Addition 1. The available addition tasks were: 3 + 1, 7 + 2, 8 + 4, 9 + 7, 12 + 5 and 14 + 7. For example, if a child easily solved 8 + 7 in Addition 1, the interviewer began this section with 9 + 7. Problems were presented in sequence until the child exhibited difficulty in solving a particular task, at which time the interviewer would suggest using pennies as an aid.

Subtraction. The interviewer said: "The next day, there are X children in the playground and Y children leave the playground to go home and do their homework. How many children are left in the playground?" Using the child's performance on addition as a guide, the interviewer began with a problem at a level the child was likely to be able to solve without adult assistance. Available problems included 4 - 2, 9 - 2, 12 - 2, 16 - 2, 17 - 2, and 21 - 2. If the child answered the question incorrectly, the interviewer guided her toward the use of pennies as an aid.

Reversibility. Each time the child correctly responded to a subtraction problem, the interviewer then said: "The X children finish their homework and go back to the playground. How many children are in the playground now?" Thus, suppose the child begins by determining that if nine children are on the playground and two go home to do homework, seven are left on the playground. If the child immediately maintains, without calculation, that nine must now be on the playground, then he or she is assumed to have used the principle of reversibility.

Representation. The child was first asked to use paper and pencil to represent pennies placed in a line on at least two separate tasks. After the child became familiar with this task, the interviewer said, "Suppose we are having a party. At the party you get X presents. Then you get Y more presents. How many presents do you have altogether?" The interviewer began by presenting a task similar to one easily solved by the child in the previous addition sections. The following tasks were available: 3 + 1, 4 + 3, 7 + 6, 13 + 5, 14 + 8, and 22 + 5. If the child provided the correct answer, the interviewer increased the task difficulty. An incorrect response prompted the interviewer to suggest the use of paper and pencil to help the child solve the problem. If the child appeared confused, the interviewer would model the use of tallies and continue to scaffold until the child understood the task at hand. Once the child successfully solved the problem, the interviewer would present an additional task before moving on to the next question.

APPENDIX C: CODING OF LEVELS OF THE CLINICAL INTERVIEW STUDY

The following is a coding scheme created to measure key strategies and principles underlying addition, subtraction, and representation.

Level 1

1. *PUSHING ASIDE*: After or as each object is counted, it is moved to the side away from those that remain to be counted. Pushing aside includes such actions as pulling out from a main pile, turning down fingers while counting, or collecting objects in one's hand. The child can easily track what has been counted and what remains to be counted, reducing reliance on memory.

2. *GROUPING*: Initially establishing small groups of objects then combining all sets thereby constructing a group larger than any one individual set to determine a solution. The child may incorporate naturally existing groups to assist him or her in finding a solution.

3. *COUNTING ALL*: Establishing groups of objects and then combining all sets to find the sum, counting every object present.

4. *SEPARATING FROM*: Traditionally a three-step process involving objects (i.e., pennies, fingers, or marks on paper). First, the child constructs a set of objects equal to the larger number of the problem. Next the child removes the number of objects equal to the smaller number (doing his or her "take away"). Finally, the child counts the remaining objects to determine the answer.

5. *SEPARATING TO*: Similar to separating from, in which the child constructs the larger set and removes objects. The child separating to removes objects until the set remaining equals the smaller number. The number of objects removed then represents the answer. The child using this strategy constantly needs to assess the status of the remaining set. This strategy is unnatural and inefficient, and therefore rare (Carpenter & Moser, 1982.

6. *AUDITORY REPRESENTATION*:   As the child determines a solution for a given problem, she drops the pennies onto the table and taps her finger, pencil, or any other object in an effort to keep track of the numbers already counted and those that remain to be counted.

7. *ASSISTED COUNTING*: The interviewer directs the child's attention toward the concrete objects used to solve a given task by tagging each object as the child counts.

8. *GUESSING*: Forming an answer based on little or no information. The child's response is a wild guess unrelated to the numbers in the task.

9. *IDIOSYNCRATIC REPRESENTATION*: Using writing to represent a number, but with no discernible relation between what is put on paper and the number to be represented. The marks are unconventional and highly personal.

Level 2

10. *TAGGING*: Touching each object (i.e., pennies, fingers, etc.) once and only once for the purpose of counting without moving the object. When using this strategy, the child must remember what has already been counted and what remains to be counted.

12. *SUBITOPRODUCTION*: Instant production of a set of a specific cardinal value without counting. The child quickly puts out $\underline{N}$ objects without enumerating them individually.

13. *PICTOGRAPHIC REPRESENTATION*: Drawing pictures in an attempt to represent a number. Generally the pictures are very detailed.

Level 3

14. *COUNTING*: The counting of concrete objects aloud or silently without actually touching the objects. Other strategies such as pushing aside and tagging include counting in their definitions, but counting as a

strategy would only be noted if the child counts a set
of objects without touching the objects.

15. *SUBITIZING*: Instant visual recognition of the cardinal
value of a set of objects. The child immediately sees
that $\underline{N}$ objects are present without counting.

16. *ESTIMATION*: An answer based on a logical
approximation. The child's response is an educated guess
directly related to the numbers in the task.

17. *MATCHING*: This strategy is seen when there is a comparison
between two sets to determine a difference. The child
showing this strategy constructs set A and then set B.
To determine the difference between the sets, the child
matches the objects, counting the objects in set A which
do not have a counterpart in set B. This strategy requires
an understanding of one-to-one correspondence.

Level 4

18. *MENTAL ENUMERATION*: Counting absent or imagery objects
either in space or in one's mind. The child visualizes
and mentally counts the objects without the use of
manipulatives. This strategy is manifested by the child
looking into space with studied concentration, bobbing
his head, or moving the eyes or lips.

19. *COUNTING ON*: Representing the number of the initial set
in a problem and then adding the number of the second set
to the first without recounting the entire group.

20. *ADDING ON*: The child starts by forming a set equal to the
smaller number in the problem. The child then continues
to add objects until the larger number is reached. The
number of objects added is the answer or the difference.

21. *COUNTING DOWN*: This strategy involves counting back from
the larger number for a certain number of steps. The child
may count back equal to the smaller number in the problem, with
the answer being the last number stated in the count back.
Or the child may count back until the smaller number is

reached; the answer then is the number of steps in the count back. The first scenario has been referred to as *counting down from*, the second is *counting down to* (Carpenter & Moser, 1982). Both counting down from and to require keeping track of the number steps counting back. The child simultaneously counts forward to keep track as he or she counts back to take away. The child may keep track with fingers or verbally through a double count.

22. *COUNTING UP*: Similar to adding on, this strategy involves counting without objects. The child starts the count at the smaller number, counting until the larger number is reached. The answer then is equal to the number of steps it took to reach the larger number. The child must keep track of these steps.

23. *QUICK RECALL*: Immediate recollection of previously learned or memorized material (i.e., rote recall of number facts).

24. *EQUALIZING*: Requires a comparison between two sets as seen earlier in matching. The child matches an object in Set A to a corresponding object in Set B. Relying on one-to-one correspondence, the child then adds objects to Set B until the two sets are equal. The answer then is the number added. A potential error lies in not accurately keeping track of what was added. This strategy, therefore, requires more memory than the matching strategy.

25. *ICONIC REPRESENTATION*: A distinct mark not directly tied to the object's appearance is used to represent each object. For example, the child draws seven tallies to represent the seven pennies. Other forms of iconic representation include Xs, check marks, or dots (not circles).

26. *SYMBOLIC REPRESENTATION*: Written numerals are used to represent a set of objects. When asked to represent seven pennies, the child writes the number "7."

Children's application of the following mathematical principle was calculated:

Reversibility

Reversibility is understanding the reciprocal nature between addition and subtraction. After responding that 10 - 2 equals 8, a child using this principle is able to determine the answer to 8 + 2 without counting or using manipulatives.

An overall strategy level was determined for each child by first identifying all of the strategies used within the addition, subtraction, and representation segments of the clinical interview. Next, the frequency of each strategy was compiled and multiplied by its appropriate level. Thus, the weight assigned to each strategy corresponded to the numerical value attached to its level. For example, if tagging--a Level 2 strategy--was used on 15 occasions throughout an interview, this frequency would be multiplied by 2 for a weight assignment of 30. The weighted strategies were then summed and divided by the total number of strategies used within the relevant segments of the clinical interview to determine the average strategy level for each child. Thus, a child who used 61 strategies, which were assigned a weight of 94, received a score of 1.54, whereas a child who used 42 strategies, which were assigned a weight of 133, received a score of 2.93.

9

GEOGRAPHY FOR YOUNG CHILDREN: MAPS AS TOOLS FOR LEARNING ENVIRONMENTS

Lynn S. Liben
Roger M. Downs
The Pennsylvania State University

Federal legislation in the form of the *Goals 2000: Educate America Act* (Public Law 103-227) has established ambitious goals for all K-12 educators. Particularly important to anyone concerned with early childhood education is the first and seemingly simple "Ready to Learn" goal: "By the year 2000, all children in America will start school ready to learn." But before those responsible for preparing children to learn can help to shape appropriate early environments, it is critical to know what children will be expected to learn once they actually enter school. Again, *Goals 2000* is prescriptive: Goal 3, "Student Achievement and Citizenship," names the subjects that should be mastered in the course of education. The list includes English, mathematics, science, foreign languages, civics and government, economics, arts, history, and--the focus of this chapter--geography.

Before plunging into details about our research and recommendations concerning geography for young children, we begin by anticipating three questions, one or more of which may well be on the minds of skeptical readers. First, is geography education needed? Second, though perhaps a prior question, is geography needed? And third, in the context of the first two questions, is developmental psychology needed? To foreshadow what follows, our answers to all three questions are affirmative. Moreover, the answers lead to the conclusion that maps and other graphic representations of place play a central role not only for education in geography in particular, but for education in general. Maps therefore become the focus of our chapter.

In the second section we present our interdisciplinary approach to maps and the person who uses them. From geography, we draw descriptions of the major dimensions along which maps vary, which, by implication, comprise the dimensions that must be understood by the map user. From developmental psychology, we draw descriptions of cognitive foundations relevant for understanding those dimensions. Given the purpose of this particular volume, we assume that the person of interest is a young child, and thus we focus on early expressions of those cognitive foundations.

In the third major section, we describe illustrative empirical findings on young children's map understanding drawn from our own program of research. Our purpose is to highlight both the strengths and weaknesses of young children's understanding. Strengths provide a foundation on which to build; weaknesses suggest areas in which instruction and appropriate preparation for later instruction are needed. In the fourth section, we discuss illustrative educational activities and materials. We purposely begin by selecting problematic programs. We do so not because we take great pleasure in being nay-sayers, but rather because these examples provide clear illustrations of our assertion that problems arise when geography and developmental psychology are not adequately considered in planning educational materials and activities. We then suggest means to foster the integration of geography and developmental psychology. We conclude with a plea that all those involved in geography education pay close attention to both disciplines as they design education programs.

ADDRESSING THE SKEPTICS' QUESTIONS

Is Geography Education Needed?

One way to answer the question about the need for education in geography is by examining the state of Americans' geographic knowledge in the decades following an era in which geography was not taught in the schools. In short, it fared poorly. During the mid-1980s, the media were filled with articles such as one reporting that "20 percent of American youths can't find U.S. on a world map" (Innerst, 1984). Stories like these led to the proclamation of "Geography Awareness Week" by the U.S.Congress and to the establishment of an annual "National Geography Bee by the National Geographic Society. Virtually everyone came to recognize, however, that Congressional proclamations, contests, television specials, and similar activities could not solve the problems alone, thus setting the context for the inclusion of geography in *Goals 2000*.

Is Geography Needed?

In one sense, answering this question returns us to the first because the very posing of this question is likely to be driven by a naive (and mistaken) belief about the nature of geography. That is, people who have not been educated in the discipline of geography are likely to equate knowledge of geography with knowledge of place location facts, for example, that Paris is the capital of France, and that Ames is in Iowa. Given the widespread nature of this misunderstanding, it is perhaps not surprising that the writers of the *Geography for Life: National Geography Standards 1994* (Geography Education Standards Project, 1994) began their definition of *geography* by saying what it is not:

> Geography is not a collection of arcane information. Rather, it is the study of spatial aspects of human existence. People everywhere need to know about the nature of their world and their place in it. Geography has much more to do with asking questions and solving problems than it does with rote memorization of isolated facts.
> So what exactly is geography? It is an integrative discipline that brings together the physical and human dimensions of the world in the study of people, places, and environments. Its subject matter is Earth's surface and the proceses that shape it, the relationships between people and environments, and the connections between people and places. (p. 18)

Given this definition of geography, it is self-evident that geography is an essential part of human knowledge and existence. Understanding geography is critical for allowing us to make good decisions about our environment; to enhance the global economy; to decide where to locate schools, roads, airports, or radar stations; and to understand and address political conflicts. The *National Geography Standards* are replete with dramatic examples of what geography is and why it matters.

In the context of providing a more informed definition of geography, it is important to add that although the examples of geographic ignorance cited earlier focused on place location facts, there is ample evidence that geographic ignorance is more pervasive. As a society, we have repeatedly made local decisions that reflect ignorance of geographic knowledge and thinking, as, for example, treating decisions about venting chemical pollutants or locating waste disposal sites without regard to their global implications; building homes, businesses, or stadiums without adequate thought to infrastructure demands; or making military or political decisions without adequate understanding of the terrain and its use by local inhabitants.

As implied by the definition from the *National Geography Standards* and implicit in the examples just given, it is not just the content of geography that is important. It is also the process of geographic thinking. At its core, geographic thinking is spatial thinking. Geography is concerned with the explanation of spatial patterns and processes, and therefore the discipline is by its nature one that requires and fosters spatial thought. In our view, spatial thinking should take its place alongside linguistic and mathematical tools as essential components of education--a point to which we return later.

We close our case for why geography is needed by focusing on the importance of maps or, more broadly, graphic representations of place. Maps play a central role in geography. Again, to return to the *National Geography Standards*, maps or other kinds of representations of spatial distributions are mentioned explicitly in 13 Standards, are strongly implied in 3 and are arguably implicit in the remaining 2. Over and over, the specific skills include map skills and spatial thinking. For example, the first standard states that students should know: "How to use maps and other geographic representations, tools, and technologies to acquire, process, and report information from a spatial perspective" (p. 61). This, like all standards, is then translated into the knowledge that children are expected to acquire. For example, the explication of the first standard for Grades K to 4 begins:

> By the end of the fourth grade, the student knows and understands:
>
> 1. The characteristics and purposes of geographic representations--such as maps, globes, graphs, diagrams, aerial and other photographs, and satellite-produced images. (p. 106)

In turn, specific behaviors are named that could be taken as demonstrations of the student's knowledge and skills, accompanied by suggested learning activities that can aid in the development of these skills. To continue with the same example,

> A. Identify and describe the characteristics and purposes of geographic representations, tools, and technologies, as exemplified by being able to. . . Interpret aerial photographs or satellite-produced images to locate and identify physical and human features.

Examine a variety of maps to identify and describe their
basic elements.

Design a map that displays information selected by the
student. (p. 106)

Maps are at the center of geography. Perhaps just as important, maps
provide an entree into graphic representations in general. These, in turn, are
critically important even for components of education that are unrelated to
geography, particularly given the increasing reliance on computer graphics for
the display and manipulation of data in many fields. For example, scientific
visualization (Haber & McNabb, 1990) and cartographic visualization
(MacEachren & Taylor, 1994) are central to contemporary work by
demographers, epidemiologists, geologists, chemists, physicists, anthropologists,
historians, anthropologists, biologists, meteorologists, astronomers, and
oceanographers (to name just a few) as they describe, attempt to understand, and
model the effects of manipulating a wide range of phenomena. We would argue
that the concepts and skills taught through geographic maps will serve children
well in developing the kinds of skills that are needed to understand and profit
from images, irrespective.of the content they represent, the particular medium
of presentation, and of the particular problem they are addressed to solve.

In light of the centrality of maps for geography per se, as well as their
utility for facilitating children's understanding of graphic representations more
broadly, the research and theory we review in the body of this chapter are
focused on maps. As might by now have been inferred, our subtitle--"Maps as
Tools for Learning Environments"--is meant to carry two meanings. First,
maps allow us to learn about the environment they represent, that is, they are
tools for learning about environments. Thus, for example, from maps we can
learn something about the proximity of two political units or about the
relationship between topography and settlement patterns. But maps also provide
opportunities to learn general concepts and skills, that is, they create
environments for learning. They provide opportunities to develop skills in
measurement, geometry, interpolation, extrapolation, pattern recognition,
planning, and so on. Having, we hope, convinced even the most skeptical
reader about the importance of geography and the necessity for education in
geography, we turn to the final introductory question.

Is Developmental Psychology Needed?

Our final question asks whether developmental psychology is needed. Our
answer to this question is also enthusiastically affirmative. We believe that
developmental psychology is absolutely essential for planning and implementing
geography education and, indeed, for planning and implementing any kind of

education. This stance rests on the fundamental belief that the processes of comprehending, retaining, and applying new knowledge or new skills are always profoundly affected by the kinds of knowledge, cognitive skills, and socioemotional history the student brings to the learning situation.

This is, of course, the core belief of constructivism to which we subscribe. Our own favorite brand of constructivism is Piagetian theory, but we are just as comfortable with a Vygotskian or Brunerian version. Although this is not the place to address theoretical controversies within developmental psychology, it is worth pointing out that, in our view, the similarities among these theorists far outweigh the differences, despite the fact that they are often pictured as competing theories in the contemporary literature and despite the fact they currently enjoy very different status. Vygotsky is very much in vogue, Piaget is very definitely in disfavor, and Bruner is very puzzlingly often overlooked.

As we read these theories, the differences are ones of emphasis rather than core beliefs. Piaget placed particular emphasis on self-constructive processes (as in accommodation, assimilation, and equilibration; see e.g., Piaget, 1970, 1985), although he too recognized the importance of the social transmission of knowledge (Piaget & Inhelder, 1969), culture (e.g., Piaget, 1972; Piaget & Garcia, 1989), the role of peers in cognitive development (e.g., Piaget, 1965), and the importance of targeted education (e.g., Inhelder, Sinclair, & Bovet, 1974; Piaget, 1971, 1973). Vygotsky placed more emphasis on the role of social context for development, attending in particular to the role of the adult (or peer) in helping bring out the potentials of the child (as in the zone of proximal development; see e.g., Vygotsky, 1962, 1978) and the importance of the social construction of knowledge (Vygotsky, 1978). But Vygotsky, too, saw as important what the child brought to those socially situated learning opportunities. Thus, the notion of a *zone* of proximal development implies that there is a range of possibilities associated with any particular child at any particular moment, as illustrated by the kinds of reasoning he reported that children of different ages brought to concept-formation tasks (see Vygotsky, 1962, especially chap. 5). Bruner paid particular attention to the cultural and educational contexts in which children were placed, arguing that differences in these contents could affect or amplify the cognitive capacities of individuals (as in the different opportunities afforded by societies in which education occurs in an immediate rather than a removed context; see Bruner, 1964) and paying sustained and explicit attention to education per se (as in his discussions of general issues in education and his design of specific curriculum units; e.g., Bruner, 1960, 1966, 1973). But again, Bruner, too, recognized important age-linked differences in the nature of children's thought, as, for example, in his discussion of expanding systems of representation (the sequence of inactive, iconic, and symbolic representation; see Bruner, 1964) or as in children's developing abilities to reason systematically (as in work on how children reason in problems such as "20 Questions"; see Bruner, Oliver, & Greenfield, 1966).

Although all three theoretical positions emphasize the gradual nature of cognitive development and attribute causal roles (albeit differentially weighted) to both self-regulated and social factors, other developmental theorists give far greater explanatory weight to biological endowment. Those holding nativist views of individual development typically believe that babies arrive with many of the cognitive accomplishments that constructivists assert develop gradually and with effort (for a particularly pointed exchange, see Haith, 1998; Spelke, 1998).

Although our theoretical stance is more closely aligned with the gradual and effortful view than with the nativsit and automatic view, we believe that it is not necessary to select between these alternatives for most of the educational matters at hand. We need only agree that, at any given point, any particular child may be prepared to benefit from certain kinds of experiences in certain kinds of ways and not in others. We return to the implications of our research and theoretical position for education in the final two sections of the chapter. Before doing so, we turn to two tasks. The first is to provide an interdisciplinary perspective for approaching geography education. The second is to illustrate empirical research on children's understanding of maps.

CONCEPTUALIZING PLACE REPRESENTATIONS AND THE PEOPLE WHO ENCOUNTER THEM

At the core of our work is the proposition that the study of place representation must involve attention to two sets of links, depicted in Figure 9.1. The first concerns the processes by which the cartographer creates a representation of the referent world; the second concerns the processes by which the child extracts (or, more accurately given our theoretical perspective, constructs) understanding from that representation. Analyzing and understanding the first of these links is rooted in geography; analyzing and understanding the second is rooted in developmental psychology.

For an audience of psychologists and educators, the importance of the links between knower and representation is well appreciated. For an audience of geographers or cartographers, the importance of links between reality and representation is well appreciated. Because the two audiences are rarely one and the same, however, most psychologists and educators approach the development of geographic curricula with a naive cartographic perspective (Downs, 1985; Downs & Liben, 1988; Liben & Downs, 1989), whereas geographers approach the development of geographic curricula with a naive knower perspective (e.g., Downs, Liben, & Daggs, 1988; Liben & Downs, 1994). In the hope of speaking to both audiences, we therefore consider each set of links in turn.

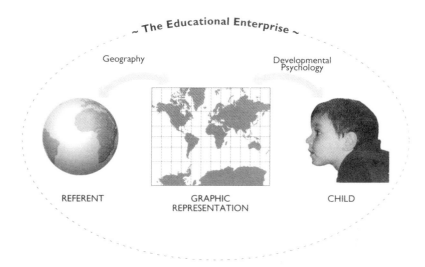

FIG. 9.1. An interdisciplinary approach to geography education.

Linking Referent and the Map

Understanding the first link--between referent and map--may fruitfully begin with a cartographic definition of a map:

> A map is a generalized, reduced, symbolic spatial representation of reality that has been transformed from the spherical surface of the earth (or any celestial body) in some dimensionally systematic way. (Liben & Downs, 1989, p. 180)

Implicit within this definition are two sets of correspondences between reality and map: representational correspondences and geometric correspondences. Representational correspondences specify what information is to be presented (e.g., information about land elevation) and the graphic means used to portray it (e.g., colors or contour lines). Geometric correspondences specify the spatial relations between reality and representation. These include viewing distance, and thus the scale of the map; viewing azimuth, and thus the orientation of the map (e.g., whether the space is viewed from the south vs. from the east); and viewing angle, and thus the kind of map (e.g., whether the space is viewed from straight down [known as a nadir, plan, or vertical view] vs. from an angle [known as an oblique or perspective map]). Thus, the process of going from a reality to a representation of that reality includes a variety of decisions about what information is to be included, at what level of abstraction, how it is to be symbolized, and how to handle the changes necessitated by going from a large, irregular, three-dimensional surface to a small, regular, two-dimensional surface.

What is especially informative about explicating these correspondences is that through them we can make explicit the point that there is not a singular, correct map of some referent. Maps are not simply miniaturizations or re-presentations of the world (see also Downs, 1981; Liben, 1999; MacEachern, 1995). Cartographers must make many interrelated decisions about various features of the map--decisions that rest on the purpose for which the map is intended. By illustration, a map of the world (small scale) could include information about major political divisions (e.g., countries, capitals) and perhaps major topographical features (such as large lakes and mountain ranges), but could not include detailed political or physical information. Although one reason for omitting much of this information is practical--it would be impossible to fit all the information on one piece of paper--an even more important reason is functional--it enables the cartographer to highlight certain ideas and relationships.

But it is not simply that content varies across maps: Spatial characteristics vary as well. For example, in designing a subway map, the cartographer includes information about order (which subway station is next), intersections (which subway stations allow transfer to other lines), and some general sense of direction (e.g., which lines run roughly north-south or east-west), but omits information about what is above ground and distorts precise metric and angular relationships that would be merely distracting for the rider (albeit essential for subway repair or rescue crews).

Similar attention to purpose is relevant for decisions about solving what cartographer's refer to as the map projection problem, that is, the fact that it is impossible to use a plane surface to represent a spherical surface without distorting some spatial feature of the referent--area, distance, direction, or shape. Again the cartographer's solution depends on the purpose for which the map is intended (see Muehrcke & Muehrcke, 1998). Thus, for example, a map designed for ship navigation is most useful if angular relationships are preserved (so that the ship's bearing may be set), even though this solution distorts land area (as in a Mercator projection). A map designed to examine agricultural production is most useful if it preserves area, even if it distorts direction (as in a cylindrical equal area projection).

Unless one appreciates the link between map function and map form, and unless one recognizes that many familiar features of maps are conventions rather than necessities, one risks harboring the erroneous beliefs (all of which we have encountered in children and adults) that north is always at the top of the page, Greenland is bigger than Brazil, and Russia is far from the United States. In short, unless one understands the processes involved in linking referents and maps, there is a risk of reifying both the maps and the reality that they represent. However, even powerful, persuasive maps with a message do little good if they cannot be understood by those who use them. This, in turn, raises the second set of links: those between representation and knower.

Linking the Map to the Knower

Given the position that representational and geometric correspondences are at the core of maps, what is most critical from the perspective of developmental psychology is characterizing the child's representational and spatial development. We thus highlight major developmental achievements in each.

Understanding "Stand For." Although the idea that one thing can be used to stand for another may seem patently obvious to an adult, there is considerable evidence that the symbolic nature of representations and the ability to use them in a stand-for relation to referents are not so apparent to very young children. Probably the most dramatic demonstration of this generalization comes from an already classic study by DeLoache (1987) using a scale model of a simply furnished laboratory room. After pointing out to young children that each element of the big room had a counterpart in the little room (e.g., a miniature blue couch and a big blue couch), a small Snoopy dog was hidden in the scale model, and the child was asked to find the big Snoopy who was hidden in the analogous place in the big room. DeLoache found that almost none of the 2 1/2-year-old children she tested could use the information from the scale model to find the dog in the big room, even though the children were almost always able to remember the original hiding location of the small dog. Interestingly, children just half a year older were able to solve the task, leading DeLoache to place the emergence of *representational insight* at somewhere between 30 and 36 months of age.

Observations by other theorists support the notion that children come to appreciate the symbolic nature of representations only gradually during the preschool years. Vygotsky (1962), for example, noted that long after children are using words quite successfully, they seem to believe that the word is inherently part of the referent itself, and thus that objects' names *must* be what they are. For example, a preschooler will assert that "an animal is called 'cow' because it has horns, 'calf' because its horns are still small" (Vygotsky, 1962, p. 29) and will reject the notion of interchanging the names *ink* and *cow* "because ink is used for writing, and the cow gives milk" (p. 29). Piaget (1929) described a similar but far more extensive and longer lasting problem of *nominal realism.* He reported that children initially believe that names emanate from things, seem to reside within those things, and cannot be changed.

Contemporary investigators have been unearthing misconceptions in young children's beliefs about the necessary links between linguistic symbols and their referents.   Bialystok (1992), for example, has shown that preschool children who know letter sounds, but cannot yet read, are likely to assume that physical characteristics of the referent (whether it is a large or small object) will be mimicked by the physical characteristics of the symbol (whether the word is long or short).   For example, when given two words and two pictures, children were more likely to match the words with the pictured objects correctly if their relative sizes matched (as in the pair *elephant* and *ant*) than when they did not (as in the pair *car* and *banana*).

Even beyond the preschool years, when the child has demonstrated representational insight and becomes more flexible about the use of linguistic symbols, children continue to enlarge their skill in exploiting representations in a stand-for relation.   Research on children's understanding of analogies and metaphors illustrates these later accomplishments.   For example, Gentner (1988) found that, whereas young children can typically understand metaphorical relations based on object attributes (such as color or shape), they are typically unable to understand metaphorical relations based on higher order relations (such as function).   Thus, for example, preschoolers are able to understand "The sun is like an orange," but not "A cloud is like a sponge."

In short, there are early tendencies to reify symbols, see them as immutable, and assume that symbols and referents share concrete characteristics --all tendencies that we show later are likewise evident in children's understanding of maps.

Understanding space.   One useful way to conceptualize children's developing understanding of space is provided by Piagetian theory.   Piaget suggested that, although even very young children can function quite well at the level of *action* (moving through space intelligently), it is over the entire course of childhood that reflective *representations* of space develop.   More specifically, Piaget and Inhelder (1956) suggested that preschoolers first develop topological concepts that concern qualitative relations such as proximity, order, enclosure, separation, and touching.   Thus, for example, preschoolers can represent relations such as *next to*, *on*, and *between* and can distinguish between open and closed figures.   However they do not differentiate between a triangle and a square or between a square and a rectangle because the latter two pairs are topologically (albeit not metrically) equivalent.

Emerging next are projective and Euclidean concepts.   Projective concepts are those dependent on point of view, for example, spatial relations such as left/right, in front/behind, up/down, or view-specific qualities such as whether an object is represented from its front or side.   Euclidean concepts are those dependent on Euclidean geometry, which establishes an abstract, stable reference system that allows measurement in all directions, permitting conservation of distance and angle.[1]

These three conceptual systems may be applied to spatial relationsin environments or to their representations. A topological description of a referent space is illustrated by a statement such as "The house is next to the railway station." A projective description of the same referent might be "The house is infront of the railway station", or, when approached from the opposite direction, "The house is behind the railway station." A Euclidean (or metric) description might read: "The house is one mile northeast of the railroad station" or might give coordinates in degrees of latitude and longitude.

Before leaving the discussion of topological, projective, and Euclidean concepts, we would like to emphasize that although the language we have chosen to use is decidedly Piagetian, this framework is compatible with the way that children's understanding of space is said to develop by scholars working outside the Piagetian tradition. That is, the Piagetian description that young children use primarily topological concepts is much like the suggestion made by others that young children rely upon local landmarks or local configurations. The Piagetian position that older children develop projective concepts is like the suggestion that children become increasingly more flexible in using alternative frames of reference. Finally, the Piagetian position concerning the late development of Euclidean concepts is comparable to the suggestion that a belated developmental accomplishment is mastering precise metrics of space (e.g., see Newcombe, Huttenlocher, Drummey, & Wiley, 1998; Presson, 1982; Siegel & White, 1975; Uttal, 1996). Irrespective of whether one uses language of *topological*, *projective*, and *Euclidean* or of *landmarks, frames of reference*, and *quantitative precision*, the general picture concerning the developmental sequence and challenges of spatial concepts is roughly the same. As with the development of representation, we revisit these concepts when we discuss children's understanding of maps later.

---

[1]There is some uncertainty about Piaget's position on the developmental relation between projective and Euclidean concepts. Piaget and Inhelder (1956) have been interpreted to say either that these two systems emerge sequentially or that they emerge in concert (see Merriwether & Liben, 1997). In any case, in later writings, Piaget (Piaget & Garcia, 1989) replaced the topological/projective/Euclidean sequence with one in which developmental progression is described as moving from intrafigural to interfigural to transfigural relations. Less important here than the specific theory is the general nature of a developmental progression that moves from a focus on (a) spatial properties of individual objects or local groups of objects, (b) objects in space in relation to the viewer, and (c) objects in space in relation to some specified, viewer-independent system (such as Cartesian coordinates).

Summary

At the core of our work is the proposition that place representations are not simply miniaturizations of reality that present the world as is, but rather are symbolic realizations of that world. Maps not only teach us that Paris is the capital of France and show us efficient routes to travel from home to the nearest railway station, but they allow cartographers to communicate (and users to discover) new spatial patterns and relations. But to understand or construct these messages, users must draw upon symbolic and spatial understanding. The previous section has reviewed the developmental course of symbolic understanding and spatial concepts. In the next section we demonstrate how development in these conceptual arenas is reflected in children's understanding and use of maps by describing illustrative findings from our program of empirical research.

EMPIRICAL ILLUSTRATIONS

Investigators studying children's developing understanding of maps have used a variety of methods that are depicted in Figure 9.2. (See Liben, 1997, for a more detailed description of these methods, the advantages of and "threats" to each.) In brief, *production methods* are those in which children have (naturally)

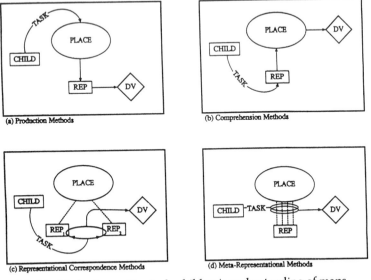

FIG. 9.2. Methods used to study children's understanding of maps, or more, generally, spatial representations of place [REP]. Dependent Variables are indicated by DV. (Reproduced from Liben, 1997, by permission).

or are given (experimentally) experience in some place (e.g., a room, building, or neighborhood), and asked to demonstrate knowledge of that space on an external representation (e.g., by drawing a map or marking a map to show particular locations). *Comprehension methods* are the inverse: children are given some experience with or information on a representation (e.g., they might examine a map of a playhouse, or are shown the location of some object by a sticker on the map) and are then asked to perform some action in the place (e.g., point from within one of the play rooms to another, or find an object in an actual room after having been shown its location on a map). *Representational correspondence* methods ask children to relate information from one representation to another (e.g., given a location shown on one map, show the same location on a map at a different scale). And finally, *meta-representational* methods are those in which children are asked to reflect on one or more of the relations depicted in the other three methods (e.g., why two different representations of the same place appear different and what might be learned uniquely from each).

In our work, we have used production, representational correspondence, and meta-representational methods. Participants have ranged from 3-year-old preschool children to faculty experts in geography. Given the purpose of the present volume on early childhood, we focus here on results from young children (but see Downs & Liben, 1991, for discussion of the continuing educational challenges throughout the life course).

Illustrative of our work using production methods is a study (Liben & Yekel, 1996) in which preschoolers were first asked to find objects (e.g., a teddy bear, lunch box) that had been placed in their classroom and were then asked to record the objects' locations by placing colored stickers on a classroom map. In a second production study (Liben & Downs, 1993), children in a kindergarten, first grade, a second grade, and a multi-age fifth/sixth-grade watched as an adult stood at a series of locations in their classroom and pointed straight ahead. Children were asked to place arrow stickers on a classroom map to show the adult's location and pointing direction. Illustrative of our work using representational correspondence methods is a study (Liben & Downs, 1991) in which first- and second-grade children were shown an aerial photograph of Chicago containing numbered locations, and were asked to place stickers to show the same locations on a map that represented (in a different scale) a portion of the area shown on the aerial photograph. In another correspondence study (Liben & Downs, 1989), first- and second-grade children were shown a three-dimensional model of the local terrain that contained colored flags; the children were asked to show the flags' locations on a contour map by using colored stickers. Our work with meta-representational methods is illustrated by an interview study with preschool children ages 3 to 6 (Liben & Downs, 1991) in which we asked questions about content, origins, and use of various place representations. All children were interviewed with aerial photographs of Chicago and their local community, as well as a Rand McNally Road map of Pennsylvania. In a second study (Downs et al., 1988), we asked elementary-school children, middle-school children, and adults to judge whether they considered various place images to be maps by asking them to respond *yes*, *no*, or *can't decide* to the question "Is this a map?"

Generalizing the findings from these diverse studies, the data show that even young preschoolers have some understanding of the representational and spatial meaning of maps but, at the same time, evidence some significant misunderstandings that seem to reflect the general course of representational and spatial development discussed earlier. We next provide examples of specific observations that lead us to these generalizations, focusing on representational and then spatial understanding.

Representational understanding. Children's general understanding of the meaning of place representations is suggested by their spontaneous descriptions of the images as a whole. For example, preschool children often greeted an aerial photograph of Chicago with spontaneous comments about its content (e.g., "a city" or "states and stuff" or "buildings") and reacted to a road map with a sense of familiarity (e.g., "I know what *that* is. . . *that's* a *real* map" and "It shows states and stuff," (see Liben & Downs, 1991). Furthermore, when we showed a variety of place representations and asked the question "Is this a map?" (Downs et al., 1988), even kindergarten children differentially accepted and rejected images that also elicit differential patterns of acceptance by adults. For example, when asked "Is this a map?", over 90% of kindergarten children answered *yes* when shown a small-scale, colored, political world map, whereas only about 35% responded *yes* when shown an eye-level photograph of the Chicago skyline. (Percentages for adults were, 100% and 70%, respectively). When asked a more open-ended question; "Do you know what a map is?" (Liben & Yekel, 1996), many preschoolers were able to say something about maps as way-finding devices (e.g., "Something you look at to show you where to go") or the storage of place information ("Something that shows the whole world around you. [It] shows where aunts and uncles live and I can see where my aunt lives"), although this knowledge was not universal (e.g., "I don't know") or vague (e.g., "What you look at sometimes"). In brief, children's success in interpreting the general place-referential meaning of maps (what we have referred to as understanding at the *holistic level*; see Liben & Downs, 1989) is relatively good among many preschool children.

Findings also suggest that young children have some understanding of the representational meaning of pieces of these place representations, or what we have called understanding of the *componential level* (Liben & Downs, 1989). To illustrate, the preschool children in our interview study (Liben & Downs, 1991) were commonly able to identify a few specific referents on various representations (e.g., buildings, roads, and the lake on the aerial photograph of Chicago; roads and rivers on the road map of Pennsylvania).

At the same time, however, preschoolers' identifications suggested some important limitations in their understanding of the abstract and arbitrary nature of symbolic representation. First, their identifications of the referent of the whole image were often unreasonable by adult standards, as, for example, when preschool children offered that the aerial photograph of Chicago showed "a big state" or "the United States" or "the whole world" and that the road map of Pennsylvania showed "Part of Africa" and, at once, "California, Canada, the West, and the North Coast" (see Downs et al., 1988; Liben & Downs, 1991). Of course, preschoolers are at a distinct disadvantage because they cannot read the titles and legends, and because they have less content knowledge about particular places. Probably more compelling evidence for deep-seated confusions are those that occur at the componential level. Particularly informative were responses in which the young child appeared to have overinterpreted the iconic (picturelike) characteristics of the representation's components.

Sometimes iconic interpretations lead to correct responses because the map-maker has used iconically motivated symbols on the map, or because there are, in fact, perceptual similarities between the referent and the image. Thus, for example, on the aerial photograph of Chicago, children often recognized roads "because they are gray" or "because they are straight"; on the road map of Pennsylvania, many children correctly identified the Susquehanna River as water, asserting that they could tell "because it is blue." However, the tendency to interpret symbols iconically often led to incorrect interpretations instead. On the Chicago aerial photograph, for example, a baseball diamond was interpreted as "an eye" and "a guitar," and a semicircular field of grass was thought to show "cheese." On the road map of Pennsylvania, the yellow areas used to show cities were interpreted as "eggs" and "firecrackers," and the Rand McNally compass rose was said to be "the sun," "a basketball stadium," "feathers," and--presumably because on the Pennsylvania map it is placed in the blue of Lake Erie--"the place where the lifeguard sits." Even when a referent was identified correctly (as in correctly interpreting a line on the road map as a road), children sometimes overextended a physical quality of the symbol to infer a similar physical quality of the referent. A striking example is when children claimed that a road shown in red on the map meant that if you stood on that road in the real world it would look red as well. These errors are reminiscent of the confusions described earlier with respect to language in which children erroneously believed that symbol and referent share surface characteristics (as in expecting that large objects have long words; see Bialystok, 1992).

Finally, we observed some interpretive confusions that we believe may stem from an overextension of graphic conventions. For young children who have relatively minimal exposure to maps, these conventional overextensions are more likely to derive from conventions in drawing rather than conventions in cartography. One example comes from how children responded to a question about whether they could find grass on the aerial photograph of Chicago. Some children rejected the possibility altogether, asserting that grass is green and the photograph was not (a response based in expectations about iconicity). Two preschoolers pointed to the bottom of the photograph, running their hands along the bottom border. Another child spontaneously volunteered that there was sky at the top. One interpretation of these otherwise puzzling responses is that they reflect knowledge that grass is at the bottom of pictures and sky is at the top. For children who have had more exposure to maps, but not yet to a great variety of them, there may be overextensions driven by cartographic conventions. In our interview study, for example, one 4-year-old child spontaneously and confidently identified the top part of the page of the road map as "the North Coast" and another said it was "Canada" (it was actually New York), identifications we speculate are the result of experiences with maps of the United States in which north and Canada are, indeed, usually at the top of the page.

Spatial Correspondences. A similar mixture of understanding and misunderstanding is evident when we turn from the representational to the spatial arena. Again, even preschool children demonstrate some rudimentary spatial understanding insofar as they are able to interpret a small, two-dimensional, vertical image (e.g., an aerial photograph of Chicago or a plan map) as a representation of a large, three-dimensional environment that they would normally experience from eye level. However, success is by no means universal. More important, the pattern of successes and failures is consistent with the pattern of individual and developmental differences in the progression of spatial concepts discussed earlier. To the extent that mapping tasks can be solved by calling on only topological concepts, even children with less advanced spatial skills (typically younger children) can perform well. To the extent that the mapping tasks require projective or Euclidean concepts, only those with more advanced spatial concepts (typically older children) do well.

Data from our interview study provide many humorous but telling illustrations of the difficulty preschool children have in understanding the scale relationships between the representation and the referent space. On the Chicago aerial photograph, for example, a child who had just successfully identified buildings as buildings, then rejected a road because it was "too skinny for two cars to fit on." The same difficulty appeared on the road map as, for example, when another child mistakenly interpreted the Susquehanna River as a road and vehemently denied that a black line could show a road because the former, but not the latter, was "fat enough for two cars to go on." (It is interesting to note that this response is actually sophisticated with respect to representational understanding insofar as the child did not assume that the blue color meant that it must be water.)   Another 4-year-old was aghast when the interviewer suggested that perhaps a particular part of an aerial photograph of the local State College, Pennsylvania region showed the university building in which his father worked.   Horrified, he responded, "Oh no it's huge. It's as big as this whole map!" while he gestured, moving his hand expansively around the sheet containing the aerial photograph.   On a plastic relief map, the same child rejected raised sections as mountains because "they're not high enough." Finally, indicative of children's difficulty in understanding scale was the finding that the boats on Lake Michigan in the aerial photograph of Chicago were identified by several preschoolers as *fish* (see Liben & Downs, 1991, for a fuller description of these results).

Other misinterpretations suggested that children also had difficulty understanding viewing angle and/or azimuth.   For example, rows of railroad cars lined up in parallel were identified as *book shelves* and tennis courts were identified as *doors*.   Similarly, in our study with a simple plan map of a preschool class (Liben & Yekel, 1996), two children identified the overhead view of a double sink as a *door*.   These misidentifications make sense if one assumes that children are interpreting components of the images as if they were being viewed from the front (as in an elevation view) rather than from overhead (as in a plan view).   In short, data from the meta-representational studies are consistent with the presumed relevance of topological, projective, and Euclidean concepts for map understanding.

Production and correspondence methods may also be used to evaluate the proposed relevance of these spatial concepts for mapping. One implication of our developmental analysis is that map-location tasks that provide many landmarks should be solved more easily by younger (and spatially less skilled) children than tasks that provide few landmarks. The former tasks can be solved by topological reasoning, but the latter call on Euclidean concepts (as when the child mentally creates horizontal and vertical axes and scale to find isomorphic locations in the two spaces).

Our data from location tasks are consistent with this conjecture as illustrated by the study in which children examined locations marked on an aerial photograph of Chicago and then placed stickers on a cartographic map to show the same locations (Liben & Downs, 1991). Consistent with the hypothesized early ability to draw on topological concepts, performance differed both across age and target locations. For example, for a unique target that was located on the end in the breakwater in Lake Michigan, correct responses were given by 29% and 70% of children in Grades 1 and 2, respectively. In contrast, for a location on a building on a city block that looked similar to many other buildings and blocks, the percentages of correct responses were 0% and 19%. Similar landmark effects were evident in the task in which children were asked to place colored stickers on a contour map to show the location of colored flags in a three-dimensional model (Liben & Downs, 1989). Contrasting percentages of correct responses for a location with a unique landmark (a flag at the end of Mt. Nittany, which, because of its shape, provided a unique landmark) versus one located in a relatively undifferentiated area (on a flat area of the valley) were 44% versus 13% for Grade 1 and 59% versus 22% for Grade 2.

A second implication of our developmental analysis is that map-location tasks that draw relatively less on projective concepts should be solved more easily by younger (and spatially less skilled) children than tasks that draw relatively more heavily on projective concepts. Thus, mapping tasks in which the referential and representational spaces are aligned should be solved more easily than mapping tasks that require the child to mentally coordinate the two spaces (e.g., by mentally rotating one of the spaces or by mentally transporting oneself to a new vantage point).

An empirical illustration demonstrating the importance of alignment comes from the task in which children were asked to place arrow stickers on classroom maps to show an adult's location and direction of pointing (Liben & Downs, 1993). The left graph of Fig. 9.3 shows data for children's responses when the maps were aligned with the classroom. (The data are given for accuracy of arrow locations; data on accuracy of arrow orientations were comparable.) About half the kindergarten children's responses, and almost all

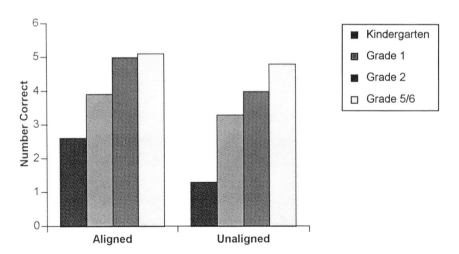

FIG. 9.3. Mean number correct, by grade, on the location task given under aligned and unaligned conditions. (Data taken from Liben & Downs, 1993.)

second-grade children's responses were correct. On the right of Figure 9.3 are data from a condition in which the map and classroom were unaligned (by 180 degrees). Performance was significantly lower in the unaligned than aligned conditions in all but the oldest grade. This pattern of findings is consistent with the notion that young children are especially challenged by the tasks that require an understanding of projective spatial concepts (or frame of reference), but that as they develop projective concepts, they can coordinate conflicting frames of reference successfully.

In summary, the predicted relation between developing spatial concepts and successes on mapping tasks was evident in a range of studies. Children's errors in identifying components of both aerial photographs and maps were consistent with a failure to have mastered projective and Euclidean concepts. Similarly, the patterns of performance observed on various place-location tasks were also consistent with the hypothesized role of projective and Euclidean concepts. Children in early elementary school grades performed relatively well when they could rely on topological concepts for task solution and relatively poorly when it was necessary to use projective or Euclidean concepts. Tasks that were problematic for young elementary school children were solved by older elementary school children who, for the most part, could be expected to have developed the more advanced projective and Euclidean skills. (See, for example, performance by children in Grade 5/6 in the unaligned condition shown in Figure 9.3).

Individual difference data also supported the theoretical link insofar as children who performed better on other (non-map) assessments of metric and projective spatial concepts performed better on mapping tasks predicted to depend on those concepts. This relationship held even when chronological age and scores on other cognitive indexes were partialed out (see Liben & Downs, 1989; 1993). In short, the way in which children understand and use the spatial properties of maps appears to be consistent with the hypothesized developmental progression of underlying spatial concepts.

Conclusions

A range of findings from our empirical work leads us to conclude that even by age 3, many children can recognize maps and other representations of place as standing for referent spaces, and some are already able to talk about map function. Despite the relative lack of explicit attention to map experiences in most homes and classes (compared, say, with an early focus on language), we observe considerable progress in children's understanding of the representational and spatial nature of maps over the early elementary school years. Furthermore, children's enthusiasm about maps leads us to be optimistic that they may well provide a valuable entree into developing skills in spatial and graphic representations more generally. Some preschool children we interviewed were so engaged that we were able to go beyond our core set of map materials for interviews that lasted as long as 45 minutes. When we entered one first-grade classroom during a several-week instructional unit, one child excitedly shouted out "The map people!", and the entire class broke into applause.

Our findings suggest that most preschool children have at least some understanding of the general representational nature of maps, consistent with the conclusion by DeLoache (1987, 1989) that representational insight is usually established by 3 years. At the same time, our empirical work has revealed that there is still much for children to come to understand, both about the representational and spatial meaning of maps. The kinds of confusions evidenced by children with respect to the representational qualities of maps are similar to those discussed by Piaget, Vygotsky, and Bruner with respect to other symbol systems. The kinds of confusions evidenced with respect to spatial components of maps are consistent with the developmental progression originally proposed by Piaget and Inhelder (1956) concerning the emergence of topological, projective, and Euclidean concepts. Although we believe that this theory is not the only one that can be used to characterize age-linked conceptual development, we would insist that *some* developmental approach is critical for identifying ways in which children should be prepared to enter school and for informing the design of curriculum to be used after they arrive. In the final section of this chapter, we turn to discussions of the educational enterprise more directly.

GEOGRAPHY EDUCATION: THE EDUCATIONAL ENTERPRISE

In the first section of this chapter we focused on the two links represented by arrows in Figure 9.1. With respect to the link between referent and representation, our argument was that place representations such as maps are symbolic representations about the referent space, not miniature re-presentations of the referent. What is provided in and communicated by the representation is (and indeed should be) different from what is available from the referent space. With respect to the link between representation and user, our argument was that users are not passive recipients of representations. On the contrary, when individuals use place representations to acquire information or to generate and solve problems about the referent space, they do so by bringing to those representations a particular combination of cognitive skills and experiences. In the preceding section, we provided illustrative empirical findings consistent with the notion that children's understanding of maps is affected by their developing symbolic and spatial concepts.

In this section, we address the educational implications of our conceptualization and empirical findings. At the broadest level, our approach to these educational implications is indicated in Figure 9.1 by the ellipse denoting the educational enterprise. Its enveloping placement is meant to imply that this enterprise--whether addressed to education in formal or informal settings--is an overarching one that must take both disciplines and both sets of links into account. Absent this integrated approach, we risk an educational curriculum that (a) contains content that is mistaken (i.e., simply wrong), (b) is mistaught and/or misunderstood (i.e., although understood by the teacher and presented accurately, is taught in a way that--given the child's concepts--is misinterpreted); or (c) is characterized by missed opportunities (i.e., fails to exploit learning opportunities to foster geographic knowledge, spatial thinking, and graphic skills). We begin with brief descriptions of materials and activities that we have encountered (and, in one case, even designed) that help illustrate the three kinds of problems. In the final section, we provide some general guidelines for moving from the conceptual world of the academy into the practical world of the classroom.

Educational Illustrations

The first examples illustrate our assertion that geographic materials are sometimes flat out wrong or misleading. One of the clearest examples comes from a children's book on maps that we stumbled on by chance in our local public library, which asserts that "North is always to the top of the map" (Rhodes, 1970, p. 46). Given exposure to a lesson like this, it is small wonder that many children automatically assume that north is up (an issue discussed again later) and have difficulty in understanding maps with other viewing azimuths (see Downs & Liben, 1991).

An example of what we would consider to be a misleading geography lesson is one described by Sachs and Banas (1987). Teachers were told to cut a world political map into horizontal strips and then ask children to reassemble the map and place name cards on it to show features such as an ocean or Brazil. To demonstrate the efficacy of the lesson plan, Sachs and Banas reported that the speed and accuracy of card placement improved with repetition and reinforcement. As discussed in detail elsewhere (Liben & Downs, 1994), activities like these seem to push for solution strategies at the graphic rather than *geo*graphic level. For example, children may reassemble the map based on finding connecting lines and colors rather than understanding relations among different physical and human features (e.g., mountains, rivers, sea ports, and population centers). Furthermore, they are likely to learn where things are in relation to the particular representation used for the task (i.e., in this particular projection, with this particular orientation, with these particular colors). Although this lesson is not factually wrong, it is, we believe, wrong in the sense of presenting a reified and hence misleading lesson about geography.

Our next example demonstrates how--even with teachers who are geographically and developmentally savvy (ourselves!)--children may misunderstand a lesson when the conceptual foundation has not yet been adequately laid. This lesson, too, concerned north. In part motivated by the knowledge that north is so often taught incorrectly by fixing it relative to the page (as illustrated by the Rhodes book discussed earlier), we began our discussion of north in first- and second-grade classes by asking students to close their eyes and point to where they thought north was. As we anticipated, responses were variable and commonly included pointing straight ahead or straight up in the air. We then discussed the notion of magnetic north, took out a compass, and had a number of children come up to the front of the room one at a time to point to north (which they discovered was over their left shoulder). In the course of these activities, one second-grade boy became increasingly agitated and eventually leapt to his feet, went over to the wall, pulled down the map, and pointed triumphantly to show everyone that indeed north as straight up. We discussed this issue further with respect to the map and placement of maps and thought that our message had been heard.

However, a few weeks later, we accompanied the first and second graders on a field trip to a recreation center. Soon after we were there, we asked everyone to close their eyes and point to north. We had anticipated that most children would recognize that they did not know and perhaps ask for compasses. Instead, we found that children now quite consistently and confidently pointed over their left shoulders! Our lesson seemed to have eliminated the fixed referent of the classroom or wall map and substituted the fixed referent of the child's own body. Viewed from the perspective of the difficulty of projective spatial concepts for children of this age, this outcome is not surprising. However, it does provide an excellent example of how well-intentioned instruction may simply substitute one misunderstanding for another.

Our final example concerns missed opportunities and comes from a short animation of a treasure hunt on Sesame Street, in which a young girl receives a map from a pirate who speaks gibberish except for the word map. The map contains iconic pictures of a tree, rock, and tree stump next to which appears a large blue "X." The animation shows the girl encountering a sequence of adults, each of whom she asks (again, in verbal gibberish) about the next landmark (the meaning of the gibberish is made clear by a picture of the landmark in a bubble over the character's head). In each case, the adult points in a particular direction, the girl heads off in the indicated direction, and she reaches the landmark. When she finally reaches the tree stump, she digs a hole, finds the treasure chest, opens it, and discovers that it contains the letter "X"!

The particular animation was developed to teach the letter "X." When considered from the perspective of enhancing children's letter recognition in preparation for later reading, the vignette is probably highly effective.

However, from our perspective--one concerned with preparing children for later map learning and for enhancing spatial concepts--the animation is less than ideal because it fails to capitalize on an opportunity to foster understanding in the spatial-graphic-geographic realm. Even worse, it probably interferes with the child's understanding of the representational nature and the spatial power of maps.

First, throughout the sequence, the child and the adults respond to a series of individual landmarks rather than to the configurational relations among them. In each case, the child asks about a single landmark and simply follows the direction in which the adult physically points. Any lesson about the power of a map to help reveal relations among landmarks was thus lost. Indeed, the route that the child travels is one that would *not* have taken if the map had been used as a map rather than as a pictorial list of individual landmarks: The child follows two legs of a triangle rather than the hypotenuse. In addition, the travel as depicted is almost impossible to combine into a coherent whole: Characters move from side to side across the screen, making it difficult to form a coherent image of the relations among screen space, the map space, and the referent space. No attempt was made to depict the girl figuring out the isomorphisms between the surrounding environment and the space depicted on the map. Finally, the closing scene in which the child opens the treasure chest and removes the letter "X" is pedagogically problematic. Adults are amused because they discover that something that is obviously (to them) meant to be an arbitrary symbol on the map (the letter "X" on the paper) turns out to be a motivated symbol for the referent (i.e., a "real" X rather than, say, a cache of jewels). However, in light of the research reviewed earlier, this ending seems destined to reinforce rather than overcome young children's confusions about the shared characteristics of symbols and their referents.

To reiterate, in our view the vignette is probably extremely effective for the purpose for which it was designed--providing repeated and memorable exposure to the letter "X." Our regret is that as is so often the case, designers appear to have considered how to help prepare children for literacy, without simultaneously considering how they might also help prepare children for graphicacy. One can readily imagine ways to modify the vignette to demonstrate the power of maps. For example, one might have had two characters leaving from the same place at the same time to find a buried treasure. One character might follow the procedure used in the vignette, going from landmark to landmark by asking directions from one to the next. The second character might instead consult a map to figure out the best route to the goal and thereby arrive long before the first character. This revision would demonstrate the advantage of considering configurational relations among landmarks, rather than considering each individually. Or one might use the original vignette or one character going from landmark to landmark, but simultaneously show an aerial view of the character's movements as the story unfolds (e.g., by having Big Bird looking down on the scene). This would demonstrate that the same event can be represented in multiple ways (by showing two representations simultaneously) and provide experience with alternative viewing angles (by showing both normal eye-level views and the aerial [vertical] view of the same content). In addition, the advantage to having a bird's eye view or a map could be implicitly demonstrated by showing the inefficiency of taking the longer path to the treasure.

Overcoming and Avoiding Educational Pitfalls

All of the preceding examples are negative ones in the sense that they provide illustrations of what not to do. We believe that the conceptual and empirical work reviewed earlier is also forward looking in the sense of providing lessons about what *should* be done. Clearly it would be impossible in just a few pages to lay out the specific implications of our work for designing a curriculum in geography or for preparing children for their later encounter with that curriculum. We can, however, provide a few principled "do's" organized as counterpoints to the three negative illustrations given above.

The first "do" is relevant to the formulation of any domain-specific curriculum: It is essential to look to the parent discipline for setting the educational agenda. By drawing from the discipline of geography, curricula will necessarily be designed to go beyond place-location lessons and avoid confining children to using only north-at-the-top, Mercator projection, water-colored-blue maps. As we have suggested elsewhere (Liben & Downs, 1994), a specific lesson from geography is the implication that, beginning early, children should be exposed to many different kinds of representations of objects and places, many different forms, and, a variety of representations that show the "identical" referent. By seeing that the apparent shape and size of, say, Greenland varies markedly from map to map, the child should be better equipped to understand how to differentiate between characteristics of the representation versus characteristics of the referent, to learn a range of subject content, and, more generally, to appreciate the value and power of different kinds of representations.

Of course it is impossible for program developers and teachers, particularly those in early childhood who necessarily cover so many content areas, to be experts in every domain in which they teach. Thus, the implication is not to demand that each individual teacher will become an expert geographer, but rather to urge that geographers be partners in curriculum development. An example of this model is that used by Children's Television Network (CTW) in planning programs for new content areas. For example, when CTW decided to introduce geography to Sesame Street, staff began by reviewing existing geography curricula for young children, asked geography consultants to review a draft set of curriculum goals, and then assembled a working group of research staff, writers, producers, and content specialists who could shape goals and consider programming possibilities (see Liben & Downs, 1994). The resulting pieces were theoretically informed by an understanding of the kinds of issue reviewed earlier. For example, one vignette produced after these collaborative workshops shows a school playground, first as a child views it during recess, and then as it is seen from increasingly distant and increasingly vertical views, culminating in a plan map. This vignette was well designed to help children to see transitions occurring across different viewing angles, azimuths, and scales, transitions that are usually invisible or ignored. Experiences like these should help prepare children for later understanding of representations of more distant geographic spaces.

Another example of integrating geography experts and teachers in productive partnerships is the nation-wide system of Geographic Alliances supported by the National Geographic Society. Each state's Alliance links university-based geography educators with classroom teachers to provide inservice and preservice workshops, field trips, materials, and mentoring programs. Grassroots activities like these fit into still larger national efforts in which members of the geography education community have collaboratively defined national standards (Geography Education Standards Project, 1994).

The second "do" is the psychological counterpart of the first--namely, that it is also important to involve developmental and educational psychologists in designing and reviewing materials. As is perhaps all too well illustrated by our own failed attempt to help children understand north, this approach is not foolproof. However, it does help identify what kinds of concepts are likely to be difficult for young children, suggest assessments to determine whether children have understood the intended concepts, and to offer ideas about revising classroom activities and materials when necessary. From a practical perspective, the involvement of developmental and educational psychologists from the academic world is often the best way to ensure that this kind of curriculum assessment and revision occurs. Classroom teachers rarely have the time or resources to do these, and professionals who develop curricula commercially (e.g., publishers) generally channel their support into the design and distribution of marketable materials rather than to the evaluation of their effectiveness.

It is important to pause here to make explicit our position about early geography education, which we take as implicit in the prior discussions as well as in our work elsewhere. We believe (and think that data support) the generalization that children of different ages and abilities bring differing concepts and knowledge to the instructional setting. As a consequence, different children take away different lessons (sometimes even confusing or inaccurate ones) from the same instructional activities and materials. We believe, therefore, that it is critical to structure activities and materials in ways that take these age and individual differences into account. We believe that, for very young children, the most important kinds of educational experiences will be those that help build the basic foundations on which later more advanced geographic concepts can be taught.

Elsewhere we (Liben & Downs, 1994) have discussed the importance of thinking about graphic readiness and developing ways to foster pre-mapping skills much as we already think about reading readiness and try to foster prereading skills. For example, premapping activities would include those that help develop the idea that any one referent can be represented in many different ways, and the idea that information available from one source (e.g., a photograph at a particular scale from a particular viewing angle and direction) is different from information available from another (e.g., a schematic plan map). In addition, we would urge the utility of producing and using maps of environments in which children live and play before turning to maps of distant, unfamiliar places that cannot be experienced directly.

However, the fact that we believe that young children have various cognitive immaturities (e.g., difficulty in understanding projective concepts, or difficulty in understanding the hierarchical nature of class inclusion relations; see Downs et al., 1988) does *not* mean we believe that geography education and mapping should be avoided with young children. We make this statement explicitly and emphatically here because our position has been misinterpreted along just these lines (see Blaut, 1997a, 1997b). We would like to avoid any further misunderstanding (see our fuller response in Downs & Liben, 1997; Liben & Downs, 1997).

Our position is most like Bruner's classic claim: "We begin with the hypothesis that any subject can be taught effectively in some intellectual honest form to any child at any stage of development" (Bruner, 1960, p. 33). We would add (as we believe Bruner implied) that a failure to make adjustments for the learner's conceptual development encourages understanding at a superficial level at best and leads to deep misunderstandings at worst. There is ample evidence for these kinds of misconceptions in various domains, perhaps most dramatically in the literature on naive physics, which has shown repeatedly that even adults who have taken college-level physics courses display deep misunderstandings of their physical worlds (e.g., McAfee & Proffitt, 1991; Roncato & Rumiati, 1986). Closer to the geographic topic at hand are the findings of Vosniadou and Brewer (1992) showing that despite the fact that children can confidently tell you (as they have been taught) that the Earth is a sphere, they respond incorrectly to questions that they have not encountered before (e.g., "Could you fall off the edge of the Earth?"). Taken together, children's responses to questions like these reveal that their underlying mental models of Earth are wrong, believing, for example, that Earth is a flattened disc or a hollow ball containing people living inside.

As a specific illustration of what might be done at the level of early preparation that builds on both geography and developmental psychology, we return to our own failed attempt to teach the concept of *north*. What the failed lesson indicates--and indeed what could (and should) have been predicted from children's more general difficulty in understanding projective spatial concepts--is that young children will have difficulty understanding the relativity of their own perspective in relation to fixed frames of reference. To prepare children for learning these geographic and spatial concepts, early experiences should develop understanding of the relativity of point of view. At a preschool level, for example, one might have matching tasks (e.g., via card games) in which *matches* require not only that the referent is the same (e.g., both pictures are of the same bear), but also that the view of the referent is the same (e.g., both show the bear from the front rather than, say, the back or either side). As another example, one might have activities in which one must find and order views (e.g., photographs) as one moves systematically around or away from some object. One might give children a particular perspective on something (e.g., a picture of the side of the school) and have the child go to a location they would need to go to see that particular view. One might also use activities that prepare children to understand that directions are related to one's initial location and orientation. For example, children who are in different positions and orientations within a room may all point to the same target (e.g., the teacher's desk) and then be asked to describe where they are pointing. Discovering that they point differently (e.g., "behind me," "in front of me," "to my side") and yet are all correct may also prepare children to later appreciate why, for example, north cannot always be straight ahead, or directly over their left shoulder!

It would be impossible to generate here the endless activities that could prepare children for later geographic and spatial competencies. Instead, we end with a third overarching "do" which is to urge that those responsible for developing educational programs and materials bring spatial and graphic representations onto center stage. We observe that most adults (including educators) give relatively little attention to graphic or spatial skills. Because there has been such an imbalance in our thinking and empirical work favoring linguistic education, it will take considerable effort to redress this problem. Consider, for example, what might happen to early education if--along with some minimal competency in verbal language that is already required for high school graduation--there were also minimal competency requirements in, say, image interpretation, mental rotation, wayfinding, or graphic production. Might we see more early educators attending to precursors of graphic, spatial and nonlinguistic, but representational, skills?

There are ample demonstrations confirming the role of early experience for later competencies. In the domain of literacy, for example, there is a large and compelling research literature showing a relation between early parent-childrearing and later literacy (e.g., see Morrow, chap. 10, this volume). In the visuospatial domain, there is evidence that greater use of certain kinds of toys is linked to better spatial skills. Indeed, the well-documented male superiority in spatial skills in both childhood and adulthood, as well as individual differences in spatial ability within sex, appears to be at least in part attributed to differential toy use and leisure activities earlier in life (e.g., Baenninger & Newcombe, 1989; Sherman, 1967; Signorella, Jamison, & Krupa, 1989).

There may be similar kinds of early experiences that facilitate children's abilities to interpret representations and eventually foster a higher level or meta-level understanding of representations (see Liben, 1999). As an example of initial work in this area, we are currently studying if and how parents call attention to graphics when reading picture books with their preschool children and what children understand from these experiences (Szechter & Liben, 1999). Similarly, we have begun to study whether experience in producing view-specific representations (photographs) affects children's spatial skills (Liben & Szechter, 1999). Although we cannot describe the findings here, we mention this work to provide concrete examples of the kinds of early experiences that might provide the foundations for developing activities useful for preparing children for more formal educational curricula on geography and other spatial curricula.

CONCLUSIONS

We close by returning to the importance of geography and to the value of a developmental approach for designing geography curriculum and preparing children to profit from that curriculum. At the broadest level, our message is that geography as a discipline is important not only because of its content, but also because of its utility for promoting spatial thinking and graphic representation. We believe these essential cognitive skills should take their place alongside linguistic tools. Children are surrounded by (and able to hear) oral language and acquire the ability to understand it without struggle. It is equally true that children who are surrounded by (and able to see) graphic spatial stimuli likewise acquire the ability to understand graphics without struggle. In the course of normal exposure to the graphics of the culture, children become able to make sense of drawings in their picture books, photographs, and other graphically presented representations. Just as the ability to understand language does not translate without instruction into an automatic ability to read text or into refined production or comprehension skills, so too, the ability to understand graphics does not translate into an automatic ability to read graphics. We have tried to demonstrate that the decoding process is not an easy one and draws on a complex set of cognitive skills. Furthermore, we have tried to argue that geography education can enhance, as well as be enhanced by, spatial thinking. Ultimately, the translation of these ideas into practice is dependent on parents, child-care providers, classroom teachers, television producers, toy manufacturers, book and software publishers, and other adults. As a consequence, to foster geography education, the first step is for adults to abandon the regrettably common belief that geography is nothing more than an endless store of place-location facts. Those responsible for designing and implementing early education must first become cognizant of the richness of the subject matter of geography and of the kinds of cognitive skills that geography education fosters. Only then will the inclusion of geography in *Goals 2000* legislation actually find its way into educational practice. Just as it is essential for those responsible for educating children to appreciate the value of the subject matter, so too it is essential for them to appreciate the qualities of the learners who encounter it. We must be continually attentive to how the materials, activities, questions, and information of the discipline are likely to be understood by far less developed and experienced minds. In short, to return to our interdisciplinary stance, it is critical to understand both the discipline and the child. We believe that we can get there from here, but to do so we must know not only where we are headed, but also have a good appreciation for where we are starting.

REFERENCES

Baenninger, M., & Newcombe, N. (1989). The role of experience in spatial test performance: A meta-analysis. *Sex Roles, 20*, 327-344.

Bialystok, E. (1992). Symbolic representation of letters and numbers. *Cognitive Development, 7*, 301-316.

Blaut, J. M. (1997a). Children can. *Annals of the Association of American Geographers, 87*, 152-158.

Blaut, J. M. (1997b). Piagetian pessimism and the mapping abilities of young children: A rejoinder to Liben and Downs. *Annals of the Association of American Geographers, 87*, 168-177.

Bruner, J. S. (1960). *The process of education.* Cambridge, MA: Harvard University Press.

Bruner, J. S. (1966). *Toward a theory of instruction.* New York: Norton.

Bruner, J. S. (1973). *Beyond the information given.* New York: Norton.

Bruner, J. S., Oliver, R. R., & Greenfield, P. M. (1966). *Studies in cognitive growth* (pp. 9-11). New York: Wiley.

DeLoache, J. S. (1987). Rapid change in the symbolic functioning of very young children. *Science, 238*, 1556-1557.

DeLoache, J. S. (1989). The development of representation in young children. In H. W. Reese (Ed.), *Advances in child development and behavior* (Vol. 22, pp. 1-39). New York: Academic Press.

Downs, R. M. (1981). Maps and mappings as metaphors for spatial representation. In L. S. Liben, A. H. Patterson, & N. Newcombe (Eds.), *Spatial representation and behavior across the life span: Theory and application* (pp. 143-166). New York: Academic Press.

Downs, R. M. (1985). The representation of space: Its development in children and in cartography. In R. Cohen (Ed.), *The development of spatial cognition* (pp. 323-345). Hillsdale, NJ: Lawrence Erlbaum Associates.

Downs, R. M., & Liben, L. S. (1988). Through a map darkly: Understanding maps as representations. *Genetic Epistemologist, 16*, 11-18.

Downs, R. M., & Liben, L. S. (1991). The development of expertise in geography: A cognitive-developmental approach to geographic education. *Annals of the Association of American Geographers, 81*, 304-327.

Downs, R. M., & Liben, L. S. (1997). The final summation: The defense rests. *Annals of the Association of American Geographers, 87*, 178-180.

Downs, R. M., Liben, L. S., & Daggs, D. G. (1988). On education and geographers: The role of cognitive-development theory in geographic education. *Annals of the Association of American Geographers, 78*, 680-700.

Gentner, D. (1988). Metaphor as structure mapping: The relational shift. *Child Development, 59*, 47-59.

Geography Education Standards Project. (1994). *Geography for life: National geography standards 1994.* Washington, DC: National Geographic Research & Exploration.

Haber, R. B., & McNabb, D. A. (1990). Visualization idioms: A conceptual model for scientific visualization systems. In G. M. Nielson, B. Shriver, & L. J. Rosenblum (Eds.), *Visualization in scientific computing* (pp. 73-93). London: IEEE Press.

Haith, M. M. (1998). Who put the cog in infant cognition? *Infant Behavior and Development, 21*, 167-179.

Inhelder, B., Sinclair, M., & Bovet, M. (1974). *Learning and the development of cognition.* Cambridge, MA: Harvard University Press.

Innerst, C. (1984, December 13). 20 percent of American youths can't find U.S. on a world map. *The Washington Times*, p. A1.

Liben, L. S. (1997). Children's understanding of spatial representations of place: Mapping the methodological landscape. In N. Foreman & R. Gillett (Eds.), *A handbook of spatial research paradigms and methodologies* (pp. 41-83). East Sussex, UK: Taylor & Francis.

Liben, L. S. (1999). Developing an understanding of external spatial representations. In I. E. Sigel (Ed.), *Development of mental representation: Theories and applications* (pp. 297-321). Mahwah, NJ: Lawrence Erlbaum Associates.

Liben, L. S., & Downs, R. M. (1989). Understanding maps as symbols: The development of map concepts in children. In H. W. Reese (Ed.), *Advances in child development and behavior* (Vol. 22, pp. 145-201). New York: Academic Press.

Liben, L. S., & Downs, R. M. (1991). The role of graphic representations in understanding the world. In R. M. Downs, L. S. Liben, & D. S. Palermo (Eds.), *Visions of aesthetics, the environment, and development: The legacy of Joachim F. Wohlwill* (pp. 139-180). Hillsdale, NJ: Lawrence Erlbaum Associates.

Liben, L. S., & Downs, R. M. (1993). Understanding person-space-map relations: Cartographic and developmental perspectives. *Developmental Psychology, 29*, 739-752.

Liben, L. S., & Downs, R. M. (1994). Fostering geographic literacy from early childhood: The contributions of interdisciplinary research. *Journal of Applied Developmental Psychology, 15*, 549-569.

Liben, L. S., & Downs, R. M. (1997). Can-ism and can'tianism: A straw child. *Annals of the Association of American Geographers, 87*, 159-167.

Liben, L. S., & Szechter, L. E. (1999, October). *Teaching children photography: Beyond point and shoot.* Presentation at the Cognitive Development Society, Chapel Hill, SC.

Liben, L. S., & Yekel, C. A. (1996). Preschoolers' understanding of plan and oblique maps: The role of geometric and representational correspondence. *Child Development, 67*, 2780-2796.

MacEachren, A. M. (1995). *How maps work.* New York: Guilford.

MacEachren, A. M., & Taylor, D. R. F. (1994). *Visualization in modern cartography.* Tarrytown, NY: Elsevier.

McAfee, E. A., & Proffitt, D. R. (1991). Understanding the surface orientation of liquids. *Cognitive Psychology, 23*, 483-514.

Merriwether, A. M., & Liben, L. S. (1997). Adults' failures on Euclidean and projective spatial tasks: Implications for characterizing spatial cognition. *Journal of Adult Development, 4*, 57-69.

Muehrcke, P., & Muehrcke, J. O. (1998). *Map use: Reading, analysis, and interpretation* (4th ed.). Madison, WI: JP Publications.

Newcombe, N., Huttenlocher, J., Drummey, A. B., & Wiley, J. G. (1998). the development of spatial location coding: Place learning and dead reckoning in the second and third years. *Cognitive Development, 13*, 185-200.

Piaget, J. (1929). *The child's conception of the world.* London: Routledge & Kegan Paul.

Piaget, J. (1965). *The moral judgment of the child.* New York: The Free Press.

Piaget, J. (1970). Piaget's theory. In P. Mussen (Ed.), *Carmichael's manual of child psychology* (pp. 703-732). New York: Wiley.

Piaget, J. (1971). *Science of education and the psychology of the child.* New York: Viking.

Piaget, J. (1972). Intellectual evolution from adolescence to adulthood. *Human Development, 15*, 1-12.

Piaget, J. (1973). *To understand is to invent: The future of education.* New York: Viking.

Piaget, J. (1985). *The equilibrium of cognitive structures.* Chicago: University of Chicago Press.

Piaget, J., & Garcia, R. (1989). *Psychogenesis and the history of science.* New York: Columbia University Press.

Piaget, J., & Inhelder, B. (1956). *The child's conception of space.* New York: Basic Books.

Presson, C. C. (1982). The development of map-reading skills. *Child Development, 53*, 196-199.

Rhodes, D. (1970). *How to read a highway map.* Los Angeles, CA: Elk Grove Press.

Roncato, S., & Rumiati, R. (1986). Naive statistics: Current misconceptions on equilibrium. *Journal of Experimental Psychology: Learning, Memory, and Cognition, 12*, 361-377.

Sachs, F. G., & Banas, N. (1987). Using the ENIGMA reading program to teach geography more effectively. *Techniques: A Journal for Remedial Education and Counseling, 3*, 121-124.

Sherman, J. (1967). Problem of sex differences in space perception and aspects of intellectual functioning. *Psychological Review, 74*, 290-299.

Siegel, A. W., & White, S. (1975). The development of spatial representations of large-scale environments. In H. W. Reese (Eds.), *Advances in child development and behavior* (Vol. 10, pp. 9-55). New York: Academic Press.

Signorella, M. L., Jamison, W., & Krupa, M. H. (1989). Predicting spatial performance from gender stereotyping in activity preferences and in self-concept. *Developmental Psychology, 25*, 89-95.

Spelke, E. S. (1998). Nativism, empiricism, and the origins of knowledge. *Infant Behavior and Development, 21*, 181-200.

Szechter, L. E., & Liben, L. S. (1999, April). *Joint picture-book reading: Early lessons in pictorial comprehension.* Poster session presented at the biennial meetings of the Society for Research in Child Development, Albuquerque, NM.

Uttal, D. (1996). Angles and distances: Children's and adults' reconstruction and scaling of spatial configurations. *Child Development, 67,* 2763-2779.

Vosniadou, S., & Brewer, W. H. (1992). Mental models of the earth: A study of conceptual change in childhood. *Cognitive Psychology, 24,* 535-585.

Vygotsky, L. S. (1962). *Thought and language.* Cambridge, MA: MIT Press.

Vygotsky, L. S. (1978). *Mind in society.* Cambridge, MA: Harvard University Press.

10

LITERACY DEVELOPMENT AND YOUNG CHILDREN: RESEARCH TO PRACTICE

Lesley Mandel Morrow
Rutgers - The State University of New Jersey

Four-year-old Michael and his mother were at the mall shopping. They approached a store and Michael piped up in a loud voice, "Look, Mommy, I can read those letters, M-A-C-Y-S. Those letters spell Sears."

Michael's mother smiled and praised him. "That was great, Mike. You got every letter right. Now let's look at the letters again. The first one you know really well."

"Oh," Michael agreed, "it's the first letter of my name and it says mmmmmm." "Wow, you are doing some good thinking today," Michael's mother assured. "So if the first letter of that word is M like in Michael, it can't say Sears. M-A-C-Y-S spells Macy's. Macy's is a department store like Sears. That's why you thought it said Sears. But looking at the letters can help you to figure out the word."

Not long ago, we would have chuckled at Michael's remarks as cute but incorrect. Today, however, we realize that he is demonstrating a great deal of literacy knowledge that deserves recognition. First, Michael not only knows what letters are; he can also identify them in a sign. Next he understands that letters spell words and that words are read and have meaning. Although Michael does not read the word correctly, he nonetheless makes an informed guess. As the vignette suggests, Michael realizes that the building is a department store. However, because he has never been to this one, he relies on his own experiences and background knowledge. He speculates that this new store goes by the name of one with which he is already familiar. Here Michael is trying out some of his literacy knowledge on an adult who he knows is interested and willing to interact positively with him. Michael's mother encourages his literacy development by offering positive reinforcement for what he knows. She also extends her support and guidance by helping with correct responses (Morrow, 1997a, 1997b; see Stipek & Greene, chap. 3, this volume).

Research in early literacy identifies Michael's accomplishments as emergent literacy behavior. Although the literacy skills and knowledge he demonstrates may seem unconventional to an adult, his performance is to be rewarded and encouraged. He uses literacy in a real context and shares his thoughts with his mother as he actively participates in their joint literacy experience. This example illustrates some of the important findings from research regarding early literacy development. Attempting to identify how literacy is acquired in early childhood, researchers observed children engaged in a variety of literacy activities, evaluating each task from the young learners' perspective. From these studies, we know that, foremost, children need to see adults model literacy activities for them. As the findings also suggest, children benefit from some direct instruction that fosters literacy development. *Direct instruction* in this chapter is defined as deliberate and systematic guidance from adults based on a planned curriculum of skills. Those who promote a direct instructional model believe that skills are acquired through the transmission of information rather than a process approach within a meaningful context. This means that teaching involves telling as opposed to students being emersed in a context in which they construct their own meaning to acquire information. Early literacy researchers need to examine explicit teaching strategies appropriate for young learners' needs. Understanding how literacy is acquired helps design developmentally appropriate strategies for instruction, whether they be through direct instruction or a constructivist model.

DEFINING EMERGENT LITERACY

The term *emergent literacy* was first used by Clay (1966). The concept assumes that children acquire some knowledge about language, reading, and writing before coming to school. Literacy development begins early and continues throughout life, and there is a dynamic relationship among the communication skills of reading, writing, listening, and speaking. Each skill influences the others in the course of development that occurs in the everyday contexts of home and community life. Clay defined *emergent literacy* as those language behaviors--demonstrated by very young children--that were not yet conventional. When children begin to read and write in a manner similar to that of adults, they are no longer considered emergent readers and writers. However, children are always emerging in their reading and writing. Therefore, we must acknowledge their accomplishments and reward their ongoing progress. Young children possess certain literacy skills, although these skills are neither fully developed nor conventional from the standpoint of mature reading and writing. According to emergent literacy theory, a child is involved in legitimate literacy behavior when he or she narrates a familiar storybook while looking at the pictures and occasionally at the print. Although the reading is not conventional, the child gives the impression of mature reading through tone of voice, attention to illustrations, and the ability to follow print with left-to-right progression across pages (Sulzby, 1985).

The emergent literacy approach to learning is different from reading-readiness approaches. Reading-readiness activities are seen as precursors to reading, and the tasks that students perform are usually not genuine reading or writing of any type. Some educators believe that students must master these tasks before formal reading can begin. In fact, advocates of reading-readiness methods favor the systematic instruction of prescribed skills (i.e., letter-sound relations). They assume that all children are at fairly similar levels of development when starting kindergarten and need these skills before attempting to read and write (Teale & Sulzby, 1986).

Alternatively, Teale (1982) adopted the emergent perspective and viewed the development of early literacy as the result of children's involvement in reading activities mediated by more literate others. The rich social interaction in these activities is particularly important to a child's development. Not only do interactive literacy events teach children the societal function and conventions of reading; they also link reading with enjoyment and satisfaction and thus increase children's desire to engage in literacy activities. Teale's emphasis on the social aspects of reading development reflects Vygotsky's (1979) more general theory of intellectual development that all higher mental functions are internalized social relationships.

PROCESSES, SKILLS, AND PRACTICES INVOLVED IN LITERACY ACQUISITION

Holdaway (1979) and others have defined four processes that enable young children to acquire literacy abilities. The first process, observation of literacy behaviors, is when children see adults read and write either for business or pleasure (e.g., writing directions and reading favorite stories at bedtime). The second is collaboration, whereby the child interacts with another individual and, in the process, receives direct guidance, encouragement, motivation, and help. The third is practice, during which time the child attempts alone what has been learned previously in cooperation with others. Whether role-playing or using invented spelling while writing, children have the opportunity to experiment without direction or adult observation, evaluate their own performances, make corrections, and increase skills. In the fourth process, performance, children share what has been learned and seek approval from adults who are supportive and interested in their progress (Smith, 1997).

Educators have also become aware of specific skills that are extremely important to literacy development--specifically, phonemic awareness and phonics knowledge (Adams, 1990; Juel, 1991). As we know, the emergent literacy perspective fosters a constructivist approach to learning with the child experiencing immersion in literacy activities and minimal direct instruction. More recently, there has been a movement toward direct instruction. Teaching skills in an organized and systematic fashion, some educators argue, is a necessity for many children. Rather than exalt one view over the other and thereby limit our full instructional power, we should consider all perspectives when designing an early literacy program.

From a statement published by the International Reading Association (1990), we have the foundations for such a program. Indeed, the following insights into what we need to know about early literacy development have strong implications for instruction:

1. Literacy development begins early in life, long before children start formal instruction in school.
2. School personnel need to recognize the literacy that children bring with them when they enter school. Early classroom experiences with reading and writing should build on the knowledge and ability that already exist in the child. This is different for each child based on his or her background.
3. Literacy involves concurrent development of oral language, reading, and writing. These language activities are interrelated; developing ability in one helps development in the others. The integration of the   literacy skills into other content areas throughout the school day helps foster their development as well.
4. Children's literature is a natural resource for literacy learning. It introduces children to books with material that is interesting and enjoyable. It provides a model of writing and language that is of high   quality. Selections to be read to children are chosen based on themes that are being studied in the classroom and topics in which students demonstrate an interest. Literature should be shared in a variety of ways.
5. Children learn best when literacy is based on functional experiences in which there is an interest and meaning or a purpose for reading and writing. The interest and meaning for reading and writing are generated when literacy activities are linked to themes studied in the classroom and to children's own life experiences.
6. Children need opportunities to learn in social settings where they can interact with adults and peers during literacy activities.
7. To meet individual needs, direct instruction of skills is necessary to guide and support learning. This instruction

should be based on the particular needs of children and should take place in small groups or in one-on-one settings.

8. There should be an organizational plan for skill development and careful selection of materials used for instruction.

9. Although children's literacy development can be described in general stages, children can pass through these stages in a variety of ways and at different ages.

10. Adults must serve as models for literacy behavior by demonstrating the use of books and print.

11. The joy of learning needs to be emphasized as a major goal. Early literacy experiences should develop positive attitudes toward reading and writing. Experiences that are meaningful and interesting, and result in success will produce such attitudes.

According to this early literacy perspective, teachers should attend to reading, writing, oral language, listening, and viewing concurrently in an integrated fashion. They must also make every effort to create meaningful and purposeful literacy activities that coordinate with other areas of the curriculum, such as social studies, science, music, art, play, and math (International Reading Association and the National Association for the Education of Young Children, 1998; Morrow, 1997a; Strickland, 1990). Through these activities, students are exposed to a great deal of children's literature. Social interaction animates each literacy experience as children collaborate, consult, and share their work with teachers and peers. In addition, teachers need to establish a scope and sequence of skills and set aside time for direct instruction. Flexibility is a must, however, as teachers balance the various types of instructional settings--formal and informal, planned and spontaneous, teacher directed and student centered. As a case in point, teachers generally focus first on letters and sounds that are used more often because they are familiar to the children. However,if a class is studying animals and learning about panda bears and polar bears, this is an appropriate time for a teacher to introduce or reinforce the sound and symbol relation of the letter"P." The basic concept for an instructional model for literacy development prevails whether we are talking about a 3-year-old or a 6-year-old. Although the skills to be accomplished are obviously different, the time spent on instruction and the amount of formal teaching differs as well. However, the debate concerning any decontextualized skill instruction and the use of a direct teaching model continue to be concerns of many early childhood researchers and teachers.

STRIKING A BALANCE IN EARLY CHILDHOOD EDUCATION

The pendulum swings frequently concerning the theory and practice in literacy and early childhood education. Philosophers who had the first impact on early childhood practices believed in the natural unfolding of the child. Their ideas, when interpreted into practice, suggested that the teacher take the role of a facilitator and invite children to explore their world as a site for active learning (Froebel, 1974; Rousseau, 1962; Rusk & Scotland, 1979). Dewey (1966) continued this tradition of the child-centered curriculum and integrated the teachings of all skills through themes that students and teachers investigated. Montessori (1965) changed some of our views of early childhood instruction by suggesting that children needed early, orderly, systematic training in skills. She supplied her teaching environment with materials for learning specific concepts to meet established objectives. Piaget's theories of cognitive development stressed that learning takes place when children interact with peers and adults in a social setting as they act on the environment (Piaget & Inhelder, 1969). Finally, Vygotsky's theory of intellectual development suggested to early childhood educators that children learn by internalizing activities conducted in the world around them. As Vygotsky explained, children emulate behaviors and incorporate new ideas into their existing knowledge. For continued development to occur, Vygotsky believed that students need guidance and direction from more literate others until they reach the *zone of proximal development*--a time where they become more self-reliant and must be given the opportunity to practice new skills learned on their own.

All of these thinkers have had an enduring impact on how we deal with literacy development in the early years. However, we often experience times when there is a strong emphasis on one theory or another. This is also when we find educators vacillating--in full swing, moving back and forth from a purely constructivist problem-solving approach where children explore their environment without specific objectives and little teacher guidance to a highly structured behaviorist perspective with an explicit, transmission model for learning.

More recently, in the heated debates surrounding early literacy instruction and developmentally appropriate practice, we have begun to hear the word *balance*. The term challenges the parochialism of current programs that pursue an exclusive commitment to one model over another. Rather than subscribe to any one approach, educators need to explore the full gamut of theoretical and pedagogical options. They must use careful judgment and select those theories and learning strategies that are optimally effective as well as appropriate to the learning styles of each child. Balance suggests that educators use some constructivist methods with problem-solving activities and more explicit direct instruction to support those inquiry processes. Thus, when preparing a balanced program, educators should use multiple strategies to meet the varied needs of students and ensure learning for all children.

According to Pressley (1998), scientific evidence justifies the explicit teaching of skills as a start for constructivist activities. However, constructivist activities permit consolidation and elaboration of skills. One methodology does not preclude or exclude the other. Balance is sensible rather than contradictory; transmission and construction are part of the same whole: Constructivist activities clarify the meaning and purpose of skills, whereas skill lessons enable knowledge construction to begin.

Balanced instruction is based on a model of literacy learning that encompasses both the elegance and complexity of the reading and language arts processes. Such a model acknowledges the importance of both the form (phonics, mechanics, etc.) and function (comprehension, purpose, meaning) of the literacy processes. It also recognizes that learning occurs most effectively in a whole-part-whole context. This type of instruction is characterized by meaningful literacy activities that provide children with both the skill and desire to become proficient lifelong readers.

RESEARCH IN EARLY LITERACY AND ITS IMPLICATIONS FOR EARLY LITERACY PRACTICE

To develop such a model--a truly balanced instructional program--we first need to explore research in several areas that affect early literacy development. The International Reading Association (IRA) along with the National Association for the Education of Young Children (NAEYC) composed a joint statement on *Learning to Read and Write: Developmentally Appropriate Practices for Young Children*. Much of what follows reflects the thinking of that statement and, moreover, shares the same commitment to balanced, integrated and developmentally sound early childhood education (International Reading Association and the National Association for the Education of Young Children, 1998). The findings on home influences, literacy-rich environments, oral language, and writing development, for example, have implications for classroom practice and, for the design of an early literacy framework.

Home Influences

Research. Many of the perspectives in early literacy come from studying homes in which children learned to read without direct instruction before coming to school, learned to read in school quite easily, and became proficient readers. Some of what goes on in these homes can be adapted as strategies in school.

These homes are rich with reading and writing materials that are used frequently by children with support and encouragement from adults. Books, magazines, newspapers, pencils, markers, and writing paper abound. Adults in these homes regularly engage in literacy activities and perform such real-life tasks as writing grocery lists, reading newspapers, and sharing recipes in the kitchen. These activities have meaning and purpose, and they draw from environmental print or print that is part of the everyday surroundings, such as cereal boxes, fast-food logos, and traffic signs. The atmosphere supports literacy involvement and social experiences as adults and children share books they have read, talk with one another, and communicate in writing (Clark, 1976; Durkin, 1966; Morrow, 1983; Teale, 1978). Family members serve as models of involvement in literacy activities. For example, they answer children's questions about books and print and, in so doing, provide informal direct instruction. They read to children frequently and reward them for participating in literacy activities.

Implications for Early Literacy Instruction. We cannot replicate these home environments in the school, because the situations are so vastly different, nor would it be entirely appropriate. By the same token, however, we can adapt elements from the home that seem to foster success in literacy development. Foremost, we can provide rich literacy environments where children are surrounded by books, writing materials, and the written word. We can make literacy learning more enjoyable by sharing what has been written and read. In the same spirit, we can allow the voluntary choice of reading and writing by scheduling periods of time in which children have the opportunity to engage in these activities independently. We can provide functional literacy experiences as well, such as writing thank-you notes to a veterinarian after visiting his or her office.

We should also avail ourselves in every way possible to make literacy a pleasant experience for the children. For example, we can read to the children and invite them to share their favorite stories with others. Finally, to succeed on all these fronts, we need to encourage participation by parents in the early literacy development of their children. We can do this by informing them about what is being learned, and what they can do to help, and by requiring them to work with their children on assignments at home. We must also invite parents into the classrooms and encourage school participation as well. Teachers need parents so that children can be successful, and parents need to assume responsibility for helping with the literacy development of their child.

Literacy-Rich Environments

Research. As mentioned, research from homes where children come to school already reading tells us that we need to be very concerned about providing literacy-rich environments in our classrooms. Studies have found that many preschoolers can read road signs, labels on food boxes, and logos. Such findings highlight the importance of providing and using environmental print in classrooms to encourage young children to read (Goodman, 1984).

Implications for Early Literacy Instruction. A literacy-rich environment supports and extends literacy development. Classrooms need learning centers equipped with materials that encourage reading and writing and help develop themes being studied. Teachers should display and discuss functional print in their classrooms. Classrooms should also include literacy centers with a library corner and a writing area with an abundant supply of materials for reading, writing, and oral-language activities. Teachers can incorporate dramatic play centers as well and, in the process, supplement those literacy activities in the library and writing areas. By performing the roles within a restaurant, for example, the children exercise their imaginations, not to mention their communication skills. The manner in which the teacher uses the print with the children differs based on their developmental levels (see Liben & Downs, chap. 9, this volume).

To further enrich these environments, teachers need to fill their classrooms with the printed word. For example, they might begin by identifying learning centers and each child's cubby with labels. Teachers can also post daily routines, helper and attendance charts, and a bulletin board for notices of classroom events. Even more, teachers might display lists of new words from units of instruction on experience charts, with illustrations next to written words to aid students who are not able to read.

Oral Language

Research. Children whose language is well developed are likely to be more successful in developing literacy skills than those who do not have a strong language base. Studies of how children learn oral language reveal that language acquisition is based somewhat on developmental maturity. However, research also indicates that children play a central role in their own language acquisition process by actively constructing language. They acquire language, foremost, through imitation; children are notorious for repeating their parents' or siblings' every word. Children are highly inventive as agents of their language development. When lacking the conventional words needed to communicate their thoughts, children simple create their own terms.

Children's first words are usually functional words, and they are motivated to continue generating language when their attempts are positively reinforced. Children who are constantly exposed to an environment rich in language and who interact with adults using language in a social content develop more facility with oral language than children lacking these opportunities (Bloom, 1972; Brown, 1973; Brown & Bellugi, 1964; Bruner, 1975; Lennenberg, 1967; McNeil, 1970; Menyuk, 1977).

Implications for Early Literacy Instruction. The implications of this research for classroom practice suggest that we should give children the opportunity to use language frequently. They need to explore and experiment with language, hear good models, and discuss topics that are of interest to them. What is more, children should play with language in social settings and receive positive reinforcement from adults for any new attempts they make. Children also need explicit guidance to advance in their vocabulary, syntax, and pronunciation skill development. They should have a great deal of exposure to children's literature as well. These encounters provide good models of language. Children also need ample opportunity to talk about books that have been read; experiences of this sort encourage the rich social interaction that is fundamental to language learning. Finally, children must be able to pursue topics that interest them. With these units of study and the classroom discussions that ensue, children have a forum for learning new words.

Writing Development

Research. Writing development begins early and continues along with reading development. Initially, children do not differentiate writing from illustration. However, some children as young as 2 years of age distinguish scribble writing from scribble drawing by separating them on the page and explaining which is the picture and which is the story. Their scribble writing progresses to letterlike forms and eventually to discernible letters, often written repeatedly and randomly on a page. At this point, some children *invent* spelling before eventually using conventional orthography (Sulzby, 1985). These categories of writing development vary among children, and some will fluctuate back and forth across categories.

Reading and writing skills build on each other, with each contributing to proficiency in the other. Historically, writing was not included in preschool and kindergarten curricula, because early theorists believed its development followed reading. Recent research about early writing, however, has challenged these traditional views. We now encourage children's first attempts at writing, although the work of 3- to 5-year-olds is not considered conventional writing. Nevertheless, praising these children's emergent writing has become standard practice in early childhood classrooms.

Implications for Early Literacy Instruction. Children learn to write outside of school by writing for a purpose, and teachers should keep this in mind when preparing activities for writing. Specifically, teachers might consider initiating pen-pal programs with another class or another school, writing invitations to parents, composing thank-you notes to class visitors, or preparing greeting cards for special occasions. Teachers could also keep a class address book in the dramatic play area. Another possibility is for children to collect their *very own words*--words that children select based on home experiences or new school experiences and then record on 3 x 5 index cards stored in file boxes or coffee cans. Teachers also need to let children share their thoughts by keeping journals or exchanging messages on a bulletin board. With thematic units, teachers are able to generate real reasons for writing. Whatever the theme, all of these activities can be used throughout the course of the unit under study. In addition, children's literature can be excellent motivation for writing experiences. Series books such as Madeline (Bemelmens, 1939) encourage writing one's own stories about the central character (Morrow, 1997a).

Many children do not write conventionally in preschool and kindergarten. We must applaud what they can do be it drawing pictures for writing, creating scribble writing, composing random letters, generating invented spelling, or producing conventional print. It is so important to encourage children by letting them know that their unconventional writing is only a beginning, and that, although these early efforts are not the same as the writing that older children can do, their work is legitimate nonetheless. Instruction in the mechanics of writing letters, spelling, and punctuation can begin with minilessons during the school year.

Reading: Knowledge About Print and Constructing Meaning From Text

Research. Mason (1984) suggested that there are three strands of reading behavior that develop separately but concurrently--attention to the functions, forms, and conventions of print, with the first of these dominating initial reading development. Children seem to learn how print functions first as they move toward reading (Goodman, 1984; Smith, 1971). Often the first words a child reads are those with meaning and purpose in the child's life, such as family names, food labels, road signs, and names of fast-food restaurants. Learning about the functions of print has been referred to as the *roots of literacy* (Goodman, 1984). Once these roots take hold, the learner's concern shifts to the forms of print, such as details about names, sounds, and configurations of letters and words. Next children become interested in identifying and using conventions of print. For example, they begin to recognize that print is read from left to right, that punctuation serves certain purposes in printed material, and that spaces serve to separate letters and words. Although recognition of the functions of print seems to dominate reading development at first, the child is at the same time capable of acquiring and learning about the forms and conventions of print as well (Mason, 1984).

Educators have become increasingly aware of the need to address phonemic awareness instruction in early literacy development because research has shown that it is a strong predictor of reading success and is also necessary for children to acquire the ability to use phonics (Adams, 1990; Juel, Griffith, & Gough, 1986). Phonemic awareness is the ability to examine language independently of meaning and manipulate component sounds. It is the knowledge that words are composed of smaller units, or phonemes. Such knowledge requires the ability to attend to a sound in the context of the other sounds in the word. For example, children demonstrate phonemic awareness when they can segment sounds in the words they say and blend those sounds together to form words.

As with any literacy skill, there are levels of difficulty in the acquisition process. At the simplest level, children are able to rhyme words and recognize rhyming words. On the next level, children begin blending phonemes and splitting syllables (i.e., segmenting the beginning sound *c* from the rest of the word *cake*). Finally, the most difficult task for children is to segment the phonemes in spoken words and manipulate phonemes to form different words (Adams, Treiman, & Pressley, 1998; Adams, 1990). Activities involving phonics-based strategies (i.e., sound symbol relations) and word-analysis strategies, such as context and syntax clues, are all considered important exercises for early literacy development.

Implications for Early Literacy Instruction. This research suggests that early instruction in literacy development focus simultaneously on the functions, forms, and conventions of print, with lessons addressing phonemic awareness, knowledge of letters, sound symbol relations, context and syntax clues, syllables, and punctuation.

In early childhood literacy programs, a great deal of emphasis should be placed on the functions of print, such as writing greeting cards or reading print that is related to children's daily lives. Through these experiences, children learn the purpose of print and how it is used. They are then able to deal with instruction involving knowledge of letters and sounds. Although teachers have been concerned about teaching decoding skills, they are now realizing that children need specific word-recognition strategies to help them become independent readers. A balance between direct instruction in these skills and instruction within the context of real literature, everyday environmental print, and theme units needs to be achieved to add meaning to abstract concepts for young children. The development of decoding skills must be put into proper perspective for teachers because it is only one among many other processes necessary for learning how to read.

Constructing Meaning From Text

Research. Experiencing children's literature is one of the most important ways in which young learners can begin to appreciate the meaningful nature of text. Studies show that children who have such meaningful encounters with books tend to develop more interest in them and in learning to read. Storybook reading enhances background information and sense of story structure, and it familiarizes children with the differences between written and oral language. They learn that printed words have sounds and print contains meaning. By listening to well-structured unfamiliar stories, children's comprehension and language skills develop. Reading to children helps them understand how print functions and how it is used. They learn how to handle books; become aware of left-to-right and front-to-back directionality; recognize that stories have beginnings, middles, and ends; and learn about authorship (Cohen, 1968; Feitelson, Kita, & Goldstein, 1986; Hoffman, 1982; Mason & Au, 1986; Morrow, 1984; Ninio, 1980; Pellegrini & Galda, 1982).

Studies also illustrate that it is not just the storybook reading that achieves these benefits, but active participation in the reading event. The intimate social exchanges of a shared literacy experience spark children's interest and motivation to read. As they pause to comment and respond during the reading, the adult and child cooperatively construct meanings. The adult helps the child understand by interpreting the written language, and the child continually refines that understanding with ongoing feedback from the adult (Morrow, 1988). To this extent, their interaction provides a direct channel of information for the child and, in addition, supports the development of emotions and cognitions critical for continued learning (see Stipek & Greene, chap. 3, this volume). These strategies, among others, have been tested to help children acquire skills. Teachers should use such strategies when sharing literature with children so as to provide direct instruction for the acquisition of comprehension skills.

Implications for Early Literacy Instruction. Strategies derived from the research on reading stories help children benefit from the storybook reading by developing concepts about books and print and by constructing meaning from the text. Some of these strategies follow.

The directed listening/reading and thinking activity (DL/RTA) provides the child with an organizational framework that can be internalized through frequent use and subsequently transferred when new material is presented. The directed listening/reading and thinking activity is a strategy that helps construct meaning about text and can be used in many different forms. With younger children, we will use the directed listening activity because they are not yet able to read. With children who are already reading, we use the strategy both for listening and reading. The basic strategy involves the following steps:

1. Before the story begins, prepare for listening or reading with discussions and questions. Provide background information or ask children to predict what might happen. Set a goal for listening or reading, such as "Try to remember which part of the story you like best." The objective for every story reading can be different.

2. Read the story with expression and show the illustrations. Pause at the natural breaks for children's reactions, comments, or questions. Encourage children to chant along with you or read some of the words. If children are reading, have them read the story all the way through.

3. Discuss the story after listening or reading. Begin the discussion by focusing on the original objective. Then allow it to go off into other directions. When children relate a story to their own life experiences, they better understand its meaning. This type of activity can be used in both small-group and one-to-one story readings, both of which have been found to increase the number and complexity of children's responses as well as their story comprehension (Morrow, 1988). Prompt children to respond, or scaffold and model responses when children do not respond on their own. For example, if a child cannot answer the question, "How did the animals act when the little red hen asked for help?" (Galdone, 1973), say, "Those animals aren't very helpful to the little red hen. Each time she asks them for help they all answer, Not I." Relate the story to your own life experiences, answer questions, and offer positive reinforcement for children's comments.

With younger children we might use all the elements outlined with every story and, of course, with less detail and time for discussions.

The DLR/TA can be used with both narrative and expository text, the only difference being the types of questions asked before and after reading. Teachers can employ this strategy with a whole group in an oral reading and thus encourage children's full participation in the reading event. For instance, the teacher might pause before a predictable phrase and let the children fill in the blank. "Are you my _____?" from Eastman's (1960) *Are You My Mother?* is a good example. With the DL/RTA format, teachers can also create favorite stories in their classrooms by performing repeated readings of the same book. Children's responses to repeated stories become more sophisticated as they interpret, predict, and make associations with real life. With each successive reading, the purposes for reading evolve, and children gradually begin to exercise higher order thinking skills. For example, once children start narrating familiar stories while the teacher is reading, they learn to focus on elements of print, asking names of letters and words.

Follow-up activities help children reconstruct meaning. Retelling engages children in holistic comprehension and organization of thought and allows for personalization. With practice, children learn to introduce a story with its setting and to recount its theme, plot episodes, and resolution. Through retellings, children demonstrate comprehension of story details and are able to sequence, add inferences and offer interpretations as well (Morrow, 1997a, 1997b). Teachers need to model retelling and support children's early attempts with verbal prompts using felt boards with story characters, presenting role movies, and manipulating puppets (Morrow, 1997b).

A Framework for an Early Literacy Curriculum

In this final section, I provide a framework for a balanced early literacy curriculum based on the research and implications for practice provide thus far. Most every instructional framework is predicated on specific and precise curricular objectives, and this early literacy program is no exception. Therefore, I begin by discussing the objectives that drive the curriculum. Each list of instructional goals--for language development as well as reading and writing development--reflects my commitment to a fully balanced program.

Some objectives invoke constructivism, whereas others call for direct instruction. Indeed, immersion and transmission models are equally represented in the curriculum overview. On the one hand, the lists identify various skills that require explicit, systematic instruction. Some examples are as follows: "The child discriminates speech sounds, identifies rhyming words, and knows what a letter is and can point to one on a printed page." On the other hand, the lists also specify skills that demand more student-centered, inquiry-based and integrated instruction. Examples include: "The child enjoys the rhythm and rhyme of poetry and other literature, asks to be read to and asks to write, and writes for functional purposes." Because the curricular goals are varied and comprehensive, the success of an early literacy program requires familiarity and facility with multiples theories and practices in early childhood education.

In the second portion of this framework discussion, I describe the instructional settings, materials, activities, learning experiences, and forms of assessment that are the foundations of a balanced literacy program. Figure 10.1 provides an overview of this framework (Morrow, Strickland, & Woo, 1998). I also elaborate on the specific strategies that teachers can use to meet the curricular goals of the program. In doing so, I portray the different reading and writing experiences--ranging from pleasure reading to phonemic awareness exercises--that are necessary for children's acquisition of literacy skills.

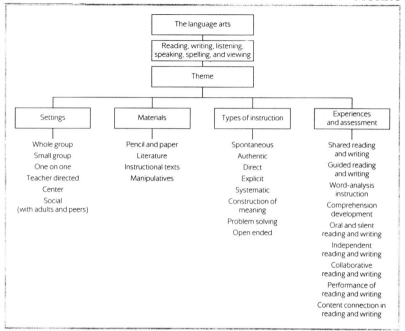

Source: From L. M. Morrow, D. S. Strickland, & D. G. Woo, 1998. In *Literacy Instruction in Half- and Whole-Day Kindergarten: Research to Practice* (Fig. 2, p. 76). Reprinted with permission of the International Reading Association.

FIG. 10.1. Strategies and structures in a balanced literacy program. (Source: From L. M. Morrow & D. G. Woo, 1998. In *Literacy Instruction in Half-and Whole-Day Kindergarten: Research to Practice* (Fig. 2, p. 76). Reprinted with permission of the International Reading Association.

Finally, in the closing section of the framework overview, I present a broad picture of the total curriculum and expound on the overall instructional context within which these literacy experiences and skills unfold. In the spirit of the International Reading Association's (1990) statement, I discuss the value of thematic, interdisciplinary units and invoke Dewey's concept of an integrated school day to foster content-area and literacy skill development. I then conclude by urging early education teachers to strike that delicate balance between immersion (or a more constructivist approach) and direct instruction by integrating literacy activities throughout the curriculum.

LITERACY OBJECTIVES FOR PREPARING AND ASSESSING LITERACY INSTRUCTION

At first glance, this first portion of the framework appears to have a more direct instructional perspective based on the current research and theoretical perspectives about children's language and literacy development discussed earlier. Although I concentrate on the skills and objectives for the acquisition of language and literacy development, I also want to reiterate that many of the stated objectives reflect a constructivist orientation as well. By the same token, it is important to note that, in addition to the skills listed on the following pages, children also need many experiences related to reading and writing. They need these experiences in varied settings with different types of instruction and instructional materials (Strickland, 1990). When designing a framework and curriculum, the first step is to articulate clear and precise goals. In that spirit, Table 10.1 provides a list of curricular objectives.

Types of Reading and Writing Experiences

If students are to develop and master these skills, then they must have varied experiences as readers and writers. This next section provides a description of some of the crucial reading and writing experiences necessary within the literacy framework. As with the curricular objectives, these literacy experiences and their respective settings, materials, and modes of instruction all characterize a balanced early literacy program with an equal measure of transmission and immersion pedagogy. Each experience is adjusted to the developmental level of the children. For example, the framework includes independent reading and writing alone or in collaboration. For children who are not yet reading conventionally, this means looking at picture story books and telling the story through the use of the pictures, or pretend reading as a result of knowing the story that had been read to the children at another time.

Shared Writing and Reading. With shared writing and reading, children write first and then read what they write. This is often coordinated with theme related activities being studied. The class usually carries out the shared writing and reading in a whole-group setting, with the teacher acting as facilitator and scribe. The session begins with a discussion of the activity and then moves to a recording on a chart written by the teacher but dictated by the children. During this time, the teacher encourages the children to use ideas and langauge relevant to the theme studied and join in as she or he reads aloud the completed chart.

After dictating the chart to the teacher, watching the teacher record the dictations, and reading what has been written, the children then examine the elements of the text with the teacher. The teacher typically invites the children to look for letters and words that they recognize, words and letters that are repeated, punctuation marks, and other features of interest to them. If the class is learning about rhymes, the children select a rhyming word from the chart. If the class has been working on specific consonant letter-sound relations, children would then locate examples. The shared writing and reading concludes as the class turns to the whole-group setting and rereads the entire chart together (Strickland, 1989).

TABLE 10.1

Curricular Objectives for Literacy Development

Language Development

Oral Expression

1.	Speaks in complete sentences.
2.	Engages freely in conversation in varied situations.
3.	Takes turns appropriately when engaged in conversation.
4.	Understands the language of others when spoken to.
5.	Pronounces speech sounds and words appropriately for age, language, background.
6.	Has appropriately sized vocabulary for level of maturity.
7.	Uses increasingly complex oral language, attending to the structural elements appropriate for age, background, and dialect.
8.	Responds to literal and inferential questions.

Receptive Learning

1.	Follows oral directions.
2.	Attends to adult models of rich oral language.
3.	Listens to a variety of literature to increase background information, langauge of books, and attention span.
4.	Attends to others when they are speaking.
5.	Discriminates speech sounds appropriately.
6.	Discriminates environmental sounds appropriately.
7.	Enjoys the rhythm and rhyme of poetry and other literature.
8.	Identifies rhyming words.

Reading and Writing

Positive Attitudes Toward Reading and Writing

1.	The child voluntarily chooses to look at books or to write.
2.	The child asks to be read to and asks to write.
3.	The child listens while being read to and watches others who are writing.
4.	The child demonstrates an interest in books by responding to stories read to him or her with questions and comments that are related to the book.
5.	The child demonstrates an interest in writing by taking the opportunity to write and by sharing what he or she has written with others.

Concepts About Books

1.	Knows that a book is for reading.
2.	Knows where the front and back of a book are.
3.	Knows which is the top and the bottom of the book.

(Continued)

4. Can turn the pages of a book properly.
5. Knows that print is to be read and pictures to be discussed.
6. Can show where to begin reading on a page.
7. Knows what a title of a book is.
8. Knows what an author and illustrator are.

Comprehension of Text

1. Retells familiar stories using pictures in the book to recall the details.
2. Retells stories in readinglike intonations.
3. Retells a story without the book and demonstrates knowledge of details.
4. Includes elements of story structure in story retelling: setting, theme, plot episodes, resolution.
5. Responds to story readings with literal, inferential, and critical questions and comments.
6. Demonstrates inferential and critical insights during story retellings.
7. Responds to literal, interpretive, and critical questions about stories.
8. Participates in story reading by reciting the story as the teacher reads.
9. Can guess words in the story based on syntax and context.

Concepts About Print

1. Knows that print is read from left to right.
2. Knows that oral language can be written down and then read.
3. Knows what a letter and word is and can point to them on a page.
4. Can read environmental print (signs, store names).
5. Can recognize some words by sight in the context of book print.
6. Can identify words that rhyme and create rhymes.
7. Can say sounds heard in a word (e.g., cat: c and at)
8. Can blend together sounds to form words.
9. Can identify letters by name.
10. Can associate sounds with letters.
11. Knows that there are spaces between words.
12. Matches spoken to printed words.
13. Identifies words by sight.
14. Uses syntax, context, and picture clues to identify words.

Writing Development

1. Level of development in writing: scribble, drawing for writing, letterlike forms, random letters/letter strings, invented spelling, and conventional spelling.
2. Writes a few words conventionally.
3. Understands the correspondence between spoken and written words when using dictation to record thoughts.

(Continued)

4.   Explores with writing materials.
5.   Copies letters and words.
6.   Writes his or her name.
7.   Collaborates with others in writing.
8.   Writes independently.
9.   Writes narrative stories and expository pieces.
10. Uses literature as a model for writing.
11. Writes for functional purposes.
12. Follows the mechanics of writing: forms upper and lowercase letters legibly, writes from left to right, leaves spaces between words, uses capital letters when necessary, uses periods and commas in appropriate places.

Reading Aloud and Responding Experiences. The modeling technique of reading aloud and responding is usually carried out in a whole-group setting. The teacher reads aloud to students and encourages responses. Students have the opportunity to hear the teacher read with expression and fluency. The selection for reading aloud should be a quality piece of literature related to themes being studied.

The read-aloud session is structured with before-, during-, and after-reading strategies. The purpose is to enhance comprehension and look at elements of print. Before reading, the teacher introduces or reintroduces the book to the children by giving the title and author. The teacher may then ask the children to use this information for predicting what the story is about. If appropriate, a brief discussion may take place about relevant concepts to be encountered.

During reading, teachers build positive attitudes by showing their own personal pleasure and interest. At times the teacher may pause and ask the children what they think might happen next or may ask them to fill in a predictable work based on the context of the story. Discussion during reading is encouraged as long as it is focused on the story. Teachers often invite children to read along with them--either by chanting repetitive phrases or narrating the entire text if it is a familiar book that has been read before. In this setting, the teacher can use a Big Book, where the print is visible and tracked with a pointer.

After reading, the teacher encourages the students to talk about the story in ways that personalize it for them. At this time, they ask questions of the teacher and of one another. Responses to the literature most often come at the end of the reading when children can discuss the story, do a pantomime of the story, role-play the story, reenact the story with puppets, or retell the story.

Guided Reading and Writing. Guided reading and writing usually take place in a small-group setting or on a one-to-one basis with the teacher and a child. Children are grouped based on their similar needs in literacy instruction. The teacher acts as a mentor and coach, offering explicit instruction and tailoring lessons to meet the children's individual needs. The materials and activities are selected very carefully with that particular child's instructional level for learning in mind.

Although there are particular components of guided reading lessons, they can vary depending on the age of the children and their needs. Guided reading can include the development of fluent reading, comprehension skills, word analysis, and writing skills. In a traditional guided reading lesson, children read or are read something that is easy and familiar for fluency and success. The child often selects the book. With preschool and kindergarten children, it may be a story they have heard. In this case, the children attempt reading behavior by reading the story from the pictures rather than the print.

While the child is reading or pretend reading, the teacher keeps a running record to evaluate progress in word analysis. This record allows the teacher to follow the text as the child is reading. The teacher marks errors and evaluates the types of miscues the child is making to devise strategies for improving independent reading fluency. Familiar materials provide a good opportunity to discuss the story being read with the aim of enhancing comprehension.

Children practice writing words they know or are writing on small chalkboards or white boards. When children do not yet write conventional words, they can use scribble writing, letter strings, or invented spelling. Additional work with words occurs as children learn about parts of words, such as common word endings, by using magnetic letters or a small slate or white board. They work on rhyming words, determining how many sounds they hear in a word, sounding parts of words, and blending them together to enhance phonemic awareness. As indicated, phonic skills are taught explicitly and within the context of authentic print.

In guided reading lessons, children also write their own stories in a notebook. Depending on the children's level of literacy development, they may scribble write, use letter strings, or use invented spelling. Print elements are discussed in the child's writing, including letters in their name or other letters they know.

Finally, the teacher introduces a new book, discusses what the story is about, and looks at the pictures with the children to predict what the people or animals might say in the story. The class discusses words from the story. The teacher may read the story first, but the children will do it alone if capable. The teacher helps the children with strategies for decoding if he or she is having difficulty figuring out words.

There are many variations to the steps in a guided reading lesson. However, what is most important is for teachers to learn as much as possible about the children with whom they are working. Such knowledge is absolutely necessary if teachers are to make the most of this small-group setting and provide students with appropriate materials and strategies that optimize learning. Indeed, this is the time and place for explicit and direct instruction.

Independent Reading and Writing Alone or in Collaboration. In early literacy programs, children need time to engage in literacy learning without the teacher, both alone and in a socially interactive way with peers. Working independent of the teacher promotes self-direction, a sense of responsibility, and self-empowerment. This provides children with practice in reading and writing for fluency and pleasure.

When deciding to work alone or in collaboration with others, children can select among several literacy options. This part of the school day can be called *literacy center time.* To establish this daily routine, teachers introduce the literacy activities by explaining a small number that are available for use at centers. Once children become accustomed to these initial activities and no longer require teacher assistance, it is time to add more items to the area. The first day that the children use the literacy center, for example, a teacher might introduce the open faced book shelves, the system for book selection, and materials for making their own books. On another day, the teacher can introduce the literature manipulative materials, such as the felt board, story characters, and taped stories with headsets. On subsequent days, the teacher can continue to build up the center by presenting additional options. However, the teacher must be careful to introduce only a few minutes at a time so as to avoid unnecessary confusion. The following strategies are designed to facilitate literacy center time:

1. Stress that the classroom be relatively quiet, with minimal movement during literacy center time.

2. Provide a list of literacy center activities where children can indicate their choices of things to do. When children have selected their activities to do during the literacy center period in advance, they know where to go and what to do.

3. Encourage children to stay with their choices for the entire literacy center session, allowing them to change once or twice if they wish.

4. Allow children to work alone or with other children in the literacy center, at their desk or table, or at other locations in the classroom.

The literacy center provides many choices for activities so that all children can immerse themselves in literature.

Integrating Literacy Activities Throughout the Curriculum

The curricular objectives, literacy skills, reading and writing experiences, instructional settings, and materials all come together to create one big picture of a fully integrated, theme-based, child-centered, and balanced early literacy program. In this final section, I present the historical precedents, contemporary practices, and benefits of integrating literacy activities throughout the curriculum.

A thematic or otherwise interdisciplinary model is well known to the early childhood curriculum. We have John Dewey to thank for the integrated school day--an interdisciplinary approach to teaching content. According to Dewey, all learning should be active, manipulative, sensory-oriented, and, above all else, based on the interests of the child. In this vein, he believed that children need time to explore and experiment in a classroom filled with interesting materials to learn. Dewey also argued that learning should be based on real-life experiences. He reasoned that, once children pursue their interests and participate in related activities, they have cause to seek out, exercise, and develop skills that are necessary to those pursuits. Skill development thus proceeds in a functional way (Dewey, 1966). For example, if the class is studying dinosaurs, dinosaurs are discussed, read about, written about, created out of clay in art, sung about at music time, and counted in math. Children in this situation become interested in a topic and use that interest as motivation to learn other skills.

However, with the advent of theme-based instruction, today's teachers are starting to move away from this practice of merely guiding students through a series of activities that focus on a specific topic such as dinosaurs. Instead, contemporary educators focus more on developing children's sense of inquiry, their ability to develop questions about a topic, determine ways to find answers to their questions, and share what they learn with others. Nowadays, teachers expose children to possible areas of interest by offering firsthand experiences as well as read-aloud sessions. The children's curiosity grows as they learn about new topics, generate new questions for further learning, and use various resources (i.e., more read aloud, simple experimentation, and questioning others) to build their information base and share what they know with the group. Rather than simply isolating the activities into subject areas, theme-based approaches invite children to learn about the world around them. Almost by default, content areas come into play naturally and nearly seamlessly. For example, when investigating a particular issue, children use math to answer certain questions; they write, dictate, or draw pictures when seeking, locating, and recording information related to those questions. They also discuss what they know and what they want to find out. In this way, the processes of listening, speaking, reading, writing, and thinking are highly integrated, operating in near unison as children learn more about topics under investigation. Activities in an integrated curriculum are designed to meet content-area and literacy objectives. For these reasons, such a curriculum makes an ideal component of a balanced early literacy curriculum framework.

    Benefits of Integrated United. A thematic-based curriculum has other benefits as well. Aside from accomplishing literacy and content-area goals, an integrated program also has the power to improve children's overall attitude and outlook toward learning. When literacy skills are developed in an integrated fashion, children see purposes and reasons for becoming literate. Because topics are generally based on interest and real-life experiences, children are more likely to be engaged and invested in their own literacy development. During an interdisciplinary investigation, for example, children are more inclined to ask for the skills that they consider necessary to participate fully in experiences that matter to them both in and out of school.

    To illustrate the benefits of an integrated approach, I offer this anecdote based on observations of a kindergarten class studying transportation. Without teacher prompting, nearly all of the children eagerly explored books available about transportation and requested additional titles on space travel. Some children even wanted maps of places not included in the center. Many requested *very own words* and asked for help preparing highway signs to show travel destinations and mileage. Several children dictated directions to get from one place to the next. With this thematic unit, the teacher created the need for literacy information. The children actively responded to that need and, as a consequence, learning became self-generated.

Closing Remarks

    Given the research on early literacy, many areas need to be focused on when designing a program. Skill development should take place in authentic, meaningful settings and in supported and guided reading as well. Studies suggest the concurrent learning of reading, writing, oral language, and listening in a meaningful way through the integration of these skills into play and into content-area teaching such as art, music, math, science, and social studies. This integration can be done through the use of themes that bring meaning and purpose to learning and provide a reason to read, write, listen, and speak. Children's literature should be a major source of these themes. Children need predictable texts with limited vocabularies so that they can begin to read on their own and enjoy some degree of success when doing so.

    The framework described needs to be organized within the school day in whole-group, small-group, and one-to-one instruction. Teachers and students must be involved in ongoing assessment to evaluate progress and plan for subsequent literacy activities and experiences. Early childhood classrooms should be designed to accommodate different organizational structures, literacy centers, library stations, and writing areas, to name a few, for learning. Classrooms need literacy and content-area materials for the guided instruction of skills and thematic instruction for integrated learning. What has been described provides developmentally appropriate practice for developing literacy skills in early childhood classrooms (International Reading Association and the National Association for the Education of Young Children, 1998).

REFERENCES

Adams, M. J. (1990). *Beginning to read: Thinking and learning about print.* Urbana: University of Illinois Center for the Study of Reading.

Adams, M. J., Treiman, R., & Pressley, M. (1998). Reading, writing and literacy. In W. Damon (Eds.), *Handbook of child psychology: Vol. 4. Child psychology in practice* (pp. 275-356). New York: Wiley.

Bemelmens, L. (1939). *Madeline.* New York: Viking.

Bloom, B. (1972). *Language development: Form and function in emerging grammars.* Cambridge, MA: MIT Press.

Brown, R. (1973). *A first language: The early stages.* Cambridge, MA: Harvard University Press.

Brown, R., & Bellugi, U. (1964). Three processes in the child's acquisition of syntax. *Harvard Educational Review, 34,* 133-151.

Bruner, J. (1975). The ontogenesis of speech arts. *Journal of Child Language, 3,* 1-19.

Clark, M. (1976). *Young fluent readers.* London: Heinemann.

Clay, M. M. (1966). *Emergent reading behavior.* Unpublished doctoral dissertation, University of Auckland.

Cohen, D. (1968). The effects of literature on vocabulary and reading achievement. *Elementary English, 45,* 209-213, 217.

Dewey, J. (1966). *Democracy and education.* New York: First Press. (Original work published 1916)

Durkin, D. (1966). *Children who read early.* New York: Teachers College Press.

Eastman, P. D. (1960). *Are you my mother?* New York: Random House.

Feitelson, D., Kita, B., & Goldstein, Z. (1986). Effects of listening to series stories on first graders' comprehension and use of language. *Research in the Teaching of English, 20,* 339-356.

Froebel, F. (1974). *The education of man.* Clifton, NJ: August M. Kelly.

Galdone, P. (1973). *The little red hen.* Boston, MA: Houghton Mifflin.

Goodman, Y. (1984). The development of initial literacy. In H. Goelman, A. Oberg, & F. Smith (Eds.), *Awakening to literacy* (pp. 102-109). Exeter, NJ: Heinemann.

Hoffman, S. J. (1982). *Preschool reading related behaviors: A parent diary.* Unpublished doctoral dissertation, University of Pennsylvania, Philadelphia.

Holdaway, D. (1979). *The foundations of literacy.* New York: Ashton Scholastic.

International Reading Association. (1990). *Literacy development and early-childhood (Pre-K through 3rd grade).* Newark, DE: Author.

International Reading Association and the National Association for the Education of Young Children. (1998). *Learning to read and write: Developmentally appropriate practice.* (A joint position paper). Newark, DE and Washington, DC: Authors.

Juel, C. (1991). Beginning reading. In R. Barr, P. Mosenthal, & P. D. Pearson (Eds.), *Handbook of reading research: Vol. II* (pp. 759-788). New York: Longman.

Juel, C., Griffith, P. L., & Gough, P. B. (1986). Acquisition of literacy: A longitudinal study of children in first and second grade. *Journal of Educational Psychology, 78,* 243-255.

Lennenberg, E. (1967). *Biological foundations of language.* New York: Wiley.

Mason, J. (1984). Early reading from a developmental perspective. In P. D. Pearson, M. Kamil, P. Mosenthal, & R. Barr (Eds.), *Handbook of reading research: Vol. 1* (pp. 505-543). New York: Longman.

McNeil, D. (1970). *The acquisition of language: The study of developmental psycholinguistics.* New York: Harper & Row.

Menyuk, P. (1977). *Language and maturation.* Cambridge, MA: MIT Press.

Montessori, M. (1965). *Spontaneous activity in education.* New York: Schocken.

Morrow, L. M. (1983). Home and school correlates of early interest in literature. *Journal of Educational Research, 76,* 221-230.

Morrow, L. M. (1984). Reading stories to young children: Effects of story structure and traditional questioning strategies on comprehension. *Journal of Reading Behavior, 16,* 273-288.

Morrow, L. M. (1988). Young children's responses to one-to-one story readings in school settings. *Reading Research Quarterly, 23,* 89-107.

Morrow, L. M. (1997a). *Literacy development in the early years: Helping children read and write* (3rd ed.). Boston, MA: Allyn & Bacon.

Morrow, L. M. (1997b). *The literacy center: Contexts for reading and writing.* York, ME: Stenhouse.

Morrow, L. M., Strickland, D., & Woo, D. G. (1998). *Literacy instruction in half- and whole-day kindergarten: Research to practice.* Newark, DE: International Reading Association.

Ninio, A. (1980). Picture book reading in mother-infant dyad belonging to two subgroups in Israel. *Child Development, 51,* 587-590.

Pellegrini, A., & Galda, L. (1982). The effects of thematic fantasy play training on the development of children's story comprehension. *American Educational Research Journal, 19,* 443-452.

Piaget, J., & Inhelder, B. (1969). *The psychology of the child.* New York: Basic Books.

Pressley, N. (1998). *Reading instruction that works: The case for balanced teaching.* New York: Guilford.

Rousseau, J. (1962). *Emile* (W. Boyd, Ed. & Trans). New York: Columbia University Teachers College. (Original work published 1762)

Rusk, R., & Scotland, J. (1979). *Doctrines of the great educators.* New York: St. Martin's Press.

Smith, F. (1971). *Understanding reading.* New York: Holt, Rinehart & Winston.

Smith, F. (1997). *Reading without nonsense* (3rd ed.). New York: Teachers College Press.

Strickland, D. S. (1990). Emergent literacy: How young children learn to read. *Educational Leadership, 47,* 18-23.

Sulzby, E. (1985). Kindergartners as writers and readers. In M. Farr (Ed.), *Advances in writing research: Children's early writing* (Vol. 1, pp. 127-200). Norwood, NJ: Ablex.

Teale, W. (1978). Positive environments for learning to read: What studies of early readers tell us. *Language Arts, 55,* 922-932.

Teale, W. H. (1982). Toward a theory of how children learn to read and write naturally. *Language Arts, 58* (8), 902-912.

Teale, W., & Sulzby, E. (1986). Emergent literacy as a perspective for looking at how children become writers and readers. In W. H. Teale & E. Sulzby (Eds.), *Emergent literacy:*

Writing and reading (pp. vii-xxv). Norwood, NJ: Ablex.

Vygotsky, L. S. (1978). *Mind in society: The development of higher psychological processes*. (M. Cole, V. John-Steiner, S. Scribner, & E. Souberman, Trans.) Cambridge, MA: Harvard University Press. (Original work published 1934)

11

IMAGINATION STYLES OF FOUR- AND FIVE-YEAR OLDS

Helane S. Rosenberg
Rutgers - The State University of New Jersey

Researchers and writers love to document the imaginative behavior of young people. Scholarly accounts of how children use their imagination in creating dramas, artworks, and stories document the diverse nature of the artistic products of children. Fictional accounts seem to capture even more of the variety and scope of whole worlds created by children. Who hasn't been delighted and touched by Alice from *Alice's Adventures in Wonderland* (Carroll, 1946), Peter from *Peter Pan* (Barrie, 1906), or Mary from *The Secret Garden* (Burnett, 1962)?

Recently, filmmakers have begun to provide us with similarly provocative portraits of young children as central characters who present themselves as primarily imaginative. Two recent films--"Kolya" and "Ponette" --let us know the minds of two young children. Kolya has thoughts and feelings that we, the audience, are permitted to hear and see. Ponette does not speak, but the filmmaker allows us to hear her self-talk and gain access to her imagery storehouse. We come to know little Ponette's inner life and actually see her imagination interchanges and her final imagination visit with her dead mother.

Although these childhood imaginations have been invented by adults, the artists creating these stories and films lead us to believe that the imagination of a child is as unique as a fingerprint and as idiosyncratic in style as the work of a mature artist. Those of us who conduct real-life arts activities with real young children describe the unique and consistent body of works of children as young as 3. The spirits of Alice, Peter, with a touch of Kolya and Ponette, together with recent developments in the field of arts education and mental imagery inform the investigation described in this chapter. It is an investigation of how four different young people create stories, pictures, and dramas. Each case also focuses on a description of the imagination style of the child.

THE ARTS AND MENTAL IMAGERY

Although there is relatively little scholarly work on the processes of imagination and art making in young children, there is a rich literature on both older children children and adult artists. Of special importance is a framework developed by Rosenberg and Pinciotti (1985, 1984, 1983) describing how artists and experienced drama participants use their images in their theatre or drama work. The authors detailed a three-part process: image, imaging, and imagination. They described an internal/external oscillation to characterize the process by which these mature artists and drama participants collect, sort, and transform their inner world into a finished art piece. This work is further elaborated by Rosenberg and Epstein (1991), Rosenberg (1987), and Rosenberg and Trusheim (1990). Most important to the work described here are the techniques in which artists talk to the work in progress, the manner in which time and space seem altered to these artists, and how a work in progress takes on a life of its own. A recent investigation by Csikszentmihalyi (1996) underscored the importance of these processes. Based on a series of interviews with creative and imaginative people, Csikszentmihalyi elaborated on the notion of *flow*. *Flow* refers to the intense concentration and altered consciousness evident in the process of art making and that may be present even in young children.

Interestingly, these ideas are consistent with accepted practice in the field of arts education (Edwards, 1997; Jalongo & Stamp, 1997; Rosenberg, 1987). Arts educators have long suggested that children as young as 3 use their imagination in consistent ways. Practitioners share stories of children whose behavior patterns become established early and remain relatively consistent. Children show strikingly stable preferences in their use of materials, including real-life experiences as opposed to fantastical episodes in their dramas and stories, and even in their creation of a consistent body of stylistically coherent work.

Gardner's (1982) definition of *style* provides a basis for the work described here. According to Gardner, *style* refers to "the characteristic features of compositions which mark the works of individuals or school independent of the content of these works (as cited in Wolf & Grollman, 1982).

In a longitudinal study of early symbolic development conducted at Harvard University's Project Zero, Wolf and Grollman (1982) identified two discrete styles in the way four girls (from a cohort of five) played with their dolls. They identified two criteria for determining style. First, "stylistic differences must be conceptualized and shown to result from differences in the quality and not the developmental level of the individual's behavior"--thus, not affected by cognitive maturity. Second, individual differences must be consistent across time.

In their study of the children's play, Wolf and Grollman (1982) noted two major styles in which children approached play materials. They described object-dependent fantasy and object independent transformational play. Object-dependent players were labeled *patterners*. Patterners preferred real-life props and objects. They used objects to represent the necessary props--a block on a plate for a piece of cake or a stick for a knife. Wolf and Grollman observed that patterners were sensitive to quantity, shape, size, and color, and excelled in visuospatial tasks and in creating designs. In contrast, the object-independent players were labeled *dramatists*. Dramatists often referred to nonpresent events, objects, or persons. They might roll imaginary dough or blow out imaginary birthday candles. Dramatists preferred open-ended props and made outlandish substitutions to fit their dramas. The object-independent children worked to maintain fantasy and sustain make-believe.

Imaginative styles were further explored by Tower (1984, 1985) with a larger sample of 4- and 5-five-year-olds. She identified two types of imagination: constructive and expressive. Constructive imaginative children operate with rules, but these can be suspended within accepted environmental constraints. Tower observed that expressive imaginative children set aside all external rules. Singer and Singer (1990) concluded that Tower's constructive imaginative children resemble Wolf and Grollman's (1982) patterners, whereas the expressive imaginative children resemble the dramatists.

About the Study

This chapter follows four 4-and-a-half to 5-year-olds during a semester in their preschool experience. Each of the children in the study took part in a series of weekly imagination/arts sessions led by undergraduate students. The findings detailed here focus specifically on two distinct imagination styles observed by the researcher.

Children in the study participated in one of two series of activities, either the Play for Success Method, an imagery-based drama, dance, and art method; or a KidPix and story-making method. Both set of experiences had been developed by the author. College student leaders conducted each session. All sessions were audio recorded and most were videotaped.

About the Play for Success Method

The Play for Success Method is a series of activities, developed by the author, for children ages 3 to 6. The approach evolved from the Rutgers Imagination Method, developed for stimulating drama and imagination in 7- to 12-year-olds (Rosenberg, 1987). The activities are broken into nine categories focusing on different content areas such as drama, movement, art, science, or math. Some are more sensory-based. All the activities have a major imagery component.

About the KidPix/Story-Making Method

KidPix Studio (Broderbund Software, 1995) is a popular commercial software program. An experience with KidPix was paired with a guided interaction in story making. In this treatment, the leader begins by explaining that the child will be using KidPix to make a picture and then tell a story. The child is encouraged to experiment with the stamp sets icons and, from these icons, to complete a picture on the screen, which is then printed. The child is then asked to tell a story about the picture. The leader re-reads the story aloud to the child. This is followed by a leader-directed discussion designed to foster story making. The leader models making a picture and creating a story that is either related to the picture or is related to the personal experience stimulated by the picture. During the modeling, the leader discusses character, conflict, dialogue, and beginning/middle/end. The child is then guided through a second picture-story-making episode.

Imagination Styles: Guiding the Investigation

Our observations have led us to believe that there were two fairly distinctive styles of imaginative behavior. These two styles crossed both types of activities; KidPix and Play for Success. Building on the work by Gardner and others discussed earlier, we developed a working list of characteristics of each category of behavior. As each characteristic emerged from the data, it was added to the list, and the tapes and notes were again scanned to see whether each child did or did not exhibit this characteristic. What evolved was a fairly discrete list of characteristics that seem to describe what I termed *imagination styles*. For the purpose of this chapter, the descriptive names given to the styles are *Pragmatist* and *Fantasizer*.

   The Fantasizer. The most distinct characteristic of the Fantasizer is her clear ability to be in what Csikszentmihalyi termed *flow*. Several features of flow exhibited by the adult artists in Csikszentmihalyi's work were demonstrated by the Fantasizers in my work. The most salient were apparent self-defined goals throughout the activity, absence of distractibility once engaged, no worry of failure, lack of self-consciousness, distortion of time, and autotelic activity (Csikszentmihalyi, 1996). Children identified as in flow played for a longer time, acknowledged the leader infrequently, and played even if other activities were going on right beside them. Videotapes of these children show them intensely involved in their activity. Field notes describe Fantasizers as focused, riveted, and "into it."

A second characteristic, implicit in the notion of flow described earlier, is internal locus of control. During the activity the Fantasizer is pleasing herself in the manner of a true artist/inventor. It is important to note that this occurs although an activity might initially be stimulated by a leader. The child is not concerned with the leader response until the story or picture is completed.

A third characteristic is a distinctive type of self-talk. Both Fantasizer and Pragmatist incorporate self-talk in their activities, but content and timing of these personal conversations are different. Fantasizers talk while they are participating in the activity. The child seems to be having conversations with his or her other self, the materials used in the activity, and the work in progress.

A fourth characteristic refers to the use of distinctive imagery-related activities. The Fantasizer uses both memory and imagination images and demonstrates internal/external oscillation, as described elsewhere (Rosenberg & Pinciotti, 1985). Memory images are those internal pictures of sights, sounds, touches, smells, or tastes that a person has experienced in everyday life. These experiences and subsequent images can be visual, tactile, olfactory, gustatory, kinesthetic, or auditory. Memory images are often powerful and can stimulate stories, drama, or artwork. Imagination images are images that are created by a person, usually combining pieces of memory images to invent a stimulating image of something that never actually existed or happened in life. A child can concoct a story about being lost in the woods and saved by a big dog named Lassie. What characterizes both memory and imagination images is that both types are personal, not generic, images.

Internal/external oscillation describes the process by which a child moves between an internal work in progress and the internal stimulating image for that piece. We have developed terminology that helps describe what we see. For example, we see a child *draw down* an image on paper. In drawing down, what we see is a child who seems to draw a picture so quickly that it seems that he or she is afraid that it might go away and needs to be captured.

A fifth variable concerns the child's response to the physical conditions and the materials at hand. For the Fantasizer, the physical space sets the stage for the success or failure of the activity. Once a Fantasizer gets comfortable, all is well--the sky is the limit. However, if a Fantasizer has a cold, feels that the room is too cold or hot, or is bothered by a smell, then nothing can happen until the situation is remedied. Observations suggest that a Fantasizer either jumps right into the activity or clearly chooses not to participate. Fantasizers seem to be sensory. The smell, sound, and taste grabs his or her attention.

The Pragmatist. In contrast to the Fantasizer, the Pragmatist is concerned with the real world around her. She is easily distracted, makes reference to time, focuses on the camera and tape recorder, and needs to be encouraged by the leader more often than the Fantasizer. Questions such as, "Is this alright?", "Can you hear me?", "How do I look?" illustrate the Pragmatist's concern with the audience. These children move in and out of the task and often look to the leader as a coach for reassurance while the improvisation is progressing.

The Pragmatist demonstrates an external locus of control. The shape of his or her participation is often very different from that of the Fantasizer. Initially, the Pragmatist may begin, stop and ask for clarification, then start up, and turn to the camera. He or she may play as long as the Fantasizer, but the level of involvement is less intense.

The Pragmatist's self-talk also differs from that of the Fantasizer. The Pragmatist uses self-talk primarily as a way to evaluate what he or she has done. For example:

"I like this stamp; it is so cute."
"I look just like a princess in this costume."

The self-self conversations we hear demonstrate reflection on the completed activity or evaluations of past efforts.

A fourth characteristic is the use of imagery. For the Pragmatist, memory images or recycled imagination images (often termed *generic images*) typically provide the internal stimulus for the activity. When questioned about what cat, for example, is the subject of the story, we find that no particularly real-life cat is the subject, merely a vaguely recollected cat. Similarly, the self provides central images. Pragmatists write about, make pictures of, and do dramas about what actually happened in their lives. Life, untransformed, is transferred to the page, the scene, or picture.

Fifth, the Pragmatist can work in less than ideal physical circumstances. Tapes reveal few comments about hot or cold rooms or headaches or colds. Pragmatists seem able to work when they are not well, although they are often distracted by their headache or sniffles. It seems as if the sensory aspects of the room or their physical condition are not part of their consciousness, although these factors may influence their behavior. A leader can count on the Pragmatist to begin to play no matter what.

Finally, the pragmatist is logical and conscientious. He tries to make sense of disparate elements, tries to find a useful procedure to get through an activity, and wants to know how he is doing. Even if he likes the magical or spiritual, the Pragmatist seems uncomfortable with an open-ended or unfamiliar activity. The Pragmatist wants to be right, to draw the correct and good picture, and to write the story that includes every single image for fear that the story without one image will not be judged well. The Pragmatist appears to be the teacher's dream because she tries hard, is predictable, and wants approval. One pragmatist, described later, quickly and efficiently mastered an art protocol and rarely strayed from creating and re-creating essentially the same picture.

Four Case Studies

To illustrate these two imagination styles, four case studies are described. Four children, two males and two females, representing the Play for Success and the KidPix/Story-Making Methods have been selected. These children provide particularly rich examples of the two imagination styles under two very different types of activity structures.

I begin with Daphna, a girl in the KidPix/Story-Making Method. I end with Benjy, a boy, in more or less the same activities. Daphna illustrates a Pragmatist, whereas Benjy is a true Fantasizer. Gabriel and Celia both participated in Play for Success. Gabriel, like Benjy, is a Fantasizer, whereas Celia, like Daphna, is a Pragmatist.

Daphna: The Pragmatist With KidPix. At the outset of our study, Daphna was 4 years and 7 months. Daphna was described as *very feminine.* She liked to wear dresses, particularly pink ones with pictures of Disney heroines. At school Daphna played almost exclusively with two or three other girls, and her favorite toys were Barbies and Magic Pony.

Initially Daphna was shy. The head teacher needed to assist Daphna to play and suggested that Daphna's friend sit next to her at the computer. Eventually during the first session, Daphna sat at the computer on her own. She remained seated during the first hour of this and every subsequent session. Daphna appeared to like the leader. Daphna told her teacher that the leader was, "Very nice and pretty and a good artist and a very good storymaker." Three characteristics of Daphna's behavior, her artwork, and her stories suggest that Daphna is a Pragmatist. First, she precisely modeled the leader. Second, she performed consistently and relatively quickly in the drawing/story-making activity. Third, her self-talk was highly evaluative.

During the early sessions, the leader demonstrated how to use the computer and the KidPix program. Daphna dutifully learned to use the mouse, scrolled through the stamps, mastered the paintbrush, created a picture, and told a story. For her first story, Daphna used the same stamps and told virtually the same story as did the leader. The leader used a few stamps from one set, put them in random order on the page, used a few more stamps from another set, and then told a short story. Daphna did the same thing.

Later she was asked to make her own picture and tell a story. Daphna picked the first stamp set on the screen, a Christmas stamp set, and placed the set around the page in random order. She went down each row and placed a few of each on the page. Daphna told her story in the same way, moving around the screen and merely adding one person or object to the tale. As Daphna told her story, the leader typed it.

> A Christmas Story. It was Christmas at Ginger Man's house.
> And they were having a big Christmas party. And they
> forgot to plant their seeds. And some animals were outside
> in the backyard and they were playing under their trees.
> And that's all.

After Daphna made her first picture and told the story, the leader praised her and tried to embellish it by connecting the images on the screen to objects from real life. During the process, Daphna saw a stamp set of animals and asked the leader to put a cat in the picture and in the story. The leader responded, "Great idea, you can put a cat into your own story."

Daphna explained, "I have two cats." Daphna seemed extremely motivated by the animal stamp set and the leaders model and was eager to make a picture and a story. Excitedly, Daphna began the process. She searched through the stamp sets and found the ones with animals. She began a unique behavior that she would continue throughout the semester. She placed a stamp on the side of the picture, looked it over, and then placed it fairly randomly within the picture. It was as if she felt compelled to use every stamp.

She told a story very similar to the one told by the leader. Daphna made herself the central character, added a cat, and seemed to incorporate some elements of "The Little Mermaid," which she had told the leader was her favorite movie.

> Rescue at Sea. A girl named Daphna and her best friend
> named Leah were sailing to New York City. They had a cat
> on their boat and the cat fell overboard. They threw the
> cat a rope. And then some other animals came from under
> the ocean and they helped the cat come back on the boat.
> Then the spider fly came and the clouds went away and the
> sun came out and a beautiful rainbow came out of the sky.
> The God of the rainbows came out of the rainbows. And
> that's the end.

During subsequent weeks, Daphna continued both to model the leader very directly and to go about the process of art making and story making in a fairly ritualized manner. If the leader were to use the art pen, then so would Daphna. Even when the leader asked Daphna to make a picture without the pen, Daphna behaved as if she were being tricked and smiled and copied what the leader had done. Only during one session at the end of the semester did Daphna specifically mention that she wanted to make her background black, "not like yours," she said to the leader.

Daphna liked the leader. She frequently asked, "Is this good? Do you like it?" Perhaps, because Daphna did not ever really seem to have an image

that she was "drawing down" on the computer, this rote approach of doing just
what the leader had done seemed the best way to solve the problem. One
wonders whether Daphna would have participated at all if no modeling had been
part of the protocol.

Watching Daphna create in the same way from week to week suggests
that Daphna was being more dutiful than inventive. Daphna's stories almost
always incorporated all the stamps, but rarely did the story *hang together* except
perhaps serially. Daphna would use a stamp set, put a few stamp sets on the
side, look at the stamp, put it into the picture in a fairly random way, and then
continue through several stamp sets until she filled up the page. Then she would
write a story that included all the stamps and announce she was finished.

Stylistically, Daphna's artwork and stories make up a unified body of
work. The piece that seems to most characteristically represent Daphna's work
is from Week 6 and is the third drawing/story of the five-part hula hoop girl
series created toward the end of the semester. Entitled, "The Hula Hoop Girl
Went to the Circus," it follows here.

> Once there was a hula hoop girl and her whole life she
> wanted to go to a circus. And she was standing outside
> and heard an elephant, giraffe, tiger, and doggy and
> everything. And reindeer. And she ran over where they
> were coming from. And it was a circus train and she got
> on and that was-the end. Oh, and it started to rain
> and rain and rain and rain. And then the sun came out.
> And big explosions came out. And then she saw, she saw
> a circus. And that's the end. No, and then a humming
> bird landed on her shoulder and became her friend. And
> she went to a circus. And that's the end.

The main action and locale of the Hula Hoop Girl parallels the
entertainment videotapes Daphna frequently views and the books she is reading.
The Hula Hoop series seems to be modeled after the Madeline books (Bemelens,
1939) and tapes that Daphna has talked about. Although children's artwork and
stories are often based on works they have read, what characterizes Daphna's
work is that it does not seem to originate from a clear internal image that she
is able to articulate. Her work seems a copy of a copy and consequently her
stories are dutiful, appropriate, but rarely inspired.

Daphna's self-talk is intriguing. She began to narrate herself almost
from the first session. Her talk is described as teenage like in nature. In an
early session, after placing a stamp on the page, Daphna says, "I like that
stamp!", "Wow, isn't that stamp so cute!", or "A cool stamp."

Later in the semester, Daphna placed a stamp on the picture and then took it out and said, "I don't want this girl, I want that one." She then replaced the stamp. After she placed a stamp of a fox on the page, she turned to the leader and chattily said in her best teenage voice, "That stamp is supposed to be a fox, but it looks more like a cat."

Gabriel: Fantasizer at Play. Gabriel was just 5 years old at the beginning of the work described here. Gabriel and his twin sister, Celia, had been part of the study since its inception. Gabriel is a gentle boy with a winning smile. His small motor skills are below average, as are his verbal skills, although when "in the flow" Gabriel seems to find just the right turn of phrase. What he lacks in these areas, however, he makes up for with enthusiasm, humor, empathy, and imagination. Gabriel was the most consistently enthusiastic participant in the study, approaching each task with real zest and a big smile.

Gabriel exemplified a Fantasizer--able to go with the flow and present in a here-and-now reality. I describe Gabriel's participation in two of the activities included in Play for Success. The first was called Magic Painting. In Magic Painting, the child is directed to paint on half a page, talk about the painting, fold the page over, and then talk about what the unfolded picture now looks like. Many children have great difficulty first in covering their piece and then allowing themselves to view the transformed picture. They have difficulty giving up control of the work to the materials.

As he began the activity, Gabriel had no plan. Gabriel described his idea and then allowed the glob to inspire him. When the paper was folded over, Gabriel explained that the frog of the original painting had gone away. He explained that "A ghost had chased him away." When the leader pointed out that there were really two frogs, Gabriel explained that the old frog had made the new one. As the leader pointed out that each object and character had a duplicate on the second page, Gabriel seemed enchanted. He proceeded to develop a complex story with clear connections to the actual picture. Not only did he include each object and his duplicate in the story, but he also included the ghost to help explain how each character had been doubled.

For Gabriel and other Fantasizers, materials seem to have magical properties. Gabriel allows the materials to speak to him. Gabriel could not explain how the picture changed. He just knew it had changed and was entirely different. Gabriel spends much of his time in this activity in experiencing the materials: the changes, the mirror image, the two of everything. Gabriel shows us that he is very much in the here and now.

The second activity was called Up in the Attic. This activity was designed to promote the exploration of a variety of costume pieces and was followed by the development of an enactment directed by the child participant. Unlike many of the other children in the study, Gabriel spent much of his initial time exploring each of the costume pieces. He viewed the pieces separately, then together, then separately again. During an almost 2-hour segment, Gabriel tried on the pieces, developed brief characterization, and then returned to costume exploration.

Initially, Gabriel took out all the hats, looked at them, put on the firefighter hat, walked around like a firefighter, and spoke few firefighter lines: "I'm Firefighter Frank and I put out fires. Here's my truck and my hose (miming both)." Then he took off the hat, looked at the other hats, selected the race car driver helmet, and briefly explored the role of race car driver. He proceeded through the hats, often returning to a hat and then going on to a new one. Although the leader was present, he showed no interest in her.

Analyses of the videotape suggest that Gabriel is in the planning stage of a potentially more detailed enactment, but not really moving ahead to the presentation. The sensory aspects of the hats and costumes and how they feel on his head and body are the true forces. Interestingly, although a full-length mirror is readily available in the classroom, Gabriel does not use it to see what he looks like wearing the costume pieces or hats. It seems as if Gabriel sees himself from within. Even with encouragement from the student leader, Gabriel is not interested in participating in an interactive enactment. Gabriel is clearly into the flow and only wants to explore. After this lengthy exploration, in which he also explores other props in the classroom (besides the ones in the truck), Gabriel indicates that he is finished.

When questioned later about this exploration in a revisitation of Up in the Attic, Gabriel recalled the costume pieces and hats. He appeared to derive intense pleasure from his recall and progressed in the revisiting of Attic activity. The tape shows that Gabriel feels each hat in the same order as before, does a compressed rehearsal of what he had done last time, and seems ready to move on. This time Gabriel is able to begin to enact a story and interact with the leader.

Gabriel seems equally successful in all art forms. He enjoyed every category of Play for Success. Interestingly, in contrast to most of the other boys in the study, Gabriel particularly liked to dress up and "try out all these people." Once we captured his attention, usually with a costume piece, prop, or some art materials, Gabriel would play until the session was over. "That truck needs me," Gabriel would say as a way to explain why he was playing with it for so long. At times, Gabriel would often not get to the larger task, such as interacting with the leader, because he spent so much time experimenting. Gabriel began with no clear plan, yet he always knew when he was done. However, if an activity did not strike his fancy, Gabriel would not play.

Celia: A Pragmatist at Play. Celia was 5 years old as the semester began. She is a twin; her brother is Gabriel, who was also in the study. Celia's parents are both professors; her mother is in her 40s, her father in his 50s. Celia had been part of the study since she was 3 and had a close relationship with the student leader. She had participated in Play for Success in visual art, music, drama, and writing.

Celia is a Pragmatist. In the following discussion, Celia's participation in several of the Play for Success activities is described. The Magic Painting Activity is described first. What we hoped to do in conducting Magic Painting with Celia was to help her let go of a very strong stimulating image. Based on prior observations, we knew that Celia liked to draw and redraw an image of herself and her best friend, Rama. Celia is very blond and Rama is very dark. Each drawing of the two--on the swings, in the park, in the sandbox--contains a yellow figure and a black one. Our objective for Magic Painting was to encourage Celia to give up control of the media and allow what she sees to stimulate the retrieval of a memory image or the creation of an imagination image. Obviously many painters and playwrights use the same stimulating image for work after work, but in Celia's case, we hoped to help her expand her repertoire before settling on that single image.

When Celia manipulated the thick paint with the spoon, it seemed quite difficult for her to draw herself and her friend. She managed to do it. When the paper was folded, Celia did not see an entirely new picture, but a mirror image of the picture of herself with her friend. Finally, when she folded one picture that did not look much like Celia and her friend Rama (more like a reddish glob), Celia did concur that this picture looked like a butterfly.

When the student leader tried to discover more about how Celia could work with this strong image, she found that Celia could see the image of herself and her friend from outside, as if she were looking at the experience. She could also place herself into the picture and describe how she went from outside the image to within it. This ability suggested that Celia has tremendous control of her imaging strategies.

In a similar activity, Straw Paintings, in which she was asked to blow three different colored paints through straws and then talk about what the three blocks looked like, Celia exhibited a premature closure (Torrance & Ball, 1992). Once she had decided what the first blob looked like, she made the other two blobs fit the category. For example, Celia described the three blobs as Frankenstein, a bumble bee, and a reindeer, and then she connected the three blobs by saying that both the bumble bee and the reindeer were in Frankenstein's tummy. She titled the work "Inside Tummy." Certainly the solution and the title are wonderfully inventive. Yet like most Pragmatists, unless the blobs were connected, Celia felt like she had not done what she had been asked.

Celia said she felt "more better" in different categories of activities. For example, when solving jigsawlike puzzle activities, like the activity Art Match, Celia was able to demonstrate a wide variety of well-developed imagery strategies and a similarly well-developed internal/external oscillation skill. For Art Match, we selected some well-known paintings of Chagall, Picasso, and

Kandinsky and provided the children with each painting in two versions: one whole and the other cut into a variety of pieces. The piece division ranged from fairly simple with both shape and subject matter clues, to fairly complex, with all pieces being similar and both shape and subject matter clues, to fairly complex, with all pieces being similar and subject of painting being very abstract. Celia seemed to match pieces almost entirely internally, mentally manipulating the pieces without physically touching them. She was quick and right on target--getting all the puzzles together in less than a minute.

In the second step of Art Match, the child is asked what the painting looks like. To do this, Celia looked at each picture as if she had never seen it, although moments before she had been matching pieces up a storm. It was almost as if she changed from a focus on the parts to the whole. She seemed to switch gears as she slowed herself down and responded. When questioned about how she had changed, Celia said, "Now I can look, before I couldn't."

Celia's preferred art form is drama. Just one costume or set piece seems to unlock an entire storehouse of images for Celia. The window frame (used here for a post office window) encourages Celia to recall her real-life post office experiences. In the tape of Post Office, we see Celia moving from being actor, to director, to playwright, to actor again. She also took on many dramatic roles in the enactment, including, of course, princess, mommy, and bride.

In another activity, Up in the Attic, a box filled with a variety of costume pieces--such as veils, crowns, long skirts, tutus, sorcerer's hat, Native American dress, nurse's cap, doctor bag, construction worker hat, tool belt, and white gloves--captured Celia's attention for almost 2 hours. The tape reveals a four-act drama. Each scene is given a name: "Indian and Wizard," "Sleeping Princess," "Princess and Prince Together," and "Beautiful Princess and Wizard." Celia played a variety of parts, all starring Celia with the leader in a variety of subsidiary roles. Celia sings, dances, and enacts wonderfully, but in a way quite typical of dramatic 5-year-olds. Although she shows talent, grace, a lovely singing voice, and model-like poses that show costumes off their utmost, Celia, when questioned, had everything planned before her arrival. When the activity was revisited about 6 weeks later, the same dramas probably stimulated the very same images.

Celia, like other Pragmatists, seems to work from memory images. In Post Office, we see Celia being Belle (from "Beauty and the Beast"), Pocahontas, or Cinderella. As we watch the drama unfolding, we see quite well-developed characterizations--Celia, walks, talks and dresses like the characters she develops, but the characters selected are quite traditional. We see a wonderful performance of recycled Disney.

Celia plays for a long time in many of the more drama-oriented activities. A quick conclusion might be that Celia is in the flow. Closer observation reveals that she moves spontaneously from one scene to another to another, rarely experiencing flow (like Gabriel might) because we could see her being aware and even commenting on the presence of the leader or the camera or being distracted by children coming or going.

Benjy: A Fantasizer With KidPix. Benjy was 4 years and 9 months when the study began. Benjy is a rambunctious, high-energy boy who loves Power Rangers action figures, eating, and his dad and his brother, in that order. He also admitted he loved his mom, although the house is "filled with guys. Even the pets are all boys." Both Benjy's mother and father have advanced college degrees and provide Benjy with strong educational models. A superficial observer of Benjy might find him not really interested in drawing or writing because he seems so action-oriented, but Benjy truly exemplifies a boy with real imagination abilities and artistic talents.

Several aspects of what Benjy did and how he did it place Benjy in the domain of the Fantasizer. First, Benjy consistently jumped right into the process. Second, Benjy exhibited sophisticated and idiosyncratic self-talk characteristics of a Fantasizer. Finally, Benjy created a body of work that depicts varied subject matter, but hangs together stylistically. This body of work over time demonstrates tremendous artistic growth. Transcriptions of the tapes reveal that Benjy viewed his work as art and understood that it was to be viewed by others and would have an effect on them.

One characteristic of Benjy's activity is his jump start. The leader would sit down with Benjy and he was off and running. He came into the semester knowing how to use the computer and discovered the stamp sets, paintbrush, drawing tools, and other aspects of KidPix on his own. The only real modeling that the leader did was demonstrating for Benjy how to connect a story to the picture and how to construct stories with a beginning, middle, and end.

Benjy seemed to work from a clear, vivid internal visual image. He seemed to be drawing down on the screen what he saw in his head. Benjy also seemed to have fluent access to his storehouse of KidPix images. He seemed able to flip through the KidPix stamps mentally, manipulate them in his head, and use that image as the stimulus for the picture.

Benjy would either really go with the activity and work solidly for the 1-hour block or he would not become involved at all. The only real refocusing tool that the leader was able to use effectively was to point to the screen and ask him to look again at what he had done.

Benjy's self-talk and personal narration was extraordinary. Benjy seemed to talk aloud to his alter ego, to the work of art both in process and completed, and to the images that seemed to exist both internally and externally. From the second session on, Benjy talked constantly while he drew. He described his actions as he worked, making statements such as, "Benjy you're going to put this mouse here and click there." He also narrated himself while he was working. "The rainbow is here and the guy is over there. I can put the pirates here, the graves there with the wolves and the bugs and the skulls here." Perhaps the narration was a focusing device or perhaps he was using the words to help him re-create the image from his head onto the screen.

Certainly most unique in his personal narration was how he talked about the stamps and the work in progress. "That stamp needs to be here. I know." In many ways, he is like a mature artist in that the work and the materials have a life of their own (Rosenberg & Epstein, 1991). During the second from the last session, for example, Benjy was looking behind him, to the screen, and then back again. When questioned, he explained, "The stamps are coming through the door." When the leader said that could not be possible, Benjy said, "Yes, the stamps are coming through the door. Here they are now." He then pointed to the picture on the screen.

Benjy truly created a body of work during the semester. From the beginning, Benjy's stories and drawings were inventive and different from those of the other children in the study. Benjy combined different elements of KidPix: the stamp sets, the paint brush, shadings, and shapes. Benjy was enchanted with the process of making art. He also understood that the art piece could affect its receiver. He often asked the leader about her response. Several times he turned directly toward her and said, "Are you really scared?" Similarly, Benjy also liked making people laugh. Benjy's drawings and stories were funny.

Benjy's last picture and story were called, "The Story of Rainbow Land." In this picture, he used only three stamps (a face, a full-body figure, and a bubble with a scene in it) but explained, "It looks like there are more because they were dancing and moving so fast."

> Once upon a time Rainbow Land was a big place. And then
> it was even bigger and bigger. If you went to the end
> of Rainbow Land, If you went to the end of the road,
> you would only see water. And nothing else. Only
> water. The guys are dancing. And everyone was dancing
> in Rainbow Land. There were only two people in Rainbow
> Land, but there looked like there was a lot because
> they were dancing so fast. The end.

A BRIEF CONCLUSION

It is hard to believe that the four children discussed herein were only 5 years old. They played, enacted, drew, and wrote with a sophistication far above their years. I present these observations to encourage educators to expand their view of the arts for young children. Certainly Benjy can be portrayed as a young Seurat and Celia as Madonna of the new millennium. More than that, however, these cases suggest that these young children, as well as many like them, offer us (their parents, their teachers, and those who study them) windows into their imaginations.

Many questions remain unanswered. Is style constant throughout life? Is style consistent across different art forms? Can style be learned? Are children capable of shifting from style to style? At what age, if ever, do these stylistic behaviors go underground? Right now, my team and I are continuing the observations of the children discussed in this chapter. They are now 6 and seem to be working within the same imagination styles. Of course, now that they are 6, they have even more to say about their imagination styles. A recently transcribed discussion between Celia and Gabriel captures the essence of the differences in style. Celia explained, "I dreamed I married a boy from preschool. He had yellow hair."

"Who is that?" questioned Gabriel, naming all the boys in preschool with yellow hair and without yellow hair. He wanted to be part of Celia's fantasy dream.

Celia dismissed him, "Oh, Gabriel, don't you know, dreams are not real. I didn't marry anybody."

Gabriel retorted, "They are real to me."

REFERENCES

Barrie, J. M. (1906). *Peter Pan in Kensington Gardens*. New York: Charles Scribner's Sons.

Bemelmens, L. (1939). *Madeline*. New York: Viking.

Broderbund Software. (1995). *KidPix Studio*. Novato, CA: Author.

Burnett, F. H. (1962). *The secret garden*. Philadelphia, PA: Lippincott.

Carroll, L. (1946). *Alice's adventures in wonderland*. Cleveland, OH: World Publishing Company.

Csikszentmihalyi, M. (1996). *Creativity: Flow and the psychology of discover and invention*. New York: Harper Collins.

Edwards, L. C. (1997). *The creative arts: A process approach for teachers and children*. Upper Saddle River, NJ: Merrill.

Gardner, H. (1982). *Art, mind, and brain*. New York: Basic Books.

Jalongo, M. R., & Stamp, L. N. (1997). *The arts in children's lives: Aesthetic education in early childhood*. Needham Heights, MA: Allyn & Bacon.

Rosenberg, H. S. (1987). *Creative drama and imagination: Transforming ideas into action*. New York: Holt, Rinehart & Winston.

Rosenberg, H. S., & Epstein, Y. (1991). Alone together: Collaborative imagery in visual art-making. *Journal of Mental Imagery, 15* (3 & 4), 157-170.

Rosenberg, H. S., & Pinciotti, P. (1983/1984). Imagery in creative drama. *Imagination, Cognition, and Personality, 3* (1), 69-75.

Rosenberg, H. S., & Pinciotti, P. (1985). The iii system: Imagery and creative drama. *Journal of Creative Behavior, 19* (2), 142-144.

Rosenberg, H. S., & Trusheim, W. (1990). Creative transformations: How visual artists, musicians, and dancers use mental imagery in their work. In *Imagery current perspectives*. New York: Plenum.

Singer, D. G., & Singer, J. S. (1990). *The house of make-believe: Children's play and the developing imagination*. Cambridge, MA: Harvard University Press.

Torrance, E. P., & Ball, O. E. (1992). *Torrance tests of creative thinking: Streamlines scoring guide figural A and B*. Bensenville, IL: Scholastic Testing Service.

Tower, R. B. (1984/1985). Preschoolers' imaginativeness. *Imagination, Cognition, and Personality, 4* (4), 349-364.

Wolf, D., & Grollman, S. (1982). Ways of playing: Individual differences in imaginative styles. *Contributions to Human Development, 6*, 46-63.

12

MEASURING RECOMMENDED PRACTICES FOR VERY YOUNG CHILDREN WITH DISABILITIES

Ellen C. Frede
The College of New Jersey

W. Steven Barnett
Rutgers - The State University of New Jersey

Theresa Lupo
The College of New Jersey

The value of educational, therapeutic, and social services for infants and young children with disabilities and their families has been acknowledged by leaders in the field of special education (Guralnick, 1997; Meisels, Dichtmiller, & Liaw, 1994; Shonkoff, Hauser-Cram, Krauss, & Upshur, 1992) and by policymakers as shown by the enactment of PL 99-457 and the Individuals with Disabilities Education Act Amendments of 1997 (IDEA, 1997). These beliefs are substantiated by both research and theory that show the importance of the first years of life for brain growth and development (Chugani, Phelps, & Mazziotta, 1987; Kolb, 1989), learning (Ramey et al., 1992), language (Dunham & Dunham, 1992), and social development (Werner & Smith, 1982). However, evidence establishing the effectiveness of early intervention for all young children with disabilities is less clear partly because methodological issues make it difficult to conduct convincing studies with this highly diverse population (Casto & Mastropieri, 1986; Escobar, Barnett, & Goetze, 1994; Guralnick, 1993, 1997; Olds & Kitzman, 1993), although meta-analyses of existing studies have shown modest positive outcomes (Casto & Mastropieri, 1986; Shonkoff & Hauser-Cram,, 1987).

It is clear that asking the question "Is early intervention effective?" is simplistic given the wide variety of intervention methods (e.g., setting, theoretical perspective, curricula, intensity); the variation in quality of the implementation of those methods; the differing targets for intervention (e.g., child, parents, the family system); and the diversity of salient child and family characteristics (e.g., type and severity of disability, socioeconomic background, family stress, child temperament and personality, and parent belief systems). The important questions to be answered are how effective are alternative interventions, under what conditions, and for which populations? Guralnick (1997) refered to research designed to answer these questions as *second-generation* research. Further, Guralnick stated that the goals of this endeavor should be to lead practitioners in their work with young children and their families and policymakers in their decision making that directly impacts the work of practitioners and the quality of services provided to children and their families.

This chapter presents results from one aspect of a research study designed to be second generation. The New Jersey Early Intervention System Study is a longitudinal statewide study that attempts to provide a comprehensive and complex view of one state's early intervention system for infants and toddlers with disabilities. Specifically, this chapter focuses on the results of the Program Quality Study that measured program practices through direct observation. To put the study in context, an overview of the theories guiding early childhood special education (ECSE) and a selected review of research on recommended practices are presented.

BACKGROUND FOR THE STUDY

Principles Guiding Early Childhood Special Education Practices

With the passage of the Individuals With Disabilities Education Act Amendments of 1997 (IDEA), the mandate for serving young children with disabilities in the natural environment is quite clear. *Natural environments* are defined in the federal law as "the home and community settings in which children without disabilities participate," (IDEA, 1997, p. 82). For young children these community settings include a relative's home, a family day-care provider's home, and child-care and preschool classrooms. In addition, the Americans with Disabilities Act (ADA) requires that community programs, such as child-care centers, may not restrict enrollment due to a disability. Thus, two fields of early childhood special education (ECSE) and early childhood care and education (ECCE) have strong reasons to collaborate and develop a common language so that inclusion in the natural environment can best meet the needs of all children. Efforts to collaborate are long standing, but not as far reaching as is necessary given the clear imperative of IDEA and ADA.

Despite commonality of purpose, there are many different variables that influence programs for young children. ECCE and ECSE programs traditionally serve different populations, have distinct but complementary goals, and are often based on different theoretical approaches (Bricker & Cripe, 1992; McLean & Odom, 1993). As Bricker and Cripe explained, intervention practices in ECSE were originally based on behaviorist philosophies that lead to highly structured, adult-directed activities designed to shape a child's responses toward a specific learning objective. The effectiveness of behavior analysis for older institutionalized populations influenced its use with younger children.

In the 30 years since the initial ECSE programs emerged, research and practice have influenced theory, and the approach has broadened to include constructivist and sociocultural theories, and practices from ECCE and other fields such as speech pathology. ECSE now emphasizes the importance of involving parents, siblings, caregivers, and playmates in intervention as part of the child's social environment and embedding objective-based interventions within child-initiated activities.

The rationale for providing services in the natural environment is twofold. The first stems from a basic civil rights view that any person with a disability has the right to be a full member of society, participating in educational and community programs. The second rationale comes from both the sociocultural approach and an efficacy view that whatever is taught in the natural environment rather than in a segregated or institutional setting will be more likely to generalize and become part of the child's repertoire of behaviors. How the rationale for natural environments is understood may affect how it is implemented. For example, if setting is all that matters because the interest is in equal access, then placing children in child-care programs but providing therapy outside of the normal routine of the center may be the service provision. However, if generalization of learning is also understood to be a purpose, then interventionists will take on a more consulting role with the parent and classroom teacher to ensure that techniques are used during the child's routine activities even when the interventionist is not present (Frede, 1998). The belief that service in the natural environment is a civil rights issue alone may lead to a continued separation of the two fields of ECCE and ECSE, whereas the second leads to a revision of the roles of special educators, therapists, and classroom teachers.

Recommended Practices in Early Childhood Special Education

According to Casto (1988), evaluations and changes in ECSE programs have been primarily based on non-experimental methods (i.e., expert opinion, tradition, personal experience, common sense) rather than research-based standards of best practice. The recent publication of the Division of Early Childhood (DEC) Task Force on Recommended Practices (1993) is an attempt to remedy this and is evidence of a consensus within the field of ECSE regarding optimal program features. The DEC Executive Board established the Task Force on Recommended Practices in the spring of 1991. DEC members, parents, and experts met to create the Recommended Practices document. Research and expert opinion influenced the establishment of a practice, but the views and perspectives of multiple constituencies in ECSE were also important. Therefore, the DEC Task Force developed a consensus across stakeholders, supported by research, expert opinion, and practitioners' and parents' experience.

The first step in this process involved identifying strands or areas of concentration and then establishing work groups in each of the 14 areas. The members of the work groups used six criteria to identify recommended practices in each area. These criteria stated that practices must be research or value based, multicultural, cross-disciplinary, normalized, and developmentally and chronologically age appropriate for children between the ages of birth and 5 to 6 years. To establish social validity and treatment acceptability of the identified practices, a randomly selected sample of teachers, parents, administrators, researchers, and other professionals in the field was surveyed to determine their level of agreement with the items and frequency of their current use (Odom, McLean, Johnson, & LaMontagne, 1995). Although the majority of the respondents across constituency groups agreed with the Recommended Practices, practitioners were apt to rate the use of practices higher than parents or representatives of higher education. According to the authors, the low ratings on the current use of such innovations in the field as child-initiated activities, family-centered approaches, and developmentally appropriate practices were distressing (Odom et al., 1995).

The DEC Recommended Practices suggest effective methods across the following areas: Assessment, Family Participation, IFSPs and IEPs, Service Delivery Models, General Curriculum and Intervention Strategies, Interventions to Promote Communication Skills, Interventions to Promote Social Skills and Emotional Development, Interventions to Promote Adaptive Behavior Skills, Interventions to Promote Motor Skills, Transition Personnel Competence, Program Evaluation, and Early Intervention with Children Who Are Gifted. To correspond to the research presented later in this chapter, the following review of the literature regarding Recommended Practices is confined to selected practices observable in an intervention session--Communication Interventions, Social and Emotional Skill Interventions, Family Participation and Service Delivery Models, and General Curriculum and Intervention Strategies.

Communication Interventions. A strong language acquisition and communication teaching component in ECSE programs is important not only because many program participants have language delays, but also because oral language is the foundation for much social and cognitive development. By preschool age (i.e., ages 3-5), children with language delays talk approximately half as much as and are less responsive to teacher and peer inquiries than typically developing peers (Warren, McQuarter, & Rogers-Warren, 1984). The DEC recommends that language interventions be considered for all children with special needs to help improve overall development. Communication includes many different methods of transmitting messages, both verbal and nonverbal:

> Communication may be intentional or unintentional; it may
> involve conventional or nonconventional signals; it may be
> expressed through linguistic or non-linguistic forms; and it
> may be conveyed through oral or non-oral (gestural, graphic,
> and written) modes. (Division of Early Childhood Task
> Force on Recommended Practices, 1993, p. 75)

To enable young children with special needs to communicate more effectively, interventionists should employ a variety of performance assessment methods to regularly refine goals and identify strategies for teaching that address each child's specific needs (Division of Early Childhood Task Force on Recommended Practices, 1993). Communication interventions range from highly structured, didactic teaching to naturalistic, child-centered methods. Highly structured, didactic interventions teach more formal aspects of language using behavior-based techniques such as modeling, stimulus control, and reinforcement. Naturalistic, child-oriented interventions teach less formal aspects of language and place a greater emphasis on communication. These naturalistic techniques also rely on adult-modeled language within the context of conversational interaction. Other methods such as milieu teaching and incidental methods combine highly structured, didactic interventions and naturalistic, child-oriented methods in varying proportions (Yoder, Kaiser, & Alpert, 1991).

Milieu techniques involve brief adult-child interactions in which instruction is based on the child's focus of attention and assistance is provided when needed. Incidental teaching refers to interactions that arise naturally during unstructured periods. It involves arranging the environment to increase the likelihood of the child's initiating language, selecting language targets appropriate to the child, responding to a child's language with a request for expansion, and reinforcing the attempt with attention and access to the object of language. Exchanges are brief, positive, and oriented toward communication. This method incorporates modeling, shaping, and reinforcement. Shaping, prompting, and contingent reinforcement occur in contexts where language will be used (Warren & Kaiser, 1986).

Warren, McQuarter, and Rogers-Warren (1984) examined the use of mands and models with young children with language delays who were socially isolated and unresponsive. (A mand is any verbalization that requires a response other than a yes/no question [e.g., "What do you want?" or "Tell me what you want."]) This technique required the teacher to determine the focus of the child's attention through observation. The teacher then requested or instructed the child to verbalize using a mand. The teacher then waited for a response. Children were praised if they responded correctly. Another strategy had the teacher provide a model for language, wait for a response, and praise or modeled as appropriate if the child did not respond correctly. Consistent use of these methods during free play increased the child's total verbalization and initiations. During fading, children maintained the improved verbalization and initiation rates and increased their mean length of utterance.

Comparing the effectiveness of a milieu language program with a behavioral didactic approach for young children with developmental delays, Yoder, Kaiser, and Alpert (1991) found that milieu teaching produced a greater increase in language development and more consistent responses to teaching. Children who benefited most from milieu teaching were those who scored lower on pretreatment variables--specifically those who did not talk, did not self-initiate, had limited vocabulary, and had less intelligible speech. However, children who benefited more from the behavioral didactic approach were those who scored higher during pretreatment--particularly those with greater self initiation, more frequent utterances, and more intelligible speech. Cole, Dale, and Mills (1991) found similar results in a comparison of incidental teaching with direct instruction.

Camarata (1993) studied the teaching of speech production in the context of naturalistic conversation for preschool-age children with communication disorders. Out of concern that drill and practice methods and imitation exercises may result in resistance to training and even disruptive behavior, interventionists made no direct requests for speech production. Instead, the environment was arranged so that there were a large number of items containing target sounds (e.g., to increase production of the /l/ sound, lions, toy lips, lambs, and lights were provided in the play area). The children spontaneously initiated verbalizations within the context of play. The children were presented with accurate models of speech if their own pronunciations were incorrect. In addition, correct pronunciations were affirmed. Camarata found that correct speech production generalized to the home and to interactions with other adults.

Because elements of both naturalistic, child-oriented techniques and structured, didactic teaching methods have shown positive results, a combined approach can be employed. If the content and timing of a mixed approach are controlled by the child rather than imposed by the teacher, children can move at their own pace and avoid feeling pressure to perform. The child-directed content helps motivate responsiveness and creates an environment in which the child is more engaged. Bricker and Cripe (1992) suggested that infants and young children benefit more from child-initiated and self-directed activities that are meaningful and responsive to children's needs. Because ECSE programs serve children with different needs and different goals, a variety of communication and language intervention techniques, rather than just one, should be employed. The most appropriate language teaching method varies depending on the child's developmental level, the type and degree of the handicapping condition, the specific child's characteristics, and the child's individual language goals (Yoder, Kaiser, & Alpert, 1991).

According to the DEC, children need frequent opportunities for both transmitting and receiving language. Communication intervention should occur with different partners, have different content, and occur in varying contexts. Implementation of language techniques should be individualized for children and applied consistently and frequently. Also, environments should be constructed to encourage communication. The language teaching methods found effective in the studies discussed earlier are consistent with these recommendations.

Socioemotional Skill Interventions. The young child's ability to establish effective and appropriate peer relationships affects cognitive, communicative, and overall social development (Guralnick, 1993; Fewell & Kaminski, 1988). Enhancing children's peer-related social competence should be a priority among early interventionists because children with disabilities often have difficulty forming such relationships.

According to Strain and Kohler (1988), social skill deficits in young children with disabilities often result in peer rejection, scapegoating, disproportionate placement in special classes, and poor self-esteem. Over extended periods of time, absence of skill and a lack of support for social development can cause emotional responses in children that are just as limiting as any primary disability (Gresham, 1982). There are a number of variables that affect these social skill deficits, including: (a) person variables, such as developmental level, temperament, physical integrity, sensory integrity, motor skills, and the ability to use toys; (b) peer group variables, their tolerance for differences, access to appropriate role models, and regularity of exposure to other children; and (c) environmental variables, such as availability and number of cooperative-use toys, teacher prompts to play together, set time and location for interaction with other children, and dramatic play opportunities (Guralnick, 1993).

Many personal and environmental characteristics place children with disabilities at risk of developing social skills deficits. Therefore, interventionists should create situations and adapt environments and materials to encourage and enable children to practice social skills. Teachers may need to facilitate, model, guide, or redirect behaviors. Learning self initiated play skills, negotiating tactics, and conflict-resolution skills helps children move toward more productive and satisfying peer relationships, which, in turn, increase their independence and feelings of self-efficacy. Inclusion in a social group allows children to experience both positive and negative emotions. Although most children learn how to regulate their behaviors in naturally occurring interactions, some may require more structured settings and situations to learn to control their responses. Children who do not learn proper emotional regulation may compensate with inappropriate behaviors such as withdrawal or aggression. Finally, social-cognitive processes involve children encoding relevant social cues, interpreting the cues, and selecting strategies and alternatives based on these. Children who cannot read social cues or have no repertoire of social strategies due to developmental or cognitive delays have difficulty interacting with peers (Guralnick, 1993).

Child-to-child communication and social skills can be enhanced by providing early intervention recipients with access to other children, frequent encounters with children with well-developed social skills, and engaging toys and materials. Adults can facilitate this process with prompts and feedback as needed. To maintain and generalize social skills, interaction should take place in multiple contexts. One means to provide these interactions is through play. Play is a rich resource for sustained peer interactions and fostering such social skills as sharing, turn-taking, and cooperation (Howes & Seward, 1987).

Odom, Peterson, McConnell, and Ostrosky (1990) found that, in regular and special early education programs, the greatest amount of time spent in socialization with peers occurred during play. Of all the play activities noted, pretending (dramatic play) produced the greatest number of verbalizations. The study also found that children with disabilities had less social interaction than did children of the same developmental level without disabilities. Children without disabilities spent nearly twice as much time in play as did children with disabilities. Children with disabilities spent most of their time in gross motor, preacademics (learning skills related to reading, writing, and mathematics), and snack. Children talked to peers least during formal language intervention, preacademic skills, fine motor, class business, and story times.

File and Kontos (1993) measured play to compare the quality of ECCE programs to that of ECSE programs. Although levels of cognitive play among both groups were similar, levels of social play were lower for children in ECSE. Teacher support for cognitive play occurred six times more frequently than did support for social play. Best practice states that interventionists who engage in responsive, supportive interactions with children allow them to maximize the learning potential of their social and cognitive play (File & Kontos, 1993). Similarly, Odom et al. (1990) found that when comparing ECCE with ECSE, the former were often more play based and child centered and contained more child-initiated activities. In contrast, the ECSE classes had substantially more teacher-directed activities.

Research in the area of socioemotional development in early intervention has tended to focus on preschool-age children. For younger children, parents are the primary social partners, and research has tended to focus on parent-child relationships. According to the DEC, socioemotional development for infants can be enhanced by assisting families in their interactions with their children. This differentiation is reflected in the Recommended Practice in the division of indicators for infants and separate indicators for children ages 3 to 5. In both age brackets, however, including the family in intervention is essential. Most learning for infants and toddlers takes place in the home, therefore, extending services and methods to parents will help promote development and generalization.

Family Participation. The DEC recommendations specify that interventionists must take the family's needs, goals, concerns, and priorities into account, thereby making intervention more family centered. It is important to consider the family's choice and pace of services desired when planning. Brinker (1992) stressed the importance of including other family members in early intervention, because they may also play an important role in the children's development. Parents can effectively promote development and further interventions at home.

Girolametto (1988) found that parents of children with developmental delays who participated in intervention programs were more responsive to and less controlling of their children's behavior than were parents who did not participate. Parents learned how to (a) follow children's conversational leads, (b) respond to children's attempts to communicate in a contingent manner, and (c) take turns in conversation and therefore encourage conversation all within the context of play. As a result, children were able to initiate on more topics, were more responsive to taking turns, used more turns, and had a more diverse vocabulary. Children who are able to engage in interaction receive more feedback on their interests and communicate attempts than do children with poor initiation and response skills (Girolametto, 1988). Parents of children with disabilities may require assistance with this interaction because these children are not as responsive.

Research from other perspectives has also shown that parents can be interventionists. Camarata (1993) studied language acquisition and mother-child interactions. This research revealed that speech production in children with language delays improved when mothers supplied accurate models of words and sentences in natural conversation and interaction.

Girolametto, Verbey, and Tannock (1994) studied the effects of parent training on the joint engagement in play interactions of preschool children with developmental delays. In this study, parents were trained to encourage their children's participation in social interaction through their own responsiveness, language models, and child-centered interactions. Mothers who received training had more mother-child interactions than those that did not receive training. Results show longer duration of engagement, greater frequency of joint engagement, and improved ability to attend.

Parents who use a responsive, child-oriented style of interaction help the development of their children with disabilities. Mahoney and Powers (1988) taught parents to use turn-taking and interactive match in their interactions with their children. Turn-taking in conversation improves balance, decreases directions, and increases responses. Interactive match involves adjusting tempo and pace of activities to meet the current developmental level and relating interventions to the child's interests. Turn-taking and interactive match are related to moderate developmental gains. The study showed that the parents were successful at decreasing their own turns and increasing their response mands and interactive match.

Eiserman, Weber, and McCoun (1992) studied parent training with preschool children with speech disorders. Parents were trained by a speech language pathologist using therapeutic techniques. Parents, including those who had previously low levels of involvement in their children's education, effectively increased their children's personal and social skills and adaptive behavior as well as their speech. The authors suggested that optimal language development occurs in a relaxed home environment where language can be spontaneous. Their results also found that generalization occurs more successfully when language intervention occurs in the context of daily living.

Service Delivery Modes and General Curriculum and Intervention Strategies. The environment in which early intervention services occur affects communication, as well as social, emotional, and cognitive development. The CEC's Division of Early Childhood (DEC) Recommended Practices indicate that programs must have a sufficient quantity and variety of age-appropriate toys and materials to meet the needs of the specific children in their programs. The environment should stimulate child choice, engagement, and initiation. The interventionists should arrange the environments so that they encourage high engagement levels for all children. One of the ways to arrange the environment is to deliver naturalistic therapies in ECCE classrooms integrated into the regular daily routine. The DEC recommends that pull-out services--those in which the therapist and child work on skills and activities in a different room or outside the context of the regular classroom routine--only be used when activity-based, routine service options have not met student needs. Although pull-out services are often emphasized in early childhood classrooms, McWilliam, Young, and Harville (1996) found that occupational therapists, physical therapists, and speech language pathologists support integrated therapy in contexts relevant to the child. They also support interdisciplinary collaboration as well as involvement of peers who do not require these therapies.

The number of children involved in each component of the intervention program can also have significant effects. In a study examining the effects of play group size on language, McCabe et al. (1996) found that, when playing in groups of four compared with groups of two, children had fewer utterances, but used more varied vocabulary. The authors concluded that play in very small groups led to parallel play and self-talk, whereas larger groups stimulated more diversity. McCabe et al. suggested that this type of environmental manipulation should be given careful consideration in planning intervention.

Adults' presentation of toys and interaction with children can also have an effect on children's play. Preschool-age children with developmental delays showed higher levels of positive emotion when adults encouraged child-centered play than when they were more directive (Hupp, Boat, & Alpert, 1992; cited in Bailey, 1994). Children construct knowledge by playing with toys, but also benefit from initiating and interacting with peers and adults in the context of play.

Consistent with the DEC Recommended Practices, Bailey and Wolery (1992) suggested that toys should be responsive, age appropriate, adapted to increase engagement and learning, include naturally occurring objects, and promote learning of skills. Materials are also important to service delivery. The selection of toys and age appropriate materials can help create environments that maximize children's opportunities to practice social and cooperative play (Bailey, 1994). Quilitch and Risley (1973) found that children engaged in social interaction more frequently when provided with *social toys* such as games or toys that could involve two to four children simultaneously, rather than *isolate toys*, such as clay or books, which would be used by one child at a time. Social toys promote sharing, turn-taking, and pretend play. Social play can be encouraged by involving peers and providing an appropriate number of toys. Programs should have enough toys so as to avoid conflict, but not so many that children do not interact with each other (Dempsey & Frost, 1993; Olds, 1979).

THE EARLY INTERVENTION PROGRAM OBSERVATION SCALE

The Recommended Practices can be used to guide, direct, and assess practice in early intervention. Although the Recommended Practices were based on research whenever it was available and clear, no direct observational research has been conducted to validate them. Research is needed to identify the extent to which the practices are implemented and to investigate the relationship between specific recommended practices and outcomes for child and family with varying characteristics (Bruder, 1997). For the present study, an observation instrument based on the Recommended Practices was developed to measure implementation and describe practices in one state's early intervention system for infants and toddlers with disabilities. In the future, reports will be presented relating practices to child and family outcomes.

Items in the Early Intervention Program Observation Scale (EIPOS) were derived from the Recommended Practices for Early Intervention from other early intervention observations scales and from recommendations of experts in the field. Two versions of the scale were developed. The Center Based Early

Intervention Program Observation Scale-Revised (CBEIPOS-R) consists of 29 items that are scored following an observation of at least one full group or an individual center-based session of the early intervention program. The Home Based Early Intervention Program Observation Scale (HBEIPOS) contains 23 items that are scored following an observation of one full home-based session. Twenty of the items on the two versions of the instrument are the same. Items are scored on a scale of 1 to 5 (1, *not evident--no aspect of the criterion is met* to 5, *fully evident--all aspects of the criterion are met*). The scale is divided into six sections that roughly mirror sections of the Recommended Practices: (a) Parents/Family, (b) Program Environment and Service Delivery (center based only), (c) General Curriculum and Intervention Strategies, (d) Communication Skills, (e) Social and Emotional Development, and (f) Motor Skills. Table 12.1 provides the number of items in each session and examples.

TABLE 12.1

Sample Items by Section from the EIPOS

Section	Sample Items
I	**Family and Parent Participation** [Three Items]
	• The family [caregiver] are involved in the session by modeling their own techniques, practicing techniques introduced by the interventionist, discussing the child's progress, and suggesting areas of possible contentration.
	• The interventionist and the family [caregiver] discuss ways for activities to involve materials that are generally found in the home, are inexpensive, and are not elaborate. They also discuss how to implement the activities in the family's [caregiver's] daily routine.
II	**Program Environment and Service Delivery** [four times for center based only]
	• Therapy is provided within the normal routine; pull out services are employed only when routine, activity-based options for services have failed to meet identified needs.
III	**General Curriculum and Intervention Strategies** [seven items for center based and eight items for home based]
	• The interventionist is responsive to and encourages infant's/child's interests, preferences, and motivation.

(Continued)

•The interventionist integrates skills from various domains within the routine activities of the home or center and makes use of naturally occurring activities for incidental teaching of functional skills.

•The interventionist uses prompting strategies, differential reinforcement, and response shaping in the last intrusive way.

IV   **Communication Skills** [four times for center-based obsersvations and three items for home-based observations]

•The interventionist encourages children to use language through a variety of developmentally appropriate techniques including milieu teaching, expansion, motherese, responsive interaction and being a conversational partner, and direct instruction and mand modeling.

•Communication partners individualize/adapt their communication to the child's linguistic sophistication and disability status to ensure that communication directed to the child is understandable.

V   **Social and Emotional Development** [eight items for center-based observations and six for home-based observations]

•When infant/child struggles attempts to do something slightly beyond his or her capability the interventionist provides scaffolding by suggesting methods, demonstrating or providing other support to allow the child to be successful.

•The infant/child is appropriately positioned for each access to objects and others.

•The interventionist helps the child identify, express, and cope with feelings.

VI   **Motor Skills** [three items]

•The interventionist adapts motor activities, materials, environments, and intervention strategies as needed to accommodate the abilities of individual children.

The purpose of the observations was to investigate regular, direct service provision. Thus, recommended practices related to assessment, individualized family service plans (IFSPs), case management, transition, program evaluation, and other areas were not included in the instrument. In addition, these are recommended practices specific to programs for infants and toddlers with disabilities. Although some of the items would also be appropriate for other ages, the instrument is not designed for use with programs serving older children.

The New Jersey Early Intervention System Study

The New Jersey Early Intervention System Study (EISS) uses a longitudinal design to investigate the cost, quality, and outcomes of early intervention for infants and toddlers with disabilities. A major goal of the study is to understand the specifics of early intervention--how it is provided to particular children and families; why early intervention practices and costs in the first 5 years of life vary; and what the consequences of these variations are for the lives and development of children and parents. Questions addressed by the study include:

1.   What services are received by children who enter early intervention prior to age 3?
2.   What is the quality of services provided, and how does it vary among families?
3.   How do variations in services affect costs and outcomes for children and families?

The Study of Program Quality that is reported in this chapter used direct observation to measure early intervention practices and contribute to answering these questions. Ultimately, the relationship of program quality to child and family outcome is analyzed. In this chapter, the results of program observations are presented, giving a description of implementation of recommended practices in direct service provision.

Models of Early Intervention Services in New Jersey

Before providing more information on the procedures and results of the Study of Program Quality, it is necessary to give a brief description of the service delivery models employed in New Jersey during the study to clarify the types of early intervention services provided.

1.   *Group center-based* services are provided at the early intervention program (EIP). Infants and toddlers with disabilities meet with therapists and other interventionists for an average of almost 1.5 hours weekly. The most typical schedule involves some time for children to be in music and snack together and other time in individual sessions with therapists, special education teachers, or teacher assistants.

Often parents are present for part of the session and leave for parent-support meetings. In some cases, parents drop their children off at the center and are not present or they observe from another location. In almost 30% of the programs, parents were not present or left for an extended part of the session. With the passage of the IDEA, this type of service is decreasing to provide services in the child's natural environment.

2.   For *individual home-based* services, an interventionist goes to the child's home, typically once per week for about 1 hour. In some cases, a single professional or primary interventionist provides all of the intervention with the child and family; in other cases, different therapists deliver therapy on different days or together. In 80% of the sessions, the parent or primary caregiver (e.g., nanny or grandparent) is present. In addition, these sessions often include other family members. Home-based services that are in the child's natural environment are increasing.

3.   *Community child care centers* are also sites where children receive services. Although provision in community child-care centers is increasing, it remains rare. In 1997, less than 4% (five children) of the sample children received early intervention services in a community program. In two of the five cases, the interventionist removed the child from the regular activities of the center and provided individual therapy. Although the location was the child's natural environment, the services were not delivered naturally within the child's normal routine--a practice that is likely to impede generalization. None of the children in the sample we observed received early intervention services in a family day-care home.

4.   *Individual therapy sessions* delivered at the EIP program last less than 1 hour on average and are the least likely to have parents present for the session. About 36% of the sessions did not have parents present. Use of this treatment format is decreasing.

METHODS

As part of the larger study, a stratified random sample of 300 infants and toddlers with disabilities and their families from across the state was obtained as they entered the early intervention system. This sample provides prospective longitudinal data on service usage, child development, and family outcomes. Children are eligible for early intervention from birth based on disability and at risk criteria, but are enrolled at any age between birth and 3 years of age. Thus, the children in the study entered at a wide range of ages. Depending on the age at which they began services, they received different amounts of early intervention before exiting at age 3. Baseline information on the sample was gathered through parent interviews and standardized assessments of child functioning and mother-child interactions. Parent interviews and assessments were conducted yearly and at exit from the early intervention system when the child turned 3. Also as part of the larger study, all center-based early intervention programs in the state were observed using an earlier version of the instrument used in the present study. The observation data to be presented here were collected on the actual services delivered to the sample children and families who were still enrolled in early intervention during the second year of the study. Thus, the sample is composed of children who entered early intervention prior to age 2, but who were at least 1 year old at the time of the observation.

By design, the sample for this part of the study is a subset of the full longitudinal sample. Many children had aged out of early intervention before these quality observations were conducted. Others were deemed ineligible for early intervention after a short time because they no longer had a disability. A few families chose not to continue in early intervention or moved out of New Jersey. These children were not considered part of the Program Quality Study because they had spent so little time in the program to accurately ensure its effect. The services for five children who were in foster-care and were experiencing changes in their foster-care arrangements were not observed. All of these children and families who still live in New Jersey continue to be part of the larger longitudinal study. The total sample size for the Program Quality Study is 149. Thirty-eight home-based observations were completed for 41 children, including one set of twins and one set of triplets. Ninety center-based observations of 103 study children were completed. This included 63 observation interventions in group sessions and 31 observations of individual therapy sessions.

CBEIPOS was also used for observing service delivery in community-based services. Five community-based observations were completed: three in group settings and two in individual pull-out therapy sessions. With the exception of three EIPs that service children with low-incidence and specialized disabilities, at least one observation of service provision in every EIP in the state is included in this study.

Prior to each observation, families were contacted to obtain consent for observations. The EIP was then contacted. Independent observers conducted each observation.

Initial interrater reliability for the observation instruments ranged from

76% to 92% with an average of 83% for exact matches. If scores of 1 and 2 or 4 and 5 are collapsed, the interrater reliability exceeded 92%. Shadow scoring of 10% of all observations showed that reliability was maintained above 90% during the data collection. The internal consistency of the overall scales was satisfactory (Cronbach's alpha = 0.92, p < .001; Cronbach's alpha = 0.84, p < .001). The decline rate for family participation in the Study of Program Quality was extraordinarily low, with only one family saying it did not want the child's program observed. Each location within an EIP was observed and treated as a separate site.

RESULTS

Table 12.2 depicts the results for each of the three types of services. Average scores are presented for the EIPOS total and for each section--Parent/Family Participation, Program Environment and Service Delivery, General Curriculum and Intervention Strategies, Communication Skills, Social and Emotional Development, and Motor Skills. The overall mean on the HEIPOS across home-based programs was 3.73 (sd = 0.62). The mean for CBEIPOS group sessions was 3.76 (sd = 0.47) and for Individual therapy sessions it was 3.66 (sd = 0.45). The slightly lower score for the individual observations may be due to the fact that fewer items on the instrument are applicable to therapy sessions involving only one child. Results are not given for community child-care centers because the number observed was so low (n = 5). In addition, service in two centers was essentially individual therapy, whereas in the other three, it was delivered in the regular routine of the program, making it unreasonable to treat the observations as one type of service.

The section of greatest concern overall was Family/Parent Participation, as evidenced by a mean of 2.63 for home-based, 2.65 for center-based group, and 2.83 for individual intervention sessions. Family members were not present for the services in a large number of observations: 5 of the 38 (13%) home-based session, 18 of the 63 (29%) group sessions, and 11 of the 31 (36%) individual sessions. The data were analyzed with these coded as missing, because it was not possible to observe the interactions.

Alternatively, it is reasonable to consider that in most of these programs where parents are systematically not included in the session, the criteria for parent/family participation are not being met. For this reason, we also analyzed the data with the scores on this section entered as "1" or "not evident" when parents were absent. If parents are not present, it is difficult to involve them in the interaction or discuss ways to use techniques in their normal routine. (In four cases, the programs normally included parents; but in an effort to prepare children for preschool, parents did not stay in the group session we observed.) These cases have been treated separately. With this recoding, the Parent/Family

Involvement scores drop to 2.40 for the home-based sessions, 2.17 for the group sessions, and 2.18 for the individual sessions.

TABLE 12.2

Mean Scores on Early Intervention Program Observation Scale as a Function of Subscale and Setting

Section	Home Based[1] Group Session		Center Based[1] Group Session		Individual Therapy	
	$\underline{n} = 38$		$\underline{n} = 63$		$\underline{n} = 31$	
	M	SD	M	SD	M	SD
Total	3.73	0.62	3.76	0.47	3.66	0.45
Parents/family	2.62	1.41	2.64	1.23	2.82	1.20
Program environment and service delivery	NA	NA	3.82	0.82	3.43	0.76
General curriculum and intervention	3.33	0.80	3.68	0.59	3.61	0.69
Communication	4.15	0.88	3.88	0.60	4.44	0.57
Social/emotional	4.33	0.70	3.95	0.64	4.38	0.53
Motor	4.45	0.66	4.78	0.48	4.23	0.98

[1]Maximum score = 5.

In earlier research on the larger study, anecdotal observations raised concerns about four areas: (a) children who were not physically impaired being strapped into special support chairs, (b) children and families who were non-English speakers receiving services in English only, (c) the limited use of primary interventionists, and (d) the number of children who were not benefiting from their session because they spent a great deal of time crying. Thus, observers were asked to capture systematic information on these areas while conducting their observations. In 8 of 63 group observations (14%), children who did not have significant physical impairments were strapped to special support chairs. This did not occur in home-based or individual sessions. Crying for a substantial amount of time as a direct result of something that happened in the intervention occurred in 8 of the 38 home-based sessions (21%), 4 of the 31 individual sessions (13%), and 29 of the 63 group sessions (46%). A small number of EIPs used primary interventionists to deliver services. Only 10 of 38 (26%) home-based programs offered primary interventionists, as did just 10 of 62 (11%) center-based programs. Finally, in 16 of the families, the primary language was Spanish. None of the seven home-based sessions and only six of the nine center-based sessions were provided in Spanish.

DISCUSSION

It is not to be expected with a comprehensive observation instrument such as the EIPOS that any program would meet all criteria fully. This is especially true considering the short duration of the observation. However, mean scores around 3.7 indicate that programs scored poorly on many items, and scores ranging between 4 and 5 would be more satisfactory.

Not surprisingly, the observations showed that qualified professionals are mostly delivering therapy-driven intervention. Techniques derived directly from the behavior analysis approach are common (e.g., using prompting and response shaping or mand modeling). The programs are well equipped to serve the children and provide physically safe environments. Interventionists used many recommended practices in motor development, cognition, and communication. The greatest strength of the EIPs is in using recommended practices that are expected to enhance motor skills. Interventionists successfully incorporate motor skills into the context of normal activities and help facilitate the use of these skills in multiple environments. In addition, concept learning is often integrated into activities, and multiple strategies are used to encourage language use.

Less obvious from the data in Table 12.2 but embedded within the ratings, several comments are noteworthy. Allowing children to take initiative and work within the child's chosen activity was rarely seen. Interventionists were less often responsive to children's initiations within interventionist-directed activities and rarely showed a responsiveness to infants by imitating the infant's actions, which is important for social, cognitive, and language development.

To maximize child progress and meet the developmental needs of infants and toddlers, families and other caregivers must be active partners in early intervention. Although a number of programs involve parents in the sessions by modeling and practicing techniques, most do not. Often there is not a balance among interactions of the interventionist, children, and family members. Dialogue between parents and interventionists (e.g., discussion of child progress and suggested areas of concentration) is also infrequent. A related concern is the scarcity of interventionists who speak the primary language of the child and family.

In many cases, intervention is not delivered as part of the family or child's normal routine, making generalizations of behaviors more difficult. In home-based sessions, interventionists often bring materials to the home, use them with the child, and take them away, further inhibiting parents' involvement and the generalization of skills. They often do not use the child's own toys and materials, nor do they discuss implementing practices in the home during routine activities such as meals, bath time, or dressing. When appropriate toys are not available in the home, interventionists rarely assist families in obtaining the needed resources. In center-based programs, pull-out therapy was often used rather than naturalistic techniques within the regular routine of the program.

One of the primary purposes of group service delivery is to provide children with opportunities for socialization. Interventionists seldom encourage child-to-child communication or interaction. Also in the area of socioemotional development, the number of crying children raises concerns. Infants and toddlers cry as a form of communication, and it is to be expected that children would cry occasionally. In the instances noted by the observers, crying is sustained, intense (not just fussing), and typically resulted from the interventionist's actions. For example, in one program, a toddler was coloring with a blue crayon; the interventionist removed the blue crayon from his hand and gave him a red one, saying, "Use this one now." He cried and is told he has used enough blue. He continues to cry for over 10 minutes. A child who is crying is not able to learn. Related to this, interventionists were rarely seen helping children cope with and identify their feelings.

These results corroborate the findings of Odom, McLean, Johnson, and LaMontagne (1995) that the more recent Recommended Practices are not being implemented widely. Of most concern for those interested in inclusion and serving young children with disabilities in the natural environment is the scarcity of the implementation of practices that correspond to the Guidelines for Developmentally Appropriate Practice. Specifically, many interventionists in this study were not seen to be responsive to children, to use naturalistic techniques such as child-initiated activities and integrated therapy, or to involve the family or other caregivers in the intervention. Although service in the natural environment is increasing, in this study, techniques that use naturally occurring opportunities to reach objectives and that reflect the new emphasis in the field of ECSE on constructivist and sociocultural approaches are not yet as widely used.

Collection of final outcome data on the sample has just been completed, and the more complex analyses of how recommended practices affect outcomes and interact with family and child characteristics and other program factors will be forthcoming. These analyses will help determine the extent to which greater use of the Recommended Practices produces more beneficial outcomes for children and families.

ACKNOWLEDGMENT

The research reported in this paper was supported in part through funding by the New Jersey Department of Health and Senior Services and through institutional faculty research funds at The College of New Jersey.

REFERENCES

Bailey, D. (1994). Toy play in infancy and early childhood: Normal development and special considerations for children with disabilities. *Technical Report No. 11: Research Synthesis on Early Intervention Practices* (pp. 1-42). ERIC Document 304 248.

Bailey, D., & Wolery, M. (1992). *Teaching infants and preschoolers with disabilities*. New York: Merrill.

Bricker, D., & Cripe, J. J. W. (1992). *An activity-based approach to early intervention*. Baltimore, MD: Brookes.

Brinker, R. P. (1992). Family involvement in early intervention: Accepting the unchangeable, changing the changeable and knowing the difference. *Topics in Early Childhood Special Education, 12*(3), 307-333.

Bruder, M. B. (1997). The effectiveness of specific educational/developmental curricula for children with established disabilities. In M. J. Guralnick (Ed.), *The effectiveness of early intervention* (pp. 523-548). Baltimore, MD: Brookes.

Camarata, S. (1993). The application of naturalistic conversation training to speech production in children with speech disabilities. *Journal of Applied Behavior Analysis, 26*(2), 173-182.

Casto, G. (1988). Research and program evaluation in early childhood special education. In S. L. Odom & M. B. Karnes (Eds.), *Early intervention for infants and children with handicaps: An empirical base* (pp. 51-62). Baltimore, MD: Brookes.

Casto, G., & Mastropieri, M. (1986). The efficacy of early intervention programs: A meta-analysis. *Exceptional Children, 52*, 417-424.

Chugani, H., Phelps, M. E., & Mazziotta, J. C. (1987). Positron emission tomography study of human brain functional development. *Annals of Neurology, 22*(4), 495.

Cole, K., Dale, P., & Mills, P. (1991). Individual differences in language delayed children's responses to direct and interactive preschool instruction. *Topics in Early Childhood Special Education, 11*(1), 99-124.

Dempsey, J. D., & Frost, J. L. (1993). Play environments in early childhood education.

In B. Spodek (Ed.), *Handbook of research on the education of young children* (pp. 306-321). New York: Macmillan.

Division of Early Childhood Task Force on Recommended Practices. (1993). *DEC recommended practices: Indicators of quality in programs for infants and young children with special needs and their families.* Reston, VA: Council for Exceptional Children.

Dunham, P. R., & Dunham, F. (1992). Lexical development during middle infancy: A mutually driven infant-caregiver process. *Developmental Psychology, 28,* 414-420.

Escobar, C. M., Barnett, W. S., & Goetze, L. D. (1994). Cost analysis in early intervention. *Journal of Early Intervention, 18*(1), 48-63.

Eiserman, W., Weber, C., & McCoun, M. (1992). Two alternative program models for serving speech-disordered preschoolers: A second year follow-up. *Journal of Communication Disorders, 25,* 77-106.

Fewell, R. R., & Kaminski, R. (1988). Play skills development and instruction for young children with handicaps. In S. L. Odom & M. B. Karnes (Eds.), *Early intervention for infants and children with handicaps: An empirical base* (pp. 145-158). Baltimore, MD: Brookes.

File, N., & Kontos, S. (1993). The relationship of program quality to children's paly in integrated early intervention settings. *Topics in Early Childhood Special Education, 13*(1), 1-18.

Frede, E. C. (1998). *Quality in early intervention: Views from the field* (Technical report of the New Jersey Early Intervention System Study). New Brunswick, NJ: Center for Early Education at Rutgers University.

Girolametto, L. E. (1988). Improving the social-conversational skills of developmentally delayed children: An intervention study. *Journal of Speech and Hearing Disorders, 53,* 156-167.

Girolametto, L., Verbey, M., & Tannock, R. (1994). Improving joing engagement in parent-child interaction: An intervention study. *Journal of Early Intervention, 18*(2), 155-167.

Gresham, F. M. (1982). Misguided mainstreaming: The case for social skills training with handicapped children. *Exceptional Children, 48,* 422-433.

Guralnick, M. J. (1988). Efficacy research in early childhood intervention programs. In S. L. Odom & M. B. Karnes (Eds.), *Early intervention for infants and children with handicaps: An empirical base* (pp. 75-88). Baltimore, MD: Brookes.

Guralnick, M. J. (1993). Developmentally appropriate practice in the assessment and intervention of children's peer relations. *Topics in Early Childhood Special Education, 13*(3), 344-372.

Guralnick, M. J. (Ed.). (1997). *The effectiveness of early childhood intervention.* Baltimore, MD: Brookes.

Howes, C., & Seward, P. (1987). Child's play with adults, toys, and peers: An examination of family and child-care influences. *Child Development, 58,* 932-944.

Individuals with Disabilities Education Act Amendments of 1997, Pub. L. No. 102 - 119. (1997).

Kolb, B. (1989). Brain development, plasticity, and behavior. *American Psychologist, 44*(9), 1203-1212.

Mahoney, G., & Powers, A. (1988). Modifying parent-child interaction: Enhancing the development of handicapped children. *Journal of Special Education, 22*(1), 82-97.

McCabe, J. R., Jenkins, J. R., Mills, P. E., Dale, P. S., Cole, K. N., & Pepler, L. (1996). Effects of play group variables on language use by preschool children with disabilities. *Journal of Early Intervention, 20*(4), 329-340.

McLean, M. E., & Odom, S. L. (1993). Practices for young children with and without disabilities: A comparison of DEC and NAEYC identified practices. *Topics in Early Childhood Special Education, 13,* 274-292.

McWilliam, R. A., Young, H. J., & Harville, K. (1996). Therapy services in early intervention: Current status, barriers, and recommendations. *Topics in Early Childhood Special Education, 16*(3), 348-375.

Meisels, S. J., Dichtmiller, M., & Liaw, F. R. (1994). A multidimensional analysis of early childhood intervention programs. In C. H. Zeanah (Ed.), *Handbook of infant mental health* (pp. 361-385). New York: Guilford.

Odom, S. L. (1988). Research in early childhood special education: Methodologies and paradigms. In S. L. Odom & M. B. Karnes (Eds.), *Early intervention for infants and children with handicaps: An empirical base* (pp. 1-21). Baltimore, MD: Brookes.

Odom, S. L., McLean, M. E., Johnson, L. J., & LaMontagne, M. J. (1995). Recommended practices in early childhood special education: Validation and current use. *Journal of Early Intervention, 19*(1), 1-17.

Odom, S. L., Peterson, C., McConnell, S., & Ostrosky, M. (1990). Ecobehavioral analysis of early education/specialized classroom settings and peer social interaction. *Education & Treatment of Children, 13*(4), 316-331.

Olds, A. R. (1979). Designing developmentally optimal classrooms for children with special needs. In S. J. Meisels (Ed.), *Special education and development: Perspectives on young children with special needs* (pp. 91-138). Baltimore, MD: University Park Press.

Olds, D. L., & Kitzman, H. (1993). Review of research on home visitation for pregnant women and parents of young children. *The Future of Children, 3*(4).

Quilitch, H. R., & Risley, T. R. (1973). The effects of play materials on social play. *Journal of Applied Behavior Analysis, 6*(3), 573-578.

Ramey, C. T., Bryant, D. M., Wasik, B. H., Sparling, J. J., Fendt, K. H., & LaVange, L. M. (1992). The infant health development program for low birth weight, premature infants: Program elements, family participation, and child intelligence. *Pediatrics, 89*, 454-465.

Shonkoff, J. P., Hauser-Cram, P., Krauss, M. W., & Upshur, C. C. (1992). Development of infants and toddlers with disabilities and their families. *Monographs of the Society for Research in Child Development, 57* (Serial No. 230).

Strain, P. S., & Kohler, F. W. (1988). Social skill intervention with young children with handicaps: Some new conceptualizations and directions. In S. L. odom & M. B. Karnes (Eds.), *Early intervention for infants and children with handicaps: An empirical base* (pp. 159-177). Baltimore, MD: Brookes.

Warren, S., & Kaiser, A. (1986). Incidental language teaching: A critical review. *Journal of Speech and Hearing Disorders, 51*, 291-299.

Warren, S. F., McQuarter, R. J., & Rogers-Warren, A. K. (1984). The effects of mands and models on the speech of unresponsive language-delayed preschool children. *Journal of Speech and Hearing Disorders, 49*, 43-52.

Werner, E. E., & Smith, R. S. (1982). *Vulnerable but invisible: A longitudinal study of resilient children and youth.* New York: McGraw-Hill.

Yoder, P., Kaiser, A., & Alpert, C. (1991). An exploratory study of the iteration between language teaching methods and child characteristics. *Journal of Speech and Hearing Research, 34*, 155-167.

Author Index

A

Abelson, R., 136
Adams, M., 255, 264
Adcock, C., 5
Ainsworth, M., 94, 109
Alessandri, R., 77
Alpert, C., 301, 303
American Association for the
  Advancement of Science,
  3, 27
Arnett, J., 123
Arend, R., 69, 93
Armstrong, J., 134
Astington, J., 54
Atkinson, J., 65

B

Baenninger, M., 248
Bailey, D., 307
Ball, O., 291
Ball, W., 97
Banas, N., 241
Banet, B., 13
Barnes, J., 66
Barnett, W., 4, 25, 297
Barrie, J., 280
Bartholomew, K., 122
Bodrova, E., 15, 27
Bond, J., 13

Barrett, K., 111
Becker, T. E., 121, 122
Beckwith, L., 68, 70
Bell, S., 94
Bellugi, U., 262
Bemelmens, L., 263, 288
Benenson, J., 67
Bennett, E., 81, 115
Bereiter, C., 5, 7, 40, 43, 52
Berger, A., 132, 137
Berk, L., 15, 27
Berman, L., 67
Bernstein, L., 67
Bialystok, E., 229
Biber, B., 7
Bidell, T., 27
Bigler, T., 27
Billings, T., 121, 122
Bigler, T., 27
Birch, S., 81, 82
Bizzell, R., 8, 10, 24
Blackwell, J., 72, 75
Blank, H., 29
Blaut, J., 246
Blehar, M., 94, 109
Bleiker, C., 49, 55, 56, 57
Bloom, B., 5, 262
Blumenfeld, P., 67, 71

Subject Index